THE POLITICAL ECONOMY OF THE
SPECIAL RELATIONSHIP

The Political Economy of the Special Relationship

ANGLO-AMERICAN DEVELOPMENT
FROM THE GOLD STANDARD
TO THE FINANCIAL CRISIS

JEREMY GREEN

PRINCETON UNIVERSITY PRESS

PRINCETON & OXFORD

Requests for permission to reproduce material from this work
should be sent to permissions@press.princeton.edu

Published by Princeton University Press
41 William Street, Princeton, New Jersey 08540
6 Oxford Street, Woodstock, Oxfordshire OX20 1TR

press.princeton.edu

ISBN 978-0-691-19732-6
ISBN (e-book) 978-0-691-20161-0

Library of Congress Control Number 2020936531

British Library Cataloging-in-Publication Data is available

Editorial: Hannah Paul
Production Editorial: Ali Parrington
Jacket/Cover Design: Layla Mac Rory
Production: Erin Suydam
Publicity: Kate Hensley & Kate Farquhar-Thomson

This book has been composed in Arno

Printed on acid-free paper. ∞

Printed in the United States of America

10 9 8 7 6 5 4 3 2 1

CONTENTS

ILLUSTRATIONS

Table

Figures

PREFACE

I BEGAN WORK on this project in 2008, during the peak of the global financial crisis. The genesis of this book was heavily influenced by the events of 2007/8. The crucial role of major US- and UK-based banks, alongside the rapid transmission of the crisis through New York and London, highlighted the importance of Anglo-America within international finance. It also spoke to the political importance of developing a better understanding of financial globalization: how it was made, by whom, and to what ends. At a moment of apparently impending financial collapse, understanding how the world had come to be characterized by a deep and dangerous form of financial interdependence took on a new sense of urgency. Existing scholarship seemed to have captured part of the story—the part that put the United States at the center of the modern post–World War II international financial system. But there was also something lacking in these accounts. They did not have the theoretical tools to make sense of an undoubted empirical truth: that, despite the comparative postwar deterioration of the United Kingdom's economy from its imperial heyday, UK capitalism continued to play a central role in the politics of international finance.

My sense that political economy scholarship had neglected the UK's role within the international economy was not only informed by the crisis; the project also took its cue from a deeper set of ideas and debates. My thinking on the topic was catalyzed by the longstanding Empire Seminars within the Department of Political Science at York University in Toronto. Sitting in those seminars, I recognized that theories of the global political economy from across the spectrum were overly US-centric. The story of the politics of the modern international financial system started and ended with the dominance of US finance as one component of the wider rise of postwar US capitalism. The UK's role as a pivotal player in the politics of financial globalization didn't receive the attention it merited—the idea of a neat postwar transition to US hegemony or imperialism (depending on your theoretical and political tastes) had consigned the UK's role to history. And so the idea for this book was born.

In the decade since I began working on this project, the legacy of the financial crisis has transformed the global economy in ways that are still not fully apparent. The formerly strong consensus around liberal approaches to managing the international economy within the West and beyond has come under significant pressure. Persistently slow economic growth and a habitual dependency on ultraloose monetary policy have created the sense of a global economy in a condition of permanent dysfunction. Within many countries, populist movements and leaders have changed the tenor of liberal democratic politics, leading to deep social and political divisions. The pro-globalization momentum that marked Western political economies from the 1990s has stalled. In the US, Donald Trump's presidency and his "America First" mantra have undermined US international leadership position and ushered in a more unilateralist moment in the global political economy. Trade policy has been weaponized to achieve national economic goals, and a more conflictual tussle over global economic and geopolitical influence has emerged between the US, China, Russia, and the European Union (EU). China's power and influence have risen dramatically over the past decade. In Europe, the crisis exposed deep divisions between southern and northern countries, while the UK has turned inward under the seemingly intractable pressures associated with the fractious politics of Brexit.

Amid these important shifts within the global economy, though, we can also see some notable continuities. While trade has become increasingly politicized in the postcrisis era, finance remains strangely immune to the political realignments characteristic of Western politics, and the challenge to liberal finance notably muted. Unlike in the aftermath of the Great Depression, no calls have been issued for the euthanasia of today's rentiers, and while trade flows are the subject of a great deal of disagreement, capital flows are not. Political parties on the left have developed some critical ideas about finance but—despite the frailty of the postcrisis economic recovery and the deep structural weaknesses of the global economy—have been too weak to build the electoral coalitions required to win state power and, consequently, unable to secure a political platform from which to institutionalize their policies. For the incumbent political parties on the right, the postcrisis response has largely been to tinker with the regulatory conditions of finance while continuing to cleave to a belief in the benefits of an open, liberalized financial system, leaning increasingly on central bank intervention through ultralow interest rates and monetary easing to manage and mask the weaknesses of liberal international finance. In practice, this has meant an increased reliance upon state intervention within private financial markets. But in the realm of ideas, the pristine preeminence of private finance has endured—albeit with the recognition of the need for some regulatory adjustment. We have not witnessed a shift comparable to that of the interwar period, when, as Keynes observed, ideas about restrictions on private finance in the form of capital controls that had previously been deeply unpopular moved from heresy to orthodoxy.

This mismatch between a newly politicized and increasingly fraught trade politics on the one hand, and the continued commitment to liberal ideas and policies governing a globalized financial system on the other, amplifies the contemporary resonance of the questions posed in this book. If we are to understand how liberal finance has weathered the crisis so effectively, we need to gain a sense of the underlying historical structures, processes, and institutional roots of modern global finance. My hope is that a sustained investigation of Anglo-America's role within financial globalization goes some way toward illuminating those historical foundations. At a time when the UK and the US are once more at the center of important transformations within the global economy—in the shape of Brexit and the Trump presidency—understanding their role in the making of modern international finance feels all the more necessary.

Beyond the intellectual challenge of explaining the role of Anglo-America in financial globalization, this book also engages with a more practical political question: What contemporary lessons can we learn from the previous efforts to democratize private finance? It is this question that motivates, in part, the reappraisal of the shift from a Keynesian postwar regulatory order in modern finance to a neoliberal approach to financial governance, and the different forms of state intervention that these frameworks involved. The breakdown of the liberal international order during the 1930s, sparked by the Wall Street crash and the Depression that followed, generated new ideas and policies for regulating private finance. These new approaches were motivated by the goal of constraining the power of private finance in the interest of the wider public good and insulating modern democracy from the vagaries of laissez-faire. As the events of 2007/8 confirmed with searing clarity, the first project to democratize modern finance was, despite its short-term successes, a failure.

Why did this previous attempt to democratize modern finance ultimately prove unsuccessful in constraining the power of private finance over the international economy? How we answer this question has very important implications for rethinking international finance and creating new policies and institutions to achieve those goals. A better understanding of why the postwar regulatory order was unable to durably bend private finance toward wider public goals of full employment, welfare, and stable economic growth is critical to thinking about how global finance might be reimagined and reorganized today. The major challenges of the twenty-first century, from climate change to staggering levels of inequality, seem to call out for a transformation of comparable scope and ambition. I hope that what follows will provide some insight into these issues.

ACKNOWLEDGMENTS

LITTLE DID I know when I began work on this project that it would occupy me for more than a decade. This book represents the outcome of that long period of researching, thinking, and writing on the topic. Completing the book has stretched and challenged me in many ways, and I have drawn on many different sources of support and inspiration during along the way. At York University, Leo Panitch and Hannes Lacher deserve special mention for their commitment, diligence, and encouragement while supervising my PhD thesis. Stephen Gill also provided important insights both at the very beginning and end of the program. Perhaps more important than the academic support I received at York, though, was the camaraderie and intellectual inspiration offered by my friends: Joseph Baines, Eric George, Julian Germann, and Sandy Hager. Their support has been indispensable.

At the University of Sheffield, Colin Hay and Tony Payne deserve a special mention for hiring a PhD student with a half-written thesis to begin work as a postdoctoral fellow at their new postcrisis research institute, SPERI (Sheffield Political Economy Research Institute). The support and opportunities provided by my time at SPERI gave me a further opportunity for me to develop this project and taught me many things, both intellectual and professional. Andrew Gamble has also been a source of inspiration and guidance, both as my external examiner for the PhD and then as a mentor back in the UK. I am very much indebted to his generosity. Scott Lavery also provided intellectual inspiration during my time at Sheffield and since, and I have benefited greatly from the work that we have undertaken together. And, at the University of Bristol, where I spent two very enjoyable years, John Downer deserves special mention for his friendship, intellectual curiosity, and support.

The final stages of this project were all completed while working in POLIS (Department of Politics and International Studies) at Cambridge. Here I have continued to receive encouragement and support, while benefiting from a hugely stimulating intellectual environment. Helen Thompson, David Runciman, Jason Sharman, and Duncan Kelly deserve particular mention for their contributions in helping me complete this book. At Princeton University Press, Sarah Caro offered encouragement early on, and Hannah Paul has since proved an excellent editor. On a more personal note, my family have been supportive of my academic journey from the start, and I am very much indebted to their love and warmth. Finally, to my partner, Solène: sharing the completion of this book with you is a cherished privilege.

ABBREVIATIONS

AFL-CIO	American Federation of Labor and Congress of Industrial Organizations
BBA	British Bankers' Association
BIS	Bank for International Settlements
BOLSA	Bank of London and South America
CBI	Confederation of British Industry
CCC	Competition Credit and Control
CD	Certificate of deposit
CDO	Collateralized debt obligation
CPE	Comparative political economy
DEA	Department of Economic Affairs
EEC	European Economic Community
EPU	European Payments Union
EU	European Union
FSA	Financial Services Authority
FDI	Foreign direct investment
FOMC	Federal Open Market Committee
GDP	Gross domestic product
GFC	Global financial crisis
G7	Group of Seven
G20	Group of Twenty
IBBS	International bank branches
IEA	Institute of Economic Affairs

IFC	International Financial Centre
IMF	International Monetary Fund
IPE	International political economy
LIBOR	London Interbank Offered Rate
MNCS	Multinational corporations
MTFS	Medium-Term Financial Strategy
NATO	North Atlantic Treaty Organization
NEDC	National Economic Development Council
OECD	Organization for Economic Cooperation and Development
OPEC	Organization of the Petroleum-Exporting Countries
PSBR	Public sector borrowing requirement
RMBSS	Residential mortgage-backed securities
S&L	Savings and loan association
SEC	Securities and Exchange Commission
SPV	Special purpose vehicle
TUC	Trades Union Congress
UK	United Kingdom
US	United States
VOC	Varieties of capitalism

THE POLITICAL ECONOMY OF THE
SPECIAL RELATIONSHIP

Introduction

Little by little, the two countries established an instinctive conjunction of financial interests, so that it seemed impossible on either side, to imagine life without it. This, and not sentiment and language, was the innermost guts of the "Special Relationship."

—SUSAN STRANGE, *STERLING AND BRITISH POLICY*

THE CLOSE postwar association between the United Kingdom and the United States is known by a single mnemonic: the "Special Relationship." It refers to an unusually close and cooperative partnership between two independent states, encompassing diplomatic, military-strategic, political, economic, and cultural spheres. For the UK, the Special Relationship has offered a means to preserve great-power status even though its capacity for unilateral action in pursuit of foreign policy objectives is greatly diminished. For the US, the UK's possession of nuclear weapons, access to political and military intelligence, and position on the United Nations Security Council are valuable appendages. Despite the occasional spat and periods of cooling, diplomatic relations between the two states have remained extraordinarily close (Watt, 1986; Curtis, 1998; Dumbrell, 2006). But for all that the concept of the Special Relationship has illuminated, it has also obscured much—for example, the *political economy* of Anglo-America, buried beneath more fashionable scholarly preoccupations with diplomacy, grand strategy, and the cultural and sentimental linkages between the two states.[1] This is a great shame because, as Susan Strange (1971) noted, it was the exchange of roles between the dollar and sterling, as well as the deep financial ties between the two states, that were central to Anglo-American unity and integration.

In this book, I examine the political economy of the relationship between the UK and the US. I do this both as a way of moving beyond the traditional preoccupations of literature on Anglo-America and, more importantly, to challenge international political economy's (IPE) emphasis upon the singularly transformative role of US power in the making of a postwar global political economy. The accent in the book is predominantly on the "Anglo" facet of Anglo-American development, because it recovers the overlooked centrality of the UK's hugely significant contribution to fashioning a postwar global capitalism *alongside* America. Throughout the book, I argue that interactive processes of "Anglo-American development" shaped the politics of financial globalization. Institutional interdependencies between private finance in London and New York City—alongside close linkages between the Anglo-American treasuries and central banks—generated a distinctive sphere of Anglo-American capitalism centered upon financial integration. Despite being increasingly uneven, as US power waxed and UK power waned, Anglo-American development was hugely consequential for both states. It had important effects on both the domestic political economies of the US and the UK as well as the wider global political economy. Domestically, Anglo-American financial integration and transatlantic regulatory interdependence destabilized the postwar architecture of financial regulation in both states, and it fueled the growth of their financial sectors and made workers more dependent upon debt. Internationally, Anglo-American financial integration spurred the wider liberalization of global finance and critically undermined the foundations of the Bretton Woods monetary regime. This book tells the story of the Anglo-American origins of modern global finance, tracing its development from nascent forms of Anglo-American integration and cooperation associated with the gold standard to the spectacular implosion of Anglo-American finance and the international economy in the global financial crisis of 2007/8.

Hegemonic Cycles, Structural Power, and Anglo-America

By recovering the UK's deeply integrated and influential role within the origins of modern financial globalization, this book challenges some of the central foundations of IPE. Within its traditional historiography, IPE has viewed modern international economic history as a cyclical succession of neatly delineated phases of liberal "hegemonic" leadership punctuated by periods of anarchic disorder. As a field that originated in an evaluation of the role of these hegemonic powers in shaping the structures of the international economic order, IPE understood the systemic transformation of global capitalism as something that grew out of the leadership efforts of a singular, dominant state (Cohen, 2008). In the nineteenth century, during the *Pax Britannica*, the UK is said to have played this role; after World War II, the baton of international leadership passed to the US, under the auspices of *Pax Americana*. The US implemented its vision of a liberal international economic order at Bretton Woods in 1944, before overseeing the globalization project in the decades that followed.

This cyclical narrative has an important blind spot: the centrality of postwar *Anglo-American development* to the politics of financial globalization. The "hegemony" story has largely interpreted the waning of the UK's power and the waxing of America's as analytically discrete phenomena. But, as this book argues, they were in fact deeply interrelated processes. This book is, then, on one level, a methodological critique of thinking about the historical development of the modern international economy as a cyclical set of transitions between different national hegemonic powers that singularly, and discretely, refashion the global system. Such an approach reads the *international* within IPE as something sociologically reductive—a by-product or outgrowth of national dynamics anchored in the dominant state of a given epoch and projected outward into the world. In doing so, it remains trapped within a form of methodological nationalism that overlooks the fuller complexity of international capitalist development across space and time.

By adopting a more complex, transnational view of power transformation, we arrive at a different account of the politics of financial globalization, one that modifies claims regarding the singularity of America's role in driving that project and draws attention to the underappreciated significance of the UK's. Consequently, this book complements and extends the efforts of scholars that have highlighted the wider significance of an Anglo-American heartland within the global political economy (Van der Pijl, 1984; 1998; 2006; Mead, 2007; Gowan, 2009). It teases out, in much finer institutional and historical detail, the processes that generated Anglo-American financial interdependence by focusing on the imbrication of Anglo-American capitalism within distinctive national and international monetary orders. However, it does not do so through formulations of the relationship between distinctive class fractions or an historical-sociological state form specific to Anglo-America (Van der Pijl, 1998, 2006), nor the specificity of Anglo-American maritime power and a shared Protestant, liberal cultural disposition (Mead, 2007).

Instead, in this book I explore the historical-institutional articulation of the functionally and politically privileged relationship between private and public finance at the heart of the capitalist state (Ingham, 1984; Wray, 2012). Using the public-private financial nexus between the treasury, the central bank, and private banking in each country as an institutional pivot, I examine the historical transformation of Anglo-American political economy through the prism of the interactive dynamics of both the domestic and international monetary orders. Domestically, I focus on the dissolution of the financial regulatory structure associated with the postwar Keynesian state and the emergence of a more liberalized financial system. Internationally, I analyze the role of Anglo-American development in both founding and subsequently undermining the embedded liberalism of the Bretton Woods monetary order.

From this alternative vantage point, we arrive at a different story about the politics of financial globalization and the role of Anglo-America within it. This book does not deny the distinctive and unparalleled importance of US power and capitalism in remaking the postwar global political economy; a wide body of scholarship has clearly and convincingly stated the case for America's central role in relaunching the liberal international economic order (Keohane, 1984; Cox, 1987; Gilpin, 1987; Gowan, 1999; Smith, 2005; Ikenberry, 2011; Konings, 2011; Panitch and Gindin, 2012). But, rather than being bound up with the familiar IPE preoccupation with arguing either for or against the notion of US hegemonic decline from the 1970s, as much of that literature has been, this book explores the long-term developmental interaction of the US with the UK as a specific analytical and empirical puzzle. This focus enables the book to make a novel theoretical contribution to our understanding of the formation of power within the modern global political economy, through a critical engagement with the notion of "structural power" that came to be associated with those authors that argued *against* claims regarding the onset of US decline, and *for* the reality of enduring US dominance (Strange, 1987; 1996; Gill and Law, 1989; Gill, 1991; Konings, 2011; Panitch and Gindin, 2012).

In its original formulation (Strange, 1987), structural power never got to grips with the complex processes of international development that generated the institutional capacities formative to America's postwar financial power. There was no sense of the historicity of structural power, because Strange's work began from the assumption of an already existing US predominance and sought only to explain its continuity. Where the story of the prehistory of US structural power in finance has been told, that history has largely been viewed as the product of an externalization of the internal dynamics of US capitalism into a largely spatially indeterminate global economy (Konings, 2011; Panitch and Gindin, 2012). Explanations of postwar financial globalization focused on the structural power of US finance have missed the transatlantic interactivity that shaped America's global financial power. Without a set of extremely particular and politically contingent institutional developments within the UK, driven by the efforts of bankers and state officials who sought to manage the distinctive challenges of the UK's transition into postimperial power, US finance could never have realized the spatial fix that brought the dollar into the City of London. In the process, the options open to US policy makers were also structured in important ways by dynamics unfolding within the UK. This was not, then, simply a case of the US having the power to "shape and determine the structures of the global political economy within which other states . . . have to operate" (Strange, 1994: 24–25). That formulation has produced a misleading interpretation of the monolithic power of the US.

It was also not, as has been argued (Burn, 1996; 2006), simply a case of the City of London, and with it the "City-Bank-Treasury" nexus at the commanding heights of UK capitalism, recovering its prewar gold standard orientation (Ingham, 1984: 131, 149). This was something qualitatively distinct. To suggest that the development of the Euromarkets and the arrival of US finance in London recovered the autonomy of the old axis of power in the City-Bank-Treasury nexus is to overlook the extent to which the arrival of the US dollar and US banks pulled US state power into the City. In doing so it fundamentally redefined UK sovereignty. In as far as the City-Bank-Treasury nexus did retain its predominance within UK capitalism, it did so by integrating itself within the rapidly internationalizing Federal Reserve-Wall Street-Treasury nexus at the heart of US capitalism. Transatlantic integration gave rise to a new order of Anglo-American finance, spatially and institutionally embedded within an Atlanticized UK capitalism. This emergent financial order was critical to the incubation of financial globalization that undermined, in synchronicity, both the Bretton Woods international monetary order and the postwar order of domestic financial regulation within the two states.

Anglo-American financial integration also sparked processes of regulatory interaction, through a transatlantic regulatory feedback loop that gave momentum to the broader international dynamics of financial liberalization. These processes led to the synthetic development of novel Anglo-American financial practices that proved central to the breakdown of Bretton Woods and the global takeoff of banking from the 1970s. Perhaps most consequentially, these dynamics would eventually sow the seeds for the global financial crisis of 2007/8. We cannot, then, credibly tell the story of the political economy of postwar global finance as a dichotomy between American ad hoc and European rules-based visions of financial globalization (Abdelal, 2007). Such a distinction misses the specificity of the UK's role within the genesis of financial globalization.

Owing to its former status as the leading sponsor of the international economic order and its possession of the City of London, as well as its tight integration with US finance, the UK's orientation toward financial globalization was distinctive from, and often contrary to, the prevailing continental position.[2] Additionally, we cannot tell the story of financial liberalization and institutional transformation within the US without properly appreciating the importance of the Special Relationship with the UK. As the book shows, momentum for the dismantling of the New Deal financial regulation in the US as well as the transformation in central banking techniques—particularly during the critical decade of the 1980s—owed a great deal to competitive interaction with UK finance. This Anglo-American dynamic is understated in the existing scholarship, which has conceived of the dynamics of financialization and liberalization within the US as largely endogenous (Krippner, 2005, 2011; Meltzer, 2009; Konings, 2011; Panitch and Gindin, 2012). The synchronized Anglo-American turn to neoliberalism was not simply the product of a shared transatlantic context of ideas or structural similarities of their political systems; Anglo-American development played a central role.

A focus on development has traditionally confined the discussion to issues of north-south inequality and the idea of divergent and asynchronous paths to capitalist modernity (Rist, 2002; Payne and Phillips, 2010). But, insofar as the institutions of capitalist sociality are always in flux, development can form the foundation for a historical analysis of *all* processes of socioeconomic change, not just those of the Global South. Turning our attention to "development" as a diachronic spatiotemporal dynamic of institutional transformation sui generis moves us away from the static tautology of US structural power and brings us toward an appreciation of the way US financial power resources were developed historically *and* geographically—not only through the endogenous growth of US economic power, but also via the expansion of US finance in and through the subordinate incorporation of UK capitalism.

In advancing these arguments about Anglo-American development, I make a wider point about the nature of order and historical transformation within global capitalism by breaking from the traditional focus upon distinctive stages of hegemonic or "imperial" rule. That tradition begins from the assumption of a dominant nation state impressing its power upon the international system in a monocausal and geographically ill-defined manner. Instead, I argue that patterns of international political-economic order are historically specific, resistant to generalization, and generated by complex and uneven coarticulations of capitalist development between and across distinctive nation-states and other scales. These developmental processes operate through and across privileged geographical sites—regional, national and subnational—that act as nodal points within global capitalism. From this emerges the sense of complex, integrated, and interdependent forms of global power, rather than a neat succession of transformations between discrete phases of global rule by a single dominant state. In an age of much more intensive and extensive globalization, that premise is more, not less, valid. Thinking in these terms provides important clues for interpreting the contemporary growth of China's international power under conditions of dense economic entanglement with US multinational corporations (MNCs) and the US dollar.

As an alternative way of thinking about the politics of financial globalization and systemic transformation, this book highlights the gradual postwar subsumption of UK capitalism within a larger, transnational sphere of Anglo-American development. In doing so, it stresses both the hugely determinative impact of the US upon the fortunes of UK capitalism and the way in which working with and through the UK also shaped the historical development of US capitalism in important ways. Most important, the book shows that, in their very interactive development, the UK and the US came to constitute something more than the sum of their parts: a distinctive Anglo-American developmental space that refashioned the global economic order, disrupting the Keynesian compromise in both states and spurring financial liberalization. The UK's role here was not merely incidental—it was integral. To frame the dynamics of postwar UK capitalism around the causes and consequences of "decline," as so much of the literature has done (Burnham, 1990; Overbeek, 1990; Gamble, 1994; English and Kenny, 2000), is to overlook the importance of the UK's role in resuscitating the globalization project, in conjunction with the US, after World War II.

Beyond its contribution to IPE, the book also challenges the understanding of Anglo-American capitalism found in comparative political economy (CPE). The UK and the US have served as the exemplars of a specific type of "Anglo-Saxon," "Anglo-liberal," or "liberal market" capitalism within CPE (Dore et al., 1999; Coates, 2000; Hall and Soskice, 2001; Hay, 2013a). This type has been comparatively distinguished from more "coordinated" (i.e., less market-dominated), "Rhenish," or "state-led" models of capitalism. The most influential treatment of this theme is found in the "varieties of capitalism" (VOC) approach (Hall and Soskice, 2001). This approach portrays the UK and the US as representative of a "liberal market economy" (LME) variety of capitalism defined by the predominance of market mechanisms in coordinating firms' activities.[3] Significantly, the configuration of Anglo-American economies around this ideal type is viewed as a product of "institutional complementarities" that arise *internally* to each model, facilitating a particular set of comparative advantages within the international division of labor.

The VOC approach has been subject to wide-ranging critique, including for (among other things) its narrow understanding of institutions, a depoliticized treatment of capitalism, and an inattentiveness to the centrality of the state (Hancke et al., 2007; Streeck, 2010a; Clift, 2014). Most important, regarding the argument developed in this book, the VOC portrayal of the UK and US economies has failed to substantiate empirically the formation of a supposedly parallel type of capitalism within the two states. Indeed, during the late nineteenth century, the UK and the US could even be seen to represent two *distinctive* models of capitalism, with UK capitalism characterized by small-scale, family-owned, "proprietary" production, while US capitalism, by contrast, was marked by an emerging "managerial" form of large-scale, technologically advanced, corporate organization in which ownership and control were separated (Lazonick, 1993). Even after World War II, the new settlement of UK social democracy and the legacy of US New Deal–era politics were substantively different, with corporatist structures of labor representation and welfarist provision of housing and health care, among other distinctions, much stronger in the former than the latter (King and Wood, 1999). How, then, did the widespread claims of a parallel liberalized vision and organizationally symmetrical capitalism in these two states gain traction?

Through its focus upon Anglo-American financial development, this book reveals that it was the long-term developmental interaction between the two states, not their internal institutional complementarities, that was central to the paradigmatic shift to a more market-oriented, "neoliberal" model of political economy during the 1980s. The comparative methodological nationalism of CPE, and the ahistoricism of the VOC approach, have rendered these important international dimensions and common lineages largely invisible. This book stresses the role of long-term and continuing *developmental interdependence* between the two states as both a driver of common features of Anglo-American capitalism (e.g., liberalized financial markets and high levels of inequality driven in part by financial sector salaries) and a cause of wider financial globalization, liberalization, and innovation. To the extent that we can draw illuminating comparative parallels between UK and US capitalism, then, we need to adopt a historical and methodologically internationalist perspective to properly understand them (Coates, 2014).

Empirically, this book breaks new ground by using original archival material from the Bank of England Archives, the National Archives, and the Archives of the British Bankers' Association. Drawing on this new evidence, as well as a novel theoretical framework, the book examines key episodes of Anglo-American interaction. From chapters 4 to 6, much of the supporting evidence is based upon archival sources: materials drawn from the Bank of England Archives in Threadneedle Street, London; the National Archives in Kew, Surrey; and the London Metropolitan Archives, London. It is only within the past decade, during the research for this book, that access to the entirety of this wide range of archival material has been possible. Under the thirty-year rule, many of the official documents pertaining to the early years of the Thatcher government only became available as of 2009. With those documents on the early years of the neoliberal transformation now available, it has become much easier to examine the development of state institutions during both the postwar period and the beginning of the neoliberal era. This also affords a much better opportunity to examine the transformation of UK capitalism within an Anglo-American horizon. We can now trace the collapse of Keynesianism, the ascendancy of monetarist ideas, and the trajectory of financial liberalization during the transition toward neoliberalism.

This archival material illuminates how influential institutions within the UK state became entangled in the relationship with the US, and how they interpreted and were impacted by that relationship. Rather than focusing on the entirety of that historical relationship, the book looks at decisive moments of Anglo-American relations in the development of the postwar global political economy. These moments were, I argue, central not only to UK development, but also to the transformation of US capitalism and the wider global political economy.[4] I set out to answer three main research questions: first, how did Anglo-American developmental dynamics shape the transition from a Keynesian regulatory order of finance to the emergence of a more liberalized financial system and the ascendancy of monetarist ideas in the UK? Second, how did these processes feed back into the development of US capitalism? And, third, in what ways did Anglo-American development both shape and reflect the broader international monetary order?

As the book demonstrates, an Anglo-American development sphere based upon increasing financial interdependence between the two states began to emerge in earnest during the 1920s, with the disastrous attempt to restore the gold standard. After the interwar years this interdependence began, tentatively, to reemerge. But it was with the development of the Euromarkets from the late

1950s that Anglo-American development began to reach a much fuller expression, shaping the crisis years of the Bretton Woods regime in the process. In the longer term, these processes came to undermine the national monetary systems and regulatory orders in the UK and the US. Bankers in London and New York pressed for financial liberalization while the development of new central banking practices ushered in the Anglo-American transition to neoliberal capitalism in the early 1980s. By 2007/8, the neoliberal model of deregulated finance and debt-driven consumption—of which the US and the UK had been the central architects—exploded to devastating effect.

The Shape of Things to Come

Although the book is geared toward motivating the broad argument for the centrality of Anglo-American development to the politics of postwar financial globalization, individual chapters engage specific debates pertinent to the different historical periods and topics under discussion. This is unavoidable, given the historical and thematic scope of the book, with many of the subtopics—such as the UK's early postwar relationship with the US and the politics of the 1976 International Monetary Fund (IMF) crisis—having spawned extensive scholarly literatures. This is not, then, simply a debate with the dominant perspectives within IPE, nor should it simply be read as such; it should also be read as a series of contributions to more discretely framed debates around political economy.

The book proceeds as follows. In chapter 1, I set out its theoretical framework, critiquing the tendency of IPE to overlook Anglo-American development, which, I argue, arises from a fixation with hegemonic cycles of rise and decline that has framed the UK and the US framed within a declinist narrative that forecloses alternative analytical strategies. I propose an alternative framework that, by building upon works that have drawn attention to the importance of financial power within the state (Ingham, 1984; Gowan, 1999; Wray, 2012; Panitch and Gindin, 2012), conceives of Anglo-American development in terms of the interdependent and coconstitutive relationship between the Federal Reserve-Treasury-Wall Street complex and the City-Bank-Treasury nexus. This developmental perspective provides important correctives to both the hegemony story and the concept of "structural power" prevalent within IPE, and it reveals the centrality of Anglo-American dynamics to cementing the international dominance of the dollar and propelling financial globalization.

Chapter 2 examines Anglo-American development from the nineteenth century to World War II. I focus on the "great reversal" in power that occurred as US development caught up to and closed the gap with the UK, after which leadership of the international monetary order came to depend increasingly upon their cooperative efforts, a process encapsulated by the ill-fated attempt to resuscitate the gold standard after World War I. The war weakened the UK and strengthened its US creditors, forcing the City to draw upon US financial support, from both private and central bankers, to relaunch the gold standard and restore sterling convertibility. Rather than viewing the failed leadership efforts of the 1920s as a consequence of the US' unwillingness and the UK's inability to lead (Kindleberger, 1973), or of the underdeveloped capacities of US finance (Konings, 2011), I emphasize the nascent but insufficient foundations of Anglo-American financial integration as a central factor in the failure of the interwar gold standard. Anglo-American cooperation was ultimately undermined by the lack of US willingness and capacity to play a greater leadership role and respect its duties and obligations under the gold standard system, leading to the collapse of the gold standard and the increasing rivalry and protectionism of the 1930s. The failure of Anglo-American management of the international monetary system in the interwar years had a formative impact upon the priorities instituted at Bretton Woods during the 1940s.

The Anglo-American crux of the international economy was reflected in the creation of the Bretton Woods framework. In chapter 3, I challenge the traditional IPE interpretation of Bretton Woods, which views it as the marker for a new era of US hegemony (Block, 1977; Gilpin, 1987; Schwartz, 2009a; Ikenberry, 2011). Stressing the "uneven interdependence" characteristic of the postwar Anglo-American relationship, I reveal the continuing mutual dependencies between the two states and their expression within the formation of Bretton Woods. The UK's role in the creation and dynamics of Bretton Woods went far beyond the ideas of John Maynard Keynes. The continued importance of both sterling as a major international currency and of the financial infrastructure contained within the City of London, allied to the international limits of private US finance, ensured that the development of UK capitalism continued to be fundamental to postwar international finance. Tracing the struggle between economic orthodoxy and emergent Keynesian ideas within the national political economies of the UK and the US, I show that the continuing relevance of pre-Keynesian economic orthodoxy—represented most influentially by transatlantic bankers—laid the basis for the subsequent undermining of Bretton Woods and the relaunching of financial globalization from the

1950s. The "embedded liberal" compromise established through Bretton Woods was critically undermined by the shallowness of its institutionalization within the Anglo-American architects: it was never embedded firmly enough.

Chapter 4 explores the way in which postwar restrictions on the use of sterling prompted UK merchant bankers to develop an innovative method for financing international trade. They tapped into the large volume of offshore dollars that had accrued because of massive overseas US spending through military aid and the Marshall Plan, using these dollars to finance trade between third parties, leading to the birth of the offshore "Eurodollar market." I challenge existing IPE interpretations of the Euromarkets that have viewed their development either in terms of the outward expansion of US financial power (Strange, 1987; Gowan, 1990; Konings, 2011; Panitch and Gindin, 2012), or as a return to the pre–World War I classical gold standard orientation of power within UK capitalism (Burn, 1999, 2006). I argue that the development of the Euromarkets represented the foundational moment in the emergence of a qualitatively distinctive form of integrated Anglo-American financial development. Construing the Euromarkets as an embedding of US structural power in international finance, the chapter suggests that coconstitutive Anglo-American developmental processes were integral to their emergence. Dynamics generated in London circumscribed and structured US monetary policy in a way that US-centric approaches overlook. The agency of City merchant bankers in constructing the Eurodollar market infrastructure, as well as the adaptation of the Bank of England and UK Treasury, did lay the transatlantic foundations for the longer-term hegemony of the dollar. But they also generated policy dilemmas for US officials and critically undermined the fixed exchange rate system agreed at Bretton Woods by creating the institutional infrastructure for vast offshore financial markets and capital flows.

After the collapse of Bretton Woods, the global economy entered a period of sustained turmoil. The oil shock of 1973 contributed to a severe "stagflationary" crisis: the combination of high inflation and low growth. The UK suffered more than most advanced capitalist states during the 1970s. Chapter 5 focuses upon the International Monetary Fund (IMF) crisis of 1976—a crucial turning point in the politics of financial globalization that has been underappreciated within IPE. Had the UK's Labour government enacted measures proposed by the party's left wing and had the City and the Bank proved unsuccessful in defending London's regulatory culture and sponsorship of the Euromarkets from threats both inside and outside the UK, then the advancement of financial globalization would have been sharply arrested.

Chapter 5 argues that the resolution of the 1976 crisis in favor of the UK's continued commitment to an open international economic order and the abandonment of Keynesian full employment reflected increased Anglo-American interdependence. Anglo-American financial integration generated a constituency of UK financiers, political forces, and institutions with an increasingly *Atlantic* orientation. Priorities among influential financial and state actors within the UK were now bound up with, and increasingly difficult to disentangle from, the interests of US finance and the US state. As the US pressured the UK through the disciplinary stance of the US Treasury and the Fed, refracted through the power of the IMF, UK officials, the Tories, and City bankers also embraced US discipline to achieve their own domestic political ambitions by undermining a Labour government that they viewed as outmoded, dangerous, and fiscally reckless. Financial, political, and policy elites within the UK made common cause with the US to overcome the challenge of a radicalized social democratic settlement promoted by the left wing of the Labour Party. I go beyond prevailing interpretations of the 1976 crisis by rejecting the binary framing of interpretations that focus on establishing a primary level of causality, either national or international, that explains the abandonment of Keynesianism by the Labour government (Ludlum, 1992; Baker, 1999; Harmon, 2008; Rogers, 2009). As an alternative, I show that postwar Anglo-American development generated an Atlanticized constituency of social forces *within* the UK, including UK financiers, political forces, and state institutions with an increasingly transatlantic outlook. These actors united with the interests of the US to defeat the challenge of a radicalized social democratic settlement that severely threatened the City's international role. Anglo-American development made it increasingly misleading to distinguish between distinctly "national" and "international" causes.

By the end of the 1970s, with spiraling inflation in the US, Paul Volcker, as head of the Fed, adopted a radical monetary stance, pushing interest rates up to record highs in order to break inflation and undermine the wage militancy of US workers. In the US this restoration of class power, underpinning the neoliberal political project, relied upon high interest rates, recession, and market liberalization. Across the Atlantic, the formula for capitalist restructuring under Thatcher exhibited remarkable parallels. In chapter 6, I depart from existing approaches to the rise of neoliberalism, which point to the significance of the ideological similarities between Thatcherism and Reaganism (Krieger, 1986: 17; Gamble, 2001: 129; Harvey, 2005: 22; Peck and Tickell, 2007: 28), excavating the processes of transatlantic institutional symbiosis that drove the synchronized embrace of financial liberalization and monetarist central banking. Uncovering these formative transatlantic dynamics leads me to challenge IPE accounts of US financialization that have overstated the endogeneity of liberalization and associated financial sector expansion (Greider, 1987: 155; Schwartz, 2009a: 211; Konings, 2011: 131–37; Panitch and Gindin, 2012: 169; Krippner, 2012: 73).

In chapter 6 I argue that the radicalization of monetary policy, regulatory transformation, and central bank innovation in the US and the UK emerged out of institutional complementarities and interdependencies generated by Anglo-American development. The development of offshore markets in the City led bankers on both sides of the Atlantic to push for further domestic liberalization, as competition between London and New York intensified. US banks pressured regulators to replicate the City's offshore conditions, which gradually eroded New Deal–era financial regulations. These dynamics, alongside the Fed's failure to regulate the Euromarkets, demonstrated both the limits on US monetary policy autonomy and the importance of the transatlantic impetus to liberalization emerging from Anglo-American financial integration. Embracing monetarism, Thatcher and Reagan made clear that price stability would be restored and that working-class solidarity would be broken. In the absence of the Bretton Woods framework, both states demonstrated their commitment to internalizing discipline through extreme applications of monetary policy and direct confrontations with the labor movement. The pursuit of price stability over and above the Keynesian commitment to full employment helped maintain the centrality of London and New York in global financial markets. Developments in the UK and the US led the way for the broader adoption of neoliberalism within the global political economy and the further development of financialization.

As chapter 7 demonstrates, these structural transformations—part of the longer history of postwar Anglo-American development—were the ultimate cause of the global financial crisis of 2007/8. The chapter echoes IPE accounts of the origins of the crisis that have recognized its distinctively Anglo-American accent (Gowan, 2009; Hay, 2013a), but it also argues that such interpretations have not sufficiently identified the systematic transatlantic developmental processes linking the reconstitution of Anglo-American financial markets. The crisis cannot be explained as an extension of internal US dynamics of financial market transformation into a "satellite" London market (Gowan, 2009). To do so, I contend, is to miss the mutual causal dependency of Anglo-American development. Modeling a comparatively specific

"Anglo-liberal" form of capitalism indicates the core features of the defective growth model that generated the crisis (Hay, 2013a), but it does not provide a sufficiently thorough historicization of these dynamics, nor does it adequately map the transatlantic developmental processes that underpinned it.

Chapter 7 argues that the Anglo-American origins of the crisis had a deep historical-institutional lineage, rooted in the transatlantic transformation from the Keynesian order during the early 1980s. This transformation was itself enabled and conditioned by previous processes of postwar Anglo-American development. The continuation of long-term transatlantic financial liberalization and integration dynamics during the 1980s and beyond placed the markets in New York and London at the heart of the institutional infrastructure that transmitted the crisis globally. Anglo-American preeminence within international banking regulation ensured that the global financial system would accommodate the enormous leveraging-up of major banks. Politically, the conversion of both the UK's Labour Party and America's Democratic Party to the virtues of financial deregulation, as well as their acceptance of the epistemic omnipotence of financial markets, laid the basis for the profoundly misplaced complacence that generated economic vulnerability on an enormous scale. Viewing the events of 2007/8 from the perspective of the longue durée of Anglo-American finance allows us to more fully appreciate the role of the nexus between treasuries, central banks, and private bankers on both sides of the Atlantic in producing the crisis.

Chapter 8 sketches out some of the major themes of the postcrisis political economy of Anglo-America. Identifying the central policy pairing between fiscal austerity and monetary loosening, the chapter draws upon accounts of the structural crisis of neoliberal capitalism (Gamble, 2014; Streeck, 2014), arguing that, despite the adoption of unorthodox monetary policy and the restoration of growth, economic recovery has failed to arrest the underlying structural crisis of Anglo-American political economies. In the postcrisis era, the reliance upon a strategy of ultralow interest rates and quantitative easing initiated by the US and the UK demonstrated the continued centrality of Anglo-American central bank leadership to the global economy. But the sluggish return to growth in the West, and the continued stagnation of living standards within the UK and the US specifically, have revealed the declining ability of neoliberal capitalism to deliver economic growth and distributional gains in amounts adequate to bolster democratic consent. The rise of antiestablishment politics in both states—and the fracturing of the longstanding neoliberal center ground of party politics—has led to new political and economic dynamics. Alongside these changes, the rebalancing of the City-Bank-Treasury nexus toward Chinese finance, the policies of Donald Trump, and Brexit are transforming the global economy. These dynamics, I argue, threaten the political economy of the Special Relationship and the wider international standing of the UK and the US.

The book concludes by reappraising the history and politics of capitalist development within Anglo-America. Viewed through a wide historical lens, a clear picture emerges: it is the postwar Keynesian transformation of Anglo-American capitalism that is the historical anomaly in need of explanation as an exceptional development, not the rise of a neoliberal order from the 1970s. Staggering levels of inequality and the limited capacity of democracy to rein in the forces of the market have been the normal condition of modern liberal capitalism. It took two violent cataclysms of total war and the existence of a Soviet alternative to shock the system into a more equitable and democratized reconfiguration—one that placed markets (albeit incompletely) in the service of communitarian ends.

That this reconfiguration was already under threat from resurgent forces of political-economic orthodoxy by the early years of the Bretton Woods order speaks to another important lesson. The postwar embedding of liberalism within the national form of the social democratic state and the international regime of Bretton Woods did not go far enough; too much power was left to private finance in London and New York. As transatlantic bankers articulated their vision in ever-bolder terms in the decades after Bretton Woods, the vision of a democratically controlled form of capitalism that could deliver sustained growth and increased equality receded further in memory. The core institutions within the state were not transformed in a manner that might enable a lasting commitment to full employment and the pursuit of more equitable and democratic goals. As we wrestle once more with the challenge of capitalist economies that produce enormous material excesses and a sense of collective disempowerment, the lessons of history should be heeded.

1

Conceptualizing Anglo-American Development

THE THEORY of hegemonic stability (HST) was foundational to the emergence of IPE. It was with the "really big question" of systemic transformation that the discipline was preoccupied during the turbulent period of the 1970s (Kindleberger, 1973; Cohen, 2008). Our understanding of the history of the modern global political economy has been shaped, since those early enquiries, by the theory's assumptions. Scholars have identified different reasons for the rise and decline of hegemonic powers, but the commitment to a cyclical view of the history of the global political economy—punctuated by periods of hegemonic order under the leadership of a dominant state—is widely shared (Gilpin, 1975, 1983; Krasner, 1976: Olson, 1982; Keohane, 1984; Cox, 1987; Arrighi, 1990). Indeed, in recent years the concept of hegemony has made a pronounced return to political economy debates. It has been applied (awkwardly) to Germany's regional leadership role within the Eurozone, with the country being chided for the "reluctance" of its leadership and the failure to properly fulfill the functions of a hegemon (Blyth and Matthijs, 2011; Bulmer and Paterson, 2013; Crawford, 2014). At a more appropriately global level, and framed more clearly within the cyclical sense of historical leadership transitions, the concept has also been resuscitated to make sense of China's intensified global influence (Arrighi, 2007; Campbell, 2008; Beeson, 2013). The impact of HST within IPE is not, then, merely a matter of historical curiosity; it is a live issue with substantial relevance to how we think about contemporary global transformations.

According to HST, the history of the modern global political economy can be divided into distinctive phases of hegemonic leadership—the *Pax Britannica* from 1815 to 1914, followed, after a disorderly and illiberal interregnum during the interwar years, by the *Pax Americana* from 1944 to 1971. Under both periods of leadership, a single, hegemonic state is said to have sponsored a largely consensual and liberal order of trade and finance by providing public goods. Militarily, the hegemon's overwhelming power ensured security and stability. While realists and liberals stressed, respectively, the centrality of the state and the importance of international regimes in cementing hegemonic governance, Marxists highlighted the importance of social classes and ideological consensus in promoting and sustaining a liberal order (Gilpin, 1983; Keohane, 1984; Cox, 1987).

Numerous authors have challenged this narrative, arguing that the case for UK hegemony during the nineteenth century is flimsy, and that the HST framework is of limited use in understanding the continuities and distinctions of the two liberal orders (Latham, 1997; Lake, 2000; Hobson, 2002; Lacher and Germann, 2012). Despite these challenges, the theory continues to influence our understanding of both past and present manifestations of order within the global political economy. This enduring influence is a problem. HST has produced a deeply misleading reading of the history of the global political economy: it views history as a sequential cycle of neatly defined periods of rising and declining power, or hegemonic leads and lags (Krasner, 1976; Helleiner, 1994: 14), and has treated the demise of the United Kingdom and the ascendance of the United States as neatly distinguished and analytically discrete (Gilpin, 1975; Keohane, 1984; Gilpin, 1987; Arrighi, 1994; Lake, 2000).[1]

This chapter establishes the book's theoretical framework by interrogating the HST narrative and its impact upon our understanding of UK and US capitalism in the postwar period. It does so by arguing that the cyclical history of hegemonic leadership within the global political economy has led to a *declinist* preoccupation within scholarship on the UK and the US, focusing on the causes and consequences of their economic and political decline. This declinist focus has foreclosed alternative ways of thinking about the transformations of capitalism *within* each country and, more important, the transformative relationships *between* the Anglo-American political economies and their effect on the global economy. Declinism has also obscured the importance of processes of Anglo-American development within the global political economy.

By shifting focus from decline to *development*, and from national power to transnational interdependence, the chapter builds an alternative theoretical framework of Anglo-American development. Drawing upon a heterodox tradition of political economy—which stresses the importance of the

relationship between private banking, treasury control, and central banking—
the chapter outlines the primary historical-institutional bases of Anglo-
American capitalism and their transnational linkages. This framework has two
major advantages. Firstly, it recovers the important and underappreciated role
of *combined* Anglo-American leadership within the politics of postwar financial globalization. And, secondly, it presents a novel way of understanding both
the emergence (and the limits) of US power within global finance, by revealing
how America's financial ascendancy was articulated in and through transformations within UK capitalism.

The chapter begins by examining the impact of declinist narratives linked
to HST upon the study of Anglo-American capitalism. In the second section, the chapter critically engages the concept of structural power and outlines a developmental approach to global political-economic order. The third
section establishes the theoretical basis for understanding the general relationship between banking and the state within contemporary capitalism.
The specific historical-institutional foundations of Anglo-American financial
development—and their role within the politics of financial globalization—
are then outlined in the fourth section. Finally, a framework for understanding
the linked transformations of domestic financial regimes within the US and
the UK and the wider international monetary order is established.

A Tale of Two Declines

The onset of decline in the UK and the US was, according to conventional
periodization, separated by almost one hundred years. The UK's descent from
the peak of its imperial power began in the 1870s, as German, Japanese, and
US late industrialization eroded the privileges of pioneering industrial status
(Gamble, 1990: 54; Pollard, 2002: 116). In the postwar period, with the UK
crippled by debts, the preoccupation with UK decline was revived. For the US,
the recognition of decline arrived in earnest during the early 1970s, as US trade
performance deteriorated and the dollar was cut loose from the fixed gold
convertibility enshrined at Bretton Woods. Yet, despite the substantial gap in
the timing of the onset of the symptoms of decline, the scholarly recognition
of the phenomenon in both states has been peculiarly parallel. This disjuncture
between the distinctive historical periodization of decline in each country on
the one hand, and the synchronized recognition of its effects on the other, is
puzzling. It is explicable, in part, by the sheer endurance and intransigence of
the UK's condition of decline, which, having first been recognized by

commentators in the 1880s, was still the prevailing framework for thinking about UK capitalism during the 1990s (Gamble, 1990). But, in another sense, the synchronicity of declinist narratives is a product of the specific historical interpretation of the international economy proposed by HST. Either explicitly or implicitly, assessment of the fortunes of both states was, from the 1970s, increasingly interpreted through this shared cyclical reading of international economic history.[2]

Scholars of UK capitalism confirmed its relative decline through an assessment of the UK's postwar standing in comparison to US hegemony—more specifically, through an examination of the early postwar relationship between the two states that affirmed the UK's newly junior status and shaped the UK's prospects for prosperity. For the US, acknowledgment of the earlier rise and decline of the UK was both a way of making sense of US power in historical terms and, simultaneously, an early warning system for detecting signs of decline and learning the required lessons from the UK case to prevent it (Gilpin, 1975; 2002; Krasner, 1976; Calleo, 2005).

The shared international history within which thinkers on both sides of the Atlantic assessed their national capitalisms created a peculiar symmetry of declinist preoccupation. Scholars of the UK made sense of the UK experience, retrospectively, through the recognition of US predominance and the broader historical analytic of rise and decline enabled by this comparative framing. US academics viewed the crisis of the 1970s through the comparative historical lens of an earlier period of UK hegemonic decline and asked whether the weakening of US predominance and the breakdown of Bretton Woods might presage a return to the fractious, protectionist, and unstable tendencies of the 1930s (Kindleberger, 1973).

Although the historical roots of the UK decline debate are deep, there remains no consensus over its principal causes (Gamble, 1990: 32; English and Kenny, 2000: 279–300). But the very fact of decline itself is accepted. The same cannot be said for the parallel debate regarding the US. This decline is far more disputed. This dispute is due in part to the way the use of the UK case as a reference point for the US led to a premature diagnosis of decline. There is still no consensus over the question of whether US power has been in retreat; while various scholars suggested that it had experienced a pronounced decline from its postwar zenith (Gilpin, 1975; Keohane, 1982; Krasner, 1982), a contending group proposed that it had been redefined rather than suffering terminal retreat (Strange, 1987; Gill, 1991; Gowan, 1999; Konings, 2011; Panitch and Gindin, 2012). The declinists, similarly to their UK comparators, pointed to numerous different causes of decline (Gilpin, 1975: 46–47; Keohane, 1982: 66–68; Krasner, 1982: 33–42).

What matters for the focus of this book is the effect of these declinist narratives on understanding Anglo-American capitalism. One of the most important consequences of the debate over US decline is the ambiguity it has produced regarding the form and extent of US power and its projection upon subordinate forms of national capitalism. As with the UK, the focus on delineating decline has relegated other questions and concerns to the wayside. IPE scholarship became too concerned with the what, why, and how of the decline of the US and to the neglect of the underlying developmental processes that defined its role within the postwar international political economy.

By already accepting the legitimacy of the hegemonic-cycles approach to understanding IPE, these accounts fixated on exploring the transition from hegemony to decline rather than tracing how the development of US capitalism continued to shape the global political economy. Methodologically, the analyses focused on US power as a predominantly national question, which overlooked the extent to which the US state had already been internationalized through the reconstruction of global capitalism after World War II; the formation of Bretton Woods; the promotion of the international role of the dollar; and the extension of New Deal institutional patterns into Western Europe with the Marshall Plan (Maier, 1977; Gill, 1991; Gowan, 1999; Konings, 2011; Panitch and Gindin, 2012).

The Development of Structural Power

In response to declinist arguments within US academic circles, scholars developed alternative theorizations. Non-American scholars based in the UK or Canada, to whom overwhelming US power still felt very real, provided dissenting points of view.[3] Susan Strange's work was foundational here: her notion of "structural power" was the fundamental conceptual innovation underpinning the argument that US power had not diminished but had in fact undergone a transformation of form and function. Strange's work served as an important corrective to the preoccupation with US decline; by shifting attention to structural dimensions of US power, she elucidated the continuing influence of the US in shaping the parameters of action within the global economy and promoting US interests.

Strange (1987: 565) defined structural power as "the power to choose and to shape the structures of the global political economy within which other states, their political institutions, their economic enterprises, and their professional people have to operate."[4] This refers to a state's capacity to articulate the boundaries of political-economic action, order the pivotal institutions of the global political economy, and thus delimit the agency of other actors. It was less about directly exercising agency and consensual leadership in relation to other states, and more about structuring the options and choices of others through the weight of US power resources. As the nature of relationships between states changed, from the mid-1960s onward, structural power became more important (553). The US benefited from this transformation, with its structural power increasing. Continued US financial and military dominance were evidence of this enduring power (Strange, 1988b: 7–8); the notion of its "lost hegemony" was a pernicious myth.

The argument that follows in this book shifts our focus from cyclical notions of hegemonic rise and decline and moves it beyond structural power arguments. It also deepens our understanding of the developmental processes that underpin forms of global order. These processes are not adequately addressed within HST; neither are they captured by the concept of structural power. This is because Strange's work contained no overarching or clearly specified theory of change (May, 1996: 185; Tooze, 2000: 286). The concept of structural power is based upon circular reasoning—the US has structural power because it can shape the choices and preferences of other actors, but it can do so only because it has already acquired structural power. Thus, while Strange captures a very important aspect of how structural power can be utilized once attained, she does not account for how such potential emerges over time. This failure creates a theoretical bias toward continuity and obscures the microdynamism of capitalist developmental processes and institutional change; Strange's conceptualization offers no sense of how the institutional infrastructure underpinning US structural power arose. Attentiveness to these dynamics matters, because it is precisely these microprocesses that feed, cumulatively, into larger macroshifts in the prevailing orientation of the global political economy. The continuity bias of structural power provides no means to understand how existing orders came to be, or how new forms of order might emerge, and what characteristics they will likely exhibit. These neglected dynamics are integral to understanding patterns of transformation within IPE.

American structural power resources were, in fact, amassed through interactive developmental processes. Particularly in matters of finance, where Strange (1994: 104) identified US structural power as crucial evidence against decline, the historical development of structural power was tightly linked to the decisions and actions of UK policy makers and financiers. US bankers and policy makers, therefore, were not always able to steer these developmental processes toward intentional policy design and strategy—to "choose and shape," as Strange puts it (1987: 565). US power did not only structure the options of other states; it was also structured by the actions of foreign states and social forces in critical ways that were hugely consequential for the type of global political economy that took shape. These dynamics do not only apply to the case of the UK, but also to other important national capitalisms too, as well as in issue areas outside of finance.[5] In this book, the argument is that in the crucial area of financial globalization, Anglo-American development was paramount.

A further limitation of structural power, already alluded to above, is that it posits a one-directional outward projection of US power onto the broader global political economy. Contrary to the notion of structural power, US policies and practices also often ended up constraining and delimiting the possibilities for US development, and US choices and options were themselves structured in important ways by other powerful state and financial actors. In relation to other advanced capitalist states, this was a case of mutual dependence, something that structural power theories have failed to capture (Culpepper, 2015). The stress placed on the capacity of the US to "choose and shape" the structural foundations of the global political economy is excessively voluntaristic, overlooking the unintended and unexpected outcomes of codevelopment between capitalist states across time and space. As formulated by Strange, structural power never came to terms with the spatially and institutionally complex processes of transnational capitalist development that generated, often quite accidentally, the institutional capacities and infrastructure that both underpinned and, crucially, constrained America's postwar power.

The lines of causality here are complex and imbalanced. US power was a much more decisive factor in the UK's postwar development than vice versa. But, despite this imbalance, an important developmental reciprocity within Anglo-America impacted the US and the wider global political economy, particularly in matters of financial liberalization and innovation: US structural power in finance emerged through transatlantic interactivity. As we shall see in chapter 4, without highly contingent and specific institutional developments within the UK, which reflected the agency of financiers and state managers as they wrestled with the distinctive challenges of managing the UK's transition to postimperial power, America's international dominance within the sphere of finance would not have been achieved, nor would financial glo-balization have intensified so successfully. UK state institutions and merchant bankers drew in US finance by transforming their institutional orientations and capacities and opening UK capitalism to US financial power. Not only this, but the particular trajectory of UK development produced its own struc-tural power resources. UK institutional configurations, policy orientations, ideas, and financial practices constrained the policy autonomy of US state institutions and shaped the business strategies of US banks as they worked through the wider structures of Anglo-American capitalism.

A note on the term "development" is required here, since it arrives laden with baggage. By "development" here I do not refer to some naïve notion of inevitable progressive change toward a predefined telos.[6] Nor do I refer to a prescriptive array of normatively desirable policy practices and institutional arrangements associated with economic and social progress and targeted at a specified group of "developing" countries (Rist, 2002). Instead, I refer here to open-ended, contingent, and contested processes of socioeconomic institu-tional transformation. This is a broader ontology of development that seeks to provide a framework for an internationally oriented historical-institutional analysis of political economy.[7] In doing so, this framework supports con-temporary attempts to reintegrate development as a fundamental component of the broader theoretical lexicon of a holistic political economy approach (Payne and Phillips, 2010). Developmental processes can, in this more foun-dational and secular sense, be capitalist or noncapitalist. But, regarding our subject matter here, they are firmly centered upon capitalist market orders.

The shift to development is also, in part, a departure from methodological nationalism.[8] Development places emphasis on the internationally interde-pendent dimensions of these changes that cut across national borders. Devel-opment processes are contestable, conditioned by a wider global context of pressures and opportunities, and punctuated by moments of crisis. These cri-sis moments can provide either the potential for an accelerated tempo and broadened scope of transformation, or for the reversal of a preexisting trajec-tory of institutional change.[9] A developmental approach requires a chrono-logically extensive conception of the developmental processes and institu-tional transformations that underpin patterns of global order. These processes can be thought of as the continual creation and re-creation of instituted political-economic orders that involve the negation of alternative devel-opmental possibilities and bear the imprint of a particular symbolic-ideological or normative content. Within capitalism, the commitment to a market-competitive and market-dependent system of private economic activity, driven by private credit creation under an enveloping price system, structures socioeconomic activity and class relationships (Ingham, 2008; Streeck, 2010b).

Power dynamics are crucial in driving these processes. They bring into being certain developmental outcomes and reigning configurations of ideas and interests by negating others. Power is institutionalized and institutions are always in flux; what varies is the tempo of their flux and the opportunities and constraints that this presents to agents (Streeck and Thelen, 2005; Mahoney and Thelen, 2010). They are thus part of a "structured historical process" (Streeck, 2010c: 661). Structural power has emphasized the "structured" nature of historical dynamics in the global political economy, and the role of US power in shaping these dynamics, but it has downplayed the temporally extensive processual dimensions of historical-institutional transformation.[10]

By drawing on insights from historical institutionalism and setting them within an international context, we can better explain the formation and dissipation of structural power resources and broader patterns of transformation over time and across space. Historical institutionalists foreground temporality as a critical factor in explaining institutional trajectories. They situate institutions within ongoing historical processes that need to be captured through a suitably broad temporal span, and they focus attention on the role of social conflicts and groupings of socioeconomic interests in shaping institutional development, treating institutions as deeply politicized entities that are produced by—and, in turn, come to reproduce—distinctive patterns of power distribution within politics and the economy (Thelen, 1999: 381–94).

Attentiveness to temporality matters because it highlights how the development of political constraints and opportunities over time creates a "different kind of political game" (Fioretos, 2011: 371). In other words, as configurations of socioeconomic interests cluster around particular institutional arrangements, the very terms and scope of political and economic contestation shift. For historical institutionalists, timing and sequence contribute distinctive features to political processes.[11] Two related concepts are particularly salient: path dependence and positive feedback.

Path dependence refers to the way in which "particular courses of action, once introduced, can be virtually impossible to reverse" (Pierson, 2004: 18). Events or decisions at critical junctures of institutional development can lead to specific historical pathways that become increasingly difficult to modify or reverse over time. These path-dependent patterns of institutional development are driven by "positive feedback"—the self-reinforcing nature of specific institutional arrangements. Once an institution or a set of institutions is established it may create two distinctive types of feedback effect. Firstly, actors adapt to the new incentive structure created by the institution, adapting strategically in ways that reflect and reinforce the logic of the wider system. Secondly, to the extent that institutions are not neutral social mechanisms, but instead reflect and reproduce power imbalances within capitalism, particular institutions and policies strengthen certain groups while undermining others.

As these distributional inequities feedback, they produce a self-reinforcing logic whereby certain policy pathways become blocked off over time (Thelen, 1999: 392–94). This leads to a situation of policy "lock-in"—changing course becomes progressively harder the longer a particular strategy or institutional arrangement is pursued (Fioretos, 2011: 371). Existing policies create combinations of resources and incentives that help shape the positions of interest groups, governing political elites, and individual actors, with political consequences (Pierson, 1993: 608). These lock-in effects contribute to path-dependency *within* particular institutions. They may also encourage the formation of *additional* complementary institutional clusters, locking in broader patterns of institutional development and interest formation (Pierson, 2004: 27).

Critics have charged historical institutionalists with overstating continuity, providing a limited conception of institutional transformation, and neglecting the importance of ideas as a causal force within political economy (Blyth, 1997, 2002; Schmidt, 2008; Carstensen, 2011). Focusing too narrowly on the relationship between distinctive socioeconomic interest groups and institutional development can lead historical institutionalists to treat social interests as given, overlooking the extent to which social interests are actually shaped by the dominant framework of ideas prevalent within a particular historical period. In this sense, actors may have more choice and room for maneuver than the constraining institutional effects of feedback dynamics and path dependency would suggest. By failing to sufficiently attend to the impact of ideas upon socioeconomic interests, historical institutionalists have struggled to capture sharp departures from existing institutional arrangements of economic governance (Matthijs, 2012: 17). Scholars of ideational institutionalism have provided important correctives to these shortcomings by foregrounding the significance of economic ideas as both the intersubjective glue of specific historical-institutional orders and the disruptors of settled policy parameters and drivers of institutional change. Clearly, then, we also need to understand how the rise and fall of specific ideational frameworks for interpreting the management of capitalism shapes the perceived interests of different actors and impacts pathways of institutional development. In the present study, I focus on the postwar rise and fall of Keynesian ideas within Anglo-America and their supplanting by monetarist and neoliberal ideas of economic governance. The role of these competing ideas has been particularly significant during times of upheaval and uncertainty within the Anglo-American economies.

Understanding the historical-institutional and ideational dynamics outlined above is crucial to capturing the emergence of different forms of rule and specific orders within the global political economy. Shifting the focus to Anglo-American development as a set of dynamic processes driven by transatlantic combinations of private and public power, occurring over different temporal horizons, and initiated by different social forces within distinctive institutional settings and spatial sites, we arrive at a more fluid and diachronically extensive notion of the formation of US financial power—one that recognizes the postwar build-up of dollar dominance and the internationalization of US banking, while also acknowledging the constraints and dependencies of that power upon the intentions, actions, interests, and ideas of UK bankers and state managers. These relational power processes feed into the composition and decomposition of historically instituted frameworks of socioeconomic power that constitute the global political economy. Nationally, the most significant postwar transformation has been the shift from the Keynesian form of capitalism to the contemporary market-liberal or neoliberal orientation. Internationally, the transition from the Bretton Woods framework to the post–Bretton Woods order is paramount. It is upon these linked transformations that this book focuses, charting the importance of Anglo-American dynamics within them.

Financial Order in Modern Capitalism

Having sketched the foundations of a developmental approach to global order, we now need to provide a more sustained theorization of the financial relationships underpinning Anglo-American development. This requires us to take two additional steps. Firstly, we need to consider the dominant institutional concentration of financial power within modern capitalism *in general*. This is achieved by identifying the functional specificities of the monetary institutions of contemporary capitalism—in other words, what they "do" within a modern political economy. The functional perspective allows us to identify a universally important concentration of financial power within contemporary capitalism grounded in the close institutional linkages between private banking, treasury control, and central banking. This functional perspective is limited, however. While a useful heuristic that enables a general appreciation of where to look to understand the central dynamics of modern financial systems, it tells us very little about the political construction of these institutional relationships, the agency of private and public financial actors within them, or the historical-institutional specificities and path-dependencies that are unique to individual national capitalist systems. It is with these more explicitly political and historical dimensions of financial development that this book is principally concerned. To move from the general functional level to the *particular* framing of the Anglo-American financial orders, we need to adopt a second, historical-institutional level of analysis. This allows us to recognize the specific historical-institutional manifestation of the financial order within the UK and the US—the way these institutions historically came to be, the politics driving their development, and their nationally distinctive features. We can then begin to outline how and why these distinctive national financial orders came to form the basis for a broader sphere of Anglo-American development during the twentieth century.

Modern capitalist economies are characterized by a specific, private credit money system. Rather than simply acting as intermediaries of existing money by connecting depositors and borrowers, private banks create new money ex nihilo (Schumpeter, 1954: 330; Wray, 1998: 79; Werner, 2005: 178; Ingham, 2008: 75). In issuing new loans to borrowers, they create IOUs, which become new deposits for their borrowers and can be used as means of payment to third parties. The creation of these new credit loans generates funding for the financing of production and financial market speculation (Ingham, 2008: 53). It also enables lenders and borrowers to finance current economic activity based on expected future returns, thus overcoming the temporal limitation imposed by a dependency on accumulated present savings. This gives the capitalist credit money system tremendous dynamism, by escaping present constraints through the provision of credit based on a future promise of loan repayment (with interest) generated through economic activity (Streeck, 2011: 156–57).

What enables private banks to create credit money that is widely trusted and accepted throughout the modern economy? The power of the state is crucial here. Ultimately, is it the sovereign authority of the state that undergirds the operation of the monetary system. States create tokens in payment (i.e., money) in return for goods and services that they purchase from society. In modern economies, they do this by fiat—writing checks that their central banks promise to accept from recipients (Ingham, 2008: 75). Alongside private banks, then, they share the monopoly on the legitimate creation of credit money. But, unlike private banks, they have a unique capacity to generate the *private demand for money* that underpins the acceptability of government IOUs as a universal means of payment within the state. This is because governments can impose *tax liabilities* that must be paid to the state on pain of imprisonment (Wray, 1998: 6–7). The sovereign chooses a money of account for the economy and imposes tax liabilities in the same unit of account—for example, pound sterling or US dollars (Wray, 2012: 42). As the government can set the acceptable means of repayment (i.e., its own government IOUs), it is able to generate and manipulate demand for its own money supply. This puts government IOUs at the top of the monetary hierarchy. Government money is the only money that is accepted for the ultimate payment of taxes. It is also the money into which bank liabilities are convertible.[12] Clearing payments between private banks are made with government money, and payments between private banks and the central bank are also settled through government IOUs. Government money is the most liquid liability used within the domestic economy (Wray, 1998: 77).

The hierarchical relationship between government and private credit money has important implications for the functional interdependencies between private banking and the public monetary power of the state embodied by the treasury (or finance ministry) and the central bank. These interdependencies form the "money market": the institutionalized creditor-debtor relationships between the state, the central bank, and the private banking system that are central to the coordination of the supply and demand of money (Ingham, 2008: 148). Private banks maintain a privileged role within the money market because they have special access to *central bank money*, which is the ultimate means through which to settle debts. This unique access to central bank money gives private banks substantial creative and structural power within the modern economy—creative power because they can generate new monetary resources to lend at interest, and structural power because they decide who has access to credit, at what price, and on what terms. Because of their special access to government IOUs, their private money has widespread credibility and liquidity within the economy; this centrality to the money system means that their failure would be catastrophic for the economy's operation. This leads to the "too big to fail" problem—borne out spectacularly during the global financial crisis—in which private banks take greater risks safe in the knowledge that government authorities cannot afford to let them fail (Culpepper, 2015).

But this is a condition of *mutual dependency*, with private banks also depending upon the institutional authority and goodwill of state institutions. The treasury and the central bank are vested with sovereign power; they form the two related components of the government account (Wray, 2012).[13] The treasury is empowered with the capacity to spend, tax, and issue public debt. Because the state is vested with the sovereign power to tax, assuming it has a credible fiscal infrastructure of tax administration, its promises to pay debts (i.e., government IOUs) are in high demand. This puts government—or "high-powered"—money at the base of money creation in the wider banking system. State spending, through the creation of deposits on the government's account at the central bank in return for government bonds, enables the creation of new reserves within the banking system. As government borrowing and spending increase the reserves of private banks, they enable increased private money creation based on those reserves. To a considerable extent, then, private money creation is dependent on the fiscal policies of the government.

A similar functional dependency exists between private banks and the central bank. The central bank sets interest rates, regulates credit supply, governs the exchange rate, and pursues price objectives while also serving as the lender of last resort to private banks. Central banks exercise an important regulatory oversight role in relation to private banks, setting the general market price for money through interest rate policy and underwriting banks' balance sheets through the provision of lender-of-last-resort facilities during times of distress. This lender-of-last-resort function is an important bond of dependency between private banks and the central bank. Without access to central bank reserves (i.e., government IOUs), private banks are unable to settle payments and are vulnerable to liquidity crises. Private bank dependency gives the central bank regulatory leverage over private money creation. There is, therefore, a fundamental interdependence between these public and private monetary institutions within capitalism.[14] Contrary to the prevailing neoliberal discourse, which tends to view "states" and "markets" as opposing interests and clearly differentiated spheres of activity, the reality of economic activity within a modern capitalist monetary system points to a much deeper and inescapable coarticulation between market and state power.[15] Any understanding of financial order within contemporary advanced political economies must, accordingly, place a special emphasis upon these monetary relations. But what makes these institutional relationships within the Anglo-American political economies uniquely relevant to understanding the modern global political economy?

Anglo-America and Financial Globalization

Having reviewed the functional interdependencies between private and state financial institutions within modern capitalism, we now need to consider the specific historical-institutional features of capitalist money markets within the UK and the US and their implications for Anglo-American development. Here I build upon a rich tradition of heterodox political economy that stresses the centrality of the historical-institutional links that have developed between private finance, treasury control, and central bank governance within Anglo-American capitalism (Anderson, 1964; Longstreth, 1979; Ingham, 1984; Gowan, 1999; Konings, 2011; Panitch and Gindin, 2012). Examining the historical connections between private and public financial authority in the UK and the US allows us to understand the institutional basis of Anglo-American development.

Within the UK context, the foundational contribution to this framework comes from Geoffrey Ingham's examination of the City of London's role within the world economy.[16] For Ingham (1984: 6) the City's centuries-old status as the linchpin of the world capitalist system inscribed a "dual character" within UK capitalism. The UK's standing as the first industrial economy coexisted with its role as the world's major commercial entrepôt—a spatial zone within which international flows of trade and credit could be generated and mediated. Although coexistent, the two facets were not equal. International commercial capitalism prevailed, exerting a greater influence on UK society. Internally, the City's primacy over maligned industrial interests was bolstered by institutional support from both the Treasury and the Bank of England.[17] By the late nineteenth century, the relationship between these three poles of institutionalized power had evolved into an integrated and interdependent system—a City-Bank-Treasury nexus.

The crystallization of this domestic institutional nexus had significant international consequences. The UK's support for free trade and the gold standard during the nineteenth century arose from an emerging commonality of interests between modernizing groups within the state and the City's commercial and wholesale banking capitalists (Ingham, 1984: 126). Within the associated regimes of free trade and the gold standard, the Bank and the Treasury arrived at a "complementary and mutually sustaining" set of policy commitments. The Treasury's parsimony and proclivity for balanced budgets was matched by the Bank's sensibility about sound money. Tasked with managing the gold standard system, in which the pound sterling was the key international currency, the Bank adopted an increasingly interventionist stance toward the money markets; it lowered or increased interest rates in accordance with the requirement to maintain the gold-sterling parity (Ingham, 1984: 132). Linkages between the Bank and the Treasury were also underpinned by structural connections with the City and its major banking institutions (Ingham, 1984: 153). These institutional linkages were reinforced by cultural crossfertilizations that centered around associations between bankers and the landed aristocracy.

Upheaval caused by two world wars as well as the departure from the gold standard in 1931 served as critical junctures that disrupted the status quo and presented opportunities for the reform of the core institutions of UK capitalism. What transpired on each occasion, however, was a gradual return to the former orthodoxy: the City-Bank-Treasury nexus. After World War II, sterling was maintained as an international currency while the Conservative governments of the 1950s restored the City to its former preeminence. These missed opportunities for radical restructuring of UK capitalism cast the die for the UK's postwar development. They also formed the backdrop for the failed attempts at industrial modernization in the 1960s, while providing an institutional basis of support for the monetarist principles and liberal international economic policies associated with Thatcherism from 1979 (Ingham, 1984). For Ingham, then, what was nationally distinctive of the institutional nexus underpinning the UK's national financial order was its deep preindustrial historical embeddedness, its early and enduring international orientation (owing both to the City's entrepôt status and sterling's centrality to the gold standard), the relative size and power of the wider financial services sector vis-à-vis industry, and a situation whereby close linkages between private bankers and state officials created a common culture that excluded provincial industrialists. These characteristics have exhibited strong patterns of path-dependency, with the early historical advantages of the City reproduced through the strategic activity of the City-Bank-Treasury nexus. Similarly, the comparatively marginalized status of industry within UK capitalism continues today.

In the US context, scholars have identified a parallel nexus of private and public financial power that, much like the UK's financial order during the nineteenth century, became progressively internationalized during the twentieth century (Gowan, 1999; Panitch and Konings, 2009; Konings, 2011; Panitch and Gindin, 2012). Peter Gowan (1999) first drew attention to the "Dollar-Wall Street Regime," in which the interaction between the Fed, Treasury, and Wall Street was central. This led Gowan to a revised interpretation of the status of the US within the post–Bretton Woods monetary order. Rather than seeing Richard Nixon's unilateral delinking of the dollar from gold as an indication of declining US hegemonic power, as the declinists had done, Gowan identified the enactment of a new international dollar standard (supplanting the dollar gold standard of Bretton Woods) as a platform for restoring the international dominance of US power (19–23).

Taking a broader historical perspective, a parallel grouping of IPE scholars (Panitch and Konings, 2009; Konings, 2011; Panitch and Gindin, 2012) have argued, following Gowan, that the US state, and the agency of the Federal Reserve-Treasury-Wall Street nexus specifically, were central to the relaunching of global capitalism during and after the heyday of Bretton Woods. They root the postwar internationalization of US finance in the long-term domestic development of US financial institutions. Beginning in the nineteenth century, US finance began to take on a distinctive national form. Tensions with populist farmers over the dynamics of banking concentration led to a comparatively distinctive financial infrastructure vis-à-vis other late developing industrializers—American banks did not exercise control over industrial firms in the way that German banks did, for example. Instead, the relationship was mediated by investment banks and the stock market (Panitch and Gindin, 2012: 29).[18] Neither did the US experience the development of a mercantile discount market for bills of exchange that was so central to the City of London's international ascendancy. US finance was on a unique path, characterized by a more dynamic, speculative, and fragmented orientation than in the UK and elsewhere (Konings, 2011: 9; Panitch and Gindin, 2012: 29). By the early twentieth century, a distinctive US financial infrastructure had emerged, with close links between banks and financial markets that enabled high levels of financial innovation and market liquidity. US entry into the gold standard helped to consolidate a financial axis centered around the primacy of the more internationally oriented New York banking community and the stock market. But US finance remained more inward looking than its UK counterpart.

One of the important specificities of the US financial system is the relatively late arrival of a central bank (Broz, 1997). US finance had been blighted by periodic bouts of financial panic and instability prior to the founding of the

Federal Reserve System in 1912. The system reflected the regional fragmentation of US banking, but its most important base would be in New York (mirroring, albeit to a much more limited degree, London's centrality in the UK
financial system), and the design of the system itself reflected the interests of
the New York bankers consulted over its formation (Konings, 2011: 60). Unlike
the UK financial system, US banks and financial institutions played only a very
partial role in international finance prior to World War I.

The crucial period of transformation for the US financial system came in
the wake of the 1929 Wall Street crash. Due to its comparatively late and limited
engagement in World War I, and the status of Wall Street as the epicenter of
the crash, 1929 served as a critical juncture in the development of US finance.
Previous path-dependent forms of development were disrupted by the shock
of the crash and political opposition to the banks' role in generating an unsus-
tainable boom, and the Depression opened political space for new ideas that
challenged the laissez-faire approach to financial governance. As part of the
New Deal package of policies rolled out under President Roosevelt, US banking was brought under a more centrally organized legal regulatory regime. In
terms of state institutions, both the Treasury and the Federal Reserve System
saw their powers to intervene within financial markets extended. By the end
of the 1930s, the US had a more fully developed money market infrastructure
(Konings, 2011: 77–78, 101; Panitch and Gindin, 2012: 58–63). This Fed-
Treasury-Wall Street nexus, which was modernized during the New Deal era,
was then progressively internationalized in the decades that followed as US
capitalists and state officials sought to steer globalization and respond to the
contradictions between domestic economic management and increasing international integration (Konings, 2011: 110; Panitch and Gindin, 2012: 1–15).
For these approaches, then, the story of financial globalization is largely one
of the internationalization of US finance—from a peculiarly dynamic and fragmented national financial system into a globalized financial system with the
dollar as the dominant international currency and US finance and the US state
at its core.

This book builds on the above accounts of the political economy of financial power in the UK and the US. But it does so by arguing that to properly
understand the politics of financial globalization, and the central role of Anglo-
American development within it, we need to adopt a more methodologically
internationalist approach, examining the interdependent transnational dimensions of the historical emergence of national financial orders within the UK
and the US and the impact of their interaction upon the wider international

monetary order. Stories of nationally distinctive patterns of path-dependent historical development overlook the critical importance of structural and personal transatlantic linkages between Anglo-American institutions and individuals in shaping the longue durée of financial globalization. It is not sufficient to read the politics of financial globalization as a simple expansion of US finance from the national onto the international scale, alongside an associated internationalization of the US state. Nor can we understand postwar global finance without recognizing the enduring significance of the City's entrepôt role and its repurposing under conditions of Anglo-American financial development. The significance of this was one of the enduring themes of global finance in the twentieth century, ultimately feeding into the global financial crisis of 2007/8.

The institutional histories and orientations of the financial systems in the two states are unique. But there is also a comparatively distinctive interdependency and commonality between the *Anglo-American* financial orders. This is the key to understanding why Anglo-American financial development sui generis, and not simply the general development of modern capitalist financial systems within states, is so important to understanding the politics of financial globalization. Here the functional and historical-institutional orientations of finance in the two states become much more difficult to disentangle analytically. The common functional responsibility of managing a dominant international currency and an international monetary order organized around it takes us some way to understanding the historical interdependency between the UK and US financial systems during the twentieth century. It created certain parallel challenges, and common institutional requirements, that incentivized cooperative and integrative endeavors. But this was also, as this book demonstrates, a deeply historically and politically contingent development, one that required sustained political agency from social forces in both states and the navigation of distinctive moments of crisis and opportunity. Dense transatlantic networks of personal and institutional linkages between private financiers and state officials involved in financial management were central to Anglo-American development, and the deeper history of these relationships provides a critical window into the making of financial globalization.

Turning to the functional parallels of Anglo-American monetary leadership, it is helpful to specify some of the requirements of an international currency. A stable international monetary order requires that the key currency country supplies an adequate volume of liquidity, that there are ways to make adjustment to national payment imbalances that might threaten the stability of the system, and that destabilizing shifts in the composition of national currency reserves do not occur (Gilpin, 1987). Under the classical gold standard, discussed further in chapter 2, the UK took on the primary responsibility for meeting these conditions. London banks provided sterling credits for use in international trade financing (Roberts, 1995: 182; Langley, 2002: 50). In theory, payments were to be settled through gold flows between countries, but in practice exchanges of sterling balances and bills of exchange were cleared and settled within the UK through London clearinghouses and UK banks. It was, in effect, a sterling-based gold standard (Ingham, 1984; Schwartz, 2009a: 162). Not only did the UK supply the liquidity; it also helped stabilize reserve movements through the Bank of England's interest rate policy. The provision of long-term overseas sterling finance by the City enabled deficit countries to avoid short-term adjustment to payment imbalances, allowing the US and other agricultural exporters to run consistent trade deficits during the 1860s and 1870s (Schwartz, 2009a). In respect of monetary policy, a "follow the leader" convention developed, through which the Bank's adjustment of its discount rate policy was used to harmonize international monetary policy and manipulate capital flows (Eichengreen, 2008). The stability of the pound was considered to be the main goal for these interventions (Knafo, 2013), but, given sterling's key currency role, these interventions also stabilized the wider regime.

As the UK's relative economic power waned during the late nineteenth century, its capacity to anchor the international monetary order also declined. This led to increasing dependency upon America's rising financial power to support the UK's return to gold in 1925. Nascent Anglo-American financial linkages became crucial to the functioning of the international monetary order. US dollar lending and the repayment of German and Allied war debts to the US began to displace the primacy of sterling in international capital flows, while New York's significance as a global financial center increased. By 1928, the dollar had overtaken sterling as the leading international reserve currency and by 1929, sterling and the dollar were effectively acting as dual reserve currencies at the center of the international monetary order. But this was not a consistent, unilinear trend—by 1933, with the dollar devalued as the gold standard collapsed, sterling recovered its leading reserve currency role (Eichengreen and Flandreau, 2009). This was a testament to the increasingly equivalent international standing of sterling and the dollar and the comparable international financial-center status of London and New York, as well as the need for increased Anglo-American cooperation in managing the international monetary order.

Even after the dollar's key currency status was enshrined at Bretton Woods in 1944, the international monetary order continued to turn upon an increasingly important Anglo-American axis. As first UK and then, increasingly, US policy makers attempted to govern the international monetary order and manage their internationalized currencies, the political economy of the Special Relationship was shaped by a politics of mutual financial dependency. The US needed to work through the regimes and institutional infrastructure established by the UK to resuscitate an integrated international financial order during the interwar and postwar periods. This meant, crucially, working through the City as a spatial site for the reproduction of international finance. Longstanding connections between private Anglo-American bankers were central to driving this, as the increasingly internationally oriented New York banking community, the Federal Reserve Bank of New York, and the US Treasury looked to UK bankers and the Bank of England to help realize their international vision. The United States needed to circumvent the limitations of its own domestic financial infrastructure and work through London in conjunction with UK banking and the UK state. The institutional foundations of modern global finance became increasingly anchored in a combined Anglo-American financial space. As the strength of the private and public financial institutions at the core of Anglo-American development increased, in tandem with the postwar resurgence of international finance, feedback effects reinforced the grip of the financial sectors over the wider national political economy of the two states. The ascendancy of economic ideas that sought to overturn postwar Keynesianism armed the supporters of Anglo-American finance with the intellectual tools to roll back regulatory constraints.

These Anglo-American dynamics are, as this book demonstrates in subsequent chapters, critical to understanding the politics of postwar financial globalization. The post-World War II domestic organization of finance in each country, the wider political organization of the international monetary order, and the transformation of banking practices were linked through an Anglo-American axis of financial development. Anglo-American developmental interdependence was prominent during the nineteenth century and grew in significance throughout the 1920s, as the UK and the US attempted to reconstruct the gold standard. During this time, the political economy of the City and sterling became increasingly intertwined with New York and the dollar. It was this nascent field of developmental interactivity between the UK and the US—hinging upon the interdependence of their respective currencies, financial centers, and relevant state institutions—that gradually reemerged during the postwar period.

With the institutionalization of US international monetary leadership at Bretton Woods in 1944, the functional responsibilities for managing the international currency shifted to the US. But this transition was marked by a continuing dependency of US monetary management upon the institutions of UK capitalism and the politics of the pound sterling. That interdependency was reflected in the shared (albeit lopsidedly American) Anglo-American creation of the Bretton Woods agreement. Although the dollar was now the primary source of global liquidity, the key reserve currency, and the effective anchor for the international monetary system (with its fixed convertibility to gold at thirty-five dollars per ounce), the management of a stable international monetary order, as well as the supply of sufficient dollar liquidity, continued to rely heavily upon the UK's role within the international financial system (Gavin, 2004: 18). Sterling remained a heavily internationalized key currency and, allied with London's continued centrality as an international financial center, its status placed a systemic significance on the monetary policy and regulatory orientation of the Bank of England and the fiscal policies enacted by HM Treasury. The decisions and dilemmas faced by UK monetary authorities in the decades after World War II played a central role in the rise and demise of the Bretton Woods order. The dollar's fate remained closely tied to that of sterling (Gavin, 2004; Schenk, 2010).

This was not, though, simply an automatic association driven by functional interdependency. Bringing these agencies on side with the US project for a more internationally integrated global financial system was a deeply contingent and political process. Functional interdependencies associated with managing the international monetary system incentivized cooperation and integration, but it was the power and preferences of private bankers and state officials on both sides of the Atlantic that propelled Anglo-American development and drove the politics of financial globalization.

Anglo-American development exerted a generative influence upon both states, but also upon the wider institutions of the international monetary order. Because of the systemic importance of Anglo-American banking, and the centrality of sterling and the dollar as the dominant international currencies, Anglo-American developmental dynamics were central to both the creation and collapse of Bretton Woods. Despite the weakening of its economic power, the UK remained central to the politics of the international monetary system. US bankers and government agencies recognized the need to articulate the country's financial power through a subordinate and increasingly integrated UK financial system that became part of a transatlantic financial axis at the heart of a rapidly globalizing political economy. For their part, UK bankers and government officials increasingly recognized the need to draw in US financial power and capacity to maintain their own national dominance and international standing. The reproduction of institutional dominance for financiers on either side of the Atlantic came to rely on the power and prospects of finance of the other. But this was not just about the cooperative attempt to maintain the power of Anglo-American finance—it was also an intensely competitive effort to maintain and augment the standing of the two states' respective financial centers, financial institutions, and currencies within the wider global economy.

These actors and interests constituted the core of the political economy of the Special Relationship. They exerted a major influence on the development of the global political economy, not only during the formation of Bretton Woods, but also the hugely important development of the Eurodollar market and the attempt to instantiate an increasingly liberalized international financial system under floating exchange rates in the 1970s and 1980s. Building upon this institutionalist basis enables us to examine key periods of transatlantic development within the wider context of the politics of financial globalization and the transformation of the international monetary order.

Regulating Postwar Finance

In what follows, the book examines the development of Anglo-American finance within the domestic and international spheres. Domestically, both states were, up until the critical decade of the 1970s, broadly reflective of the "Keynesian compromise" that shaped the principles and methods of macroeconomic intervention during the early postwar decades and legitimated a distinctive regulatory approach toward finance. Under the Keynesian paradigm, technocratic government agencies were tasked with determining the aggregate level of economic output in accordance with the pursuit of full employment. Navigating a middle course between the laissez-faire approach of classical liberalism and the state planning of socialism, the Keynesian political economy relied upon indirect means to shape market choices (Hall, 1989: 6). By manipulating the key levers of monetary and fiscal policy, governments could manage aggregate demand within the economy (Skidelsky, 1979). Keynes rejected the traditional emphasis on balanced budgets. Instead, he argued that government should "spend against the wind," cushioning the economy from the depressive effects of the business cycle by spending countercyclically. This would require running a budget deficit during the recession. Conversely, governments should run a budget surplus to head off inflationary risks during periods of strong growth, when aggregate demand was likely to outstrip supply (Hall, 1989: 7; Keynes, 2018).

In broad terms, the regulation of finance under the Keynesian state in the UK and the US relied upon the direct administration of the money supply through quantitative limits set upon interest rates and lending volumes. This was part of a wider comparative tendency within advanced banking systems (Grossman, 2010; Altamura, 2016). In the US, the regulatory framework took on a formalized, legislative character, prompted by the banking collapses that followed the Wall Street crash (Krippner, 2011: 60). The Banking Acts of 1933 and 1935 put in place several epochal changes to the regulation of US finance. Federal deposit insurance was introduced to protect depositors, while commercial and investment banking were separated under Glass-Steagall provisions. Banks were prevented from dealing in most financial assets other than treasury bonds, with the intention of reducing financial risk and separating banking and corporate interests. Regulators wanted to ensure that banks were also prohibited from paying interest on demand deposits, and the independent Fed was given the power to set interest rate ceilings on time and savings deposits under Regulation Q while control over monetary policy was centralized within the Federal Reserve Board under the 1935 Act (Krippner, 2011: 60–61; Konings, 2011: 83). These changes were united by a common anticompetitive thrust that sought to constrain market forces with the aim of reducing the possibility of bank failure, resulting in a highly segmented financial system (Grossman, 2010: 246–50; Krippner, 2011: 60).

In the UK, by contrast, the regulatory apparatus remained distinctively informal, reflecting the longstanding "club governance" approach characteristic of UK finance (Moran, 1991)—this despite the landmark nationalization of the Bank of England in 1946. Similarly to the US, the system relied upon official controls on lending volumes and the restriction of competition within the sector. Up until the late 1960s, UK banking was dominated by a small group of five big players, with the system highly compartmentalized between different types of banks that organized tacit monopolies over sections of the loan market and avoided direct interest-rate competition (Michie, 2016: 162–167).

TABLE 1.1. Keynesian and Neoliberal Financial Orders Compared

Keynesian financial order	Neoliberal financial order
State legal-administrative controls over money supply	Market-based approach to money supply
Use of quantitative lending limits	Removal of administered controls and quantitative limits
Credit supply shaped in accordance with government policies	Interest rates/prices as primary determinant of credit supply
Constraints on competition within the sector	Increased competition within the sector

The system of administrative controls in place allowed the governments of both states to shape the supply of credit in accordance with the principles of Keynesian macroeconomic management. In the UK, the Bank of England's close linkages with the large banks enabled it to shape the rate of interest and adjust credit supply in accordance with government policies (Ross, 2004: 304). During times of monetary restraint, made frequent by the specific context of the "stop-go cycle," the Bank could impose quantitative ceilings on bank lending to limit credit supply. The compartmentalization of the sector enabled the Bank to push on specific pressure points within the financial system in pursuit of government policy (Michie, 2016: 162–67). In the US, interest rate ceilings associated with Regulation Q led to a tightly limited credit market and had an important countercyclical effect: when the economy threatened to overheat, rising market rates available on treasury bills and corporate debt outstripped the Regulation Q ceilings and triggered disintermediation from the banking sector, with deposits withdrawn to be reinvested more profitably. This dampened lending, cooled the construction and housing industries, and checked inflationary growth. As market rates fell, money flowed back again into the banking sector (Meltzer, 2009: 1066; Krippner, 2011: 62).

Internationally, the domestic Keynesian financial order was paralleled by the postwar "embedded liberal" compromise set in place at Bretton Woods. Echoing the domestic Keynesian mediation between the polarized alternatives of laissez-faire and state planning, the embedded liberal compromise sought to reconcile international economic liberalism and openness with national sovereignty and domestic interventionism (Ruggie, 1982: 393). In a crucial departure from the classical gold standard, controls were now permitted to prevent destabilizing capital flows that might threaten domestic macroeconomic autonomy. Exchange rates would be fixed to the US dollar, but with some scope for adjustment incorporated. In the most significant turn to multilateralism, the IMF was created, to provide balance of payments financing to cushion economies from the most intense pressures of market-led international economic adjustment (Eichengreen, 2008: 91).

From the 1960s, Anglo-American financial development played a central role in disrupting not only the domestic financial orders of the UK and the US, but also the Bretton Woods international monetary order. At the heart of this process was a transatlantic regulatory feedback loop between financial institutions and regulatory authorities in London and New York. The feedback loop transmitted competitive market pressures and monetary dynamics across the Anglo-American financial space and affected both private and public institutions. For private banks and other financial institutions, it generated pressures to develop new financial products and practices in order to defend and extend market share; for state institutions, it increased financial sector lobbying pressure to promote pro-market regulatory reform. And it prompted state authorities to develop regulatory and policy innovations in response to the challenges that transatlantic financial market interdependence and integration posed to sovereign control over the national monetary space. The transatlantic feedback loop is evidence of the reciprocal institutional sensitivity of finance in the UK and the US: it demonstrates the need to read the transformation of their respective national capitalisms through the shared context and generative dynamics of Anglo-American development.

Bankers in the UK and the US lobbied their national monetary authorities to enable further liberalization, to ensure the maintenance of competitive advantages, while central banks were forced to adjust their regulatory stance in response to the new challenges and jurisdictional ambiguities thrown up by the Euromarkets. The influx of US banks into the City during the 1960s increased the competitive pressure on London institutions and destabilized the prevailing regulatory order. However, it also generated feedback pressures on the US New Deal regulatory regime as US banks pressed for the recreation of offshore regulatory permissiveness within the US onshore market. Synthetic forms of Anglo-American financial innovation emerged as new products and techniques were developed. These dynamics paved the way for the financial liberalization that gathered momentum on both sides of the Atlantic during the 1970s and 1980s. Over time, they led to the breakdown of the domestic administratively determined quantitative limits used to regulate postwar banking in the UK and the US. Internationally, Anglo-American financial development fostered the growth of international capital markets and facilitated

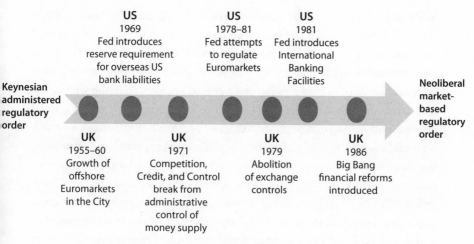

FIGURE 1.1. Timeline of transatlantic regulatory dynamics

volumes of capital and banking techniques that overwhelmed the Bretton Woods system of fixed exchange rates.

These dynamics were facilitated, intellectually, by the ascendancy of monetarism within the UK and the US, which was part of a wider transatlantic resuscitation of free market doctrine in the form of neoliberalism (Van Horn and Mirowski, 2009: 140; Stedman-Jones, 2012: 4). Gaining prominence from the late 1960s, as sustained inflation blighted Western political economies, monetarist critics of Keynesian policy highlighted the inflationary consequences of government fiscal intervention. Restating the neoclassical commitment to market equilibrium, they argued that the maintenance of price stability was the only means of achieving full employment and thus the primary goal of economic management, and that monetary policy was the only tool for realizing this objective (Clarke, 1988: 323).[19] With prominent monetarists like Milton Friedman arguing that the rising inflation of the 1960s and 1960s was primarily driven by the expansion of the money supply, Keynesian-era administrative tools for determining credit levels came under attack. Instead, free market mechanisms to govern the money supply, determining the supply and demand through the price mechanism of interest rates, were increasingly advocated and gradually applied to the regulation of banking. Friedman's technical monetarism, ardently applied during the early years of the Thatcher and Reagan governments, proved unsuccessful and politically contentious, sparking tensions between fervently pro-monetarist executives and reticent central banks in both states. But the failure of Friedman and the monetarists led to a turn to a broader set of neo-Austrian and supply-side doctrines that criticized obstacles to market forces, the monopoly power of trade unions, and progressive taxation (Clarke, 1988: 328).[20] The political and ideational struggle over the governance of money represented a crucial bridgehead in the wider neo-liberal transformation of the state (Stedman-Jones, 2012: 212), with a general emphasis upon market disciplinary regulatory restructuring through an attack on foundational structures of postwar capitalism (Peck, 2010). Institutionally, the focus upon price stability and monetary policy emphasized the importance of central banking, spurring the widespread adoption of central bank independence (Burnham, 2001). Regarding the governance of finance, the arguments proposed by monetarists helped to legitimize the development of a market-based and price-determined regulation of banking using interest rates and the abandonment of administrative constraints on lending. But, as this book demonstrates, the committed application of these ideas to the policy realm only made sense within a wider context of Anglo-American developmental interdependence. The structural, personal, and strategic linkages between Anglo-American institutions and financiers generated competitive pressures and internationalist social forces that aligned with ascendant free market doctrines.

Anglo-American developmental processes were not confined to dynamics of financial competition and integration. They also took on more explicitly intergovernmental forms of political interaction. At times, they were driven by US leverage power "pushing in" on the UK, as in 1944/45 and again in 1976. At these moments, some UK state officials resisted the imposition of US power and pushed back against it. But at other moments in the lineage of Anglo-American development, it was more a case of bankers and officials within the UK "pulling in" and soliciting US power to further their own ambitions. This was exemplified by the emergence of the Eurodollar market, with the City seeking to restore its international standing by drawing in the dollar and embracing US financial power.

The US has also retained the disciplinary option of "pulling out" its support for the UK, particularly during the crisis years of Bretton Woods, when the UK was heavily dependent upon recourse to financial backing. Over time, these combinations of pushing in, pushing back, pulling in and pulling out have been part of a dynamic reconfiguration of sovereign power between the UK and the US as features of the uneven coarticulation of Anglo-American development. Throughout these processes there have certainly been plenty of instances (perhaps most notably in 1976) of the application of US structural power, using the centrality of the dollar in unison with explicit bilateral political pressure to incentivize certain policy choices and behavioral patterns within the UK state. But that very structural capacity was itself built upon decades of Anglo-American development that gave the US increased leverage over the UK through the international primacy of the dollar. With the UK more closely integrated within an Anglo-American developmental sphere, however, US policy makers and bankers had to deal with their own constraints and difficult choices brought about by tighter integration between New York and London. Anglo-American development involved sovereign constraint and compromise from both sides.

Reorienting the study of the postwar international monetary order around Anglo-American development offers a new interpretation of the origins of financial globalization. It demonstrates how the functionally privileged institutions of modern financial systems develop through historical time and across geographical space. It reveals the politics, the events, and the economic ideas that account for the comparative importance of finance within the development of modern capitalism in the UK and the US. It enables us to move beyond the cyclical rhythms and historical inaccuracies of the HST narrative. It offers a more historically oriented and geographically sensitive approach that places the power and agency of private and public financial actors at the center of the politics of financial globalization. And it helps us to move beyond static conceptions of monolithic US structural power by revealing the transatlantic institutional interdependencies that both enabled the rise of dollar dominance and constrained US policy autonomy. The following chapters mobilize this theoretical framework to explain decisive moments in the political economy of the Special Relationship, while situating them within the broader transformation of the international monetary system.

2

The Great Reversal

IN THE middle of the nineteenth century, the United Kingdom was at the peak of its power, having achieved naval dominance and with it unprecedented pre-eminence at the center of the burgeoning world economy. Sterling functioned as the primary trading and reserve currency around the world, and the City of London was the hub of international finance. The spoils of empire had conferred enormous wealth upon the members of the UK's ruling elite, who invested their capital globally, to handsome reward. Britannia's supremacy looked set to endure indefinitely.

Beneath the veneer of enduring power, though, UK predominance had already reached its zenith; it would rapidly diminish during the latter decades of the nineteenth century. The rise of the US would play the leading role in this transformation. The interactive development of the two states became increasingly central, not only to their own futures, but to the future of the international economy. Once a mere colonial province of the British Empire in the eighteenth century, the US had become, by the end of World War I, an industrial peer and a financial rival.

This chapter examines Anglo-American development from the nineteenth century to the outbreak of World War II. The period is important not only because of the great reversal in Anglo-American power dynamics, but also because the developments of the 1920s and 1930s were instructive for the postwar planners who drew up the Bretton Woods Agreement. As the US rapidly caught up with the UK, increasing transatlantic economic interdependence meant that the future of the international economy came to rest upon the potential for a twin pivot of Anglo-American cooperation. The national development of both states was increasingly expressed within and through the development of the international monetary order, as reflected in the politics of the gold standard.

The central argument advanced in this chapter is that US economic catch-up and the deterioration of UK power fostered further political and economic interdependence, as expressed most clearly in the intertwined fortunes of London and New York, alongside sterling and the dollar. Uneven economic development and the shock of World War I undermined the UK's capacity to singularly underpin the international monetary system. Greater cooperation between Anglo-American bankers, central bankers, and government officials became central to the maintenance of a liberal international monetary order. The City-Bank-Treasury nexus was forced to draw in US financial power in order to restore its domestic and international hegemony, in a manner that foreshadowed the way the City would draw upon the dollar's strength under the Bretton Woods system. However, due to its reliance upon personal links between financiers and government officials rather than deep institutional linkages and multilateral forums, Anglo-American interdependence produced only fragile and tendential cooperation. The depth required to coordinate a broader revival of the global economy, particularly in the wake of the Great Depression, was not achieved. These processes anticipated later (and more deeply institutionalized) patterns of Anglo-American development, but were limited by the continuing political and economic competitiveness between the two powers, the toxicity of postwar debt negotiations, and the fragile multilateral structures within which this nascent Anglo-American development was embedded.

Anglo-American relations continued to be marked by sharp rivalries, with the US seeking to employ UK war debts as a lever to weaken UK power and clear the way for US expansion, while tensions over war debts limited the potential for cooperation between the two treasury departments. Ultimately, the informal and ad hoc patterns of Anglo-American cooperation proved too weak to hold together the reconstructed gold standard; the politics of sterling and the dollar were fundamental to both its collapse and the emergence of rival financial blocs during the 1930s. This was not, then—contra Kindleberger's (1973; 1981) famous interpretation—merely a failure of the US' unwillingness to lead and the UK's inability to do so. It was also a consequence of the enduring deficiencies of the US financial system to play an internationally calibrated role (Ingham, 1984: 203; Konings, 2011: 71). Only after World War II, with the creation of the Bretton Woods agreement and a UK weak enough to accept US supremacy, would the two states play a formalized role within an increasingly multilateral international monetary system centered around the dollar.

This chapter begins by reviewing Anglo-American economic development during the nineteenth century, outlining the role of the classical gold standard at the heart of industrial, trade, and financial links between the two states. It goes on to explore the impact of World War II in altering the financial balance of power between the UK and the US as well as forging closer private transatlantic financial ties. Despite accelerating US development, it took the outbreak of World War II to really close the financial gap between the two states, by eroding the UK's creditor status and dragging it into the disciplinary orbit of its new US paymaster. In the following section, the chapter examines the failed attempt to restore a postwar gold standard. The narrowing financial divide between New York and London meant that the two financial centers, and their respective currencies, came increasingly to form a dual Anglo-American axis within the international economy. This foreshadowed the centrality of these two centers within the Bretton Woods system in the post–World War II era. Finally, the chapter discusses the breakdown of the restored gold standard and the emergence of the separate currency and trading blocs that preceded the outbreak of World War II. Ultimately, the informal structures of Anglo-American cooperation at the center of the reconstructed gold standard proved too weak to prevent the international economy from fracturing into rival spheres of influence during the 1930s.

Economic Interdependence and the Gold Standard

Although US secession from the British Empire was both violent and rapid, a remarkable degree of cultural and economic affinity survived. The mutual trade dependence of the two nations was inescapable. Early industrial development boosted the Atlantic slave trade and the southern plantation system. UK workers, who emigrated to the US in large numbers during the nineteenth century, brought with them the skills of industrial production. In the 1820s and 1830s, it was Lancashire specialists who were largely responsible for introducing Calico printing to New England (Temperley, 2002: 35–36). UK methods were imported too, with techniques originating from Leeds and Sheffield employed in the iron and wool industries. The UK accounted for around half of US exports in 1850, with the US deriving one-third of its imports from the UK (Holmes, 1976: 11).

There was a strong reciprocal dimension to the balance of Anglo-American trade, enough to suggest that the two states were "closely interrelated parts of a single fast-developing web of global credit and commercial enterprise"

(Temperley, 2002: 36). The US relied on the import of UK-manufactured and semimanufactured goods, and a torrent of UK capital, which poured into the US in unparalleled volumes, nourished its prodigious industrial output. In 1854 a quarter of UK overseas investment was in US assets; by 1870 it had reached 27 percent of total foreign investment before declining prior to World War I. The UK was heavily dependent upon imports of US grain and other raw materials (Holmes, 1976: 10; Sharp, 2002: 2).

The international monetary order based on the gold standard was central to Anglo-American economic interdependence. The UK originated the classical gold standard system of payments and played the primary role in coordinating it. The convertibility of sterling (the world's principal trading and reserve currency) into gold on demand was at the heart of the system. Bills on London, denominated in sterling, became a widely accepted means of payment for international trade. By 1914, the City already hosted branches of some seventy-four foreign banks (Roberts, 2013: 24–29). The City was also home to the most sophisticated clearing mechanisms in the world, and the predominance of the UK as a foreign investor and trader meant that over 60 percent of world trade was denominated in sterling (Eichengreen, 2011: 15).

By the early twentieth century, the gold standard was widespread internationally, with the US having moved onto it in 1879. Under the system, countries promised to exchange currency for gold at a fixed price, with the national money supply underpinned by a correspondent level of gold reserves. The widely shared commitment of governments to maintain convertibility was the cornerstone of the system. Markets had confidence that the required policy measures would be taken in order to maintain the fixed value of currencies in gold terms, and the commitment to convertibility generated the level of confidence required for an extensive system of international trade and capital flows (Eichengreen, 2008: 6–29). The UK's economic preeminence was crucial to the stability of the system. UK international lending, which served as the major source of liquidity for international trade and investment, was supported by capital goods and merchandise exports that boosted the country's balance of payments (Block, 1977: 13; Ahamed, 2009: 423; Eichengreen, 2008: 41; Schwartz, 2009a: 161). In practice, gold exports to settle payments played only a very limited role. Liquidity within the system was actually based upon an expanding supply of various forms of credit issued in London, rather than any major increase in the supply of metallic money. And, rather than settling payments through gold flows between countries, the system relied upon exchanges of sterling balances and bills of exchange among UK and foreign banks (Schwartz, 2009a: 161–62).[1] These features attested to sterling's position as the dominant currency. As a result, the Bank of England played a coordinating role at the head of a "follow-the-leader" convention within central banking, according to which changes in the Bank's discount rate would be followed by foreign central banks (Eichengreen, 2008: 41; Knafo, 2013).[2]

As Anglo-American trade and UK investment into the US both quickly expanded during the nineteenth century, a transatlantic market in financial assets used to fund trade and settle payments became increasingly fundamental to the gold standard (Schwartz, 2009a: 162). Given the UK's financial ascendancy, it was no surprise that US traders relied upon London as the primary source of international credit. Although US financial dependence was a consequence of UK financial power, it was also in part a result of the relatively underdeveloped nature of US financial markets. The US financial system was born out of its UK counterpart, but it began to diverge from the UK model in significant ways during the nineteenth century (Konings, 2011: 9). Compared to the UK model, the US financial system remained fragmentary and lacked an overall network power of concentrated and integrated credit relations. This meant that US traders remained dependent upon the UK financial system. Without a central bank until the creation of the Federal Reserve in 1913, the US financial system was much more prone to crises, experiencing numerous banking panics in the century before World War I (Broz, 1999: 39).

The gold standard's reliance upon the UK was, paradoxically, both the source of its strength and its fundamental weakness. As the UK lost ground to competitors toward the end of the nineteenth century, its status in the financial system began to weaken. The US led the pack of late industrializing countries that began to outdo the UK (Schwartz, 2009a; O'Brien and Williams: 2013; Gamble: 1990). Railway mileage in America, an important indicator of industrial development, expanded rapidly between the 1850s and 1880s, fostering a large internal market (Holmes, 1976: 13; Walton and Rockoff, 2005: 312–15). Railway expansion also played a critical role in the increasing concentration of ownership in the US and the associated development of the holding company. A great wave of industrial mergers during the 1880s and 1890s gave birth to giant enterprises. The US was much less reliant upon foreign trade for its industrialization, benefiting from the existence of an increasingly large internal market and a generous endowment of natural resources (Holmes, 1976: 74; Temperley, 2002: 66; Walton and Rockoff, 2005: 45).

The US also benefited from the relative advantages of early industrial backwardness (Gerschenkron, 1962). Here, the connection to the UK was particularly important. Transatlantic flows of people, capital, and industrial know-how furnished the country with access to technologically advanced methods of industrial production and plentiful investment, allowing it to catch up with the UK. The UK, by contrast, had begun to exhaust many of the comparative advantages associated with its earlier pioneering industrial status.[3] This was reflected in its increasingly ossified industrial structure by the late nineteenth century (Cain and Hopkins, 2016: 121). The UK's traditional, family-based, "proprietary capitalism" placed substantial limits upon the growth of the firm (Lazonick, 1993: 24).[4] The US, by contrast, developed a series of cutting-edge approaches to the organization of industrial activity within "managerial capitalism."[5]

Equipped with a more comparatively advanced model of capitalist production from the late nineteenth century, the US began to overtake the UK in the race toward the advancing frontiers of industrial modernity.[6] The UK was still reliant on the older industries of the first industrial revolution: coal, steel, iron, and shipbuilding. Its "gentlemanly" culture of capitalism, in which the fusion of aristocratic and City-based financial services power lay at the heart of national politics and culture, effectively stifled the representation of industrial interests (Cain and Hopkins, 2016). This helps explain the long continuation of the UK's commitment to free trade despite increasing demands for protection from industrial centers such as Birmingham.[7] Contrastingly, prominent late developers such as the US and Germany embraced the protectionist ideas of Alexander Hamilton and Friedrich List to shelter their infant industries and carve out shares of the world market (Chang, 2003).

By the eve of World War I, then, the developmental gains of the US and the deterioration of UK industrial competitiveness had considerably altered their economic relationship. From 1870 to 1914, US growth outpaced that of the UK (Holmes, 1976; Gamble, 1990; Schwartz, 2009a). Overall, economic primacy had shifted toward the US, which surpassed the UK as the world's biggest manufacturing nation (Allen, 1956: 29; Dimbleby and Reynolds, 1988: 34). By 1912, the US was also the world's largest trading nation (Eichengreen and Flandreau, 2009: 4). The UK's trajectory was starkly opposite. Between 1870 and 1910, its share of world manufacturing capacity decreased from 32 percent down to 15 percent, with her share of world trade decreasing from 25 percent down to 14 percent in the same period (Temperley, 2002: 89). Now it was the UK who looked to the US for the latest techniques in manufacturing as the former relationship between pioneer and laggard was reversed. In chemicals, automobile manufactures, industrial management, and electrical goods,

Germany and the US led the way (Schwartz, 2009: 152).[8] The great reversal had begun to gather momentum.

In one crucial area, however, the US remained some distance from reaching the level of UK power. The sterling-based international financial system centered in the City of London remained dominant, and the UK continued to perform the role of creditor to the world.[9] International loans raised in the City were borrowed and repaid in sterling (Roberts, 2013: 21). Merchant banks in the City had broad international networks of overseas correspondents and were able to generate large volumes of trade acceptances, which were then transacted within large and liquid secondary markets comprised of individual and institutional investors (Eichengreen and Flandreau, 2009: 4). These institutional endowments helped to secure the City's role at the heart of international finance.

Although the US had caught up in terms of industrial prowess and merchandise exports, its financial system remained insufficiently mature to service international markets. Despite the rapid growth of US exports, the dollar was barely used for the provision of trade credit and US banks were insignificant players in international trade financing (Eichengreen and Flandreau, 2009: 4). This marginal role was linked to prohibitions that prevented national banks from establishing branches overseas. They were also forbidden from dealing in trade credit up until the Federal Reserve Act of 1913 (McGuire, 1971: 429). The lack of foreign branches made it very difficult for US banks to support their clients abroad. Although private banks such as J. P. Morgan and Company were not burdened with these restrictions, they still did not move into the financing of US foreign trade on a large scale. The major problem for US banks was the cost advantage enjoyed by London. Interest rates and risks were lower there, as the existence of a broad population of investors to whom trade acceptances could be resold gave the market a highly liquid character. The well-developed market meant that there was little uncertainty over the price that could be obtained when discounting a bill. London benefited from a central bank that would step in to rediscount banks' securities when they needed to cash them, with the effect of stabilizing the market (Eichengreen, 2011: 17–20).

War and Anglo-American Finance

It would take the outbreak of war in 1914 to unseat the UK's financial predominance. The war's first significant impact was the major financial crisis that broke out in July 1914. Prompted by Austria's bellicose ultimatum to Serbia in the wake of the assassination of Archduke Franz Ferdinand, the crisis engulfed London and prompted the convulsion of its financial markets on a scale never witnessed before. With war now appearing inevitable, the markets rapidly sought to shift into safe and liquid assets, particularly gold. As assets were liquidated en masse and loans were called in, the markets broke down. Contagion spread through international markets, disrupting foreign currency exchanges and leading to the shutdown of virtually all of the world's securities and commodities markets by August. Facing huge demand for its discount window facilities, as investors looked to cash in their bills of exchange, the Bank of England was forced to suspend the Bank Act and remove restrictions on the supply of banknotes.[10] And, in a sign of the increased centrality of Anglo-America to the functioning of the international monetary system, fluctuations in the sterling-dollar exchange rate disrupted crucial trade and investment links between the two states.[11] This prompted UK officials to visit US bankers in Washington, DC, at the behest of US Treasury secretary William McAdoo, in an attempt to stabilize the exchange rate and facilitate US payments to London-based creditors. The crisis demonstrated both the City's vulnerability and the increased importance of bilateral Anglo-American ties to the functioning of the international payments system (Roberts, 2013: 5–23, 74).

With widespread financial instability and obstructions to trade and capital flows, the war brought an end to the gold standard. Increased rivalry and military tensions within Europe undermined the financial solidarity that supported the system. Countries then sought to cordon off their gold supplies and suspend convertibility in order to pay for essential materials (Block, 1977: 14; Eichengreen, 2008: 42). At the outbreak of war, the US remained the junior partner in the Anglo-American relationship. By the time peace fell across Europe in 1919, a radical turnaround had occurred. War sapped the UK's strength while swelling US coffers and emboldening her leaders. The UK was now forced to go cap in hand to her US ally. The sudden weakening of the UK's comparative financial advantage and the reversal in economic status created the conditions for greater financial interdependency between the two states. The primary mechanism of this reversal was the power of credit: it was a lever of power that the US would pull to great effect to dislodge European predominance in the post-war world.

Although the reversal of credit-debtor relations was enormously significant for intergovernmental relations between the two nations, it also reflected the increased importance of private transatlantic banking connections. During the three years of US neutrality, from 1914 to 1917, the House of Morgan banking dynasty supplied liquidity to the Allied war effort.[12] Not only did the House of Morgan raise funds through placement of UK and Allied bonds in the New York money market; by 1915 it was also the exclusive purchasing agent for all Allied acquisition of goods from the US (Burk, 1985: 19; Chernow, 1990: 187).

By the late 1860s, the House of Morgan organized most UK investments in the US. These investments were large. By 1869, Europeans owned around $1 billion of US government bonds and around $465 million of US corporate securities (Corey, 1969: 87). More than any other activity, it was railroad expansion that accounted for the largest amount of foreign investment. The investment bank oversaw centralization, enabling it to acquire overall discretion over the paramount issues of business management. J. P. Morgan's predominance heralded the more general historical shift toward the investment bank's strategic control over US industry at large. Having achieved unprecedented consolidation in the control of assets within the nation, the House of Morgan looked abroad for new opportunities. Nearly all the industrial combinations controlled by Morgan took a dynamic role in America's budding imperialism, investing large amounts of capital overseas (Corey, 1969: 333). This was part of a larger competition with European investors in China and Latin America. Morgan's overseas ambitions received active encouragement from the government (Corey, 1969: 333; Chernow, 1990: 132).

The US government had adopted a stance of formal neutrality toward the belligerents. This foreclosed the possibility of the US Treasury raising funds for the UK through placements of UK bonds in America. Private banking was the only remaining alternative. The House of Morgan duly stepped forward. An avowed anglophile, John Pierpont Morgan spent half of every year in the UK (Dimbleby and Reynolds, 1988: 45; Ovendale, 1998: 12). Crucially, the House of Morgan had no major linkages to German industrial firms, leaving the way clear for unrestricted engagement with the Allied cause (Burk, 1981: 27). This engagement came at huge risk: if the UK lost the war, Morgan would likely be bankrupted. But, beyond the raw profit motive, genuine Anglo-American patriotism—conveyed in private communications between the US and UK branches of the bank—played an important role in the decision (Burk, 1985: 27).

By 1915 Morgan's had become the sole purchasing agent for the Allies. Not only did Morgan's purchase goods; they also initiated an expansion of new productive capacity to meet surging Allied demand. Financiers and manufacturers came together to accept huge contracts from the UK government (Burk, 1985: 24). The disordered competition and inflation that attended early Allied purchasing was brought under control by the Morgan monopoly. As Allied orders increased, the UK's financial dependence increased accordingly. Already by October 1915, the House of Morgan had arranged a loan of $500 million to be spent by the Allies on US purchases. By the war's end, the House of Morgan had raised over $1.5 billion in Allied credits (Corey, 1969: 423; Chernow, 1990: 200).

Private lending was virtually extinguished once the US Treasury monopolized the creditor function on joining the war. The US government established sweeping control over the US economy, setting prices and directing industry (Corey, 1969: 426; Burk, 1985: 57). As a consequence, Morgan's power was greatly diminished, with the government placing loans and organizing purchases. The wartime state of emergency enabled a massive reassertion of government sovereignty over economic activity.

Undoubtedly, America's participation in the war swung the conflict in the Allies' favor, and its vast resources were immediately brought to bear on the war effort. But it also meant that the legacy of inter-Allied borrowing would be intensely politicized, creating a major bone of contention in the postwar political economy. Although temporarily maligned, the House of Morgan continued to play a key role in Anglo-American relations in the postwar period of reconstruction and uncertainty. Indeed, its efforts were central to the disastrous attempt to restore the gold standard during the 1920s, as fragile cooperation between Anglo-American bankers became increasingly important in shaping the international economy.

Resuscitating the Gold Standard

As the guns fell silent across Europe in November 1918, the dust settled upon a radically altered landscape. Many of the old certainties of the international order had been shaken at their foundations, none more so than the UK's position at the apex of international power.[13] The war greatly destabilized the international economy, which was blighted by overproduction, overcapacity, and rising inflation (Holmes, 1976; Frieden, 2007; Schwartz, 2009a). While US industrial power had increased, European economies had been gravely weakened, and their currencies experienced sustained instability (Eichengreen and Temin, 2000: 194). Having focused inward on the requirements of the war economy, the Europeans ceded much of their international economic advantage. Their positions as suppliers of capital and manufactures to the world were now inverted—they depended upon imports of capital, manufactures, and raw materials from the rest of the world as their trade positions deteriorated rapidly. The US, conversely, had more than doubled its exports between 1914 and 1917, running a trade surplus of almost five times its prewar level and benefiting from booming agricultural exports to the UK (Frieden, 2007: 130).

For the UK, economic adjustment to the postwar world would be particularly painful. Two of its key industries, shipbuilding and steel, were hit hard by overproduction and overcapacity. International competitors had emerged, and world demand had slackened. To add to this, UK industrial dominance in coal and textiles was also under threat.[14] The UK experienced a worsening balance of trade during the 1920s as imports remained high but exports declined markedly.[15] Reliance upon traditional industries (e.g., coal, steel, textiles) hamstrung the possibility of export-led growth in a more competitive world market (Moggridge, 1972: 29, Dimbleby and Reynolds, 1988: 97). Even the UK's longstanding predominance in "invisibles" was under threat— around seven hundred thousand tonnes of merchant shipping were lost during the war.

Nowhere was the transformation of UK power more evident than in the reversal of its financial status. No longer creditor supreme to US industrialization, the UK was now heavily indebted to the US. By March 1920, the UK's overall public debt stood at £7.8 billion. During the 1920s, debt servicing consumed a staggering 40 percent of the UK's budget (Temperley, 2001: 123). Most of this was owed to the US government and would have to be repaid in dollars. The UK's trade deficit with both the US and Canada made this difficult, as did the increasingly protectionist stance of the US during the 1920s (Hudson, 1972; Holmes, 1976; Schwartz, 2009a).

These changes drastically undermined the UK's position in the international economy (Block, 1977: 14; Langley, 2002: 60; Konings, 2011: 71). As UK power waned, US ascendance accelerated. The interactive fortunes of sterling and the dollar were central to this process. From 1915, sterling's value relative to gold had fluctuated, reducing its reliability as an international trading and reserve currency. By contrast, the dollar remained pegged to gold during the period. Because of the dollar's greater stability, importers and exporters in Latin America, Asia, and the US decided that the dollar was a more appealing unit through which to conduct their business. Although the UK pegged sterling to the dollar from 1916, the fears of investors and traders were not allayed. The UK had run up massive wartime budget deficits and was experiencing substantial inflation. The markets rightly anticipated that the pound's value would fall once US support for the currency was withdrawn at the end of the war (Eichengreen, 2011: 27).

The UK's diminishing power contrasted starkly to US ascendance, a process encapsulated by the rise of the dollar and the now unrivaled international supremacy of the US in industry, trade, and finance (Frieden, 2007: 132). The war led to a massive expansion of US export business as the US became the "factory and grainery to the world" (Eichengreen, 2011: 26). US businesses were the primary beneficiaries of the withdrawal of European producers from foreign markets during the war. The war had also severely disrupted the credit mechanisms in place before 1914. German and UK banks were forced to turn to their counterparts in New York for the acceptance of bills to purchase imports from the US, Asia, and Latin America (Eichengreen, 2011: 26). This expansion of dollar-denominated trade credit was part of a broader decentralization of credit relations that damaged sterling and empowered the dollar (Schwartz, 2009a). Consequently, New York emerged as the leading center for the transmission of international credit. From 1921 to 1924, the value of new issues of foreign securities in New York stood at $2,373 million, compared to a meager $917 million in London during the same period. Between 191 and 1929, over $1 billion of loans per year flowed out of New York (Frieden, 2007: 141). World War I had set in place a "competitive duality" between New York and London as the world's major international financial centers, with New York growing increasingly powerful (Langley, 2002: 61). This was the beginning of the substantial competitive interaction between London and New York that, as subsequent chapters show, would prove to be so critical to the politics of financial globalization in the post–World War II era.

The dollar's rise was not, however, exclusively a consequence of sterling's demise. It also reflected the growing capacity of US financial markets. The creation of the Fed in 1913 was crucial in this respect. The US system now had a central bank that could act as a lender of last resort and play a market-making role to extend the liquidity of trade acceptances in the US market (Broz, 1999; Eichengreen and Flandreau, 2009: 7; Konings, 2011: 73). The Federal Reserve Act also empowered national banks to deal in trade credit for the first time and enabled them to establish branches abroad. By the end of 1920, US banks were operating 181 branches abroad (Eichengreen, 2011: 18–28).

Despite this enhanced financial infrastructure, the US lagged behind the UK in terms of the maturity of its financial system and its suitability to play an international entrepôt role. While the UK's dominance had been rooted in its supremacy in world trade, its massive overseas investments, and a highly liquid discount market, the US was not yet comparably internationalist in orientation nor sophisticated in its market infrastructure (Ingham, 1984: 188, 203; Konings, 2011: 72). In terms of the two currencies' reserve status—an important indicator of international currency dominance—the dollar overtook sterling as the lead international reserve currency during the mid-1920s. But the dollar's rise was not linear; after dollar devaluation in 1933, sterling regained its former primacy (Eichengreen and Flandreau, 2009: 379). An increasingly dualistic interwar international monetary order, based on sterling and the dollar, foreshadowed the postwar centrality of interdependent Anglo-American finance. US finance did not supplant its UK counterpart in a neat, staged transition between hegemonic powers.

The demise of the UK's independent financial capacity, and the immaturity of the US alternative, were both crucial factors in the disastrous attempt to resuscitate the gold standard during the 1920s. Banking interests in both states shared a desire to return to an integrated international financial system, but they differed in the preferences for the configuration of the system and lacked sufficiently robust institutional linkages to maintain cooperation in the face of acute postwar economic challenges. Reactivation of the gold standard was made more difficult by negotiations over war debt repayments, currency values, and trade relations, which soured diplomatic relations and impeded cooperation between the UK, France, and the US (Clavin, 1996: 1). The 1920s witnessed intensive financial rivalry between the UK and America. The UK had a number of goals that shaped the approach to international reconstruction: a financial bloc centered in London was identified as a means to maintain sterling's international role. The UK also sought favored status in Russian relations, the reduction of war debts, and a regulated system of world capital flows as well as stability in world prices. In all these endeavors the UK was opposed by the US (Costigliola, 1977: 914; Watt, 1984: 49).

Contrary to the UK, the US intended to rebuild the world economy on the basis of a free market rather than regulation and special privileges. These tensions foreshadowed the differences of opinion that would emerge during the Bretton Woods negotiations. The US turned to the "Open Door Policy" to achieve its aims.[16] This stance was motivated by a desire to ease industrial, agricultural, and capital surpluses through outlets in the international market (Costigliola, 1977: 915). But it was also beset by a major contradiction. Although pushing for open markets internationally, the US was insistent upon the maintenance of her own high tariffs and full war debt repayment (Hudson,

1972; Block, 1977; Konings, 2011). This made it very difficult for European countries to earn the currency required to pay off their debts to the US.

War debts proved the most rancorous issue in the great-power diplomacy of the period. The burden of the debts, imposed on top of the European loss of export markets and overseas investments, had a crippling effect on the economic recovery of the major European powers. The UK and her allies were prevented from raising dollars through exports by the imposition of the Fordney McCumber Tariff in 1922 (Hudson, 1972: 9, 18). The US expected the Allies to repay debts not by boosting their export growth (as this would likely damage US industry), but rather through painful austerity at home.

Further signals of America's intention to dismantle UK power were indicated in its lenient stance toward Germany. By reestablishing Germany as the UK's rival, the US sought to check the UK's postwar power. The UK was trapped in a vicious cycle. Declining world prices in the later 1920s and the growing demand for dollars weakened sterling and served to increase the real burden of the UK's war debts. But this was not, as others have argued (Hudson, 1972: 33), simply a case of US belligerence against the UK. There is no doubt that insistence upon the repayment of war debts played a significant role in the failure to restore a stable interwar economy. But there were also important cooperative tendencies driven by the transatlantic banking community. Private banking power played a major role in solidifying Anglo-American relations and spurring the reconstruction of the international monetary system during this period.

Although the negotiations and contestation over war debts were intense, the UK and the US cooperated effectively in their attempt to reestablish the gold standard. The primary motivation for the UK's desire to return to gold was the need to restore London as the premier financial center of the world (Clarke, 1967: 72; Dimbleby and Reynolds, 1988: 90).[17] But the need to maintain imperial unity around the dominant role of sterling in the face of the rising US challenge provided the wider political context (Costigliola, 1977: 923). With the increase in trade financed in dollars during the 1920s, the UK feared a gold standard based upon the dollar as a mortal threat to the international role of sterling.

For the City and the Bank, the restoration of the gold standard was integral to maintaining sterling's dominance. The UK government also stood to benefit from a return to gold, with increased confidence in the pound expected to reduce the cost of new government borrowing and help service the huge national debt. It was further hoped that the return to gold would increase the City's contributions to national revenue and provide a firm financial base for industry. The attitude of UK industry was less enthusiastic about the return to gold, but it was the City that held sway (Boyce, 2004: 215–20). Not for the last time, the privileged status of the City would lead the UK toward economic disaster.

Despite the coolness of industrial opinion, the decision to return to gold won the day. This was in large part a consequence of the predominance of gold standard thinking among UK bankers and government officials. The UK had been on the gold standard from 1717 to 1914, interrupted only by a brief interval during the Napoleonic wars. By the 1830s the gold standard had become "an unquestioned article of faith to most economists and bankers," and it remained so until 1914 and was still central to their thinking during the 1920s (Moggridge, 1972: 2; Eichengreen and Temin, 2000: 183). The support of the Treasury, in favor of the interests of the Bank and the City, was also crucial. The Treasury's need to finance the national debt gave it a natural interest in the health of financial markets, which overlapped with that of the City and the Bank. In line with its traditional balanced-budgets orthodoxy, the Treasury believed that the gold standard could exert an important disciplinary effect upon UK workers and government expenditure (Boyce, 2004: 222). There were, nonetheless, concerns about the potential impact of returning to gold. Winston Churchill, the chancellor of the exchequer, expressed concern that the higher interest rates required to return to gold might severely retard the progress of trade, industry, and employment. The increasingly influential John Maynard Keynes was also an outspoken critic (Ahamed, 2009: 172). Montagu Norman, the governor of the Bank, assuaged Churchill's concerns by claiming, entirely disingenuously, that there was no relationship between the gold standard and domestic conditions (Eichengreen and Temin, 2000: 194). It was the City-Bank-Treasury nexus, then, that was central to the UK's desire to return to gold.

This return was, though, impossible without broader international support; Anglo-American cooperation was critical. The new gold standard system emerged on an ad hoc basis, owing to the nonparticipation of the US in the 1922 Genoa Conference. Led by the UK delegation, the subcommittee on financial questions produced a report recommending that countries should negotiate an international convention that would permit their central banks to hold an unlimited amount of foreign exchange reserves. The intention was to overcome the gold supply problem that threatened to limit the scope for international economic growth by moving on to a gold exchange standard under which reserves could also underpin the monetary base (Eichengreen and Flandreau, 2009: 385). The conference also sought to promote international cooperation, with central banks expected to work together to maintain stable prices and fixed convertibility through an appropriate adjustment of interest rates.

The UK's view on international monetary issues shaped the Genoa proposals. The holding of exchange reserves would benefit the UK, as they would most likely be held as sterling balances in London (Eichengreen, 2008: 60; Eichengreen and Flandreau, 2009: 386). Bringing foreign-exchange reserves to London would restore its international position and reconstruct the international payments mechanism that had operated prior to the war. But the follow-up meeting of central banks proposed by the subcommittee to work out the details never occurred. This was due to a lack of US support, with Fed officials resentful of the Bank's leadership of the meeting and political interests within the US skeptical of both the gold exchange standard and the need for formalized central bank cooperation.

The US was in a strong bargaining position. By the end of the war, it had the largest gold supply in the world, which would make it potentially the vital player in a restored gold standard. This situation produced resistance to the need for a gold exchange system (Ahamed, 2009: 95; Eichengreen, 2008: 61). Although the Genoa proposals were not adopted, the role of the League of Nations in attempting to organize multilateral solutions to international economic problems as part of an oversight role, throughout the 1920s and into the 1930s, formed a template for the eventual development of much more thorough multilateral regimes within the Bretton Woods system (Pauly, 1997: 47–59).

Genoa demonstrated that although leading social forces in both the UK and the US shared a commitment to rebuilding the world economy, "their contrasting positions of ascending and descending power led to considerable disagreements as to the appropriate organisation of world finance" (Langley, 2002: 63–64). This prevented the establishment of a broadly agreed multilateral framework for restoring the gold standard and meant that ad hoc central bank cooperation between the UK and the US would be essential to the revival of the international monetary system, when sterling was restored to gold convertibility in 1925.

Within the context of these broader Anglo-American disagreements, the banking communities on both sides of the Atlantic functioned as the engine in driving cooperation forward (Burk, 1991: 126). US international bankers supported the plan to restore sterling's convertibility to gold at the prewar parity because they viewed it as critical to stabilizing the entire European monetary system, which was a necessary precondition for the realization of US economic ambitions. Internationalist sections of US capital, exemplified by Wall Street bankers, tended to take a more lenient approach to the question of war debts and pushed for a more constructive engagement with European politics. Although divided over the best means through which to supplant the UK, US bankers viewed a shared Anglo-American restoration of the international monetary system as the best means to establish US banking predominance internationally. But, within the context of an isolationist Republican administration, the capacity to pull US diplomatic power along with them was limited (Block, 1977: 15–18; Konings, 2011: 74; Chernow, 1990: 227).

Once again, the House of Morgan was at the fore of cooperative efforts with central bankers from both states. The key figures were Montagu Norman, chairman of the Bank of England, and Benjamin Strong, head of the Federal Reserve Bank of New York. The importance of the relationship between the two men reflected the growing significance of Anglo-American central banking to the international economy, with the rise of the dollar and the weakening of sterling bringing about a dualistic pattern of central bank leadership. Indeed, because of the heavy exposure of New York financial houses to European war debts, the New York Fed frequently appeared to be more concerned with its relationship to the Bank of England than it was with the Federal Reserve Board in Washington (Konings, 2011: 66).

On a personal level, Norman and Strong were close friends who had developed enduring personal ties during the war, and both aimed at the restoration of the gold standard and increased autonomy for Central Banks (Chernow, 1990: 244; Ahamed, 2009: 92). Norman recognized that he would need to draw upon US financial power to restore the City's position. This realization stemmed in part from the increased interdependence of New York and London money markets after the war. The Bank of England had reluctantly placed an embargo upon foreign loans to all but the Dominion countries after the war (Ahamed, 2009: 210). The restrictions were initially put in place because the Treasury wanted to make sure that there was a ready market for UK government and corporate stock sales, but they were subsequently extended to keep domestic savings and gold reserves from flowing out (Attard, 2004: 196). As part of this effort, Norman actively diverted business to New York to decrease the pressure on sterling and the London capital market. In fact, Norman had even suggested that Dominion countries should raise funds in the New York capital markets. For Norman, the restoration of sterling's standing as the foremost international currency was paramount above concerns with London's predominance as a capital market (Attard, 2004: 211).

Norman's recognition of the need to draw in US financial power to restore the City was also based on the fact that sterling alone simply wasn't strong enough. By building up Wall Street linkages, Norman hoped to recover the City and the Bank's financial preeminence. Just as it would do from the 1950s, with the birth of the Euromarkets and the importation of dollar business into London, the City looked to draw in US financial power to restore its own predominance. Norman's relationship with the House of Morgan was a critical component of this strategy to draw in the US; at a time when Anglo-American rivalry was on the rise in other areas, the House of Morgan's London branch, Morgan Grenfell, became an important link between the City and Wall Street. The US Morgan partners in New York shared the appetite of their London colleagues for getting the UK back onto gold, which they saw as a way to protect exchange rates from manipulation by politicians. The US Treasury gave its approval for the New York Fed and the House of Morgan to coordinate the UK's return to the gold standard (Chernow 1990: 273–75).

The integral question in the run up to restoration was—at what dollar price should the pound be fixed to gold? It was decided that sterling should be restored at the prewar parity of $4.86, despite the dissenting voice of John Maynard Keynes, who believed that the pound was overvalued by 10 to 15 percent (Eichengreen, 2008: 57). UK financial leaders feared that if the pound returned to gold at under $4.86 foreign investors would lose confidence in sterling, taking even more of their business to New York (Costigliola, 1977: 923). Money markets on each side of the Atlantic had become more tightly intertwined than ever before with the city's rise. Crucially, this meant that "changes in the attractiveness of New York as a deposit center for secondary money markets or changes in New York's volume of lending affected the sterling exchanges independently of the position of the UK pattern of settlements and balance of payments at the time" (Costigliola, 1977: 34–6). This degree of interdependence made central bank cooperation imperative. Strong and Norman enabled sterling's return to gold through a cooperative strategy dealing with relative prices, interest rates, and stabilization credits (Clarke, 1972: 75). By making sure that interest rates were kept higher in London, the Fed and the Bank of England created conditions that drew capital away from New York. The New York Fed and J. P. Morgan provided $200 million and $100 million, respectively, in support of sterling's return to gold (Hogan, 1977: 73; Chernow, 1990: 276). The centrality of London and New York to the resuscitation of the gold standard during the 1920s anticipated their interdependent role within the postwar Bretton Woods order. US financial ascendance was gradually de-privileging the UK's singular role within the international monetary system and driving a much more interdependent Anglo-American axis upon which the system increasingly rested.

Beyond the return to gold in 1925, the early-to-mid-1920s had marked the high-water mark of interwar Anglo-American cooperation over international finance. During the war, a grouping of cooperatively inclined Anglo-American bankers emerged, with shared values and goals. These bankers wanted governments to remove themselves from business, pushed central banks to regain control over national currencies and stabilize exchange rates, and looked to the funding of war debts and the return to gold to prevent the political manipulation of currencies (Dayer, 1991: 158).

Simultaneously, however, US and UK bankers were also rivals. Bankers from both nations strove to achieve dominance within international markets. By the end of the war, the US had established a foreign banking system (Abrahams, 1969: 572). Both Strong and Norman intended to establish their own national currencies as the major unit for international trade and attempted to convince foreign governments to hold their reserves in dollars or pounds (Dayer, 1991: 159–60). This tension had been in evidence during negotiations over how the reformed Reichsbank should hold international reserves earlier in the decade. The US wanted Germany's foreign exchanges to be held in New York, in order to be readily convertible into gold. The UK viewed the potential transfer of reserves to New York as a threat to sterling's credibility. Eventually, the UK triumphed in this negotiation, but the effect was to increase the pressure for a swift return of sterling to convertibility with gold.

Nevertheless, financial relations between the two powers were part of an emerging "informal entente" between the two states (Hogan, 1977:77). After the war, UK elites realized that they would have to relinquish their hold on areas of the world formerly under their domination. This meant rescinding some control over international finance, resource development, and communications. The UK saw that cooperation with the US would avoid unprofitable competition and prompt the US to share some of the burden of managing world order. From the US perspective, the Republican government of the 1920s wanted cooperation based upon private programs organized and orchestrated by business and financial leaders. The upshot of this was that both domestic and international arenas of public policy became largely a private concern (Hogan, 1977: 1–7).

The Republicans promoted the role of private finance in the reconstruction of the European powers.[18] Groundwork for cooperation was laid when the Congressional War Foreign Debt Committee cancelled 50 percent of the combined Allied debt in 1922, after the UK had made a desperate last-ditch attempt to soften terms with the Balfour Note. The accord over debt was crucial to Anglo-American cooperation. It alleviated, at least temporarily, a major source of disquiet between the two powers and represented "the first block in an incipient structure of Anglo-American cooperation" (Hogan, 1977: 56).

The House of Morgan's involvement in Anglo-American attempts to restore sterling's convertibility and finance European reconstruction was symptomatic of a broader trend in international affairs: the involvement of private bankers in political as well as financial discussions with governments. The 1920s were an age of unprecedented prestige for the international banking community, with central bankers in particular now a major focus of public attention (Ahamed, 2009: 9). Private bankers laid out political requirements for securing loans. The Anglo-American financial community was the most internationally influential of all. During a time of great economic and political uncertainty, cooperation between Anglo-American financial communities provided a vital impetus in integrating the economic strategies of the UK and the US. The emerging accord between the two states during the 1920s manifested itself in cooperation between private and central bankers as well as a common approach toward war debts and reparations (Hogan, 1977: 77). Anglo-American bankers had grown accustomed to working with one another, finding this easier than managing their respective treasuries. Governments on both sides of the Atlantic saw the importance of their respective financial communities. In a deeply undemocratic manner, private bankers often made decisions of enormous political significance during the 1920s.

From Depression to War

Despite the centrality of Anglo-American financial cooperation to rebuilding the postwar international economy, the latter 1920s were marked by a rapid disintegration of efforts to cooperate as the flimsily reconstructed gold standard collapsed (Hogan, 1977: 220). Sterling proved to be grossly overvalued, as Keynes had rightly noted. European exports were more competitive, and an overvalued currency hindered the UK's economic recovery during the second half of the 1920s. The fundamental conditions underpinning the classical gold standard were no longer in place. The mechanisms of adjustment, which relied upon wage deflation to correct balance of payments deficits and boost competitiveness through a downward shift in prices, could no longer be applied without political resistance. The global political economy had undergone a major structural shift. The growth of trade unionism, working-class parties, and unemployment benefits all contributed to the slowing down of wage adjustment, which meant that austerity could not be imposed upon workers as easily as it once had been, and central bankers were not nearly as insulated from political pressures as they wished to be (Eichengreen and Temin, 2000: 192; Frieden, 2007: 13).

This reality was clearly demonstrated in the UK. Ever since returning to gold, the Bank of England had been battling losses, as gold was hoarded by France, Germany, and the US. With gold holdings now so overwhelmingly concentrated in the US, European countries, particularly the UK and Germany, were left facing major supply shortages (Ahamed, 2009: 164). Although the UK had been keen for other countries to hold sterling reserves rather than underpinning their monetary base exclusively with gold, French officials viewed the proposals made by the UK at Genoa as a "British ploy to fortify London's position as a financial centre at the expense of Paris." They preferred to hold gold instead, and they built up huge reserves on the back of an undervalued franc. Capital inflows into Germany, with the US the major source, led to a tripling of the Reichsbank's gold reserves between 1924 and 1928. This absorption of gold by France and Germany put increased pressure on the Bank of England (Eichengreen, 2008: 65).

In response to these pressures, the Bank would raise Bank Rate to pull in gold and limit domestic liquidity through the imposition of austerity. But this strategy could no longer be undertaken with the ease of the prewar period. Persistent high unemployment, remaining above 10 percent throughout the 1920s (Frieden, 2007: 139), meant that Montagu Norman was increasingly constrained by the political implications of raising rates (Attard, 2004: 205). Churchill demanded that Norman reduce Bank Rate in 1925; after initially resisting, Norman agreed to do so (Boyce, 2004: 226). The gold standard had not provided the desired degree of insulation from political pressure. When a coal strike morphed into a general strike in 1926, the political opposition to the dictates of the gold standard grew even stronger (Block, 1977: 17; Eichengreen and Temin, 2000: 193). The UK's weakening balance of payments, with the overvalued pound pricing UK goods out of foreign markets, further undermined the maintenance of convertibility and led to increasing tensions between the City and UK industrial producers (Boyce, 2004: 216). The UK's preoccupation with her position vis-à-vis the US and the dollar led policy elites to neglect the problem of undervaluation from her European competitors (Costigliola, 1977: 927–8). Once convertibility had been restored, the coordination required to prevent the UK experiencing shortages of gold did not arise.

The decisive blow to the postwar gold standard came from the dynamics of the US economy and the Fed's attempts to manage them. As the US economy prospered during the 1920s and war debt repayments were collected, gold flowed into the country. By 1926, the US held nearly 45 percent of the world's gold supply, with one-quarter of this "free gold," meaning that it was above and beyond the 40 percent backing for the money supply mandated by the US gold standard law. But rather than allow the domestic money supply to increase in response to these inflows, as gold standard protocol dictated, the US sterilized the gold inflows and refused to permit US prices to increase and allow other countries to adjust (Block, 1977: 21; Eichengreen, 2008: 65–67; Ahamed, 2009: 170).

Rejecting the traditional gold standard relationship between the gold supply and the money supply, Benjamin Strong at the New York Fed devised a new and expanded mandate for central banking. No longer was the Fed exclusively concerned with stabilizing domestic prices (although this remained its primary objective); it was also attentive to the need to respond to fluctuations in the level of domestic business activity by making appropriate adjustments to the credit supply. Strong's new monetary policy principles augured the expanded central bank mandates of the modern era, but the domestic concerns of the Fed were now jeopardizing the entire international payments system. By hoarding gold and failing to allow a commensurate increase in the money supply (with an associated increase in demand for imports and higher US prices that would dampen exports) Strong was undermining the gold standard system by forestalling the adjustments that would help correct international imbalances (Ahamed, 2009: 171).

In addition to these US policy failures, the weaknesses of the newly inaugurated Federal Reserve System also caused problems and symbolized the inadequacy of America's institutional capacity for international financial leadership. The exact locus of power within the system was unclear, which resulted in internal struggles. The Federal Reserve Board in Washington, DC, was hamstrung by a vague mandate and a lack of precisely defined purpose.

Ambiguities and tensions within the Federal Reserve System left it ill suited to play its emerging global role with genuine conviction (Ahamed, 2009: 176).

A bad situation became much worse in the final years of the 1920s. A booming New York stock market had fueled an increasingly speculative pattern of investment and reoriented the interests of US investors away from Europe and toward opportunities at home. This effectively cut European countries off from the capital inflows upon which they were dependent to service war debts. The US stood at the center of a complex payments triangle in which US private financial inflows funded Germany, which then made debt repayments to the UK or France, who in turn made payments to the US (Schwartz, 2009a: 168–171; Konings, 2011: 74). When the Fed raised interest rates to stem the boom, Europe was deprived of essential capital inflows and forced to pay higher interest rates on existing loans (Eichengreen, 2008: 69). Once the private loans to Germany began to dry up, the system came under increasing strain, but the US steadfastly refused to annul the debts. The Wall Street crash in October 1929 sent the stock market into free fall. Within a month, by October 1929, shares on Wall Street had lost 40 percent of their value. Around six thousand US banks closed between 1929 and 1932. By 1933 unemployment had reached 25 percent and economic output had fallen by one-third (Dimbleby and Reynolds, 1988: 110). Overall, the US contribution to international financial development during the interwar years was "more destructive than constructive" (Konings, 2011: 75).

Developments in the US had a major impact upon the UK. The imposition of tariffs abroad and the collapse of world trade associated with the Depression undermined the invisible earnings that had supported the UK's balance of payments. Between 1929 and 1931, the UK experienced a major deterioration in its trade balance and a massive collapse of its invisibles balance. UK exports declined by 31 percent in the same period. In this context, it became increasingly difficult for the UK to maintain sterling's value against gold. The UK initially benefited as investors retreated from the dollar after 1929, but pressure soon turned to sterling in 1931. Despite increases to Bank Rate, the UK continued to suffer from capital outflows until currency traders eventually provoked a major sterling crisis (Block, 1977: 28; Janeway, 1995: 265; Eichengreen, 2008: 78–82). A worsening budget deficit prompted a run on sterling. In a humiliating twist, the Labour prime minister Ramsey Macdonald appealed to J. P. Morgan for assistance, but was told that he must cut social security spending and balance the books to receive funds (Temperley, 2002: 129; Allen, 1955: 760). Morgan's power had enabled the imposition of conditionality upon a UK prime minister. The Labour government acceded to the deficit cuts and received a $200 million credit from Morgan (Chernow, 1990: 330; Ahamed, 2009: 427). But these actions were not enough, and the UK abandoned the gold standard on September 20th, 1931 (Clavin, 1996: 19).

The departure from gold was, however, by no means inevitable. The structural factors undergirding the UK's international monetary position were now certainly far less auspicious, and the potential political resistance to austerity greater. But, were it not for the leadership vacuum presented by the illness of Bank of England Governor Norman during the peak of the crisis, the UK might have staggered on. The decision to abandon sterling's fixed convertibility arose in part due to the successful efforts of deputy governor Ernest Harvey to temporarily suspend convertibility against the wishes of Norman (who preferred the traditional medicine of further interest rate hikes). Harvey believed that a temporary suspension would maintain the long-term prospects of the gold standard by preventing an election that he feared would weaken the power of gold standard supporters. But the devaluation did not lead to the runaway inflation that orthodox theories predicted. Instead, as Keynes had long argued, it stimulated recovery (Morrison, 2016).

The UK's devaluation of sterling symbolized the termination of the interwar gold standard (Eichengreen, 2008: 82). By 1932, the international monetary order had fragmented into three distinctive blocs, and by April 1933, Roosevelt had devalued the dollar (Clavin, 1996: 83). Anglo-American tensions were further aggravated by the collapse of the gold standard. The goodwill of US financiers toward the UK lessened due to increased speculation against the dollar amid rumors that the Bank of England had spread information about America's weakening economic position. Similarly, the UK's creation of an Exchange Equalization Account to manage sterling's floating value was viewed by skeptical US statesmen as a mechanism to competitively depreciate sterling against the dollar (Clavin, 1996: 21–22). The war debt issue had already recurred from 1929 to 1931, with the UK and the US at loggerheads once again over the issue of full cancellation. Tensions over the naval balance between the two nations also reemerged in the later 1920s. Growing Japanese power raised US concerns over the potential of a combined Anglo-Japanese naval threat in the Far East. The UK went to great lengths to make clear that this was not a realistic possibility, but to no avail. Wrangling over the Washington Naval Treaty continued to blight diplomatic relations between the two powers (Allen, 1955: 734–50).

The UK eventually defaulted on its remaining debt to the US. Amid a rapidly worsening international economic climate, the UK abandoned its longstanding commitment to free trade. At the Ottawa Conference in 1932, the

UK moved to Imperial Preference and discrimination against US goods. As the storm of the Depression raged, the UK sought refuge within protected imperial markets. Sterling could no longer function as the international "top currency" (Strange, 1971: 55). Instead, Montagu Norman established an exclusive "sterling area" of dependent colonial territories that traded in sterling with the UK at its center. The international monetary system had fragmented into rival currency and trading blocs and would not be restored on an effective multilateral basis until the 1950s. The structures of Anglo-American cooperation at the core of the reconstructed gold standard had proved too weak and the international economy was thrown into lasting turmoil that fed directly into the exacerbation of geopolitical tensions and the outbreak of World War II.

Informal cooperative efforts between the UK and the US failed to stabilize the interwar economy. But important changes in multilateral thinking occurred during the Depression era. Multilateral attempts to solidify the key currencies and escape the Depression, led by the UK at the 1933 World Economic Conference in London, failed to produce consensus. Bankers cleaved too close to their vision for the international economy and the old gold standard orthodoxies of thought (Pauly, 1997: 64). Although they found some common ground over currency matters, tensions between governmental offices on each side remained considerable (Clavin, 1996: 195). After 1933, however, the Economic and Financial Organization of the League of Nations began to develop a new model, which became a direct forebear to the fuller, formal multilateralism of the IMF. The final economic studies carried out by the league shaped the postwar settlement, by forming a new consensus that was institutionalized through the 1944 Bretton Woods Agreement. Under the new consensus, obstacles to trade would gradually be removed, and transparent, monitored agreements would facilitate an orderly approach to exchange rate adjustments. The scope for countercyclical fiscal and monetary policies, as well as capital mobility, would be shaped by the need to liberalize trade and promote a stable system of exchange rates (Pauly, 1997: 73). Although the endurance of the old orthodoxies had brought the world economy to ruin, the seeds of a new international monetary order were beginning to be sown.

The Past as Prologue

From a colonial dependency late in the eighteenth century, the US had become the foremost industrial power in the world by the eve of World War II. As this chapter has demonstrated, uneven patterns of Anglo-American development closely tied US ascendancy to the gradual diminution of UK dominance. Benefiting from the privileges of backwardness and easy access to UK finance, labor, and industrial expertise, the US rapidly closed the economic gap between the two powers. In matters of finance, the process of catch-up was slower than in the industrial sphere; it took the shock of war to catalyze transformation. But the diminution of the UK's role at the center of the international monetary system, when it came, was similarly linked to the rise of US economic power.

Transformed by war, transatlantic financial relationships became, paradoxically, both a source of contestation and a fulcrum of cooperation. It was the outbreak of war that enabled the Morgan banking dynasty to attain such a significant role at the heart of Anglo-American financial cooperation. The war also had the effect of drawing the UK into a debtor relationship with the US government that soured intergovernmental relations in the 1920s, inhibited multilateral cooperation, and increased UK dependency upon US financial power. This was not the last time that the vulnerability of debt dependency would characterize the UK's relationship with the US and open spaces for US policy ambitions. At the end of World War II, and again during the IMF crisis of 1976, the US would make use of UK financial vulnerability to achieve its ambition of a liberalized international financial system.

Transatlantic relations during the interwar period were peculiarly paradoxical. The Anglo-American relationship was marked by bitter political disagreements between governments over the repayment of war debts; at the same time, it was also defined by central bank cooperation and the growing importance of an Anglo-American banking community that spanned the Atlantic. By the 1920s, a form of private international governance, led by private and central bankers from the US and the UK, had begun to play a central role in international politics. But, due to the difficult negotiations between the Anglo-American treasuries over the issue of war debts, cooperation between private and central bankers outstripped the capacity for intergovernmental alignment. The private Anglo-American financial governance of the 1920s did, nonetheless, provide important clues as to the longue durée of Anglo-American development. By the 1980s, after decades of postwar globalization and the breakdown of the Bretton Woods order, Anglo-American private and central bankers would once more be central figures in governing international finance.

The pattern of increasingly intertwined Anglo-American monetary politics during the interwar years would continue to be crucial to the wider international political economy under the Bretton Woods system after World War II.

The rise of US financial power on the global stage emerged through its integration with UK capitalism and the political economy of Anglo-American development. But even though the UK and the US managed to resuscitate the gold standard through sporadic and ad hoc cooperation, the absence of a firmer multilateral commitment to economic cooperation and the policy blunders of US financial authorities played an important part in the breakdown of the interwar gold standard and the disintegration of the liberal international order. This was not merely a case of a failure of US leadership, but also a product of the inadequacy of US financial capacity to supplant the UK's position as the linchpin of the international economy. These deficiencies were set within a wider Anglo-American relationship that, still marked by considerable geopolitical rivalry and mutual suspicion, could not sustain the requisite level of cooperation to maintain the gold standard and reconstruct a liberal financial order. Anglo-American development had begun to remake the international economy, but the institutional foundations and alignment of transatlantic interests required to reconstruct the architecture of international finance would not emerge until after another catastrophic war.

3

Bretton Woods and the
Keynesian State

AFTER THE devastation of World War II, the United Kingdom and the United States were once again at the heart of efforts to reconstruct the international monetary order. But with the UK now gravely weakened by its role in a second major war in less than thirty years, the great reversal in power reached terminal velocity. By the end of the war the predominance of the US was beyond doubt. The UK's junior role in the political economy of the Special Relationship was clearly evinced by US leadership of the Anglo-American negotiations that produced the Bretton Woods agreement of 1944.

Bretton Woods is conventionally recognized as the marker for a new stage of hegemonic world order led by the US (Block, 1977; Gilpin, 1987: Schwartz, 2009a; Ikenberry, 2011). It signifies the final power transition between UK and US international leadership and concludes the disorderly and anarchic inter-regnum of the interwar years.[1] This chapter moves beyond existing IPE accounts of Bretton Woods by adopting a process-based approach that examines the formation and foundations of the agreement in conjunction with the patterns of state formation and the transformation of policy ideas within the Anglo-American political economies.[2] Rather than viewing the agreement as a neat transition to a postwar stage of US international hegemony, this chapter highlights important continuities with longer-term dynamics of Anglo-American development. Grounding the Bretton Woods international order in deeper historical trajectories of Anglo-American institutional development reveals the limited institutional embedding of Bretton Woods' principles within the two founder states, and the inefficacy of initial attempts at postwar multilateralism.

Existing explanations of the collapse of Bretton Woods have stressed either the prevalence of general, system-wide crisis tendencies and logical contradictions (Triffin, 1966; Gilpin, 1987); the causal significance of the contradictions of US international power (Strange, 1987; Konings, 2011; Panitch and Gindin, 2012); or the rise of neoclassical economic ideas that gradually displaced the agreement's Keynesian origins (Best, 2005). These explanations have much to their credit, but they have overlooked the specific role of Anglo-American development in first laying the basis for Bretton Woods and then generating—within a distinctive transatlantic space of financial transformation centered in the City of London—influential dynamics that simultaneously weakened both the domestic Keynesian order and the Bretton Woods agreement. The UK's role in the creation and continuation of the Bretton Woods order was not confined to the ideas of John Maynard Keynes. The continued importance of sterling as a major international currency, and of the financial infrastructure contained within London (not least the international gold market), allied to the international limits of private US finance, ensured that the development of UK capitalism would continue to be fundamental to the prospects of post-war finance.

Anglo-American relations after the outbreak of war came increasingly to be characterized by "uneven interdependence": a reciprocal dynamic in which both states recognized their mutual dependence upon the developmental trajectory of the other, even though US power was clearly predominant.[3] Uneven Anglo-American interdependence was central to both the creation of Bretton Woods and, as we will see in the following chapter, its demise. The UK was financially dependent upon the US, but US state officials and the New York banking community perceived that the realization of their postwar ambitions required the UK to adopt a multilateral approach toward the international economy.

Within this broader context of uneven interdependence, critical divisions existed between different departments of state in both the UK and the US. Exploring the struggle between economically orthodox ideas and an emergent Keynesian approach within both states, I argue that the persistence of pre-Keynesian economic orthodoxy, represented most influentially by bankers on both sides of the Atlantic, provided the foundation for the eventual undermining of Bretton Woods and the reemergence of financial globalization in the 1950s. Orthodox ideas within private and central banks proved very difficult to displace, despite the increased prominence of Keynesian approaches to economic management. Early struggles for influence over the postwar economic agenda, on both sides of the Atlantic, laid the groundwork for the eventual undermining of the domestic Keynesian compromise and the wider Bretton Woods order. Embedded liberalism did represent an important policy compromise, but it was an ambiguous one that still contained plenty of scope for conflict over differing interpretations of the agreement (Best, 2005: 54). The term itself is something of a misnomer—the guiding economic principles of the agreement were never fully institutionally "embedded" within the core Anglo-American political economies.

The chapter begins by exploring Anglo-American institutional transformations at play during the interwar and wartime periods, arguing that these processes are central to understanding the political economy of the early postwar years. This duration established the conditions for uneven interdependence between the UK and the US. The next section stresses the need to disaggregate their national interests to trace longer-term institutional developments, including the growing but limited influence of Keynesian thinking within Anglo-American treasuries, and their impact on internal policy tensions within both states. The chapter then investigates the connection between Anglo-American institutional orientations and policy priorities during the Bretton Woods negotiations, and it reviews the uneven synthesis of Anglo-American interests reached within the final Bretton Woods agreement, highlighting the role of the New York financial community in first proposing an alternative "key currency plan" and then loosening the stringency of the new framework. Finally, the chapter concludes by identifying the role of pre-Keynesian Anglo-American institutional continuities based around the power of central banks in weakening the nascent Keynesian policy framework and laying the basis for financial globalization in subsequent decades.

The Continuity of Process

Understanding the postwar Anglo-American context requires dismantling the traditional analytical division between "wartime" and "postwar" to unearth the continuity of developmental processes across the two periods. This allows us to evade a cyclical, stage-based explanation of international order. Chapter 1 outlined the importance of variable tempos of continual institutional transformation for driving changing patterns of global order.[4] These processes of institutional transformation were underway during and after the war, but they were manifested in different strategies and outcomes across the period. Changes in institutional structure, often of a gradual and incremental kind, present alternative opportunities and constraints to social agents (Streeck and Thelen, 2005; Mahoney and Thelen, 2010). This was the case for the US and the UK. Many of the conditions of the postwar world were molded during the war, particularly bilateral relations between the two powers (Kolko, 1968: 7; Hudson, 1972: 37; Dobson, 1995: 72). Negotiations over Lend-Lease were central here. The war rapidly exhausted the UK's financial assets. Gold reserves that had stood at $4 billion in 1938 were down to $1 billion by September 1940. The UK government nationalized private overseas investment holdings of citizens to meet the mounting costs of war. As the UK's reserve position worsened, they turned to the US, resulting in the Lend-Lease agreement of 1941. The pressures of war created institutional vulnerabilities within the UK while reinforcing the organizational capacity and relative resource base of US institutions, opening UK actors to the exercise of US power.

Lend-Lease ensured that the UK would no longer need dollars to purchase US goods, abating the pressure on reserves (Skidelsky, 2000: 100). The cost of transactions was deferred until after the war. But the agreement was not only a strategy to bolster the UK's resistance to Nazi Germany; it was also a lever with which the US could ensure the UK's postwar dependence, win commitment to the end of UK trade discrimination, and gain access to formerly exclusive areas of UK interests (Hudson, 1972: 44; Dobson, 1986: 32; Frieden, 2006: 255). This was not, though, simply a case of US domination over the UK. Lend-Lease also pushed the two states closer toward cooperative integration by intensifying the pooling of resources (Ovendale, 1998: 47). Financial integration was matched by integration in the technological and intelligence fields (Ovendale, 1998: 45; Dobson, 1995: 74). There was enormous transatlantic exchange of administrative capacities too.[5]

The alliance of World War II was much closer and institutionally deeper than that forged during World War I and a departure from the mutual suspicion of the 1930s (Kolko, 1968: 13; Dimbleby and Reynolds, 1988: Saville, 1993: 64).[6] But the quid pro quo for this integration was retrenchment of UK sovereignty, with the US now permitted to audit UK finances under the terms of the Lend-Lease agreement (Temperley, 2002: 162; Dobson, 1995: 72). The autonomy of the UK government and Treasury was circumscribed by growing fiscal dependence in a process that extended the reach of US power into the institutions of the UK state. This was a continuation of the constriction of UK sovereignty that emerged due to financial vulnerability in the interwar period and continued after World War II. By undermining the UK's capacity for unilateral action, it created the opportunity for Anglo-American cooperation at Bretton Woods. This enabled the gradual multilateral consolidation of US structural power in international finance around an axis of transatlantic cooperation.

War acted as a crucible for the transformation of UK sovereignty, permitting an unprecedented degree of cooperative subordination to the US. But this was not an entirely one-way street. The US depended upon the UK's institutional capacity and global influence in trade and finance. This gave the UK considerable bargaining power and created a relationship of uneven interdependence. As the key currency proposals of the Federal Reserve Bank of New York and US international bankers after the war made clear, the New York financial community recognized that they needed to restore sterling's international status alongside the City's entrepôt role to realize their vision for the postwar world economy (James, 1996: 65–66; Langley, 2002: 72). Just as Montagu Norman had looked to boost the City's status through drawing in US support, the New York bankers now looked to reestablish the City and sterling as integrated components of their attempt to establish international financial dominance. The wartime relationship also gave rise to important processes of state formation and the dissemination of new policy ideas in both states.

Anglo-American Institutional Transformation

The paramount wartime development within the UK state was the temporary demotion of the Treasury. For most of its history the Treasury was at the core of UK power, exerting a powerful and continuous influence upon the development of society (Roseveare, 1969: 9). War acted as a catalyst for its evolution. But the Treasury's fortunes during and after World War II were mixed. From 1939 until 1942, the Treasury lost its traditional sway over policy and prestige, with alternative institutional sites absorbing some of its former power (Roseveare, 1969: 325, 273; Weir, 1989: 65).[7]

The interwar years and the attempt to restore the gold standard had internationalized the Treasury's role. Its finance department undertook multilateral efforts to rebuild the international monetary system, alongside the finance ministries of other countries, through the League of Nations. This new formalized activism—a break from the informal evolution of the classical gold standard—was evidenced in the prominent role of Treasury officials during the 1922 Genoa Conference organized through the League of Nations (Roseveare, 1969: 261).[8] During the 1930s, Treasury representatives were frequently present in the foreign embassies of the major powers. This was part of the new, expanded function of the Treasury, reflecting the "breadth and intensity of

Britain's monetary problems" as it attempted to restore the gold standard based on its gravely weakened interwar political economy (Roseveare, 1969: 261).

Synchronous to this expansion of Treasury mandate was the gradual diffusion of Keynesian ideas. A parallel process was occurring in the US, but the comparative advancement of Keynesian ideas within the two states diverged substantially. In the UK, the more centralized pattern of prewar Treasury control over the wider state apparatus, alongside more formalized rules of civil service advancement, limited the capacity of policy outsiders and innovative ideas to transform established administrative practices. In the US, by contrast, the Depression-era government had a less centralized and more mature administrative structure, allowing the easier introduction of new ideas and the creation of new economic advisory groups (Weir, 1989: 60–63).

Keynes's personal participation within national government was a feature distinctive to the UK. The travails of the interwar economy spurred the progress of his thinking. He outlined a clear alternative to incumbent orthodoxy in his 1929 pamphlet for the Liberal Party: *Can Lloyd George Do It?* But while the implementation of Imperial Preference and protectionist measures during the 1930s represented a practical rupture with traditional orthodoxy, the progress of Keynesian thinking within the UK was limited.[9] Politically, the Labour Party had reaffirmed its commitment to socialist principles after the failed Labour government of 1929–31. In doing so it rejected the class compromise that underpinned Keynes's technocratic vision for a managed market economy (Weir, 1989: 57). Keynesian advocates of increased public spending and macroeconomic management were appointed to the newly created Economic Advisory Council in 1930, from where they advised the government throughout the 1930s. The economic recovery that followed from the ending of the gold standard also opened some space for Keynesian ideas within the Treasury (Morrison, 2016: 199). But Keynesian advocates failed to convert its dominant pattern of thinking (Weir, 1989: 55). The Treasury's centralized control over the wider state formed a powerful obstacle to the admittance of new ideas.

The limited gains of Keynesian advocates did not, though, preclude other important changes occurring within the Treasury. The rising power of the labor movement and the catastrophe of the break from gold in 1931 led to the expansion of the Treasury's power, with the influence of the City and the Bank diminished due to their implication in the failed return to gold. Using its increased influence, the Treasury pushed for a monetary policy more germane to the fulfillment of domestic policy imperatives rather than maintaining external balance. An Exchange Equalization Account was established, under the

Treasury's mandate, to offset the impact of short-term gold movements upon domestic monetary dynamics while the Treasury also maintained surveillance over the foreign lending of City firms (Helleiner, 1994: 32; Eichengreen and Temin, 2000).

Crucially, though, these changes were driven more by pragmatism during crisis rather than a deep intellectual conversion to Keynesian ideas (Roseveare, 1969: 261–268; Weir, 1989: 54; Cronin, 1991: 131). In the fiscal realm, the Treasury remained largely committed to the old orthodoxy of balanced budgets.[10] It had certainly not adopted the Keynesian tolerance for budget deficits, nor the priorities of full employment and countercyclical stabilization. Treasury support for low interest rates was more a reflection of the need to finance national debt at low cost than a desire to stimulate domestic expansion. It was not until the outbreak of war that old attitudes began to break (Hall, 1986: 72; Weir, 1989: 54; Helleiner, 1994: 32). The incompleteness of the Treasury's Keynesian transformation would prove critical to the development of the UK's postwar political economy.

With the arrival of Churchill as prime minister in 1940, the focus shifted toward securing raw materials for the war effort, and spaces opened for greater Keynesian influence. Consequently, the Treasury was subordinated to other ministers and departments.[11] But, as the war effort matured, the relevance of the Treasury was reestablished. Securing finances for the war effort, and the related dollar diplomacy with the US, became increasingly prominent issues (Roseveare, 1969: 273–74). As the Treasury's centrality was restored it underwent a transformation of purpose (Green, 1992: 203). After the budget of 1941, the first to publicly endorse Keynesian principles and national income statistics, the Treasury's domestic role was extended to include responsibility for the aggregate balance of resources and demand in the economy (Roseveare, 1969: 274; Hall, 1986: 72; Weir, 1989: 66).[12] This represented a break from balanced-budgets, Gladstonian thinking. The Treasury was now partially responsible for price levels, savings incentives, and the level of capital investment.[13] Acceptance of this expanded mandate by the wartime Treasury marked an important victory for Keynesian ideas in the struggle with classical economic orthodoxy (Roseveare, 1969: 276; Weir, 1989: 66). The creation of a new economic section within the war cabinet, staffed by several Keynesian economists, helped transmit Keynesian ideas within the government in a top-down process (Weir, 1989: 66).

The transformation of the Treasury's responsibilities disrupted its traditional relationship with the Bank. Prior to the war, the Treasury's domestic role was limited to the management of government finances. This meant that the Bank was the Treasury's principal point of contact with the wider economy (Green, 1992: 203). Under its increased remit, the Treasury was now brought into regular contact with a wider range of actors, diluting the traditionally privileged role given to the Bank. Indeed, Keynes's relationship with the Bank was difficult, and Keynesian ideas of monetary management were met with skepticism (Fforde, 1992: 33; Cairncross, 1995: 71). But both the triumph of Keynesian ideas and the disruption of the Treasury-Bank relationship were inconclusive. By the early 1950s, a more traditional orientation of institutional power had been restored, opening the way for the integration of Anglo-American financial power that would follow with the development of the Euromarkets.[14]

Within the US state, comparable processes of institutional and ideational transformation were underway. But here the advance of Keynesian and proto-Keynesian ideas was, despite the absence of Keynes himself from government, initially more rapid (albeit similarly incomplete). Prior to the Depression era, the US government had cleaved to balanced budgets orthodoxy much like its UK counterpart. Budget deficits were viewed as inescapably inflationary, regardless of whether there might be some underutilized capacity in the economy (Salant, 1989: 33). But during the 1930s, the terrain of economic ideas began to shift. The initial academic response to the Depression had relied upon laissez-faire doctrines and continued faith in the capacity of the private sector to lead a recovery if natural equilibrium was allowed to return. Cleaving to neoclassical assumptions, this perspective deemed state intervention unnecessary. But with Roosevelt's Democratic administration from 1933, economic ideas within the state underwent a substantial transformation. A range of new intellectual approaches emerged, more disparate than those in the UK. These included a conviction in the merits of administered prices, as well as diagnoses of both "secular stagnation" and "underconsumption" that called for greater government intervention to stabilize growth (Blyth, 2002: 50–51).[15]

Despite the gradual emergence of these ideas, Roosevelt's first administration advocated a balanced budget and moved to cut government expenditure during his first year in office. A lack of Treasury support for Keynesian-type proposals hamstrung efforts to deal with unemployment (Sweezy, 1972: 119). It was only during Roosevelt's second administration, from 1937, that explicitly Keynesian doctrines and the development of national statistics based on Keynesian principles began to gain widespread traction (Salant, 1989: 37). They did so in a more pronounced fashion than in the UK (Weir, 1989). The publication of Keynes's *General Theory* influenced economists in major US universities, with young graduates recruited into government agencies involved with the exercise of fiscal and monetary policy. Already, by 1934, Federal Reserve chairman Mariner Eccles, had begun to bring in like-minded economists to the government and tapped into early Keynesian graduates (Sweezy, 1972: 117; Salant, 1989: 37–39). This was a notable contrast to the Bank of England, in which no comparable break with orthodoxy had been achieved and clashes with Keynes were common during the interwar years (Fforde, 1992: 33; Skidelsky, 2000).

By the end of the 1930s, Keynesians occupied important positions throughout the Treasury, Budget Bureau, and Department of Commerce (Weir, 1989: 55). Their advancement within the Treasury was noteworthy because its power relative to other US institutions had increased (Helleiner, 1994: 30; Sarai, 2009: 76). The Treasury supplanted the State Department, Fed, and private bankers (e.g., the House of Morgan) in taking responsibility for international financial negotiations (Panitch and Gindin, 2012: 71). Roosevelt's administration blamed the New York financial community, and the House of Morgan specifically, for the catastrophic failure of the interwar monetary system (Helleiner, 1994: 30; Ferguson, 1995: 114; Fraser, 2005: 338–39). Government borrowing during the New Deal expanded the market in Treasury bills as private investors increased their holdings. The Treasury bill market became important to the restoration of Wall Street. In response to the banking crisis, Congress granted extended authority to the Fed. The 1935 Banking Act expanded the Fed's powers (Brinkley, 1996: 81). But, as fiscal policy came to dominate monetary policy, the Fed's remit was subsequently subordinated to Treasury imperatives during the war (Epstein and Schor, 1995: 7).

US state formation during the 1930s was also driven from below. A surge of labor radicalism pushed Roosevelt toward drastic social reforms and opened political and institutional spaces for the emergence of Keynesian ideas. Under the Wagner Act, trade unionism was legalized, with the specific aim of boosting purchasing power (Blyth, 2002: 67). The Social Security Act founded the US welfare state with nationwide provision of unemployment and retirement benefits and was similarly justified on the basis of its capacity to increase purchasing power in the economy (Brinkley, 1996: 202; Blyth, 2002: 65; Panitch and Gindin, 2012: 59). Both acts reflected ascendant underconsumptionist ideas and had the effect of boosting demand through redistribution (Blyth, 2002: 64). These changes greatly enhanced the administrative capacities of the American state. In 1938, a "grand truce" with capital was instantiated (Brinkley,

1996: 89). The truce was a product of meetings held by Roosevelt with moderate trade unionists, bankers, and industrialists; out of it emerged a transformation in economic thinking that mirrored the advancement of Keynesianism within the UK Treasury. The US Treasury recognized the need for deficit spending to stimulate demand and investment (Panitch and Gindin, 2012: 62). As was the case with the UK, this represented a break from the traditional balanced budgets orthodoxy of the gold-standard era. And, just as with the UK, the break was not comprehensively institutionalized.

Preparing for Bretton Woods

Institutional transformation and Keynesian advancement within both states shaped the negotiations that led to the Bretton Woods agreement. For both the UK and the US, the formulation of policy positions on the future of the international monetary system proved divisive, reflecting the new patterns of power that had evolved within each state. In the UK, it caused a major split between the Bank of England and the Treasury. Keynes, a contentious figure, represented the Treasury in its negotiations with the US and divided opinion within the UK state. The UK's commitments to maintaining sterling as an international currency, and the desire to remain outside of an integrated European Payments Union, caused major tensions with the US Treasury.

US policy makers identified the sterling area and imperial preference as major obstacles to the reconstruction of an open international economy after the war (Kolko, 1968: 246; Ikenberry, 2001: 186).[16] US priorities eventually converged around a commitment to multilateralism and currency convertibility, international free trade, exchange rate stability, and European integration (Hogan, 1984: 289; Hearden, 2002: 59). But, as with the UK, there were differences and conflicts between institutional interests that emerged while planning for the postwar order.

During the war the contending interests of the US Treasury and the State Department created friction over numerous issues, with disagreements over the future of Germany particularly prominent (Skidelsky, 2000: 133). Treasury secretary Henry Morgenthau mistrusted UK motives and hoped to establish US financial hegemony after the war by exhausting UK financial assets (Skidelsky, 2000: 98). In general, however, the Treasury was staffed by progressive New Deal figures such as Morgenthau and White, who, notwithstanding their desire to supplant the UK's role in the world, favored more heterodox blueprints for the postwar international economy that would allow greater scope for deficit spending and insulation from deflationary pressures.[17] The prevalence of these ideas within the US Treasury provided an important foundation for the agreement with Keynes and their UK counterparts.

By contrast, the State Department, headed by Cordell Hull, was principally concerned with dismantling the UK's Imperial Preference system and creating the kind of open-world economic conditions that had underpinned the gold standard era (Skidelsky, 2000: 126; Ikenberry, 2001: 176).[18] Both the Treasury and the State Department were in agreement, though, about the importance of the UK accepting multilateralism and currency convertibility at the earliest possible date. They viewed the UK as a key cog in the effort to restore the international economic order (Block, 1977: 41).

While US officials harbored clear objectives for the postwar international economy, the UK's leaders lacked cohesive political-economic aims (Skidelsky, 2000: 137). The Foreign Office underestimated the coherence of US postwar ambitions and objectives and clung to the old priorities of the British Empire (Saville, 1993: 65). UK and US officials expected to emerge from the war in different circumstances. The UK had lost trade share and assets while accruing debts (Frieden, 2006: 262). The US had experienced the exact opposite. These differences, between debtor and creditor nations, were reflected in the divergent priorities for Bretton Woods (Pauly, 1997: 82). The UK wanted an arrangement that would allow them to borrow without the imposition of stringent conditionality, while the US favored a system that would tie their lending to the adoption of policy imperatives (Skidelsky, 2000: 182; Frieden, 2006: 259).

Within the UK, Keynes's personal intellectual vision came to shape the Treasury approach to the Bretton Woods negotiations. His bold proposal for the postwar international monetary order hinged upon the creation of a new international bank, the Clearing Union, which would issue an international currency, the "bancor." The currency was intended to displace gold as the reserve anchor for the international monetary system. The Union was tasked with cushioning adjustment to balance of payment imbalances through rules that would govern individual countries' accumulation of both overdrafts and surpluses on the bank. Countries would be allotted a quota with the Union. For debtors, the quotas determined the extent to which they could borrow (with interest rates rising as debts increased). For creditors, the quota set the limit beyond which countries had to pay charges to the Union as a tax on excessive surpluses (Keynes, 1941; James, 1996: 36–37).

A crucial feature of this system was that it allocated responsibility for adjustment to *both* debtor and surplus countries. This would remove the possibility of surplus countries failing to adjust by hoarding reserves and constricting the money supply, as the US and France had done during the 1920s. Under the Union, creditor countries would be forced to take expansionary measures. Keynes also wanted the IMF to have the power to force surplus countries to revalue their currencies. The plan envisaged more punitive consequences for surplus countries, and it was clear that Keynes's target here was the US (Eichengreen, 2011: 46). Intellectually, his proposals reflected his desire to avoid deflationary beggar-thy-neighbor policies and guarantee international conditions conducive to domestic full employment. This would be achieved by providing deficit countries with the space to avoid immediate adjustment (through bancor overdrafts), encouraging surplus countries to reflate their economies (through taxes on bancor credits), and stimulating demand for deficit countries' imports (James, 1996: 36–37; Schwartz, 2009a: 194). It also demonstrated Keynes's faith in the technocratic regulation of the international economy through a depoliticized, multilateral institution and a truly international currency (Skidelsky, 1979).

The Bank of England (representing banking and financial services) disagreed with Keynes's general plans, although they did accept the need for capital controls (Fforde, 1992: 33; Cottrell, 1995: 110; Cairncross, 1995: 71). In contrast to his idea for an international clearing union based on the bancor, the Bank favored a different approach. It was skeptical of what it perceived as the utopian ambitions of Keynes's Union and worried about its impact on the sterling area (Kynaston 2012: 410). The Bank's vision reflected continuity with the wartime system based on payments agreements and the sterling area's preservation, countering the US Treasury and State Department's demands for its liquidation. The Bank preferred to build on the use of sterling and the dollar in existing international payments arrangements rather than attack the sterling area payments system. The problem for the Bank was that its influence over monetary policy was reduced under the postwar Labour government (Cairncross, 1995: 70–71).[19]

UK and US state formation, and the advancement of Keynesian and proto-Keynesian ideas, were reflected in the planning for Bretton Woods. The two chief architects of the plan, John Maynard Keynes and Harry Dexter White, representing the UK and US treasuries respectively, were determined not to replay the failings of the interwar years and to advance the interests of their respective states to the greatest degree possible. Despite the different interests of the UK and the US, which became increasingly apparent as the negotiations wore on, both men converged upon a common commitment to the implementation of capital controls (Pauly, 1997: 93; Frieden, 2006: 258). In fact, the US Treasury had already been in contact with its UK counterpart after 1936 over the possibility of cooperative efforts to control flows of hot money as part of the Tripartite Agreement between the UK, France, and the US (Helleiner, 1994: 31; Bordo et al., 2015: 5). These bilateral contacts foreshadowed the collaborative planning undertaken in preparation for the Bretton Woods agreement and reflected the continuity between postwar developments and interwar Anglo-American interdependence.

Both Keynes and White were critical of the orthodox economic thinking associated with the gold standard. They viewed the implementation of capital controls as an essential precondition for the kind of international monetary system that would protect the policy autonomy of the interventionist welfare state from disruptive international capital movements, while also providing conditions suitable for the continuation of economic planning processes that had been developed during the 1930s. Their convictions on capital controls were rooted in a shared belief that the maintenance of fixed exchange rates and a liberal international trading system was not compatible with a fully liberal financial order. Keynes and White were not, though, opposed to all forms of capital flows. Both men accepted the need for "productive" (as opposed to speculative) capital flows and were in support of equilibrating flows that would help correct, rather than aggravate, balance of payment imbalances. Despite these caveats, Keynes and White identified the right of states to control capital flows as a cornerstone of the postwar international monetary system. Their thinking embodied a critical appraisal of the interwar monetary system and reflected a marked departure from the liberal financial principles of the gold standard (Helleiner, 1994: 33–38; Pauly, 1997: 92; Frieden, 2006: 258).

The Key Currency Plan

The shared commitment to capital controls contained in Keynes's and White's early drafts was not received well by all quarters. New York bankers were troubled by White's emphasis upon capital controls and feared that they would lose the highly profitable business of receiving European capital flight, which had benefited New York during the 1930s (Helleiner, 1994: 39). Many international bankers in the US felt that a return to the gold standard system would best serve their interests (Frieden, 2006: 257). Too much emphasis upon capital controls might impede the bankers in their quest to establish the international predominance of US banking, a goal they had held since the 1920s (Block, 1977: 52–53).

Competing visions for postwar international monetary arrangements demonstrate the reemergence of prewar complementarity between bankers in New York and London. Anglo-American financial cooperation, between private and central bankers alike, had been foundational to the international reconstruction efforts of the 1920s. But, as we saw in the previous chapter, these informal efforts were not enough to hold the interwar gold standard together. The impetus for restoring the Anglo-American axis of international financial power now came from the US and was encapsulated by the key currency plan proposed by John Williams, the head of the Federal Reserve Bank of New York, as a critical riposte to White's planning for Bretton Woods (Mikesell, 1945: 565; James, 1996: 65–66).

The Key Currency Plan rested upon the belief that restoring the stable convertibility of the world's two foremost currencies, sterling and the dollar, would provide the surest route to rapid international economic recovery (Mikesell, 1945: 565; Helleiner, 1994: 41; James, 1996: 65–66). The US would provide the UK with a substantial loan to underwrite the restoration of sterling's international role. The loan would then enable the UK to swiftly return to convertibility and pursue multilateral trade policies, restore London as an international capital market, and foster UK cooperation with the US in the shared management of the international monetary system (Block, 1977: 52). Crucially, the plan would require the removal of all controls on sterling and the dollar. As such, it stood in direct tension with White's endorsement of mandatory capital controls and demonstrated the frictions between the more restrictive approach of the US Treasury, and the desire for a speedier push toward fuller financial liberalization favored by New York bankers and the influential New York branch of the Fed. Not only did the plan challenge the direction of White's planning; it was also based upon a serious underestimation of sterling's postwar maladies. The UK's exposure to massive sterling balances accumulated by its imperial territories during the war had rendered the pound incredibly vulnerable to a mass sell-off in favor of much-needed dollars once convertibility was restored.[20] These problems would be highlighted by the sterling crisis of 1947.

Despite the plan's grave flaws, the New York financial community enthusiastically rallied and proceeded to publicly champion it (Mikesell, 1945: 564–565). Lamont, chairman of J. P. Morgan, suggested that a better plan would be to have US and UK bankers create a dollar-pound exchange ratio to which all other currencies were tied (Hearden, 2002: 61). Randolph Burgess of the Na-tional City Bank was keen for the US government to give the UK a direct credit of $2 billion in order to provide liquidity. Similarly, Winthrop Aldrich, chair-man of Chase National Bank, identified the UK's need for dollars to purchase US goods as the crux of the postwar financial conundrum, arguing that this problem "should be faced squarely because it would be in the interest of the US to have a strong British economy" (Hearden, 2002: 63). Aldrich's critiques of White's plan had a big impact and forced the alternative proposal onto the policy agenda (Helleiner, 1994: 43).

The plans reflected continuity with financial cooperation between the Anglo-American banking communities during the 1920s. Once again, US bankers preferred an international monetary system based upon a cooperative axis of private power in London and New York. The stance of the New York banking community was lenient compared to the hardball tactics of the Trea-sury under Morgenthau. The bankers recognized the significance of the City's role as a critical nodal point within a restored international monetary system; their long-term plan to establish dominance in international finance required them to work through the City of London, breaking down the sterling area by restoring sterling's convertibility and then using the UK as a twin engine alongside US financial power, to boost world trade and foster a broad climate of multilateral trade and investment. To this end, they tempted the UK with the possibility of much-needed dollar loans in return for opposition to the US Treasury's vision for monetary reform. But Keynes's instincts were to work with the US government (Steil, 2013: 4).

The strategic thinking of New York bankers attested to the continuing cen-trality of Anglo-American developmental dynamics, expressed through the interdependence of the dollar and sterling alongside the City and New York. Although the United States's financial power had been greatly augmented by its participation in two world wars, as well as by the exhaustion of UK power, the Key Currency Plan demonstrated the extent to which New York bankers still depended upon the City's international role to achieve their long-term ambitions. This pattern of mutual (but increasingly uneven) dependence would continue to define Anglo-American development as the politics of financial globalization unfolded in the decades after Bretton Woods. The Bretton Woods Agreement, and the system it inaugurated, need to be understood within these longer-term processes of Anglo-American development.

Criticisms raised by New York bankers proved too strong for White's origi-nal plan to survive intact. Bankers voiced their discontent within Roosevelt's

administration and Republican congressional success in 1942 further strengthened their hand. The bankers' opposition to White's plan symbolized the continuing tensions of New Deal-era politics. Although some bankers had initially
supported the New Deal, principally because they saw Roosevelt's agenda as
a means to loosen the House of Morgan's firm grip over New York finance,
their appetite for further initiatives that might shake up the US financial system was limited once this goal had been achieved (Helleiner, 1994: 43–44;
Ferguson, 1995: 148–49). Their lobbying efforts ensured that White's revised
plan placed a greater emphasis upon the need to permit productive capital
flows.

Given the centrality of Anglo-American banking cooperation to the resuscitation of the gold standard, one might have expected the key currency plan
outlined by the New York Fed and Wall Street to have received a welcoming
reception over on Threadneedle Street. But the opposite was in fact true. The
Bank of England joined forces with the UK Treasury in order to resist the
amendments to White's plan that had been compelled by New York bankers.
The Bank insisted that an explicit guarantee of the right to use exchange controls to limit capital flows be included in the final agreement (Pressnell, 1986:
140, 148–49; Fforde, 1992: 40–43).

The Bank's surprising endorsement of capital controls was explicable in
terms of its reorientation toward the protected sterling area during the 1930s
and its continued concern over the perilous state of the UK's balance of payments. Bank officials believed that the best way to restore sterling's international role, at least in the short to medium term, was to maintain and extend
the sterling area. Sterling was too weak and UK reserves far too low to move
toward convertibility in the immediate future. The Bank's preferred strategy,
which received the support of some within the Treasury, was to continue the
wartime sterling arrangements, to maintain a common dollar-saving import
policy for all sterling area countries, and to continue to control the movement
of capital from the sterling area to the rest of the world (Fforde, 1992: 40; Helleiner, 1994: 45; Newton, 2004: 261). This might be possible, the Bank believed, if cohesion within the sterling area was maintained and threats were
made to block the sterling balances of countries that threatened to liberalize
their exchange controls or abandon dollar discrimination. But, despite its
seemingly heterodox endorsement of capital controls, the leopard had not
changed its spots entirely. The Bank's plan for the continuation of a restrictive
currency bloc would require domestic economic policies that put reconstruction plans on hold and prioritized the achievement of external balance

(Newton, 2004: 261–262). Clearly, the Bank had not lost its traditional preference for austerity and the privileging of external currency stability.

Even though it showed an appetite for capital controls, the Bank did nonetheless find common cause with New York financiers over a different issue.
Bank officials and the City shared the New York bankers' antipathy toward the
potential for multilateral oversight and international public financial institutions (Pressnell, 1986; Fforde, 1992: 33; Kynaston, 2011: 410). The US bankers
were worried that public financial institutions might reduce the control of
private and central bankers and lead to inflationary dynamics by creating too
much policy space for expansionary national economic programs (Best, 2005:
53–54). Their preference was for the maintenance of the old gold standard
system of financial discipline, whereby capital flows could work to ensure deflationary measures in the interest of maintaining convertibility (Block, 1977:
53). These concerns were echoed by the Bank of England, which also felt that
the international monetary system should be shaped by bankers.

Bretton Woods Is Born

The agreement that was eventually set out at Bretton Woods in 1944 reflected
a compromise between the original interests of the planners in which US priorities were clearly dominant. It also contained amendments that reflected the
lobbying efforts of the bankers. Ultimately, Keynes's vision for the International Currency Union and the bancor lost out. From the US side, Harry Dexter
White had a different vision. He wanted the establishment of two institutions—
an International Stabilization Fund and a Bank for Reconstruction (Skidelsky,
2000: 244).[21] In conjunction, these two institutions would prevent the collapse of the monetary and credit system, enable the restoration of foreign
trade, and supply reconstruction capital and relief (Panitch and Gindin, 2012:
74). Under White's plan for an International Stabilization Fund, there were
limits to free capital movement internationally, and the Fund (which eventually became the IMF) would—similarly to Keynes's vision—provide financing so that countries could avoid deflationary measures and restore external
balance (Block, 1977: 41). Members could refuse inward investment and req-
uisition foreign investments of nationals to counter the threat of capital flight
(Skidelsky, 2000: 245).

But, crucially, the New York banking lobby was successful in toning down
the commitment to cooperative capital controls, to the extent that by the time
the Joint Statement was announced in 1944, "almost all mention of the

obligation to cooperate in controlling undesirable flows had been removed" (Helleiner, 1994: 47). In the absence of cooperation, controls would inevitably prove much harder to enforce. Keynes's plan for the bancor credit was also rejected in preference for a system based upon the centrality of the dollar, which would be tied to gold. White had been clear about his conviction in the centrality of the dollar to any postwar international monetary system throughout the negotiations (James, 1996: 50). The US was unwilling to cede the privileges associated with its national money becoming the international currency. This was a move of the utmost importance. It ensured that much of the fate of Bretton Woods and the maintenance of an appropriate supply of international liquidity would depend not on the decisions of a technocratic multilateral institution (as Keynes had hoped), but on US economic policy. As the US began to run sustained current account deficits during the 1960s, the system would come under increasing strain.

White was also skeptical of Keynes's attempts to shift the burden of adjustment onto surplus countries and to allow debtors to draw upon US reserves to finance their deficits (Schwartz, 2009a: 195). Advancing US interests, as the dominant international creditor country, White's plan substituted Keynes's automatic taxes on surplus countries for a vague possibility of penalties for countries that ran perennial payments surpluses (Eichengreen, 2011: 46). In place of generous overdrafts with the IMF, the US pushed for a system that allowed temporary trade discrimination against US exports to achieve adjustment, with IMF credits playing a smaller role (Schwartz, 2009a: 195). Indeed, as soon as the serious discussions began, it was White's plan that became the central focus, with America's superior power reflected in the bargaining pattern between Keynes and White (Block, 1977: 48).

The final agreement departed from the previous gold standard regime of the interwar years in significant ways. Firstly, although they were fixed, exchange rates were now made adjustable. Secondly, controls were now accepted as a legitimate means to regulate international capital flows and provide a degree of insulation for domestic policies. Finally, the IMF was established, with a mandate to conduct multilateral oversight of national economic developments and provide balance of payments financing to countries in need (Eichengreen, 2011).

Overall, these arrangements embodied the commitment to "embedded liberalism": a normative framework that sought to steer a middle course between what were seen, considering the travails of the interwar years, as two extreme orientations within the international economic order. On the one hand, avoiding the unilateralism and beggar-thy-neighbor policies of the 1930s by creating a multilateral framework of institutionalized cooperation to regulate fixed exchange rates, build toward currency convertibility, and maintain an open and liberal orientation. While on the other hand, tempering the liberal excesses of the classical gold standard era by creating a system of protective capital controls and a multilateral international body (the IMF) to shelter nations from the most extreme pressures of market speculation and deflationary balance of payments adjustment. These international measures would facilitate domestic macroeconomic intervention to attain the newly ascendant goals of full employment and welfare provision (Ruggie, 1982).

Embedded liberalism was not, though, built on firm foundations. Indeed, the term is something of a misnomer in the institutional sense—it was never fully "embedded." Firstly, the defeat of Keynes's deeper multilateral vision for the international monetary system left the US dollar as the central reserve currency and US economic policy as the central driver of international monetary politics. This proved to be highly destabilizing to the system and established an enduring tension between US policy autonomy and international regime stability. Secondly, as has been less widely recognized, the agreement was never fully institutionally embedded within the founding Anglo-American states. Only by examining Bretton Woods in conjunction with the longer-term development of its founder countries, as a process rather than a snapshot of postwar institution-building, do we come to appreciate its fragile basis.

As we have seen, the New York banking community objected to the disruption of the classically liberal principles that had governed the international financial system under the gold standard.[22] Their views gained renewed prominence with the death of Roosevelt and the accession of Harry Truman. And, in the UK, the Bank remained committed to sterling's international role, wedded to existing structures of central bank cooperation, and hostile to the multilateral (and, in its view, US-centric) thrust of the IMF (Kynaston, 2011: 410).[23] Once the City and the Bank began to push for the restoration of London's international role under the first postwar Conservative government, market innovations and developing infrastructure fatally undermined the Bretton Woods system. Within both states, internal tensions over the correct vision for postwar economic strategy and the limited advancement of Keynesian ideas prohibited a firmer Anglo-American platform for Bretton Woods.

Orthodoxy Resurgent

Although Keynesian ideas made rapid progress within state institutions in both the UK and the US during the war, their comparative political and institutional consolidation during the postwar period diverged. In the UK, the institutional future of the Keynesian approach to economic management was initially unclear by the war's end. The newly elected Labour government favored planning rather than indirect Keynesian intervention through the market, and in the first years of the new government neither Keynesians nor more orthodox figures were clearly in control of economic policy making (Weir, 1989: 67).[24] But the central policy commitment of the Labour Party to the achievement of full employment, through the 1944 Employment White Paper, created a political foundation for that explicitly Keynesian goal. However, although the ends of the White Paper were partially Keynesian, the policy means were not. The commitment to full employment itself was conditional upon a number of other factors—the recovery of international export markets, the achievement of competitiveness, and wage and price stability. In terms of the means, the White Paper accepted the stabilizing effects of public investment, but it rejected deficit financing and remained committed to a balanced budget over the economic cycle. The political progress of Keynesian ideas was thus significant but nonetheless tendential (Clarke, 1988: 249).

Convincing the Treasury to durably convert to Keynesian principles was another matter altogether. Treasury officials opposed Beveridge's landmark welfare schemes on grounds of cost, demonstrating that they had not accepted the Keynesian argument that the welfare state's contribution to demand would stave off a postwar depression and thus ultimately pay for itself. It took some time before budgetary policy was formulated in accordance with Keynesian principles, and it emerged largely as consequence of tireless pressure from the Economic Section, which pressed the Treasury to adopt Keynesian principles (Weir, 1989: 69). The year 1947 represented a turning point, with a deflationary budget inspired by Keynesian techniques of demand management that sought to reduce inflation without abandoning the goal of full employment. But even when Keynesian fiscal measures were introduced, it was often in the guise of ad hoc crisis measures (Clarke, 1988: 261).

The more fundamental tension that arrested the progress of Keynesian policies was of a structural kind. It lay in the frequently conflicting requirements of sterling's international currency role, the interests of the City of London, and the domestic commitment to welfare and full employment.[25] This tension was reflected both in the relationship between the Bank of England and the Labour government, and divisions within the Treasury itself. It meant that the impact of Keynesian ideas led to "a pattern of policy that was not that different from past practice as one might have expected" (Hall, 1986: 69). Inside the Treasury, the increasingly important Overseas Finance Division was much more likely to align with the Bank's priorities of external currency stability rather than domestic expansion and full employment. These tensions became increasingly apparent.

They were also reflected in Keynes's thought. Keynes was committed to a liberal, multilateral international economic order very much in keeping with the longstanding interests of the City (Cottrell, 1995: 210; Green, 1992: 198). Although there were frictions with the Bank over the timing of a return to sterling convertibility, Keynes's ultimate ambition was to restore London's international role (Hall, 1986: 211). Notwithstanding the failure to deeply institutionalize Keynesian thinking within parts of the postwar UK state, then, the strategic failures that led to the revitalization of the City and undermined Keynesianism within the UK were also very much a product of the inconsistencies and contradictions within Keynes's own thinking. This would be reflected in the policy contradictions thrown up by simultaneously attempting to reflate the postwar economy, while also addressing balance of payments crises associated with the restoration of sterling's international convertibility, UK deficits, and the endemic vulnerability caused by the sterling balances.

Overlapping interests between internationalist elements in the UK and those in the US gradually began to emerge after 1947, in the aftermath of the UK's disastrous attempt to restore sterling to convertibility under pressure from US bankers. But there was plenty of fractious bargaining between the two states before a clearer bilateral pattern of cooperation emerged during the 1950s. America's attempt to corral the UK into convertibility was an expression of the shifting domestic balance of power following the death of Roosevelt in 1945. Roosevelt's death brought about a reconfiguration within the US state; New Deal figures such as Morgenthau and White were now sidelined, and US bankers took up important roles within the new Truman administration (Prins, 2014). The State Department began to exert a greater influence upon US foreign policy, with policy makers looking much more favorably upon the Key Currency Plan. State Department planners had been unhappy with the extent to which Bretton Woods had departed from gold standard principles and believed that the five-year breathing space granted to the UK before it had to restore convertibility had been too generous. Their opportunity to impose this new vision, which sought to restore sterling to convertibility well before the five-year period had elapsed, arose during the Washington Loan negotiations in 1945. Beneath the formal multilateralism of the new Bretton Woods Agreement, then, the Anglo-American bilateralism of the Key Currency Plan was, in effect, resuscitated (Hudson, 1972: 155). In practice, the international monetary order had departed much less from the prewar Anglo-American cooperative financial axis than the Bretton Woods principles suggested.

The Washington Loan negotiations were sparked by the US abruplty terminating the Lend-Lease arrangement at the end of the war. This left the UK vulnerable and desperate for additional dollars (Cairncross, 1985: 4). Keynes was sent over to Washington, DC, to negotiate for additional funding, but with the US position having hardened under the increased influence of the State Department, he was only able to secure funding at the expense of a commitment to restore convertibility by July 1947 (Saville, 1993: 150; Newton, 2004: 260). While Keynes won support for the loan agreement within government, the Bank and sections of the Treasury were opposed to the restoration of convertibility. Keynes had proposed that the UK's military expenditure should be cut and that all sterling balances should be blocked for five years in preparation for a smooth transition to convertibility that would insulate the reconstruction program from currency shocks. But the attempt to block the sterling balances was a failure, particularly after Keynes's death in 1946. The Bank was only willing to negotiate a scaling down of the balances with creditors rather than unilaterally blocking them, as Keynes had wanted; it feared bringing about the demise of the sterling area and with that sterling's status as an international currency. The Bank's refusal to compromise on the issue of sterling balances greatly heightened the risk of convertibility and resulted in the disastrous flight from the pound that occurred as soon as convertibility was restored (Cronin, 1991: 162). Crucially, the calamitous attempt to restore convertibility "meant the collapse of Keynes's efforts to establish an international context which would support British reconstruction," while the Bank's role in the failure reflected its "continuing dissent from the reconstruction consensus and preoccupation with the external status of sterling" (Newton, 2004: 265).

After the failure to restore convertibility, a consensus briefly emerged around the need to maintain sterling as an inconvertible currency. The maintenance of inconvertibility received support both from Keynesians and those officials within the Bank and the Treasury who were principally concerned with sterling. The Bank viewed the continuation of bilateral arrangements as an improvement from possible bankruptcy, while Keynesians supported controls that would insulate the domestic economy from dollar shortages. But this consensus was extremely fragile, and it began to break down when sterling came under renewed pressure in 1949. Tensions between the Bank's concerns for sterling and the Treasury's concern with domestic expansion resurfaced. The Bank increasingly pushed for public expenditure cuts and interest rate hikes to stabilize the pound, but its proposals were rejected by the chancellor, Hugh Dalton, who considered public expenditure cuts politically unacceptable (Cairncross, 1985: 165–188).

Disagreements over the future of sterling, and the balance between international and domestic goals, reflected the limited structural transformation of the UK's postwar political economy. The enduring influence of the City and the failure of the Labour government to secure greater control over investment weakened the basis for a Keynesian full employment strategy. Despite the nationalization of the Bank of England, it remained under the effective control of the same private bankers that had previously governed it and retained a high degree of operational autonomy (Roseveare, 1969: 321; Cronin, 1991: 168; Green, 1992: 204). There was no clear Labour vision of how a central bank might operate in a mixed and planned economy (Kynaston, 2011: 422–24). After 1947, there was a retreat from the wartime physical controls on prices and production, which were replaced by monetary and fiscal management techniques (Green, 1992: 204). Exclusive reliance on monetary and fiscal methods of economic management augmented the role of the financial sector and money markets in shaping policy. Although, from 1947, the Treasury was made solely responsible for planning, its concern with industrial issues extended only to the point at which they affected the balance of payments and the status of sterling (Saville, 1993: 170).

Robot and the Fragility of Bretton Woods

The limited institutionalization of Keynesian commitments to full employment and macroeconomic management vis-à-vis the external priorities of sterling and the City was highlighted under the Conservative government of 1951 (Cronin, 1991: 189). Under the Tories, the Bank of England regained the initiative in monetary policy.[26] With the Conservatives keen to restore the City's international position and sterling's international role from 1951, the proponents of a new external policy were presented with an opportunity. George Bolton at the Bank advised the chancellor to promote "progressive convertibility," by incrementally moving toward full convertibility (Newton, 2004: 270). But US financial support for such a move was not forthcoming, with the Truman administration now prioritizing European integration through the European Payments Union.[27]

In December 1951, the Conservatives reopened the City as a center for foreign exchange dealing (Strange, 1971: 64).[28] By early 1952, after intense covert planning, the Bank and the Overseas Finance Division in the Treasury launched Operation Robot, attempting a unilateral restoration of convertibility at a floating rate, without US financial support (Burnham, 2003: 41). Robot involved making convertible all sterling balances that were not blocked by the government, blocking those held outside of the sterling area, and, crucially, abandoning the fixed exchange rate commitment established at Bretton Woods and allowing the pound to float. The architects of the plan envisaged that it would restore sterling's international role and draw other European countries into a sterling-area "payments club" in which currencies would float against the dollar. They saw no less than a total subversion of the multilateral commitment to fixed exchange rates established at Bretton Woods (Burnham, 2003: 1–10). Operation Robot reflected the enduring unilateralism of UK state institutions and their initial disregard for the priorities of Bretton Woods.

The scheme neatly illustrated the limited progress of the embedded liberal compromise at both the international and national levels. Internationally, the operation of the Bretton Woods system was conspicuous by its absence after the IMF's inaugural meeting in 1946. An acute dollar shortage in Western Europe meant that European economies required bilateral US dollar aid supplied by the Marshall Plan to function (Schwartz, 2009a: 203). Sterling's disastrous return to convertibility in 1947 had set back the Bretton Woods ambition for a swift return to currency convertibility. Western European currency convertibility would not be achieved until 1958. The world economy continued to be characterized by the existence of discriminatory trade blocs, exemplified by the sterling area, and bilateral trade and payments agreements. Bretton Woods' flagship institutional creations, the IMF and the World Bank, played a marginal role in the world economy (Hudson, 1972: 285; James, 1996: 58; Burnham, 2003: 3–10).

Domestically, Operation Robot caused a battle within the government and revealed a deep schism between those who supported Keynesian ideas of postwar reconstruction and those who prioritized the traditional goals of external balance and a stable pound. Operation Robot was incompatible with the postwar domestic policy consensus of welfare and full employment, with its implementation requiring severe deflationary measures. Tighter monetary policy and spending cuts, proposed by senior Treasury and Bank officials, would have been required to stabilize the pound. Keynesian economists within the civil service rejected the plan because it would return macroeconomic policy to prewar priorities (Newton, 2004: 271–272).

Keynesian policy approaches specified a more passive role for monetary policy (James, 1996: 178). Keynes noted its inability to pull the economy out of depression and stressed the need for greater reliance upon fiscal policy. Of the two major macroeconomic levers, then, fiscal policy was accorded greater priority (Friedman, 1968: 1–2). Public works programs would boost demand and then loose monetary policy could help sustain the recovery as a subsidiary measure. From the later 1930s, Keynes became increasingly dubious of monetary policy as a tool to curb booms too. Fearing that once interest rates began to spiral upward, monetary authorities would find it hard to turn them back, he advocated greater reliance on trade policy, fiscal policy, and careful planning of public investment as measures to cool the economy (Moggridge and Howson, 1974: 239–44). Full employment was prioritized over price stability and external balance as the goal of macroeconomic policy. Indeed, a modest rise in Bank Rate in 1951 had been heralded as the "return of monetary policy" in the UK (Fforde, 1992: 315). Operation Robot threatened to give much greater momentum to this restoration of monetary policy activism. The Bank's continuing attraction to the prospect of a floating pound, which was still entertained by the governor as late as 1958, reflected a desire to free up monetary policy as an instrument of macroeconomic control (James, 1996: 100).[29]

The plan was eventually rejected by the Cabinet for being too risky, but it demonstrated clearly the growing influence of the Bank and the continuity of prewar policy priorities both within the Bank and sections of the Treasury. The plan made a mockery of the UK's supposed Keynesian consensus. The Bank had been waiting for its opportunity to restore the international orientation of the City and sterling, whatever the cost for reconstruction efforts and full employment. Operation Robot was a precursor to the longstanding tension within the UK's postwar economic development, which reflected the incomplete progress of Keynesian ideas. Keynesian commitments to full employment were politically consolidated, being accepted by both major parties (Gamble and Walkland, 1984). But, institutionally, the external requirements of sterling and the City that were privileged by the Bank frequently required interest rate hikes and spending cuts that undermined domestic growth. These tensions played out in the UK's troubled postwar stop-go cycle.

Developments within the UK intersected with a comparably incomplete consolidation of Keynesian policies in the US. Here the institutional embedding of Keynesian policies was weaker. Institutionally, the lack of centralized power equivalent to the UK Treasury (despite the wartime growth of the US Treasury's power) enabled the continued existence of competing interests within state institutions and inhibited attempts to consolidate wartime planning agencies like the National Resource Planning Board (Weir, 1989: 70). The weaker status of Keynesian policies was also reflected in the fate of the Full Employment Bill of 1945. While Keynesians had wanted the bill to specify a mandatory policy commitment to full employment and the identification of investment and expenditure as the primary technical mechanisms, the final Employment Act of 1946 removed these commitments and mandated only what the president was permitted, rather than directed, to do. Targets of maximum employment and production were set, but there was no commitment to the actual means of realizing these goals (Salant, 1989: 47). The diluted commitments in the bill reflected the active opposition of organized business interests. Businesses opposed the legislation because they feared that its promise of full employment threatened the existence of a competitive labor market. Bearing the imprints of its US stagnationist orientation and the postwar progress of stagnationist ideas within government, the draft bill also identified the inadequacies of private investment for maintaining aggregate demand. This alarmed businesses by threatening to legitimize permanent compensatory spending by government (Blyth, 2002: 82). US Keynesianism also rested on weaker bipartisan political foundations and, often being conflated with a desire for planning by its critics, aroused long-standing opposition to federal centralization (Weir, 1989: 75–79).

In the monetary sphere too, Keynesianism fell short of a lasting transformation of the US state. During the war, the independence of the Fed was restricted by the imperatives of war financing.[30] For the first time in its history, elected officials rather than unelected Fed members controlled monetary policy (Epstein and Schor, 1995: 7). This ushered in a unique phase of public control over the Fed that paralleled the restricted autonomy of the Bank in the UK. The project was short lived, however; by 1951 the Federal Reserve-Treasury Accord had restored the independence of the US central banking system and freed the Fed from the obligation to support the US government bond market by ensuring that public debt could be financed at low interest rates. The wartime arrangement had facilitated massive fiscal expansion, but it had also undermined the Fed's capacity to control inflation as it was forced to buy US government bonds every time long-term interest rates threatened to rise above the agreed level (Axilrod, 2011: 25–26). As had been the case in the UK, this outcome represented the limitations of postwar Keynesian transformation by opening the door to the reassertion of monetary and central bank predominance within macroeconomic policy. The Fed had been worried by the inflationary effect of wartime financing and wanted to raise interest rates to end the easy money policies of the wartime years (Konings, 2011: 111). It successfully lobbied prominent members of the banking community and associated business interests to push for independence in the face of Truman's administration and figures within the Treasury who had sought to hand control of monetary policy over to the president (Epstein and Schor, 1995: 28).[31]

By winning this battle, the Fed and its allies ushered in a "Conservative Keynesian" policy framework.[32] In restoring the independence of monetary policy from governmental control, the accord between the Fed and the US Treasury laid the foundations for the tight monetary policies of the 1980s and 1990s, which would be used to restore the power of capital and break working-class aspirations, shattering the Keynesian promise of full employment (Epstein and Schor, 1995: 28). The accord was a way to prevent radical forces within any government administration from pursuing inflationary policies. In this sense, then, the roots of tighter monetary control were actually implanted during the 1950s, with macroeconomic policy priority given to the need to manipulate short-term interest rates in order to control inflation and shape aggregate demand (Panitch and Gindin, 2012: 86–87).

In both the UK and the US, then, despite the progress of Keynesian policy proposals, older imperatives of central bank control over a more activist monetary policy began to reassert themselves by the early 1950s. The restoration of the Bank of England's power over monetary policy in the UK was mirrored by the reestablishment of Fed independence in the US. This represented the resurrection of banking power in both states in the early postwar period.[33] As the 1950s progressed, the restoration of central bank power would be central to the continuation of Anglo-American development and the politics of financial globalization.

Within the UK, the reemergence of the City-Bank-Treasury nexus, after a period of internal contestation between different power centers within the state, was a defining feature of the broader postwar period. The restoration of the nexus exemplified by Operation Robot and the gathering momentum toward the restoration of convertibility within both the Bank and the Treasury by the early 1950s were key to the restoration of the international economy around the Anglo-American financial axis that US bankers had long desired. During the 1950s and 1960s, the City-Bank-Treasury nexus would increasingly come to be articulated through the Federal Reserve-Wall Street-Treasury nexus in the US, as the two states played central and interdependent roles in the politics of financial globalization.

The reorientation of state institutions toward this Anglo-American financial axis was assisted by enduring ties between private bankers on both sides of the Atlantic. Just as it had done during World War I, the House of Morgan played a significant role. Lamont championed the UK cause during the war, pushing for Roosevelt to lift the arms embargo on the UK and assisting the UK ambassador, Lord Lothian. Morgan Grenfell, the UK wing of the House of Morgan, was depopulated during the war as many of its senior staff took up public positions within government. This was a logical extension of the bank's prewar role as "something of a branch office for the Bank of England, the Treasury, and the Foreign Office." Tom Catto, a senior Morgan Grenfell partner, was appointed to the role of "special advisor" to the wartime chancellor, Kingsley Wood.[34] Lamont maintained a distinctive diplomatic channel with Catto at the Treasury. Anglo-American financial power was in this way implanted within, and channeled through, the dominant institutions of governance (Chernow, 1990: 460).

Undoubtedly, these informal channels were weakened by the growth of multilateral institutions and the new climate of public accountability that followed the end of the war. An informal partnership of the Fed, the Bank of England, and the House of Morgan, which had virtually run the international monetary system in the interwar years, was gradually supplanted by the World Bank and IMF (Chernow, 1990: 486). But, until the late 1950s, as we have seen, the reach of these multilateral institutions and the Bretton Woods commitment to currency convertibility and fixed exchange rates remained circumscribed. Within the US, rival investment banks had used the New Deal–era hostility toward the "Money Trust" to promote reforms that would weaken the House of Morgan's control over US finance (Konings, 2011: 80).[35] This weakened its status as a conduit of Anglo-American financial coordination.

But the weaknesses of early postwar multilateralism presented opportunities for the continuing influence of powerful, personal, bilateral Anglo-American financial ties. Catto served as head of the Bank of England from 1944 to 1949, an appointment that was interpreted as reflecting the need for a close postwar relationship with the US (Chernow, 1990: 476). Although the UK's relative power had decreased, US bankers continued to recognize the importance of sterling and the City for the realization of their ambitions. New York was undoubtedly the world's premier financial center, and the City experienced only stuttering recovery in the early postwar years. The continuation of wartime controls confined London merchant banks to sterling area loans. Members of the banking community in London viewed these controls as onerous impediments to growth (Roberts, 1992: 313).

The sentiments of London's merchant banking community toward the postwar international monetary order are exemplified by the thoughts of one of its most prominent figures: Siegmund Warburg, the head of the famous Warburg merchant bank that would, as the following chapter demonstrates, play a leading role in the emergence of the Eurobond market during the 1960s. In a demonstration of the continuing importance of transatlantic linkages between London and New York, Warburg made several business trips to New York from February 1946 to scope out the potential for business ties with the prominent investment bank Kuhn Loeb. By the end of 1948, Warburg and his colleagues had made fourteen trips to the US. But Warburg was disappointed with the meager outcomes of these trips and began to grow increasingly frustrated with the postwar order (Ferguson, 2010: 159–60).[36] By 1950 Warburg was calling for a currency union between North America and Western Europe (Ferguson, 2010: 164). These attempts to restore Anglo-American financial links would become much more important as the decade wore on.

The Shallow Roots of Embedded Liberalism

In the face of resurgent policy orthodoxy, based in the Bank of England, the City, and the Treasury, the UK's postwar Keynesian compromise never stood much of a chance. By the early 1950s, traditional policy orientations were in the ascendancy within parts of the Treasury and the Bank. Politically, the Conservative government resumed its traditional support for the City of London. This provided fertile conditions for the reassertion of the Bank of England's control over monetary policy and a broader privileging of sterling within the core financial nexus of the UK state. As this chapter has argued, the limited headway that Keynesian thinking had made within the Treasury before and during the war left the path open for the reassertion of the old gold standard concerns. Policy became increasingly focused upon a strong pound and the appropriate deflationary medicine required to achieve external balance. The Labour government, despite nationalizing the Bank of England in 1946, was unable to thoroughly institutionalize an alternative set of economic priorities within the core institutions of the UK state.

The restoration of orthodoxy within the UK also owed much to the enduring influence of the New York banking community within the US. Domestically, their attempts to bring the UK and sterling into a multilateral international economic order were at first thwarted by the more gradualist approach to achieving UK convertibility endorsed by the US Treasury under Roosevelt. Internationally, the Bank's commitment to bilateralism in the early postwar years presented a major obstacle. But despite the failure of the New York bankers and the State Department to restore sterling's convertibility on a lasting basis in 1947, it was not long before the City-Bank-Treasury nexus began to embrace the multilateral vision that the New York financial community and the US state had sought to promote all along.

Dynamics between the UK and the US (and within each state) were central to the way the postwar international economic order unfolded. Keynesian ideas made a significant but crucially limited advancement within each country. Beneath the multilateral ideals of Bretton Woods, the importance of bilateral Anglo-American financial relations continued to be foundational to the structure of the postwar international economy. Viewed in the fuller history of Anglo-American development, it is clear that the traditional influence of private and central banking was, despite Keynes's desire for the "euthanasia of the rentier," not sustainably subordinated to the new embedded liberal vision.

By the time that Bretton Woods came into full operation, with the restoration of European currency convertibility in 1958, the erosion of Keynesian commitments within both states and the reemergence of central bank autonomy, already underway by the early 1950s, would be central to the breakdown of the fixed exchange rates and selective capital controls at the heart of the Bretton Woods agreement. Bretton Woods formalized the dollar's place as the dominant international currency, but it was Anglo-American development that continued to play a primary part in generating the conditions that would facilitate the dollar's growing structural power. The agreement reached in New Hampshire in 1944 cannot be taken as the marker of a discrete phase of unilateral hegemony; both the formation and the eventual breakdown of Bretton Woods should be interpreted through the historical processes of Anglo-American financial interdependence and the gradual formation of an Anglo-American financial order. From the late 1950s, the uneven interdependence of

Anglo-American development expressed itself in the emergence of the Euro-markets and the continued interactivity of sterling and the dollar, alongside London and New York, as both the UK and the US struggled to manage their balance of payments deficits under the Bretton Woods order. In the process, Anglo-American developmental dynamics played a critical role in the decomposition of the Bretton Woods order and the gradual rise of the alternative monetary system that emerged in the early 1970s.

4

The Euromarkets and the Crisis of Bretton Woods

NO EVENT contributed more to Anglo-American financial integration than the emergence of the Euromarkets.[1] As the Cold War order crystallized, Soviet officials, fearing seizure of dollar assets by US authorities, deposited their holdings with European banks (Burn, 1999: 229). In 1955, the Midland Bank used these holdings to finance domestic activity during a period of tight money in the UK (Schenk, 1998: 224). So began the most important development in the postwar history of international finance. The Euromarkets became the crux of a new wave of globalization. At the heart of this process lay the deepening integration of New York and London, and of the United States and the United Kingdom, as pivotal players in a resurgent global political economy.

This chapter argues that the development of the Euromarkets represented the foundational moment in the postwar intensification of Anglo-American financial development. Contending the notion of a postwar order shaped predominantly by the outward expansion of US financial power, the chapter suggests that coconstitutive Anglo-American developmental processes were the generative force that produced the Euromarkets. The agency of City merchant bankers in constructing the Eurodollar market infrastructure, and the institutional adaptation of the Bank of England and UK Treasury, laid the transatlantic foundations for the hegemony of the dollar. Their actions structured the policy dilemmas faced by US officials and critically undermined the fixed exchange rate system agreed at Bretton Woods by creating the institutional infrastructure for vast offshore financial markets and volatile capital flows.[2]

For the UK, the Euromarkets revitalized the City and enabled the merchant banking community to maintain influence within the corridors of power. In the process, the City became an offshore outpost for US finance and the UK state was drawn more tightly into the embrace of globalizing capital markets. For the US, the Euromarkets were paradoxical—in the short term they became a major constraint upon the capacity to regulate domestic monetary policy and spurred domestic financial deregulation. But in the long run, they enhanced US power by deepening the dollar's international dominance.

The chapter begins by reviewing existing IPE accounts of the Euromarkets, suggesting that they have neglected the significance of Anglo-American development. The link between domestic financial conditions in both the UK and the US, and the wider context of Bretton Woods, are then examined with a view to understanding the dynamics that produced the Euromarkets. The chapter subsequently explores the impact of US banks' arrival in the City, arguing that US entry set in motion a "transatlantic regulatory feedback loop" that destabilized the regulatory orders on both sides of the Atlantic and fostered the deeper integration of Anglo-American finance. The challenges presented by the Euromarkets, alongside the shared experience of sterling and the dollar as key reserve currencies blighted by chronic payments deficits, stimulated increased transatlantic monetary policy interdependence, diminished US and UK policy autonomy, and drove a wedge between the Anglo-American payments deficit countries and major surplus countries during the protracted attempts to stabilize Bretton Woods. The penultimate section of the chapter assesses the role of the UK's merchant banking elite in transforming the fiscal basis of the UK state by opening it up to the Euromarkets. Finally, the chapter concludes that the Euromarkets represented a decisive moment in the transition toward financial globalization, undermining the basis of both the Keynesian financial order and Bretton Woods while placing Anglo-American developmental dynamics at the center of global transformations.

States, Markets, and the Euromarkets

The debate over the Euromarkets has focused upon three main themes—firstly, attempting to identify their specific historical origins; secondly, understanding their relevance to the UK's national development; and, finally, their relevance to the international transformations associated with the collapse of the Bretton Woods system. Within the IPE literature, a subset of scholars has argued that the emergence of the Euromarkets was functional to the deepening of structural and financial power associated with US hegemony or imperialism.[3]

IPE literature on the Euromarkets has been criticized for reducing the debate to a simple dichotomy between state and market. Responsibility for the development of the Euromarkets is then accorded *either* to state agencies *or* market operators. In reality the responsibility for the emergence of the Euromarkets is hard to pin down in bifurcated terms. In the UK the pivotal institution, the Bank of England, acted as an interface between the state and the market and played the roles of "poacher" and "gamekeeper" simultaneously. Blurring the boundary between state and market renders conventional IPE accounts of the Euromarkets highly problematic.

Gary Burn's (1999) excellent corrective to the "states versus markets" dichotomy has captured many of the institutional and historical specificities of the Euromarkets' origins. Burn's account, however, neglects the substantive impact of Anglo-American development in recalibrating global capitalism, concluding instead that the Eurodollar market's ultimate significance lay in its restoration of the pre-1931 City-Bank-Treasury nexus (2006: 184). This overlooks the way in which the UK state was qualitatively transformed through its incorporation within an Anglo-American developmental sphere. The City did not regain its former autonomy through the Eurodollar market; the reemergence of its domestic hegemony through the arrival of the US dollar and US banks in London drew US state power into the affairs of the City and redefined UK sovereignty. Power did remain concentrated within the City-Bank-Treasury nexus, but it was now articulated through, and embedded within, a new, fundamentally distinctive, order of Anglo-American finance. This new order of Anglo-American finance, rooted within an Atlanticized UK capitalism, proved central to the incubation of financial globalization and liberalization that gravely undermined, in tandem, the Bretton Woods monetary order and Keynesian monetary orders in the UK and the US.

Theorists of US global power view the development of the Eurodollar market and the breakdown of Bretton Woods as a result of the international expansion of US finance (Konings, 2011; Panitch and Gindin, 2009, 2013). These approaches overlook the emergent Anglo-American field of developmental interactivity that was fundamental to financial globalization. As this book has argued, we need to look beyond the expansive dynamics of US finance and toward the coconstitutive developmental processes that occurred through the interaction of bankers and monetary officials in the City and New York. This requires that we deprivilege the exclusive role of an outward expansion of US finance or unilateral "structural power." The UK's causal force in authoring financial globalization is rendered invisible in these US-centric accounts. The

City becomes an analytical vacuum into which US banks simply move in the face of limits upon their internal development. This focus omits the way in which US structural power was constituted *through* transatlantic interactivity. Without highly contingent and specific institutional developments within the UK that reflected the agency of specific social forces and state managers as they wrestled with the distinctive challenges of managing the UK's transition to postimperial power, there would have been no spatial fix for US finance. As this chapter demonstrates, UK state institutions and merchant bankers pulled in US finance by adapting their institutional orientations and capacities and Atlanticizing UK capitalism.

This required a redefinition of sovereignty, both in terms of the spatial extension of regulatory responsibility for the Bank of England and the embedding of the fiscal basis of the Treasury within the Euromarkets. The undertheorized status of the constitution of political-economic space in US power approaches leads to an underappreciation of the centrality of the City's entrepôt role in furthering globalization (Garrod, 2015). The intersection of capitalist and state agency, through the lobbying power of influential merchant bankers, was central. In broader terms, the UK's longstanding entrepôt role was redefined through "offshore" to cope with the demise of sterling and to harness the dollar.[4] It is not enough to extrapolate financial globalization from the "development of US finance"; we need to problematize "Anglo-American development" as the creation of a distinctive form of transatlantic political-economic space, more broadly. US banks may have filled that space, but it was the UK state and UK bankers that constructed the offshore environment that enabled financial globalization through the City and integrated Anglo-American capitalism.

This was not, therefore, simply a case of the internationalization of the US state, but rather a synthetic form of Anglo-American development that ensured that the US Federal Reserve-Treasury-Wall Street nexus was articulated in and through the City-Bank-Treasury nexus in the UK. In the process, both national capitalisms were transformed, with a reduction in monetary policy autonomy and a deeper integration of their respective financial systems. The postwar period was not only about the US state structuring the options of other national capitalisms; its own policy options and business strategies were structured by developmental dynamics driven by social forces in the UK. Understanding this is crucial to understanding the subsequent role of Anglo-American leadership in driving forward the politics of financial globalization.

The Bank, Sterling, and City Internationalism

During the postwar era the UK's place in the world was rapidly and radically reconfigured. As we have seen in chapter 3, the UK was levered into accepting a junior role in the relationship with the US. Bretton Woods heralded the dollar's emergence as the key international currency, and its steady displacement of sterling continued throughout the 1950s and 1960s. Militarily, the UK also had to adjust to new realities. The humbling abortion of the Suez intervention in 1956, at the US' behest, encapsulated the impotence of the UK's attempts to pursue independent imperial objectives and spelled the end for UK unilateralism vis-à-vis the US.[5]

But the UK was not alone in riding a rising tide of change. By the mid-1960s the Bretton Woods framework was unraveling. The uneven development of national economies placed mounting strains upon the international monetary order.[6] Within Europe, increasing payment imbalances strained relations between members of the European Economic Community (EEC) and generated pressures for a deeper form of monetary integration that would stabilize European exchange rates and create a parallel set of commitments to those enshrined at Bretton Woods (Apel, 1998: 29–34; Giordano and Persaud, 2013: 7). The emergence of powerful current account surplus countries, like Japan and West Germany, drove a wedge between their interests and those of the two main deficit states, the UK and the US. Finally, the growth of inflation and the contradictions of the Triffin dilemma revealed some of the fundamental design flaws in the Bretton Woods order (James, 1996: 154–57). By 1971 the fixed exchange rate system had collapsed, with Richard Nixon unilaterally delinking the dollar from gold. It was within this context of international tumult that policy makers within dominant institutions of the UK state designed and implemented their strategies in the decades after World War II.

After surviving a temporary diminution of its powers, the Bank of England regained influence by the time the first postwar Conservative government came to power in 1951. Despite the failure of the Operation Robot plan, senior officials at the Bank continued to map the route to convertibility. As advisor to the governor of the Bank, George Bolton had worked on various proposals for the reestablishment of convertibility. Bolton went on to play a leading role in the emergence of the Eurodollar market later in the decade. By March 1954 the London Gold Market had been reopened, further strengthening the City's international role. All restrictions upon the movement of nonresident sterling outside of the dollar area were removed as sterling edged closer to full convertibility. The Bank of England was keen to go further, but the government thwarted its ambitions (Burn, 2006: 82).

The Bank Policy Rate was kept high from 1954 to 1957 as sterling came under repeated speculative attack. This was part of the much-maligned "stop-go" cycle, discussed in the previous chapter, that bedeviled UK policy during the 1950s and 1960s. Periods of domestic expansion resulted in balance of payments deficits that prompted speculative movements against the pound. Fearing devaluation, policy makers enacted deflationary measures to curb domestic consumption and expansion in the hope of restoring a healthier payments position.[7] Throughout the 1950s and 1960s, the UK experienced major sterling crises. The decline of sterling's stability and appeal were inextricably linked to the general waning of UK power in the postwar era.

The continued sterling crises of the mid-1950s produced tensions between the Bank and the Treasury. When the governor suggested that Bank Rate be increased to 7 percent in 1957, Harold Macmillan and his chancellor, Peter Thorneycroft, disagreed and suggested that the clearing banks reduce their lending instead. The banks refused to comply and Governor Cobbold refused to persuade them to accept the government's request. Thorneycroft was outraged and began to look for ways to give direct instructions to the banks and enforce Treasury control over lending. In response, Cobbold effectively threatened to make the government bankrupt by refusing to meet its checks. After this fearsome restatement of the Bank's independence, Thorneycroft eventually backed down and averted a major crisis for the UK state. This was an important moment in the postwar history of UK capitalism: in winning the contest with the Treasury, the Bank had secured control over monetary policy and, consequently, of the banking sector and the City more broadly (Fforde, 1992: 679–93; Burn, 2006: 86). This control was a vital precondition for the Bank's capacity to shape the environment within which the Euromarkets would take root.

Bank Rate did eventually rise to 7 percent, but Macmillan won a ban on refinance credits and sterling credits for financing international trade as a quid pro quo for the increase. These dynamics fostered the immediate conditions within which the Eurodollar market really began to flourish. Raising Bank Rate increased the cost of credit for the UK economy while the ban on refinancing credits and the use of sterling credits for financing third-party trade left UK merchant banks in need of an alternative medium for financing international business (Schenk, 1998: 223; Burn, 2006: 86). The measures raised questions about how financing needs would be met with restrictive monetary policy and exchange controls in place. The answer was the Euromarkets.[8]

Although the first instance of Eurodollar deposits may have occurred in mid-1955, involving the Midland Bank (Schenk, 1998: 224), the market really gathered momentum from 1957 (Martenson, 1964: 14; Bell, 1973: 8). George Bolton, a merchant banker and former advisor to the governor of the Bank, played an influential role. Bolton had left the Bank after becoming dissatisfied with the pace toward convertibility. He became chairman of the Bank of London and South America (BOLSA) in 1957, and once there he imbued the bank with the belief that sterling's use as an international reserve and vehicle currency would "virtually cease" soon. Bolton's convictions led him to shift BOLSA out of sterling business and into dollar-denominated activity (Burn, 2006: 104; Capie, 2010: 182–85).

By the late 1950s, then, sterling's perennial problems had lessened its appeal as a stable medium for international exchange. In this context, it was not surprising that the dollar, now the linchpin of the international monetary order, became a much more attractive vehicle for financing trade. With sterling weakening and subject to restrictive controls on its employment for trade, UK banks were only able to maintain their international standing by switching to the dollar. Decolonization had already precipitated a rapid loss of market share for UK merchant banks in some countries, notably India, where whole markets were lost due to nationalization. These problems were rooted in the broader diminution of UK power. Banks that had grown up financing UK overseas trade now found themselves with less business and a declining customer base. Their status as sterling institutions, once a tremendous source of strength, was now becoming a weakness (Jones, 1993: 248–87). Not surprisingly, then, it was the merchant banks that led the Euromarkets charge and set the stage for the City's rebirth.

The offshore status of the Eurodollar market made it unique. An informal approach to regulation in the City allowed the Euromarkets to flourish and effectively split the UK banking system into a much more stringently regulated domestic banking market and a permissive international market (Burn, 1999: 226; Palan, 2006: 27–32).[9] Expatriate dollars were deposited on a short-term basis, within a market that paralleled the more restrictive official market. This fertile regulatory climate was traceable to the classical gold standard era. The laissez-faire regulatory context established during the nineteenth century, defined by the intimate relationship between the Bank and the City's merchant banking community, was generally left intact after World War II despite Bank nationalization (Roseveare, 1969: 321; Cronin, 1991: 168; Green, 1992: 204; Burn, 2006: 16).

But to explain the Eurodollar market in terms of the unique regulatory context of the City and the demise of sterling is insufficient. Interactivity between the dollar supply, US monetary policy within the Bretton Woods system, and the status of the City as an entrepôt center gave the development of the Eurodollar market a peculiarly Anglo-American dimension. To apprehend this dimension, we need to turn our attention toward US financial development under Bretton Woods.

American Development and Bretton Woods

In the US, the postwar regulatory climate was markedly different from the UK's permissive conditions. In the aftermath of the Great Depression, US monetary authorities introduced "Regulation Q" and the Glass-Stegall Act (Bell, 1973: 9). Regulation Q capped the interest rate that US banks could offer for depositors, while Glass-Stegall maintained a strict division between commercial and investment banking. Despite this restrictive regulatory context (and partly because of it) US finance experienced a prolonged period of growth after the war. New Deal policy makers promoted the expansion of mortgage and consumer lending in order to pull US citizens into an intricate web of financial relations (Konings, 2011: 100).

The Federal Reserve was central to this growth dynamic. After the Great Depression and during the war, the Fed played second fiddle to the Treasury. It forwent its status as the "bankers' bank" to directly serve the government's requirements (Konings, 2011: 101). It did this by assisting the Treasury's debt-funding efforts. The Fed agreed to maintain fixed interest rates on long-term government bonds while limiting fluctuations in short-term rates in order to finance the war at affordable rates (Epstein and Schor, 1995: 7; Axilrod, 2011: 25). In doing so it relinquished some influence over liquidity creation. Because banks could sell practically any amount of government debt that they wanted to at desirable rates, these government securities became highly liquid assets, which were put to use in the expansion of US commercial banking after the war.

By the later 1950s, however, US banks were pushing against the limits of New Deal regulations. Their ability to expand their base of profitable loans was increasingly constrained by limited funding supply. Regulations circumscribing expansion of branches and capping interest rates, made these obstacles hard to overcome. Additionally, banks faced a disintermediation problem—nonbank financial institutions, offering higher rates, were drawing away deposits, while the Federal Reserve-Treasury Accord of 1951 freed the Fed from its obligation to stabilize the market for government securities. As interest rates rose, investors shifted into commercial paper and Treasury bonds, which now offered higher yields (Konings, 2011: 107).

American banks responded to these constraints through an unprecedented domestic merger wave between 1955 and 1961.[10] By 1961, at the end of the wave, a massive increase in the concentration of bank deposits had occurred. The ending of the merger wave coincided with the appointment of James Saxon as comptroller of the currency. Saxon enthusiastically promoted bank expansion and the relaxation of New Deal–era restrictions (White, 1992: 7). By the end of the merger wave, the five largest banks in New York accounted for 75 percent of deposits, with the same banks responsible for 77 percent of total commercial bank loans (de Cecco, 1976: 386).

Internationally, the desire to support the rapid expansion of US corporations overseas during the 1950s and 1960s also brought banks into tension with regulations (Cohen, 1986: 24; Sylla, 2002: 54). The Treaty of Rome and formation of the European Economic Community (EEC), along with the restoration of full currency convertibility in Western Europe in 1958, signaled to US multinationals that Europe was now ripe for investment—they could evade the EEC tariff barrier by investing inside member countries, and the restoration of convertibility removed obstacles to repatriating profits. Between 1955 and 1965 US manufacturing foreign direct investment (FDI) in Europe tripled (Panitch and Gindin, 2012: 113–14). By the late 1950s and early 1960s, then, US banks were pushing at the limits of New Deal regulations. Although this framework had nurtured the development of US banking, it had become an obstacle to further growth. Regulation Q acted as a disincentive for US banks to compete with their European counterparts, enabling the Europeans to attract dollar holdings by offering higher yields.[11]

While US banking encountered these limitations, policy makers within the US were also increasingly discontented. The contradictions of the Bretton Woods system within which US power was internationally intertwined were posing a mounting problem and threatening to limit US freedom of action in the international arena. The problem involved the role of the dollar and the status of the US within the system. During the 1950s the US made the supply of international liquidity a cornerstone of its foreign economic policy (Block, 1977: 110). European countries suffered from a "dollar gap," which limited their capacity to purchase US imports required for postwar recovery. But US liquidity supply was not an act of benevolence; the Marshall Plan Aid and war spending on Korean rearmament that boosted the European dollar supply was also intended to raise demand for US exports and stimulate expansion of international trade.

Boosting international dollar liquidity enabled European countries to return to convertibility in 1958 without making painful deflationary commitments. But America's role as the world's central banker was deeply contradictory. In the long run it threatened to undermine the keystone of the Bretton Woods system—the dollar's fixed convertibility to gold at $35 per ounce. By the late 1950s the "dollar gap" had been transformed into a "dollar glut" as European recovery enabled central banks to build up stockpiles of dollar reserves. In 1958, the US balance of payments deficit led to a run on the US gold stock for the first time. This was a landmark moment, after which US policy began to shift from one of liquidity pumping to attempting to strengthen the payments position.

European countries were caught up in the effects of changing US monetary fortunes. The massive postwar inflow of US Marshall Plan Aid had been essential to restoring continental European economic vitality by addressing the dollar gap and providing liquidity needed to boost intra-European trade and foster payments integration through the EPU. But the weakening of the US balance of payments undermined the dollar and rapidly began to transform its status from savior of Europe's postwar economy to a potential saboteur of continental monetary stability by the 1960s. This altered status was first demonstrated with the gold crisis of 1960. With confidence in the dollar weakening, the price of gold in the London market (reopened by the Conservative government in 1954) increased from thirty-five to forty dollars per ounce as investors moved out of the dollar and into gold, transgressing the fixed dollar-gold convertibility established at Bretton Woods. In a foretaste of the deeply politicized monetary relationship between the US and West Germany that unfolded throughout the rest of the decade, President Eisenhower wrote to Chancellor Adenauer pleading for help in stabilizing the dollar and threatening to pull out US troops from Germany if his requests were refused. These pleas fell on deaf ears, with Adenauer playing dumb, suggesting that he didn't understand balance of payments issues (Gavin, 2004: 45–51). As the Bretton Woods order began to show early signs of strain, the authorities of the EEC began to consider forms of deeper European monetary integration and exchange rate stabilization that would, eventually, create a parallel regional structure of monetary union outside of the multilateral vision of Bretton Woods (Tsoukalis, 1977: 53).

The US balance of payments deficit became the dominant issue of international monetary politics for the next fifteen years (Block, 1977: 140). The problem was known as the "Triffin dilemma." Robert Triffin had identified a crucial weakness of the Bretton Woods system. He realized that the deficit of the US had become the key source of international liquidity and that running a continuous deficit would be critical to supplying the dollars required for financing international trade, exchange, and the build-up of reserves (Gowa, 1983: 42). But here was the bind: if the US kept running a deficit, then confidence in the dollar's fixed convertibility to gold would be imperiled. This could lead to a run on the gold stocks, forcing the US to float the dollar and terminate Bretton Woods in the process. This was, of course, the eventual outcome, when Nixon unilaterally delinked the dollar from gold in 1971. But the stage was set for the 1960s as a decade in which the crisis of Bretton Woods gathered momentum.

These international dynamics stimulated the growth of the Eurodollar market. Flows of expatriate dollars were swollen by the vast liquidity expansion undertaken by the US. This fed directly into the capacity of London banks to absorb these deposits by offering interest rates higher than those permissible under Regulation Q. The existence of the Eurodollar market provided a further problem: it limited the efficacy of deficit reduction measures introduced by the US during the 1960s. These measures would, inadvertently, provide a massive stimulus to the market.

Eurobonds and the Paradox of the Eurodollar

As US officials grappled with mounting balance of payments problems in the early 1960s, they started to lay the groundwork, quite unintentionally, for the development of the second component of the Euromarkets—the Eurobond market. The first-ever Eurobond issue was signed in July 1963; it was made to the Italian company Autostrade and guaranteed by the IRI, a financial and industrial holding company owned by the Italian state. George Bolton, so influential to the development of the Eurodollar market, was involved once again, smoothing the progress of this landmark bond issue by employing his influence with the Bank (Kerr, 1984: 14).

The issue was signed by S. G. Warburg & Co., the UK merchant banking house. Siegmund Warburg, the paternalistic head of the bank, was a longstanding advocate of European integration. For Warburg and other Eurobond pioneers, the revival of London's role as an international capital market dealing in foreign currency was a mechanism for promoting the UK's entry into the EEC. They hoped that this would enhance the UK's membership prospects by turning the City of London "from a liability into an asset" (Ferguson, 2010: 204). Unbound from sterling, the City would be beneficial to the future of the EEC.

Despite Warburg's European ambitions, the roots of the Eurobond market lay, at least in part, in signals given out by US Treasury Secretary Douglas Dillon and a wider US reluctance to capitalize on the shift of the international bond market to New York.[12] As the US payments problem deepened, Dillon began, from 1962, to encourage the Europeans to establish their own international capital market.[13] His remarks did not fall on deaf ears, with European banks discussing his suggestions at length (Kerr, 1984: 17). What Dillon did not realize was that he was unwittingly encouraging the development of an offshore bond market comprised principally of dollar-denominated issues. By promoting a European capital market, Dillon thought, the US Treasury would be able to relieve pressure from the capital outflows associated with the New York bond market (Burn, 2006: 147). Rather than tightening controls at home, Dillon wanted to push the Europeans into liberalizing their capital markets, taking pressure off the US.

Dillon's signals encouraged both Warburg and Bolton to travel to the US in 1962, to gauge the US mood. On returning to the UK, Bolton encouraged the Bank to clear the way for Eurobond issues, and by early 1963 the approval of the chancellor and the Inland Revenue were secured. For their part, the European financial community had been keen to see the practice of international bond issuing returning to London. Syndication practices in the US had reduced the potential for commissions and fees that the Europeans could charge, as the US authorities had insisted that US investment houses must play the lead role in the syndication, charging accordingly (Kerr, 1984: 17). The restoration of a European long-term capital market would prove crucial in the decades to come.

By the early 1960s, the US was aware of the Eurodollar market. The Fed most likely didn't hear about it until 1960. But upon discovery it became concerned about the market's impact on both the US payments position and the international financial system. The Federal Reserve Bank of New York sent two staff members to London in 1962 on a Eurodollar fact-finding mission. When US bankers read their report, they lamented the presence of Regulation Q and the evidence that the locus of international lending had begun to shift across the Atlantic (Burn, 2006: 142–43). US bankers began to pressure authorities for a comparable liberalization of the onshore US market—this was the first sign that the Euromarkets were generating a feedback loop that would disrupt the regulatory context in the US. The feedback loop would shape private and public institutional adaptation within Anglo-America in the decades that followed, gradually transforming the domestic financial orders in critical ways.

The Fed's peers in the US Treasury knew even less about the Eurodollar market during the early 1960s. According to archival evidence, the term wasn't used until 1961. And President Kennedy wasn't briefed on the existence of this new market in London until 1963. This was a major problem, as the Eurodollar market was beginning to have an impact on the US payments position by this point. Not only were US dollar outflows drawn in by the Eurodollar markets higher interest rates, but, by acting as a transmission belt between the US and European money markets, the Eurodollar market was undermining US attempts to wrestle with the balance of payments. By generating a growing pool of dollars that could quickly move from the dollar into gold or other currencies, the market increased the dollar's vulnerability to speculative attacks. But, although there was only a partial awareness of the problems the Eurodollar market was causing, there was an increasing realization of the opposite effect. By encouraging private creditors to hold onto their dollars the Eurodollar market was keeping dollar holdings out of official central bank reserves and preventing a continuing decline in US gold reserves, thus strengthening the dollar and keeping Bretton Woods intact (Burn, 2006: 147).

This, then, was the paradox of the Eurodollar. The Euromarkets were simultaneously intensifying the vulnerability of the dollar to speculative attacks, while also contributing to the deepening of dollar hegemony by massively expanding the scope for dollar-denominated business. These dynamics relied heavily upon the continued existence of favorable regulatory conditions in the UK and the willingness of London bankers to press for deeper ties to US finance. The Eurodollar paradox would serve as a major contributory factor to the demise of Bretton Woods. By cementing the dominance of the dollar as the world's premier international currency, the Euromarkets paved the way for Nixon's unilateral break from Bretton Woods and the establishment of a dollar standard.

The Parallel of Deficits

During the 1960s, monetary policy on both sides of the Atlantic became increasingly concerned with fighting a rearguard action against the pressures and contradictions threatening to undermine Bretton Woods. The divergent interests and fortunes of surplus and deficit countries under Bretton Woods drove a wedge between the advanced capitalist states. These politics played out in a decade-long struggle over the future of the Bretton Woods system, with surplus and deficit countries pushing for different solutions to problems that had already become endemic.

On the surplus side of the negotiations, France, West Germany, and the other EEC surplus countries were the key players. On the deficit side, an important symmetry emerged between the two key reserve currency states: the US and the UK (Tsoukalis, 1977: 66; Gavin, 2004: 126). Both states suffered chronic payments deficits, with high exposure to external liabilities. Not surprisingly, then, the 1960s witnessed a series of measures, on both sides of the Atlantic, to prop up the ailing Bretton Woods framework. Through this process, a high degree of central bank cooperation developed, particularly between the Fed and the Bank, as it became increasingly clear that collaborative action was required to reinforce the system. Through this interaction, too, the Euromarkets received a major impetus. Crucially, Anglo-American monetary cooperation preceded the deeper European monetary integration that got underway from the later 1960s, as increasing balance of payments disequilibria and divergent national economic performance between EEC member states prompted a drive to deepen regional commitments to exchange rate stabilization and cooperation. Despite the multilateral vision enshrined at Bretton Woods, the centrality of the Anglo-American relationship continued within the system. The Key Currency Plan envisaged by New York bankers became the de facto basis of a system that relied upon US and UK deficits for the supply of liquidity. Such a system was critically flawed; by 1957 short-term dollar and sterling liabilities to foreigners were already nearly twice the size of total gold holdings outside of the two states (James, 1996: 154). The promise of fixed gold convertibility that underpinned the system was, as Triffin had foreseen, a fiction in practice.

As the US arrived at a fuller recognition of the gravity of the problems facing Bretton Woods, it began to embark upon concerted international action to stabilize the system. These efforts drew in many of the advanced capitalist states through the Group of Ten (G10) and generated increasingly politicized struggles over the international monetary order that helped solidify Anglo-American cooperation in the face of opposition from powerful surplus countries. For the UK, the shared deficit status encouraged a more generous attitude from the US toward the management of sterling crises and the UK's borrowing from the IMF. But relative US leniency was prompted more by fears over the destabilizing effects of a sterling collapse upon the dollar than any sense of fellowship.

With the start of the Kennedy administration in January 1961 and the continued deterioration of the US payments position, US efforts to stabilize Bretton Woods intensified. Reeling from a drain on US gold reserves, Kennedy's administration focused on the twin goals of eliminating the payments deficit and cooling speculation against the dollar (Bordo et al., 2015: 106). Kennedy's Undersecretary of the Treasury, Robert Roosa, organized a series of swap arrangements between central banks and made efforts to expand the IMF's resources through the General Agreements to Borrow (GAB). Swap arrangements provided standby credit lines between central banks that could be used to defend existing exchange rate parities.[14] The activation of swap lines indicated the increased intervention of the Fed to manage the international monetary system. By the end of 1962, the Fed had established swap lines with eight European central banks and the Bank of Canada. These arrangements provided the equivalent of up to $900 million in foreign exchange to be used to defend the dollar's value. This network of central bank swap lines orchestrated by the Fed continued to grow throughout the decade, having evolved from a short-term facility in 1962 to a much larger and more intermediate-term facility by the closing of the gold window in 1971. Between 1962 and 1969, the Fed presided over swaps totaling almost $7 billion in value, as it used foreign exchange reserves acquired from one central bank to substitute for unwanted dollars held by a third-party central bank, thus preventing it from converting excess dollar holdings into gold (Eichengreen, 2008: 127; Bordo et al., 2015: 151–54). These early attempts to stabilize the international monetary order of the 1960s anticipated the expanded role that the Fed would play almost half a century later, with the expansive dollar swap lines it extended to foreign central banks in the wake of the 2007/8 global financial crisis.

Roosa also introduced "Roosa Bonds": nonnegotiable US government bonds denominated in foreign currencies and sold to foreign central banks. These were intended to transform excess dollar holdings of foreign central banks into longer-term debt, reducing the level of liquid funds that could be mobilized in speculation against the dollar (Block, 1977: 179–180). The US Treasury also made use of the bonds to acquire foreign exchange for use in intervention operations to stabilize the dollar (Bordo et al., 2015: 163).

The establishment of the "London Gold Pool" in late 1961 was another crucial development. The pool was formed in response to the 1960 "dollar crisis," during which speculation in the private gold market in London had pushed the price of gold to forty dollars per ounce, jeopardizing confidence in the dollar's convertibility to gold at thirty-five dollars per ounce (Gavin, 2004: 45;

Panitch and Gindin, 2012: 123). Bilateral Anglo-American cooperation had stabilized the market in 1960, with the Bank of England acting in concert with the US Treasury to drive down the price of gold by the end of 1960 (Bordo et al., 2015: 177–78). Under the gold pool, a number of countries agreed to intervene to stabilize gold prices around the thirty-five-dollars-per-ounce commitment enshrined at Bretton Woods.[15] This multilateral action reduced pressure on the US gold stock and stabilized gold prices (Block, 1977: 178). It also demonstrated the continued importance of London as a site within which the fortunes of the international monetary order—and the dollar in particular—were partly determined. The existence of the private gold market in London placed the UK financial market infrastructure and the Bank of England at the heart of the system. After the reopening of the London market in 1954, it rapidly became the most important international free market for gold and a crucial indicator of the level of confidence within Bretton Woods. The Bank acted as the gold pool consortium's agent in the London market and determined the appropriate amount of gold sales in keeping with stable prices (Bordo et al., 2015: 177–78).

Within the IMF, the US Treasury sought to expand the availability of multilateral lending capacity to supplement the foreign currency balances available to the Exchange Stabilization Fund. These efforts led to the creation of the General Agreements to Borrow (GAB) in December 1961, which was intended to act as an additional supply of liquidity for the US. Underwritten by the G10 countries, the GAB supplied the IMF with an additional $6 billion line of credit from participating central banks of balance of payments surplus countries to be used to support the chronic deficit countries: the US and UK (James, 1996: 161; Eichengreen, 2008: 116). Through the IMF, the US could exchange dollars for foreign currencies and then use these currencies to mop up dollars in the private market and redeem the excess dollar reserves held by foreign central banks. It was hoped that this would stabilize the dollar's value and strengthen US gold reserves (Bordo et al., 2015: 108).

In the UK, the declining value of sterling and the deterioration of the balance of payments were increasingly apparent by the early 1960s. In March 1961, European central banks intervened heavily in foreign exchange markets on behalf of sterling, while the UK drew $1.5 billion from the IMF, with a further $500 million made available under a standby arrangement (Eichengreen, 2008: 123). By that summer, the chancellor had announced plans to restrict private investment outside the sterling area. This was a highly significant step: it deviated from the recent trajectory of exchange control liberalization. The

Bank's monetary policy during the early 1960s was focused principally upon defending the pound, with the central goal of maintaining parity with the dollar at $2.80 (Capie, 2010: 193).

By the mid-1960s, on both sides of the Atlantic, the problems were intensifying. Successive US administrations attempted stopgap measures to rectify the balance of payments deficit and restore confidence in the dollar. The outgoing Eisenhower administration had already issued an executive order that prohibited US citizens from collecting gold coins along with measures to boost exports and increase tourist receipts (Eichengreen, 2008: 126). President Kennedy then further intensified restrictive measures.[16] The Interest Equalization Tax, introduced in 1964, imposed a 1-percent tax on foreign security issues in the US. The tax was strongly opposed by investment bankers, stockbrokers, and Republican congressmen, but was passed into law nonetheless (Gowa, 1983: 55).

Efforts at restraining capital outflows under Kennedy were extended by the Johnson administration. By 1965 inflation was on the rise as Johnson attempted to fund his Great Society project in conjunction with increased spending on the Vietnam War, without offsetting tax increases. The war was having a sustained inflationary impact upon the global economy and shaking confidence in the dollar. Vietnam forged a clear link between the fate of US foreign policy and the sustainability of the international monetary system. As the payments problem intensified in tandem with the war effort, Johnson's administration introduced the Voluntary Credit Restraint Program in 1965. The Fed's Board of Governors oversaw its management, with the mandate to ensure that corporations and banks did not substantially increase their export of funds (Gowa, 1983: 56). Johnson further requested that the Department of Commerce steer the repatriation of overseas US investment.

Meanwhile, in the UK, the election of Harold Wilson's 1964 Labour government, within the context of a deteriorating balance of payments, had spooked the markets, bringing speculation against the pound to a new level of intensity. The previous year had been marked by an extremely harsh winter, Charles de Gaulle's veto of UK EEC membership, and a high degree of preelection uncertainty (Eichengreen, 2008: 125). These factors combined to produce an extremely challenging context for Wilson's new government. In August 1964, an additional $1 billion standby credit was arranged with the IMF and a further $500 million of funds were secured from various foreign central banks.

This was not, though, a challenge that the new government faced alone. The US was increasingly drawn into the management of the UK's monetary policy.

The US had long recognized the significance of sterling to the stability of the postwar system (Eichengreen, 2008: 123). Although the dollar was the world's dominant currency by 1945, sterling was still its major rival and, as such, a pillar of the international currency markets, whose price fluctuation would inevitably have systemic ramifications. But it was clearly an increasingly fragile pillar at its $2.80 parity with the dollar, and from 1964 supporting the existing rate became a fundamental component of US international monetary policy. Sterling was the first line of defense in maintaining the integrity of Bretton Woods and the stability of the dollar. While the pound was weak it was certain to draw some of the speculative pressure away from the dollar, but if the pound were devalued then the dollar would undoubtedly be subjected to firmer scrutiny (Block, 1977: 185). Added to this was a simmering geopolitical consideration: thewillingness of the US to support sterling was linked to the UK's presence in South East Asia. The State Department made clear that support for sterling was contingent upon the UK acting as a bulwark against communism in the region (Gavin, 2004: 130). Furthermore, the US relied upon the Euromarkets to meet the capital needs of US MNCs abroad within a context of domestic restrictions on capital outflows and deficits fueled by Vietnam (Schenk, 2010: 10, 167). Anglo-American monetary cooperation was tightly linked to these geopolitical considerations.

For his part, Wilson was an advocate of the Anglo-American relationship. He feared that any devaluation of the pound would be viewed as an abdication of the UK's international obligations (Block, 1977: 188). The rise in Bank Rate undertaken in 1964 was a landmark event: it was the first time that there had been open consultation with US monetary authorities in the run up to a rate adjustment (Capie, 2010: 193). Already in 1963, the governor of the Bank had consulted Bill Martin, the head of the Fed, about the need to coordinate future Anglo-American rate changes so as to minimize the impact of interest rate differentials (which would inevitably lead to destabilizing capital flows).

These interactions were a symptom of a deepening Anglo-American monetary cooperation. They were also a symptom of the broader intensification of the role of the Fed and the US Treasury in managing international monetary affairs during the 1960s (Panitch and Gindin, 2012: 123; Bordo et al., 2015). Private central bank power was dramatically restored during the 1960s, in what was in many ways the postwar heyday of central bank cooperation. US institutions were not alone in contributing to the strengthening of international financial cooperation; the Bank of England also played an active role. Indeed, it was the Anglo-American coordination of monetary policy during the 1960s that lay at the heart of the broader network of cooperation between central banks and finance ministries. The connectivity between UK and US monetary policy prompted Humphrey Minors, the deputy governor of the Bank, to remark in a letter to Bill Martin that "what when I was a boy was a purely domestic concern of this institution, now looks like being a matter of argument not merely between the City and its West End Branch, but even between our two governments" (Capie, 2010: 194). The Bank's international significance was further amplified by the staggering growth of the Euromarkets from the mid-1960s.

But to the extent that the shared status as reserve-issuing deficit countries and the integrative effects of the Euromarkets incentivized closer Anglo-American cooperation, it also drove an ever-wider wedge between deficit and surplus countries from the mid-1960s. This was borne out most spectacularly with the disruptive behavior of France under de Gaulle, and the toxic negotiations between the US and West Germany over the link between German surpluses and US troop presence in the country.

Major Western governments were preoccupied with the question of monetary reform focused on sustaining Bretton Woods. This reduced the space for progression toward regional monetary union in Europe and preoccupied the EEC Monetary Committee between 1964 and 1968. However, this did not prevent the French government from pursuing a distinctive vision for international monetary reform. In 1963, both the French and Dutch governments had begun to press for the creation of a new Composite Reserve Unit (CRU) to substitute for the dollar's international role. This position ran against the US and UK desire for an extension of credit facilities. The French finance minister, Valéry Giscard d'Estaing, saw the CRU as vehicle to reduce the power of the dollar and sterling by providing an alternative currency unit and a common EEC position on monetary reform (Tsoukalis, 1977: 63).

Then, in 1965, President De Gaulle gave his infamous press conference, excoriating the dollar's "exorbitant privilege" and openly politicizing international monetary discussions (Eichengreen, 2008). De Gaulle hoped to use the EEC and reform of the international monetary order as a medium to restore France's great-power status. The US and the dollar-based international currency system were perceived as the primary obstacles to this goal. De Gaulle also took a dim view of the UK's role within Bretton Woods, viewing it as a "Trojan horse" for US power, having vetoed the UK's attempt to join the EEC in 1963 (Tsoukalis, 1977: 58; Gavin, 2004: 92). De Gaulle began converting French dollar holdings into gold and encouraged other countries to follow suit

(Gavin, 2004: 92–120; Bordo et al., 2015: 179). UK Treasury officials responded to de Gaulle's attacks by warning the US that without a strong response a vacuum would be created within which French ideas could be brought to the fore during IMF discussions (Gavin, 2004: 125). These tensions were reflected in highly politicized debates between the US, the UK, and France regarding Anglo-American proposals for Special Drawing Rights (SDRs) to be issued via the IMF (James, 1996: 171). But, after a declaration of support for SDRs in March 1968, and after France had been weakened by the political and economic crisis of May 1968, they were eventually introduced in 1969, as a supplementary international reserve asset to reduce pressure on gold and dollars (Tsoukalis, 1977: 70; James, 1996: 173)

West Germany, the beneficiary of a healthy current account surplus, also applied increasing political pressure on the US deficit position. The Germans took a more measured approach, though, and mediated between the French and the Americans. Germany's security dependence on the US gave the Americans greater leverage than they possessed with France. As the US and UK positions within Bretton Woods weakened, the security guarantee offered to Germany became increasingly contentious. West Germany had agreed to purchase military hardware from both states as part of "offset agreements" in which the cost of security provision by the US and the UK would be offset by German purchase of Anglo-American military exports. Regarding the US, the agreement also involved an informal commitment by the Bundesbank to hold its dollar reserves in interest-bearing securities rather than converting them to gold or selling them to those likely to buy gold. As these agreements unraveled around 1966, with both the US and the UK seeking ways to reduce the costs of military expenditure due to balance of payments difficulties, the relationship with West Germany became increasingly fraught (Gavin, 2004: 138–163). In this way, geopolitical considerations sharpened the division between the Anglo-American deficit countries (net security suppliers) and the European surplus countries (net security recipients).

It was within this transatlantic context of balance of payments crises, deepening political divisions between deficit and surplus countries, policy transformations, and growing Anglo-American coordination of monetary policy that the next stage in the development of Euromarkets got underway. It did so as part of a broader transformation in the international monetary system that saw intensifying cooperation and attempts at coordination as the crisis of Bretton Woods deepened. As the Euromarkets developed, the goals of stabilizing Bretton Woods and restoring Western unity became even more remote.

The Americans Arrive in the City

US banks arrived in London en masse during the 1960s. By 1975, fifty-eight US bank branches had been established in the City (Sylla, 2002: 66). This led to a synthesis of Anglo-American banking practices, increased Anglo-American interest rate interdependence, and constraints upon the autonomy of policy makers on both sides of the Atlantic. It also transformed the Bank's institutional orientation toward a transatlantic outlook. The US takeover offered both a challenge and an opportunity for policy makers and bankers alike in both the US and the UK. For the Bank of England, the arrival of the Americans raised crucial questions about responsibility and sovereign authority for foreign banks, while for UK bankers it presented a potential competitive challenge. For both the Bank and the bankers, it was also a major opportunity. By invigorating and expanding the scope and depth of the Euromarkets, the US invasion offered UK bankers the chance to take a bigger slice of a rapidly growing pie, even if their relative share was declining. Buoyed by the Euromarkets, UK banks' gross foreign currency liabilities increased by 50 percent per year between 1965 and 1968 (Altamura, 2016: 18).

The US influx boosted the standing of the Euromarkets and, by association, the Bank. This was reflected in the Bank's status as the epistemological authority on the Euromarkets. The arrival of the Americans enabled the Bank to reassert its centrality and significance within the UK state and international financial community. It was through its interconnection with offshore US finance and deepening ties to the Federal Reserve-Treasury-Wall Street nexus that the Bank recovered its prewar international prestige within an international order dominated by US power. But the arrival of the Americans also raised troubling questions about the status of UK merchant banks and increased the UK's sensitivity to US economic policy. The "spatial fix" of escape into the City necessarily brought up complex questions regarding sovereign authority. US banks now depended upon a foreign central bank, but the Bank would be expected to hold closer ties to the old order of the City's banking elite than to the US interlopers.

For the US Treasury and the Fed, the US takeover of the Euromarkets was similarly Janus-faced. By escaping the New Deal regulatory parameters and dependence upon the domestic dollar supply, the US banks had gravely undermined the capacity of US fiscal and monetary policy to control banking. This would become all too clear from the mid-1960s. But they had also alleviated some of the pressure on the US balance of payments, by tapping in to

Percentage

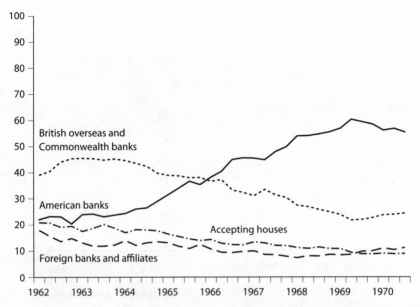

FIGURE 4.1. Current account deposits of overseas residents: London banks, 1962–1970

offshore dollar flows and intensifying the global standing of the dollar as a vehicle currency.

The scale and pace of the US capture of the Eurodollar market in particular was breathtaking (see fig. 4.1). Current account deposits of overseas residents represent Eurodollar market deposit-taking and increased dollar deposits account for the increase overwhelmingly; we can see that UK Overseas and Commonwealth Banks experienced a major loss of relative market share, with their share of Eurodollar deposits dropping from c.40 percent in 1962, to c.25 percent in 1970. Accepting houses also experienced a severe contraction of their market share, from 20 percent down to 8 percent between 1962 and 1970. For US banks the story was very different; their share of Eurodollar deposits rose precipitously, from just over 20 percent in 1962 to around 55 percent in 1970.

By disaggregating deposits into sterling and nonsterling, we get a clearer picture of the vast takeoff in Eurodollar deposits (see fig. 4.2.). For US banks, the growth in deposits of overseas residents was overwhelmingly accounted for by a sharp increase in nonsterling (i.e., dollar) deposits. The low level of sterling deposits remained remarkably stable over this period.

£ Millions

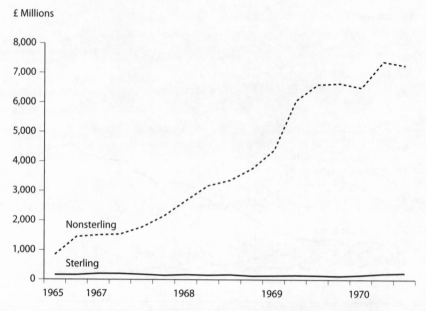

FIGURE 4.2. Current account deposits of overseas residents: US banks, 1965–1970

Contrastingly, UK Overseas and Commonwealth banks (fig. 4.3) experienced much more gradual increases in the volume of nonsterling deposits from overseas residents. Whereas US banks experienced a sevenfold increase in the volume of overseas nonsterling deposits between 1965 and 1970, UK Overseas and Commonwealth banks experienced a threefold increase. Despite the paucity of their gains in relative terms, overall UK banks participated in a level of market expansion unimaginable without the influx of US banks and the enormous US corporate client base that they brought with them.

How did the Bank of England respond to the Americanization of the Eurodollar market? The following archival evidence provides significant insights. The Bank really took notice of the US banks from 1963. The regular meeting of Eurocurrency experts at the BIS (Bank for International Settlements) provided a forum where the Euromarkets were discussed, and, in their reports on the 1963 BIS meeting, Bank officials acknowledged that London branches of US banks were more active than before in the Eurodollar market, with US businesses borrowing there rather than from New York. [17]

Correspondence between the Treasury and the Bank provided the primary channel of policy formulation around the Euromarkets; Bank officials outlined the parameters of their responsibility for Eurodollar activity in these

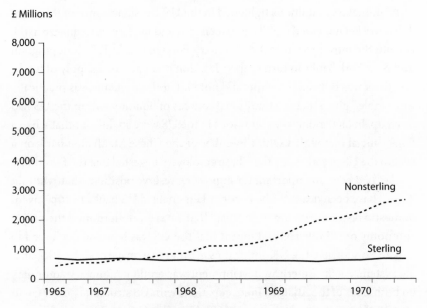

£ Millions

FIGURE 4.3. Current account deposits of overseas residents: British overseas and
Commonwealth banks, 1965–1970

exchanges. The archival record makes clear that the Bank was the primary
source of official epistemic authority on the subject of the Eurodollar market.[18] The Treasury and the Cabinet Office would turn to the Bank for information and advice about the burgeoning offshore trade.[19]

In correspondence between the Bank and the Treasury, Bank officials made
clear that what applied for UK banks, regarding the Bank stepping in as a
lender of last resort, "cannot be held to apply in the same measure at all to the
London branches or subsidiaries of foreign banks."[20] Officials concluded that
their responsibilities in times of crisis should not extend beyond supporting
UK banks. London branches of foreign banks were not viewed as the responsibility of UK authorities but rather those of their head offices. Beyond the
head offices, national central banks from the originating country would take
ultimate responsibility. This discussion occurred within a context whereby
London branches of US banks now accounted for 30 percent of deposits in the
Eurodollar market. Crucially, then, the City's hosting of foreign banks and
Eurodollar business did not entail a corresponding globalization of the Bank's
function as lender of last resort. As the transformation of the international
financial system accelerated, the Bank was at the heart of the process, carefully
navigating its way through processes of institutional learning.

As monetary conditions tightened in the US, the significance of the Euro-dollar market increased rapidly. Between 1965 and 1966 a credit squeeze in the US and the introduction of the Voluntary Foreign Credit Restraint program lead New York banks to turn to their London branches for a supply of funds. The Bank was fully aware of this and noted that this dynamic was practically "inevitable," given that the traditional sources of liquidity within the US had dried up. In fact, monetary conditions in the US were so difficult that when a Bank official met with a senior member of the Chase Manhattan bank on a visit to the US in early 1966, the Chase employee suggested that the Eurodollar market had been so important for improving reserve positions that "without it, we'd have been dead."[21] The Euromarkets enabled US banks to circumvent domestic restraints on credit in a way that severely undermined the policy autonomy of US officials and meant that the US was increasingly forced to look to London and the UK authorities in order to manage its domestic bank-ing system. Anglo-American development was eroding monetary autonomy on both sides of the Atlantic. Preoccupations with US structural power fail to capture this pronounced increase of US dependency upon UK state agency.

The Bank's own statistics on lending from London branches of US banks to their New York counterparts suggest that in the first seven months of 1966, the figure stood at £500 million, with a staggering £230 million of that lending occurring in July alone. Bank officials also noted that US banks had been pre-pared to pay "somewhat over the market rate" for money in order to attain funding.[22] By drawing upon offshore Eurodollars, US banks were able to evade the constraints imposed by US monetary policy. In this way, the capacity of US monetary policy makers to regulate the flow of domestic credit was drasti-cally undermined by Anglo-American financial integration. London's offshore role punctured a hole in US monetary management, demonstrating the sub-stantial impact that the market innovation of UK merchant bankers had wrought upon US capitalism.

Johnson's restrictive measures and the credit crunch implemented by the Fed in 1966 marked a watershed in the orientation of US banks toward the Eurodollar market. Prior to this, US banks had only borrowed passively, with overseas branches placing excess deposits with their head office. Now they borrowed actively, with their foreign branches soliciting deposits to finance domestic operations (Kane, 1981: 13). No longer taking only a passing interest in the market, they now identified Eurodollar expansion as integral to their business strategy.[23]

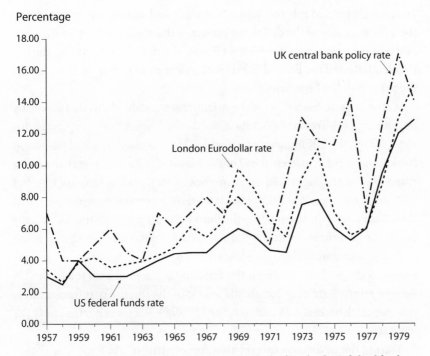

FIGURE 4.4. Comparative interest rates, 1957–1980: Bank of England, US federal funds, London Eurodollar

The Bank's position within the City enabled it to effectively gauge the intensity with which the Eurodollar market was being shaped by changes in US monetary policy. As more US banks set up shop in London, their role in funneling funds back to their US head offices led to an increasing interactivity of interest rates on either side of the Atlantic. As we can see in figure. 4.4, a triadic interaction of interest rates evolved during the 1960s: that between Bank Rate, the Eurodollar Rate, and the Federal Funds Rate.

The principal relationship here was between the Eurodollar Rate and the Federal Funds Rate, with the absence of interest rate ceilings enabling the Eurodollar Rate to be set consistently above that of the US money market rate, with the effect of drawing money out of the US capital markets and into London. Figure 4.4 shows that the UK Bank Rate was consistently the highest of the three. This was partly a function of the need to maintain the attractiveness of sterling holdings in the light of the emergence of the Euromarkets, but it was also a measure of sterling's general weakness. However, given the increasingly limited role for sterling as a trade and investment currency, and the dominant role of the dollar, the impact of the sterling rate upon the price of dollar borrowing was not without limits. The differential between the Eurodollar Rate and the Federal Funds Rate was more important with respect to the price of dollar borrowing.

Authorities on both sides of the Atlantic were aware of this dynamic early on. During a US Treasury meeting in April 1963, Robert Roosa expressed discontent with the UK monetary authorities. He suggested they had pushed up Bank Rate in order to keep ahead of the Eurodollar Rate. While in the past a rising rate for sterling would only have been considered in terms of its effect in drawing money out of dollars and into sterling, it was now understood that the UK action might also push up the Eurodollar Rate, aggravating US balance of payments difficulties through the resultant capital outflow (Burn, 2006: 158). This dynamic is clearly evidenced in figure 4.4, which shows that Bank Rate was the highest rate, with the Eurodollar Rate beneath it and the US Federal Funds Rate consistently the lowest of the three. Apart from a three-year period, between 1968 and 1971, the UK Bank Rate was continuously the highest.

During the mid-1960s this relationship intensified. As figure 4.4 shows, there was a strong correspondence between the Eurodollar Rate and the US Federal Funds Rate. This graph clearly indicates the fact that, although the Eurodollar Rate was kept marginally above the Federal Funds Rate during the early 1960s in order to draw money away from the US capital market, as the US tightened its monetary policy from the 1960s the Eurodollar Rate spiked in response to a massive surge in demand. This was a result of precisely the factors that the Bank had recognized: by drawing funds from their London branches the New York banks were pushing up the price of Eurodollar borrowing.[24] We can see this in figure 4.4, with the two spikes in the Eurodollar Rate that pushed it well over the Federal Funds Rate from 1965 to 1967 and then again from 1968 to 1971.

Anglo-American financial development in the City restricted the autonomy of US policy makers, necessitating greater cooperation and openness with UK counterparts. Eurodollar movements exerted sustained pressure upon the international monetary system. Large-scale US borrowing introduced a "permanent element of demand" shaped by economic conditions within the US (Kane, 1983: 13). This had the effect of integrating the US, Eurodollar, and European markets much more tightly. As a result, European capital markets became more exposed to fluctuations in US monetary policy, creating a form of a hub-and-spokes relationship (Bell, 1973: 62; Kane, 1983: 13). These developments contributed to the increasing international monetary disorder of the later 1960s and early 1970s, the twilight years of Bretton Woods.[25]

The funneling of Eurodollars into the US money markets was discussed at the BIS meeting in 1966. A federal representative highlighted the granting of loans by US bank branches to the head offices of US corporations, who then lent the money to their overseas subsidiaries—a method devised explicitly to circumvent the Interest Equalization Tax. When asked about the attitude of the US authorities toward this borrowing, given that it weakened the impact of US monetary restraint, Samuel Katz of the Fed replied that the borrowing was not a serious problem, due to its small size. Significantly, Katz added that these borrowings were in fact "welcome," in that they had the effect of strengthening the dollar's position and easing the US balance of payments.[26] But as the Eurodollar market's integration with the US money market intensified during the latter 1960s, the attitude of the US hardened. This tougher stance would culminate with a failed attempt to win tighter regulation of the markets. In the following decades, Euromarkets dynamics hosted in London were a continual thorn in the sides of US policy makers.

The US position was detailed by Andrew Brimmer, a member of the Fed's Board of Governors, in a presentation at the LSE in November 1969. Brimmer's talk came after a period of chaos in the international gold market in 1968 had drawn even more restrictive responses from Johnson in order to prevent capital outflows. Further investments in Western Europe were banned, tighter constraints were imposed upon bank lending, and suggestions were made to limit US travel abroad and reduce foreign exchange costs incurred as a result of overseas military expenditures. Although these measures did nothing to curb the longer-term weakness of the US balance of payments, US banks keenly felt their effects.

In response to the surge of US bank borrowing from their London branches in 1968, Brimmer suggested that although the Eurodollar market was based in London, "its basic driving force during the last year has centred in about a dozen large banks in the United States."[27] These banks had turned to the Eurodollar market in order to compensate for the loss of domestic deposits. Brimmer acknowledged that the bidding for Eurodollar funds by US banks had pushed up the Eurodollar Rate and made monetary management in the US more difficult. US policy makers were now a victim of the success of the dollar, finding their actions and autonomy severely constrained by the satellite role of the Euromarkets. By constructing the Euromarkets and drawing in the dollar, UK merchant bankers and the Bank, in conjunction, set in motion dynamics that curtailed the scope of US policy makers. The limits of US structural power were not, therefore, simply the result of developmental "contradictions" (Konings, 2011: 80). They were shaped by the agency of UK merchant bankers and the Bank of England as they used offshore to resuscitate the City's entrepôt role.

The Transatlantic Regulatory Feedback Loop

A transatlantic regulatory feedback loop emerged during the 1960s and stimulated processes of financial deregulation and central bank policy transformation that gathered pace in the decades that followed. The transatlantic feedback loop consisted of highly interactive and competitive financial regulatory transformations in the UK and the US, centered upon a transatlantic spatial axis of London and New York. Bankers in the UK and the US lobbied their national monetary authorities to enable further liberalization to ensure the maintenance of competitive advantages, while central banks were forced to adjust their regulatory stance in response to the new challenges and jurisdictional ambiguities thrown up by the Euromarkets. By increasing the competitive pressure on UK banks, the US influx destabilized the prevailing regulatory order within the City. These dynamics would pave the way for the financial liberalization that gathered momentum in both the UK and the US during the 1970s and 1980s.

Interdependent monetary dynamics between the US and the Euromarkets during the later 1960s began to affect the regulatory stance of the Fed. Indeed, the St. Louis Fed acknowledged in 1968 that Eurodollar dynamics were "having an increasing effect on domestic credit conditions and monetary policy decisions." The market had also become a "conspicuous factor" in policy decisions regarding the balance of payments and central bank cooperation (Federal Reserve Bank of St Louis, 1968: 104). In August 1969, the Fed introduced a 10-percent marginal reserve requirement for US bank liabilities to overseas branches and on funds acquired by overseas branches from their US head offices while also adjusting the required reserve level for other channels of offshore funding. The Eurodollar market was driving regulatory transformations on both sides of the Atlantic. Anglo-American developmental dynamics, gathered around financial integration, were central to regulatory transformations in the world's two most important financial centers.

The Fed's policy adjustment marked the beginning of a decades-long process of transatlantic regulatory interactivity that, as we will see in subsequent chapters, proved foundational to the emergence of liberalized global financial markets. In addition, and more specifically, it marked the beginning of the Fed's sustained attempts to bring the existence of an offshore market for dollars (a precondition for continuing international dollar hegemony) into harmony with the domestic macroeconomic priorities (a precondition for economic policy autonomy). The Eurodollar market shaped transatlantic regulatory transformation as authorities in the UK and the US attempted to come to terms with the shifting architecture of international finance. Not only did these dynamics disrupt Anglo-American regulatory orders and banking practices; they also pulled European banks into London to access the Euromarkets and escape more restrictive onshore regulation in their domestic markets (Altamura, 2016: 29). The transformative effect of the Euromarkets, driven by increased Anglo-American developmental interdependence, spread throughout the advanced capitalist states of the West.

For their part, US officials allowed Eurodollar expansion, but they certainly did not devise it as a strategy for augmenting US financial power. Any benefit they eventually derived was unintended at the outset.[28] Nevertheless, there were certain regulatory changes undertaken in the US in order to facilitate internationalization (Brimmer and Dahl, 1975: 343). On balance, though, the regulatory and policy context within the US was more disabling than encouraging, with tight money in the US and attempts to restrict lending from domestic offices the principal policy catalysts for international expansion (Battilossi, 2002: 62; Misrachi and Davis, 2004: 118).

Once the Eurodollar market emerged, though, US policy makers certainly did seek to make use of it in order to promote their perceived national interests. It began to embody an infrastructure through which US financial power could operate. But the benefit of an increasingly global reach for the dollar was balanced by the costs of rapid offshore market development. The Eurodollar market was not simply an offshore appendage of US power; it also presented an enormous challenge to US policy sovereignty in the macroeconomic arena. How could US authorities manage the balance of payments and achieve price stability when a major focal point of dollar business lay outside of their territorial control? Transatlantic financial linkages meant that decisions taken by UK authorities in London could be rapidly transmitted into the US financial system. US monetary authorities were coming to terms, in a complex and contradictory fashion, with an enormously fluid period in the history of the international monetary order as the crisis of Bretton Woods intensified.

For the Bank, the regulatory pressure emanated from the arrival of US banks with large deposit bases and a desire to push against the dealing limits put in place for UK banks. Bank officials were keen to "forestall any Treasury worrying" regarding dealing limits.[29] As US banks entered the market, they had the effect of pushing up the level of dealing limits. It was thought that an attack on the policy of limits would be an embarrassment to UK banks, which needed them to effectively conduct their operations. The Bank's adoption of a new policy, allowing larger dealing limits, was seen as "a purely defensive one forced on us by the very large number of US banks now coming to London." But in insisting upon the maintenance of dealing limits, Bank officials also believed that they were acting in the interests of the Americans, by preventing them from being associated with any decline in sterling's position.[30] By this point, then, the Bank had already begun to act on behalf of the interests of US banks.

There was general concern about the arrival of the Americans, too. Bank officials reflected that people were "constantly wondering aloud whether the large and seemingly never-ending influx of US banks into London is an unalloyed benefit." Regarding competition with UK banks, it was inferred that UK banks' willingness to help their US counterparts suggested that the newcomers were not viewed as an existential threat. Where competition for clients did appear likely, it was anticipated that the greater impact would be upon the UK-based US subsidiary clients of other US banks. In fact, the inflationary impact upon City rents generated by the Americans was viewed as potentially beneficial. It might push more peripheral players to relocate away from the City, freeing up space for more substantial businesses to move in.[31]

On balance, the Americanization of the Eurodollar market appears not to have been viewed as a major concern for the Bank in terms of any perceived threat to the profitability of UK banking interests. Where concern did arise, it was more a question of how the Bank ought to adapt its regulatory stance and continue to safeguard sterling. Both on the question of lender-of-last-resort responsibility and the issue of dealing limits, it was clear that the Bank was rapidly recalibrating its policy.

In doing so the Bank was adapting to the Euromarkets and creating a new form of overlapping financial sovereignty constituted through Anglo-American development. Although hosting a growing number of foreign banks, a key component of the Bank's institutional functions—its role as a lender of last resort—remained exclusively national. Simultaneously, the presence of US banks brought the lender-of-last-resort responsibility of the Fed into London. The Euromarkets produced a fracturing of jurisdictional authority that spawned ambiguity over regulatory responsibility and spurred the evolution of regulatory regimes to clarify the situation in the following decades. Clarification required central bank cooperation and appreciation of the increased interdependence of transatlantic monetary policy, while also having much broader ramifications for the development of international financial supervision.

The Bank's experience with the Eurodollar market and its discussion as early as 1964 of the limits to jurisdictional authority over foreign bank branches during times of crisis were the progenitors of the "home-country rule."[32] Home-country rule attributed the responsibility for defining and regulating financial institutions to the state. States would look to one another, rather than to supranational organizations, in order to legislate and enforce collective agreements on supervision (Kapstein, 1996: 9). Not only did the Bank stumble across this innovatory principle in responding to the problems raised by the Euromarkets, it also led the development of this principle internationally.

The regulatory challenge provided by the Euromarkets and a series of major banking crises during the 1970s led to an acceleration in the development of international banking supervision (Capie, 2010: 588; Goodhart, 2011: 4).[33] As the banking crises of the early 1970s unfolded, the governors of the G10 central banks met to hammer out proposals for international supervision. These meetings produced the Basel Concordat, which was circulated widely among central banks and supervisory authorities (Capie, 2010: 627). The Bank played the lead role in these discussions, providing the first two chairmen of the committee. The Basel Committee on Banking Supervision, as it came to be known, had a strong UK makeup from the start (Goodhart, 2011: 44). This reflected the Bank's unparalleled epistemic authority in these matters.

Therefore, in addition to the increasingly active stance taken by US authorities in managing the international monetary system, we must also acknowledge that the Bank of England was fundamental to the advancement of the supervisory framework required to keep pace with financial globalization. Key developments such as the Basel Committee of Bank Supervisors stemmed from the initiative of the Bank of England and drew upon the institutional learning that it had undergone during the 1960s. New York and London were functioning as the twin pivots of financial globalization, and their attendant monetary authorities played an integral role in laying the institutional groundwork for this process. The Fed-Wall Street-Treasury nexus was increasingly articulated through and with the Bank-City-Treasury nexus as part of an Anglo-American twin-engine vehicle of financial globalization. Geographically, the City of London became central to the interaction of Anglo-American developmental dynamics. This was part of a transatlantic paradox: sterling's decline was accompanied by the City's rebirth, while the dollar's ascent led, counterintuitively, to the diminution of New York's status. Offshore was a distorting mirror through which transatlantic development was reflected.

This was a major departure from the sheltered politics of the interwar years, where the restrictive sterling area had been assembled as a bulwark for UK trade predominance within the Commonwealth. Now sterling was no longer the centerpiece of a rival currency block and foundation of UK banking dominance, but an increasingly marginal component of a rapidly expanding international financial system that hinged upon the dollar. In a matter of several decades, the financial markets of the UK and the US had become integrated more completely than ever before.

Not only did Eurodollar business restore the City's centrality within the international financial system; it was now a nodal point in the global extension of US capital markets and US banking, and the hegemony of the dollar. The City had become the "banker to the dollar" and was now increasingly defined by its "enclave function" within the UK economy (Coakley and Harris, 1983: 23). It was once again a mediator between the borrowers and lenders of the world, but, unlike in the nineteenth century, the business was denominated in dollars rather than sterling and the major players were US banks, not UK banks. And, crucially, the City could continue to play this part regardless of the health of UK factories, UK merchants, and sterling (Coakley and Harris, 1983: 23).[34]

The evolution of the City's role had important consequences for UK banking. US banks brought new management techniques and financial innovation into the London market—most notably, the introduction of Certificates of Deposit in May 1966, a move mirrored by the issuing of sterling certificates of deposit (CDs) by UK banks from 1968.[35] The negotiability of CDs, pioneered in the US money markets earlier in the decade, enabled them to function as liquid assets (Bank of England, 1966: 398; Oxford, 2008: 75). US banks also introduced the "going concern" approach to lending, with future expected earnings rather than the resale value of their assets now the principal criterion for evaluating a borrower's creditworthiness. US banks imposed covenants through which they monitored the profitability of borrowing businesses, which led to an intensified role for banks in restructuring business operations in periods of crisis (Coakley and Harris, 1983: 138–40). The growth of offshore banking increased competition for deposits denominated in major currencies, with the US banks competing for sterling deposits after establishing a foothold in London. This had the effect of increasing the competitiveness of the sterling deposit market (Aliber, 1985: 83; Jones, 1991: 125).

UK banks were forced to respond to the competitive challenge posed by the Americans. While the merchant banks were prominent players in the first decade of the Euromarkets, their limited deposit bases restricted their capacity to compete as the markets grew in size (Jones, 1993: 326). The UK clearing banks, which didn't make a sustained entry into the Euromarkets until the 1970s, had been sheltered from competition through their cozy relationship with the Bank of England and the interest rate cartel that they had long maintained (Jones, 1991: 135). The entry of the Americans provided a competitive jolt to the UK banks, shaking them out of their torpor (Moran, 1986: 22).

With international banking rapidly reconfigured, the national regulatory frameworks within which it was embedded were placed under mounting strain as the effects of the transatlantic feedback loop mounted in step with deeper financial market integration. By increasing the competitive pressure on UK banks, the US influx destabilized the prevailing regulatory order within the City. In the postwar period, the Bank had relied upon its relationship with a concentrated and cartelized banking sector to manage monetary policy and control credit levels. As the number of foreign banks in London grew, the Bank found it increasingly difficult to rely on its traditional relationship with a closed network of dominant UK banks (Moran, 1986: 2; Michie, 2004: 44). Economic planning and government management of financial markets became much harder. Credit markets were increasingly responsive to global demand fluctuations rather than the requirements of the UK government.

To compete with their well-capitalized US counterparts, UK banks moved toward universal banking and away from traditional divisions between merchant and commercial banking (Battilossi, 2002: 114–16). These transformations required a corresponding regulatory recalibration, and the Conservative government's Competition Credit and Control policy offered exactly that. It disrupted the trend of credit rationing by administrative decree, which had proliferated during the tight-money policy of the 1960s, freeing up credit markets by substituting price levels for government controls as the decisive determinant of credit levels (Moran, 1986: 30). As we shall see in chapter 5, this had serious implications for the stagflationary crisis of the 1970s.

The origins of the deregulatory dynamics of the 1970s and 1980s can thus be located within the transformation of financial markets during the 1950s and 1960s. Mirroring the imperatives of Competition Credit and Control and increasingly conscious of the competitive challenge that the City posed to New York, deregulation began to gather pace in the US. Nixon called for the gradual phasing out of interest rate ceilings in 1973 while the Securities and Exchange Commission (SEC) brought about New York's "Big Bang" in 1975, breaking from its longstanding support for the cartel-like organizations that had dominated US capital markets since the 1930s (Panitch and Gindin, 2012: 149). From the late 1970s, the problem of growing foreign competition for securities business—with the London challenge central—further challenged the SEC's regulatory stance (Landau, 1987; Longstreth, 1988). As we shall see, regulatory transformations in the US then fed back into the UK, with the further liberalization during the 1980s and Thatcher's own "Big Bang" carried out after UK officials had visited the US in order to learn from its US regulatory apparatus (Moran, 1994: 168).

The Fiscal Basis of the UK State

Not only did the Euromarkets recalibrate regulatory frameworks and integrate Anglo-American monetary policy; they also fed back into the domestic foundations of the UK's political economy by reconfiguring the fiscal basis of the UK state. UK merchant bankers were able to use the momentum generated by the Euromarkets to leverage their own power and influence within the government. In the process, they helped steer the UK down a developmental path corresponding to their interests.

As the UK's balance of payments problems intensified during the 1960s, the coalition of forces behind stop-go came apart and support for alternatives gained momentum. Opponents of stop-go called for domestic expansion, modernization, and indicative planning (Jessop, 1980: 32). Crucially, the Conservative Party began to rethink their stance on state intervention. In the early 1960s the Conservatives began to enact their plans; they established the National Economic Development Council (NEDC), which served as a tripartite medium for national planning. They encouraged rationalization and modernization, introducing an incomes policy and applying for UK membership in the EEC (Jessop, 1980: 33).

Labour began to give planning increased priority under Wilson's administration (Roseveare, 1969: 326; Jessop, 1980: 39; Overbeek, 1990: 7). This was

part of the Labour government's broader economic strategy for raising investment levels, increasing exports, and replacing imports deemed inessential
(Roseveare, 1969: 343). Labour's newfound commitment to planning was
embodied in the establishment of the Department of Economic Affairs (DEA)
in 1964, along with the establishment of the Industrial Reorganization Corporation, which was formed in 1966 in order to intervene directly in the rationalization of industry and accelerate the process of merging and regrouping
among UK companies (Brittan, 1971: 319). The DEA took responsibility for
prices, incomes, and industrial policies and was primarily responsible for the
preparation of the National Plan and regional policy (Brittan, 1971: 315).

However, the development of the new planning apparatus was doomed
from the beginning. The new agencies were separate from the "central axis" of
state power (the Bank and the Treasury), and the division of responsibility
between the DEA and the Treasury was ambiguous (Jessop, 1980: 40; Brittan,
1971: 312). Economic planning in the UK had traditionally been constrained
by the domineering power of the Treasury-Bank relationship, and the creation
of the DEA was unable to overcome this. The DEA was involved in a losing
struggle for supremacy with the Treasury, which retained primary control over
public expenditure and public investment (Roseveare, 1969: 344). The Bank
and the Treasury were able to maintain the traditional priority of the balance
of payments and the reserves over and against the commitment to growth and
full employment entailed by support for planning (Jessop, 1980: 40).

The indicative nature of the new planning was a serious limitation. When
the NEDC and the DEA drew up their proposals, there were no specific policy
tools for securing either direct or indirect compliance with the specified
growth targets (Jessop, 1980: 41). When Wilson's government was faced with
the choice between devaluation, as a precondition of planned growth, and
deflation, to safeguard the reserves, it opted for the latter (Jessop, 1980: 40).[36]
The modernization efforts of the 1960s failed to restore competitiveness to UK
business (Gamble, 1990: 119). Even after the devaluation of 1967, which effectively ended sterling's international role, the government continued to prioritize deflationary measures (Jessop, 1980: 40; Cassis, 2010: 202). This failure
was in no small part down to the Labour government's fear of alienating the
US through devaluation (Brittan, 1971: 292). With the dollar under increased
pressure during the 1960s, the US feared that a UK devaluation would dent
the market's confidence in the dollar (Gowa, 1983: 39).

As the relentless stop-go cycle deepened the UK's industrial crisis, the
Euromarkets increasingly shaped the fiscal strategy of the UK state. The

Eurobond market in particular became highly significant. With an intensifying fiscal crisis, Eurobonds were touted as a potential source of funds. Already in 1961, the White Paper on the "Financial Objectives of the Nationalised Industries" suggested that nationalized industries needed to make a reasonable rate of return on the capital invested. Nationalized industries would have to contribute to their own capital needs, charging prices that realistic in light of the underlying costs. These were more demanding objectives than the prior goal of simply breaking even (Brittan, 1964: 96). It was within this context of transforming the raison d'être of the nationalized industries that the question of Eurobond borrowing took center stage.

Within the Treasury, the possibility of easing access to Euromarket funds was discussed at length. This followed hot on the heels of the renewed sense of crisis that swamped the UK after devaluation in 1967. The Treasury and the Inland Revenue discussed the possibility of easing access to the Eurodollar market for UK traders. The motivation here was the perceived benefit to the UK balance of payments, with reserves to be strengthened if UK traders borrowed outside of the sterling area to finance domestic investment.[37] In order to encourage Eurodollar borrowing, proposed new legislation sought to make more interest on foreign borrowing tax deductible.

These proposals were not well received by the Inland Revenue, which expressed concerns about the potential impact of a relaxation of borrowing controls upon offshore tax havens.[38] The Treasury and the Bank overrode its concerns. In a meeting between Treasury and Bank officials the increased balance of benefits payments post-devaluation was stressed. With confidence in sterling low, it was felt that any measures that could help bolster the UK's reserve position were to be encouraged.[39] The move toward greater Eurodollar borrowing would have an additional benefit. It was, in fact, partially devised to reduce the UK's exposure to destabilizing short-term capital movements.

By expanding the financing options available to firms, the proposal would lead to "the average lengthening of our borrowing abroad," a step that was seen as a "modest but significant step in line with the Government's policy of reducing the country's sensitivity to short-term flights of funds." Increases in reserves derived from this practice would, it was understood, be a "very real gain" and "would be recognised as such in every financial centre in the world."[40] The Bank firmly supported the proposal, and the Treasury agreed that the Inland Revenue's tax objections were "insubstantial."[41] By the end of May 1968, the chancellor of the exchequer had concluded that the balance of payments benefits outweighed the tax difficulties.[42]

Quite perversely, the growing offshore market that had enabled the numerous movements of hot money was now viewed as the most viable means of insulating the UK from speculative movements.[43] Capital controls were ruled out, and the solution appeared to be an even tighter integration with the vicissitudes of the Euromarkets. The Euromarkets were both the malady and cure. And, in a peculiar Anglo-American parallel, the Euromarkets had begun to serve as a key strategic arena for the management of the balance of payments in both states.

The increased appeal of the Euromarkets as a source of funds was not purely circumstantial. From the mid-1960s, merchant bankers began to actively press the government to promote Eurodollar borrowing. Treasury officials reported to the Inland Revenue that "merchant bankers at home and abroad have been urging for some time that if certain tax impediments were removed UK firms and public bodies would be able to raise large sums in medium and long-term issues of Eurodollar bearer bonds."[44] Foremost among these merchant banker advocates was, unsurprisingly, Siegmund Warburg himself.

In 1965 Warburg had joined with Hambros and Rothschild to push the Bank of England to exempt foreign bonds issued in London from paying stamp duty. They also pressed the Treasury to lift the requirement that income tax be deducted from interest on bonds issued by companies based in the UK (Ferguson, 2010: 225). Warburg was keen to accelerate the liberalization of London's services for international investors, viewing this as essential to achieving European integration. Harold Wilson had come to lean heavily upon Warburg for financial advice during the 1960s.[45] And, although Warburg had vociferously lobbied Wilson to avoid devaluation, the firm nonetheless "stood ready to advise the government not only on currency questions but also on the finances of nationalised entities like the National Coal Board" (Ferguson, 2010: 285).

Long-term borrowing requirements of the nationalized industries had, since 1956, been financed wholly through the exchequer.[46] This meant that their borrowing requirements were aggregated with other government borrowing. Between 1962 and 1967 the funds required for borrowing had grown from £432 million to £1.1 billion. The problem then became one of financing investment without further weakening the UK's balance of payments. Within this context, the intervention of two different interests was crucial.

Firstly, the IMF recommended in the summer of 1967, after agreeing to loan to the UK, that the nationalized industries "be required to make a greater contribution to their own requirements so as to reduce the burden of the Exchequer."[47] The IMF was beginning to have the sort of transformative impact upon UK development that it would exert more strenuously during the 1970s.

Concurrently, the merchant bankers—and Warburg in particular—were continuing to advocate for greater Euromarket borrowing for the government, local authorities, and the nationalized industries. Rather ambiguously, Warburg declared to the exchequer that borrowing from the Euromarkets would be "good for the credit."[48] He subsequently raised the issue with the minister of power and commented that the UK was making less use of the Euromarkets than Germany and France.

An unwritten alliance between the IMF and the City's merchant bankers was pushing the UK deeper into the embrace of private capital markets and transforming the fiscal basis of the UK state. Whereas past studies had concluded that the overall benefits of increased Eurodollar borrowing would be negligible, the deteriorating fiscal climate and the intensive lobbying campaign of the merchant banks, aided by IMF prescriptions, proved game-changing. The lobbying efforts of Warburg and others bore fruit: in 1969 the Gas Council raised £31 million through deutschmark-denominated Eurobond issues, and by October 1971 UK public sector agencies had raised £51 million through this channel (Ferguson, 2010: 285). This was not, then, simply a case of the outward expansion of US finance, or of the restoration of the old order of UK capitalism, but, rather, the further intensification of a qualitatively distinctive Anglo-American sphere of development. Enabled by the agency of merchant bankers based in London, the Euromarkets fundamentally Atlanticized UK capitalism, bringing about a structural transformation in the orientation of key state institutions through which they embraced the emergence of offshore Euromarkets finance.

The Euromarkets had intensified banking power in the UK, not only by pulling US banks into the UK en masse, but also by energizing City merchant bankers' efforts to use their privileged access to the Treasury-Bank nexus to render government fiscal policy compatible with their interests. Borrowing costs were higher for individual Eurobond issues offered by public sector agencies than for the exchequer, borrowing through its own aggregate account. No wonder Warburg and his kin were so keen to advocate this course of action; their presence helped ensure that financing public sector utilities was achieved not through progressive taxation or government management of the banks, but through the embrace of private capital markets. Within a Bank of England that had long stood for the traditional Gladstonian orthodoxy of balanced budgets and a Treasury that had been converted to Keynes only in technique, not thought, they found fertile soils for their arguments to be implanted (Roseveare, 1969: 325).

By the late 1960s a creeping monetarist influence was exerting itself within the Treasury. Whereas leadership over monetary policy had traditionally been left up to the Bank until the 1960s, the Treasury now became more involved with the measurement of the money supply (Brittan, 1971: 80). Geoffrey Bell, a leading advocate of the new quantity theory of money, took a position within the Treasury's finance division. Bell and other officials began to take an interest in the flow of money throughout the economy and had begun to calculate figures for Domestic Credit Expansion by the beginning of 1969 (Brittan, 1971: 81). From the mid-1960s, the finance side of the Treasury began to recover some initiative on overseas matters from the Bank. Sterling's problems could no longer be remedied with short-term credits from other central banks but needed regular recourse to the IMF instead. Increasing contact with the IMF, which dealt directly with the Treasury, augmented Treasury influence (Brittan, 1971: 80). With Roy Jenkins as chancellor after the devaluation of 1967 (discussed in the following chapter), IMF prescriptions were enacted through attempts to control the money supply to limit consumption and restrain imports (Panitch and Leys, 1997: 109).

Although the IMF prescriptions targeted the money supply (much like the monetarists) through a focus on the measurement of "domestic credit expansion," they were distinct from the Anglo-American monetarism that gathered force in subsequent years. Rather than stressing the exclusive role of the money supply in generating inflation, the IMF approach was motivated by an attempt to move from discretionary to rules-based macroeconomic policy making. Thus, it was in this support for rules over discretion that the emerging IMF approach bore some resemblance to monetarist doctrines. But even here the overlap was distinctly limited: the DCE targets were far more tendential and negotiable than the fixed policy rules outline by Friedman and other monetarists (Clift and Tomlinson, 2012: 478–82). Nevertheless, by homing in on and politicizing the money supply, IMF supervision put the question of monetary targets fully on the macroeconomic policy agenda (James, 1996: 191). This opened a policy space that the monetarists would soon occupy.

Anglo-American Finance and the Crisis of Keynesianism

The birth of the Euromarkets represented a defining moment in the postwar history of Anglo-American development. By creating the conditions to host a major offshore dollar market, the merchant bankers of the City drew US financial power into London. In doing so, they transformed the landscape of international finance, generating the infrastructure for a vast pool of mobile capital that gradually overwhelmed the capacity for central banks to maintain the fixed exchange rates promised at Bretton Woods. The Euromarkets produced new regulatory dilemmas on both sides of the Atlantic, prompting regulatory innovations such as the development of home country rule, giving the Bank of England a leading role in the politics of financial globalization alongside the Fed and the US Treasury. Deeper market integration between London and New York, allied to the increasingly intertwined fortunes of sterling and the dollar as key reserve currencies, within a context of chronic Anglo-American payments deficits, incentivized ever-deeper Anglo-American monetary cooperation during the crisis years of Bretton Woods. complicating US attempts to adjust. But the UK did not, as this chapter has demonstrated, move in this direction independently; the power of US finance was crucial in giving the required weight and depth to the Euromarkets. It was a truly Anglo-American process that would have been impossible without developmental interaction that had antecedents that reached back into the 1920s.

Static typologies of hegemony miss the significance of this expression of US power within the institutional fabric of the UK. By focusing predominantly upon America's postwar might, scholars have neglected the extent to which the UK's role as a key nodal point in the articulation of financial globalization was fundamental both to the collapse of Bretton Woods and the birth of a new order of globalized finance. US ascendancy was articulated in and through UK decline, as the states' developmental paths occasioned a constitutive interaction within the City. It was the UK's peculiar imperial history and longstanding commitment to an open international financial order, in contrast to the controls put in place by other European states, that enabled US banking to break through its national boundaries, reconfiguring the international monetary system in the process.

We can only understand the Euromarkets through this Anglo-American lens. By neglecting this kind of analysis, scholars of UK development have often understated its significance. Arrival of US banks into the Euromarkets meant that decisions taken about the City were inevitably also decisions taken about US banking. Hosting the Euromarkets posed serious constraints upon the policy autonomy of the UK state. Crucially, discussions about the nationalization of key City institutions, which gathered momentum during the 1970s, would unavoidably become discussions that threatened the position of internationalized US banks in London. The US had a more obvious and active stake in the UK's political economy than ever before.

Yet this was not simply a case of US structural power shaping the policy options open to the UK. The Euromarkets would never have been possible without the initiative and agency of merchant bankers and state officials in London, whose actions created an infrastructure for financial globalization and the international hegemony of the dollar. The feedback effects of the Euromarket development also constrained the policy autonomy of the US in crucial ways: rendering national attempts to regulate financial flows less effective, weakening the New Deal regulatory architecture, spurring transatlantic policy interdependence, and contributing to the breakdown of Bretton Woods. Borne out by the agency of UK financiers and the Bank, the Euromarkets created a distinctively transatlantic form of political-economic space, one that long proved a thorn in the side of US monetary policy makers. The Euromarkets, as we shall see in subsequent chapters, became increasingly politicized as the Bretton Woods order finally broke down in the early 1970s. They would continue to be a central issue in the decades that followed, lying at the heart of the interbanking lending "credit crunch" during the global financial crisis of 2007/8.

The Euromarkets were also deeply paradoxical. Although they constrained US policy autonomy and weakened the New Deal regulatory architecture, they also generated the institutional infrastructure that would underpin the dollar's global dominance, and, with it, America's exceptional financial power, for decades to come. Anglo-American development in the City laid the offshore market infrastructure of US structural financial power.

Through the Euromarkets and the entrenchment of dollar hegemony, the Fed's global role was augmented. This was evidenced by effect its policies had in pushing up interest rates in the Eurodollar market and shaping the geographical flow of Eurodollar funds from the mid-1960s. The City had recovered its role only through the acceptance of a particular place within a US-led and US-dominated monetary order: *as* an archipelago into Europe and the wider world for US capital markets. We need not explain the UK's acceptance of this role as a result of "hegemonic lag" (Helleiner, 1994: 99). It was the outcome of the active lobbying and business practice of the City's merchant bankers, who successfully innovated to create the Euromarkets and then waged, as we have seen, an effective campaign to pull the UK deeper into the clutches of the Euromarkets, transforming the fiscal basis of the state. In doing so, they excluded potential alternatives for the postwar state.

The Eurodollar embrace was a constraint that fatally undermined the UK Keynesian experiment. The UK willingly subjected itself to market discipline that weakened the pound and intensified the disastrous stop-go cycle of post-war recovery. As the City became ever more globalized and banks began to push against the existing regulatory framework, it became increasingly difficult for the Bank and the government to control credit to the extent required for a Keynesian growth strategy and economic planning. The rise of financial power through the Euromarkets would be foundational to the development of neo-liberal policies that gathered momentum during the crisis years of the later 1970s. This was not, however, simply a return to the gold standard–era structure and orientation of the City-Bank-Treasury nexus (Burn, 1999: 227). While power did remain concentrated within the City-Bank-Treasury nexus, it was now articulated through, and embedded within, a new order of Anglo-American finance.

Anglo-American dynamics also took on a much wider international significance through the Euromarkets, driving the decomposition of Bretton Woods. As both states wrestled with the crises of the Bretton Woods system during the 1960s and were increasingly pitted against surplus countries in the negotiations over international monetary reform, they responded to these challenges in a way that spurred the further growth of the Euromarkets. In pursuing their own distinctive strategies of national development, and through the constitutive interaction of these strategies, the UK and the US sowed the seeds for a new order of liberalized international finance. The flows of hot money unleashed by the Eurodollar market destabilized both sterling and the dollar during the 1960s and 1970s (Strange, 1972: 198; Bell, 1973: 67; Higonnet, 1985: 36; Overbeek, 1990: 109). By increasing the exposure of these two key currencies to speculative attacks, the Eurodollar market played a central role in the collapse of fixed exchange rates.

During the 1970s, as the international monetary order continued to come apart, a new era of financial discipline was born. Floating exchange rates and capital flows began to exert the kind of disciplinary pressure toward balanced budgets that had not been effectively enforced under Bretton Woods.[49] The oil crisis of 1973 combined with a crisis of profitability and increased working-class militancy to spark a world crisis and years of stagflation in the West (Glyn and Harrison, 1980: 21; Brenner, 2002: 18). The UK felt these pressures more acutely than any other developed nation. When the Labour government was forced to go, cap in hand, to the IMF once more in 1976, the US seized the opportunity to impose discipline upon what it viewed as a spendthrift the UK living beyond her means. As the UK's Keynesian compromise entered its death throes, Anglo-American dynamics would come center stage once again.

5

In the Eye of the Storm

THE INTERNATIONAL monetary system designed at Bretton Woods finally imploded during the 1970s. The terminal balance of payments deficits of the United Kingdom and the United States reached their day of reckoning. The United States' eventual answer to the Triffin dilemma was the closing of the gold window, abruptly imposing an impromptu dollar standard and restoring national policy autonomy. Without the power to enact similar unilateral measures, the UK's status as a tottering key currency component of Bretton Woods produced graver consequences. Facing a sterling crisis of unprecedented proportions, the UK became the first major casualty of the post–Bretton Woods financial order and turned to the IMF for emergency funding. This brought the UK into the orbit of US disciplinary power.

The UK's 1976 IMF bailout was a crucial turning point in the politics of financial globalization. While the 1970s have been canonized as a decade of critical systemic transformation within IPE (Strange, 1972; Helleiner, 1994; Gilpin, 2000; Frieden, 2006; Cohen, 2008; Stein, 2010), the international significance of the UK's national crisis has received much less recognition.[1] The implications of the UK's 1976 crisis for the wider global political economy were far-reaching. They prompted deep concern within the commanding heights of US capitalism and the City. This was a critical juncture within the political economy of Anglo-American development.

Had the protectionist measures and nationalization of major clearing banks advocated for by some within the Labour Party and Cabinet actually been adopted, further Anglo-American financial integration and liberalization would have been halted, and with it the wider momentum of financial globalization would have stalled. The City's infrastructural and spatial centrality, heightened by its increasing relevance to European liberalization and integration after the UK's accession to the EEC in 1973, meant that threats to liberal finance in the UK were threats to liberal finance internationally. Politically, the will of UK politicians and regulators to defend the Euromarkets during the early 1970s was critical to maintaining expansion of private international capital markets at a time of uncertainty and growing demand for capital controls.

The UK's sponsorship of liberal international finance and the City's entrepôt role might well have been abandoned in 1976. That they were not was in part due to the resistance that proposals from the Labour left met from opponents within the Cabinet, the Treasury, the Bank, and the City. But it was also due to the persistent pressure exercised by officials within the US state. With Anglo-American developmental processes now having deeply embedded the centrality of the dollar within rapidly globalizing private financial markets, the US leveraged its structural power in global finance to discipline the UK state. It did so through the provision of conditional dollar financing mediated by the IMF.

This chapter argues that the resolution of the 1976 crisis in favor of the UK's continued commitment to an open international economic order and the abandonment of Keynesian full employment reflected the increased interdependence of Anglo-American institutions and interests. Anglo-American financial integration generated a constituency of UK financiers, political forces, and institutions with an increasingly *Atlantic* orientation. Priorities among influential financial and state actors within the UK were now bound up with, and increasingly difficult to disentangle from, the interests of US finance and the US state. As the US pressured the UK through the disciplinary stance of the US Treasury and the Federal Reserve, refracted through the power of the IMF, UK officials, the Conservative Party, and City bankers also drew US discipline to what they understood as an outmoded, dangerous, and fiscally reckless Labour government. These actors made common cause with the US to overcome the challenge of a radicalized social democratic settlement promoted by the left wing of the Labour Party. Labour's plans to transform UK economic policy threatened to severely jeopardize the City's international role, imperiling its status as an offshore market for the dollar. For the US, the deepening financial integration of and monetary interdependence between the two states heightened exposure to the political-economic vulnerabilities of London and the UK economy while deepening the centrality of the City to financial globalization. By 1976, the US had run out of patience with the UK and was considering direct supervision of the UK Treasury by its US counterpart.

My argument here challenges incumbent interpretations of the 1976 crisis by rejecting a binary distinction between "national" and "international" dynamics. Existing scholarship has attempted to clearly establish a privileged level of causality to explain the abandonment of Keynesianism by the Labour government (Ludlum, 1992; Baker, 1999; Harmon, 2008; Rogers, 2009). These scholars elevate the importance of national policy changes while downplaying the significance of US influence upon the UK's chosen course of action (Ludlum, 1992; Baker, 1999; Harmon, 2008; Rogers, 2009). By cleaving to a misleading distinction between national policies and international pressures, they overlook the formative influence of Anglo-American development upon UK policy and understate the significance of US disciplinary power, alongside the IMF, in reconstituting the UK state during the critical decade of the 1970s.[2] As we saw in the previous chapter, the Bank and the Treasury were already deeply embedded within the networked connections that had been constructed with the US during the attempts to forestall the collapse of Bretton Woods during the 1960s. In this context, separating out national and international interests within the politics of the IMF crisis becomes much harder.

The chapter begins by examining the strained politics of Anglo-American monetary relations and the wider crisis of the Bretton Woods system. It goes on to explore the defense of the Euromarkets against attempts at regulatory encroachment led by West Germany and reviews the unraveling of the UK's domestic Keynesian compromise, before turning to the acute sterling crisis that fostered increasing hostility and political opposition toward the Labour government by the City, prompted the consideration of protectionist measures, and led finally to an approach to the IMF. The focus then shifts to the attempts by the US Treasury and the Fed to use the crisis to discipline the UK state, pressuring the UK Treasury to remain open to the international liberal order and demanding domestic austerity. In the penultimate section, the chapter charts the transatlantic rise of monetarist ideas during the 1970s, demonstrating their impact in hardening the stance of the US toward the UK and boosting support for austerity from within the Treasury, the Bank, and the City. Finally, the concluding section frames the UK's symbolic break from Keynesianism in 1976 as a turning point in the politics of financial globalization.

The Death Throes of Bretton Woods

The roots of the 1976 crisis lay in the persistent UK balance of payments problems of the 1960s, during which the US grew increasingly frustrated with UK profligacy. Lyndon Johnson's administration was exasperated by the failure of the Wilson government to arrest the decline of sterling and forestall fears of devaluation. The acceleration of the UK's balance of payments crisis during Wilson's government was the beginning of the process that gradually drew the UK closer into the disciplinary orbit of US power. The head of the Fed, Bill Martin, took an increasingly firm stance toward the UK from 1965, urging much sharper cuts to public spending to calm the markets (Schenk, 2010: 161).

With the UK in dire need of funding to support sterling, Martin and Johnson appeared to have reached the end of their tether. Martin proposed that massive pressure be applied to the UK to force a more comprehensive package of spending restraint. If that failed, sterling should be abandoned altogether, with the US instead turning to the IMF to construct a package to protect the dollar.[3] Johnson described Wilson as a "drunk and reckless boy," writing checks that he could not honor (Schenk, 2010: 162). The impression of a fiscally incontinent Labour government was becoming deeply entrenched. Treasury Secretary Fowler did, though, temper Martin and Johnson's plans. Fowler knew that the actual costs of abandoning sterling would, as we saw in the previous chapter, be very high, resulting in termination of Bretton Woods. Instead, it made more sense for the US to continue to contribute to multilateral support for the UK.

The negotiations from 1965 exhibited important precursors to the austerity measures imposed in 1976, with conditions stipulated on action over wage restraint, prices, and government expenditure (Capie, 2010: 207).[4] During this period, sterling's weakness exposed the UK to the US plan for rebalancing the international economy. The US vision emphasized restrictive monetary policy and credit control rather than the industrial policy favored by the Labour government (Schenk, 2010: 190).

During the 1960s, then, many of the patterns of the 1970s negotiations were already discernible. As they would be in 1976, the Bank of England and the Treasury were notably more receptive to IMF calls for austerity than the UK government. As the UK drew upon the IMF repeatedly during the 1960s, the surveillance and conditionality attached grew incrementally, with a focus upon the imposition of monetary and fiscal restraint through quantitative targets. But there was also a crucial difference in the UK's relationship to the IMF after the breakdown of Bretton Woods. When the UK government turned to the IMF in 1976, after the termination of fixed exchange rates, they would no longer benefit from the necessity of US fiscal support that had been a product of the shared fates of sterling and the dollar as the two key currencies under Bretton Woods.

The creeping imposition of Fund conditionality during the 1960s, despite its limited efficacy in practice, represented an important departure from the UK's traditional dealings with the IMF. The UK was the heaviest drawer on the Fund's resources during the first quarter century of its life. As a powerful key currency country, the UK could make drawings with scant oversight or conditionality. The UK's heavy and regular use of IMF funding began before the conditionality principles of the Fund's lending were firmly established.[5] US proposals for amending the IMF Articles of Agreement to include a statement that balance of payments financing was not an unqualified right were initially resisted by other members. By 1950, the US had successfully campaigned for the acceptance of a conditionality principle linked to IMF funding. By the end of that decade, the major elements of conditionality were in place, but the conditions tended to be used only in negotiations with developing countries (Harmon, 1997: 21–27).

Conditionality emerged, therefore, because of US power and the desire to use the Fund as a source of disciplinary control over countries facing balance of payments difficulties. The IMF had only partial autonomy from US power. The US was the largest single contributor of funds to the IMF, and it wielded exclusive veto over Fund policies. Added to this, the Fund's basis in Washington, DC, ensured a spatial and symbolic proximity to US power (Burk, 1994: 354). From the mid-1960s, Britain was drawn progressively deeper into this disciplinary trap, having to accept an ever-higher degree of conditionality and surveillance as a quid pro quo for the support of sterling.

Tense Anglo-American negotiations and the increasing UK dependence upon IMF funding were precursors to the collapse of Bretton Woods. Once the pound had been devalued in November 1967, pressure on the dollar increased almost immediately (Block, 1977: 193). Demand for gold had become increasingly linked to expectations about sterling, meaning that devaluation prompted over $3 billion worth of gold sales on the London market by the Gold Pool members. Of this $3 billion, the US share accounted for $2.2 billion. Conviction in the official dollar-gold price, and with it the bedrock of the Bretton Woods system, was now gravely undermined (Gavin, 2004: 166; Bordo et al., 2015: 180).[6] The gold market crisis shattered confidence in the dollar's fixed convertibility and effectively sounded the death knell for Bretton Woods. Sterling's plight had been central to its broader destabilization, signaling that in practice the postwar international monetary order had been an Anglo-American key currency system.

Between 1970 and 1971, the dollar came under renewed strain. On coming into office Nixon had sought to curb inflation, which had risen steadily during the 1960s, by raising interest rates, with the federal funds rate hitting 9 percent. However, the effect of the rate rise created instability within the US financial system, provoking a crisis within the commercial paper market and leading to the insolvency of Penn Central, one of the largest corporations in the US. In response, the Nixon administration began to reduce interest rates, and it suspended regulation Q ceilings to boost liquidity for the banking system (Kane, 1983: 51; Greider, 1987: 488; Panitch and Gindin, 2012: 138–39). With the dollar in distress in the international markets, Nixon switched tack, reverting to incomes and price controls and shying away from monetary tightening (Widmaier, 2016: 110–18).

Nixon's administration was forced to pull back from efforts to choke off inflation. The Fed prioritized its lender-of-last-resort role and pumped liquidity into the markets. Despite the curtailment of anti-inflationary policy, the Fed's initial move to raise interest rates to arrest inflation anticipated the more sustained effort to reduce inflation under the stewardship of Paul Volcker (Panitch and Gindin, 2012: 138–39). The Fed's U-turn in 1970 demonstrated the impact of financial market developments (sponsored by central banks) on restricting the scope for central bank action. With more and more businesses now entangled in expanding financial markets, tight money threatened to spark off a financial crisis.

More immediately, the Fed's measures had a major impact on Eurodollar flows as US banks became less dependent upon Eurodollar borrowing and began to unwind their Eurodollar positions. The availability of low-cost funds led to large European capital inflows, which contributed to crises of the deutsche mark and the dollar (Strange, 1972: 198; Block, 1977: 197). The failure to rescue the dollar through the imposition of tight money at home also ensured that other solutions would have to be found in response to the problems of Bretton Woods.

Defending the Euromarkets

This period of financial instability had major consequences for the international monetary order. In response, Western European and Japanese monetary authorities pushed for cooperative capital controls and the regulation of the Euromarkets. Within Germany, the Bundesbank developed an increasingly critical stance on the Euromarkets from 1969. Indeed, the Germans fast

became the most active opponents of Eurodollar funds, fearing that they nega-
tively affected attempts to implement domestic anti-inflationary monetary
policies. Growing German pressure placed the Euromarkets—and questions
over the pace of their unregulated growth—at the heart of international negotiations. Germany was soon joined by Switzerland and the Netherlands in
pressing for greater regulation of speculative international capital flows. By
1969, the topic of Eurodollar market control was also central to French discussion at the Banque de France. The US sided with the continental European
perspective as well, with William McChesney Martin, chairman of the Fed,
suggesting at a speech in Basel that "a case can be made for giving to an international institution some responsibility for supervising these markets." Ottmar Emminger, vice president of the Bundesbank, produced a document exploring the prospects for "Joint Supervision of the Euro-Currency Market" by
the end of 1970 (Altamura, 2016: 35–37).

In February 1971, the Europeans proposed a Standing Committee on the
Euromarkets to replace the existing Basel annual meeting of Eurocurrency
experts. Emminger continued to push for regulation of the Euromarkets
through his role as chairman of Working Party 3 within the Organization for
Economic Cooperation and Development (OECD) from 1969. At the first
meeting of the new standing committee, both the Germans and the Americans
decided that the central banks involved in the meeting should not increase
their total placements in the Euromarkets, thereby avoiding further inflation.
In the politics surrounding these attempts to regulate the rapidly growing international financial markets based in London, it was the Bank of England that
emerged as "the strongest advocate of the Euromarkets," supported by smaller
countries such as Belgium and Luxembourg, while the Bundesbank led a "conservative wing" within the G10 (including the Netherlands and Switzerland)
and drove initiatives to curb its further growth (Altamura, 2016: 92). The trend
of further financial liberalization was now in serious jeopardy.

The UK's position on the issue of capital controls and the Euromarkets was
uniquely contradictory. The specificity of its stance on capital controls and
financial regulation during the crucial years surrounding the Nixon shock is
missed by the suggestion of clearly distinguished European "managed" and
US "ad hoc" approaches to globalization (Abdelal, 2007). The UK's unique
status within a wider field of Anglo-American financial development gave it a
distinctive position in 1970s debates about the future of the international monetary order. Anglo-American financial integration in London made the City
structurally dependent upon the continuation of unregulated short-term

capital flows. This meant that UK intransigence presented a regulatory dilemma for states such as the US and Germany, who were looking to find ways to reorganize international monetary relations to rein in domestic inflation and pursue macroeconomic goals.

UK authorities shared the broader Western European commitment to maintaining the system of fixed exchange rates, but were very hesitant to countenance restrictive measures that might endanger the future of the Euromarkets. In defending the Euromarkets, UK authorities aimed to protect the major channel through which disruptive capital flows could run, imperiling the system of fixed exchange rates in the process. Throughout 1971, UK Treasury officials closely monitored the emerging position of the international community with regard to the Euromarkets, paying particular attention to the increasingly important bilateral discussions between the US and West Germany.[7] The pressure over the Euromarkets' apparent culpability for international financial instability grew to such a degree that the governor of the Bank of England dedicated his speech to the Bankers' Club of Chicago to a defense of the Euromarkets, cautioning against measures to regulate Euromarket activity.[8] The Bank of England decided not to resist proposals for an international committee to supervise the Euromarkets, but also recognized that, during a time of international monetary uncertainty that posed challenges to London's international standing, "the loss of the Euro-dollar market to London would be another serious blow" (Altamura, 2016).

In a testament to just how important the Euromarkets had become for the UK's international economic policy, the concern for their defense from regulatory encroachment was articulated at the highest level of UK government. Briefing prime minister Edward Heath for his meeting with the French president Pompidou, Treasury officials stressed that although the UK preference was for the maintenance of the Bretton Woods system, Heath should be "defensive if Pompidou complains of the Euro-dollar market as an amplifier of the US deficit." Although the UK should express support for international discussions over methods to curb excessive Eurodollar flows, which were underway through the BIS, OECD, and EEC, Heath was instructed to make clear that the Eurodollar market was not the source of the trouble.[9]

The US, for its part, attempted to muddle through the international monetary discussions of the early 1970s. The Nixon administration prioritized national autonomy above the maintenance of the Bretton Woods regime; it was unwilling to countenance the sort of subordination of domestic economic priorities to international imperatives that had led the UK into the disastrous stop-go cycle in pursuit of a stable pound. Ultimately, the rules of Bretton Woods were viewed as a potential limitation to the management of the US economy. Within the calculations of the US policy elite, Bretton Woods would only be maintained if it did not restrict America's capacity to set domestic economic policy and foreign policy autonomously (Gowa, 1983: 13–22; James, 1996: 243; Frieden, 2006: 341).

Nixon's administration was unwilling to endorse international monetary reform and opposed, in principle, the extension of capital controls (Stein, 2010: 40).[10] Despite these convictions, they adopted a pragmatic approach to policy, maintaining the existing capital controls into the early 1970s and implementing wage and price controls as part of the package that delinked the dollar from gold in August 1971. This practical stance was on display again in 1972, when the US supported West Germany's turn to capital controls to prevent disruptive deutsche mark inflows as traders moved out of sterling (James, 1996: 240).

Under Nixon's administration, the power to shape international monetary politics rested overwhelmingly with the Treasury. Particularly in the committee known as the "Volcker Group" after its chairman, Paul Volcker, the undersecretary of the Treasury for monetary affairs who "for all practical purposes was Treasury."[11] The Volcker Group was united in a commitment to prioritize national interests over the wider interests of the international system (James, 1996: 211). In policy terms, their consensus ensured that devaluation, deflation, and constraints upon US foreign policy—all measures that might have prolonged Bretton Woods—were foreclosed as potential options (Gowa, 1983: 62–99).

Mirroring its centrality in the construction of Bretton Woods, the US Treasury was now central to its dismantling. The Nixon administration closed the gold window over the weekend of August 13, 1971, after a final meeting to discuss their options at the president's Camp David retreat, imposing a 10-percent import surcharge onto other countries in order to push them to revalue their currencies, sparing the US the humiliation of having to devalue the dollar (Eichengreen, 2008: 131). As a quid pro quo for the currency realignments, Western Europe did manage to secure a commitment from the US to retain its controls on capital exports (Helleiner, 1994: 104).

But that commitment was to be short lived. The US wanted to make sure that, despite the ending of Bretton Woods, US deficits could still be covered by foreign capital inflows while the private outflows of US investors would continue to have access to foreign capital markets. The retreat from Bretton

Woods could not mean a retreat from the openness of international financial markets upon which US economic strategy so depended (Panitch and Gindin, 2012: 130–31). By 1974, the US would announce that the program of capital controls in place since the 1960s would be abolished, reversing the commitments made at the Smithsonian Agreement of December 1971 (Helleiner, 1994: 110; Hudson, 2003: 363)

In effect, the US had pushed other states onto a dollar standard by breaking the link to gold. They had then encouraged the major capitalist states to accept new exchange rates with the Smithsonian Agreement (Hudson, 2003: 348).[12] Although the Western Europeans and the Japanese were reluctant to move toward a system of floating exchange rates, they recognized that maintaining fixed rates was simply too difficult, politically, within a context of liberalized financial markets, speculative capital flows, and growing international payment imbalances (James, 1996: 235). This was particularly the case of the US, which was simply unwilling to set domestic monetary and fiscal policy objectives in line with the new parities in the Smithsonian Agreement. By loosening monetary policy in a bid to win reelection, Nixon, with the support of the Fed, stoked a rapid increase in the money supply and shattered confidence in the new parities (James, 1996: 238). Although the US offered pragmatic support for capital controls during acute periods of strain within the foreign exchange markets, the administration did not seriously consider adopting permanent and rigid exchange controls. By 1973, controls were only countenanced on a temporary basis and for balance of payments purposes (Panitch and Gindin, 2012: 145–46).

Instead of actively addressing its payments deficit, as had been unsuccessfully attempted during the previous decade, the US now adopted a different strategy in the wake of the collapse of Bretton Woods. They pushed for a realignment of exchange rates from other countries intended to boost US competitiveness in foreign trade (Block, 1977: 198). This new strategy was born out of a growing awareness of the spectacular structural financial power of the US. The construction of a dollar standard, untethered from the obligation to honor convertibility to gold, gave the US enhanced capacity to shape the flow of world credit by controlling the supply and availability of dollars (Strange, 1987: 586–89). As we saw in the previous chapter, the financial innovation and market expansion associated with the Euromarkets had created an international market infrastructure, hosted in the City, that had deepened the international power of the dollar.

Prior decades of Anglo-American financial development helped generate the global reach of US financial power by promoting the dollar's wider use and enhanced liquidity. This structural power of the dollar would—not without some irony, given its centrality to the restoration of London's international role—now be brought to bear upon the UK through the conditionality of the IMF crisis. But the context of an emerging post–Bretton Woods international monetary order, in which there was no longer a shared political commitment to maintain the dollar's fixed value, would increase the centrality of rapidly growing private financial markets in determining the dollar's international standing. The continued operation of the City's vast forex markets became an increasingly critical infrastructure underpinning the dollar's international reach. With it, the importance of maintaining the UK's commitment to an open liberal international system increased too. The dollar's structural power rested upon the maintenance of a distinctively Anglo-American financial space that heightened the sensitivity of US capitalism to the political and economic dynamics of the UK during a decisive decade for the future of globalization.

Consensus Unraveling

The UK suffered under the new international order that emerged from the wreckage of Bretton Woods. This was in part due to the world recession experienced from 1970 to 1971 as governments sought to contain rising inflation by implementing fiscal austerity measures and with monetary tightening (Roberts, 2016). That recession was the precursor to nearly a decade of international economic instability and rising class conflict as workers took to the streets to defend their living standards in the face of rapidly rising inflation and low growth—in other words, "stagflation" (Glyn and Harrison, 1980: 1). By the beginning of the decade, the UK lagged behind other advanced industrialized capitalist states, with industrial productivity only one-third of the US level and roughly two-thirds of French and West German levels (36). The long-term postwar decline of UK capitalism, particularly within industrial production, was coming to a head by the 1970s as the golden age of capitalism that had been underpinned by Bretton Woods expired.

The UK's plight during the early 1970s was not purely a consequence of an increasingly challenging capitalist world market. It was also a direct result of the policies enacted by the Conservative government of Edward Heath, elected in 1970. Heath's government adopted a radical market-centered policy of revitalization for UK capitalism in anticipation of the full-blooded monetarist program that Thatcher would implement at the end of the decade; it also gave new priority to the fight against inflation and viewed the disciplining impact of market forces, rather than an interventionist industrial strategy, as the best route to enhanced competitiveness (Clarke, 1987: 406; Matthijs, 2012: 90).

A cornerstone of the new government's strategy to combat inflation was the implementation of restrictive trade union legislation through the Industrial Relations Act. Heath's policies set the tone for the way in which the distributional struggles of the 1970s—between capital and labor in the context of low growth and high inflation—would be repeatedly conducted through state policies that sought to impose the costs of the economic difficulties upon the living standards of UK workers. Alongside the restrictive policy on the unions, the Heath government attempted to rationalize UK capitalism by allowing bankruptcies for uncompetitive industries, cherry-picking efficient sectors of the nationalized industries to be handed over to private control, and pushing membership of the EEC to subject UK firms to the panacea of European competition.

The impact of these policies was an unqualified disaster. The restrictive strategies that comprised the first phase of the Heath government floundered. The rationalization measures did not restore competitiveness, but did provoke a period of economic stagnation. The antiunion measures were even less effective. Rather than demoralizing and debilitating the labor movement, the new Industrial Relations Act galvanized union solidarity and sparked a wave of political strikes. Soured relations with the union movement eventually led to the Heath Government's downfall in February 1974 (Glyn and Harrison, 1980: 57–68).

Perhaps the most disastrous innovation of the Heath government, though, came with monetary policy. In a continuation of the Tories' longstanding role as champions of financial power in the UK, the Heath government sought to unshackle UK banks from restrictive constraints on lending through the introduction of "Competition, Credit, and Control" (CCC) in 1971 (Roberts, 2016: 31). This policy framework came as a direct response to the changing landscape of international banking and finance, of which the development of the Euromarkets in the City had been by far the greatest catalyst (Moran, 1986: 22; Battilossi, 2002). Anglo-American developmental dynamics that had been at the heart of the Euromarkets' emergence now fed back into the disintegration of traditional monetary policy as the transatlantic regulatory feedback loop further disrupted the Keynesian financial order. The intellectual ascendancy of monetarism increasingly inspired the construction of new regimes of monetary control.

In response to the intensification of international competition in banking brought about by the rise of the Euromarkets, UK clearing banks pushed for the unraveling of quantitative restrictions over their lending to compete with their better-capitalized international rivals. During the 1960s, the London clearing banks had been specifically targeted for the adoption of interest rate limits and portfolio controls. They were also subject to a "Special Deposits" scheme, whereby the Bank of England could call in special deposits to be frozen as part of efforts to control the flow of credit through administrative decree. These restrictions hampered the ability of the clearers to compete with international banks and the new building societies.[13] As the market share of the clearers contracted, the efficacy of a monetary policy framework based upon regulating their intermediation decreased accordingly (Artis and Lewis, 1981: 1–6). Lending ceilings had been removed in April 1967 but were reinstated around the time of devaluation—a move that was met by the clearers with a furious response. Ceilings had, in any case, become more and more difficult to enforce, given the way the development of offshore had punctured the national regulatory system. CCC arose out of a growing dissatisfaction with controls over lending and a concern within the Bank and the Treasury that UK banking needed to be made more competitive (Capie, 2010: 427–37). The transformations associated with the globalization of banking, hosted in the City, were rapidly corroding the foundations of UK monetary policy.

The goal of CCC was to transform monetary policy by removing quantitative restrictions upon bank advances and abolishing the cartel arrangements that controlled clearing bank interest rates. Where controls did remain, they were either reduced or extended universally to level the playing field. Crucially, the new policy hinged upon a commitment to the primacy of competition and market forces as the means of achieving credit control objectives. Under the new policy, monetary aggregates were attributed greater significance than before, with their rate of growth now controlled through the market mechanism of interest rates, influenced by the Bank's open market operations (Artis and Lewis, 1981: 7–8; Moran, 1986: 30; Capie, 2010: 500–507).

The focus that CCC attributed to monetary aggregates was evidence of the creeping advance of monetarist ideas within the UK state. The rise of monetarism was the key policy strut of the fight against inflation during the 1970s. Intellectually, it was rooted in a conviction in the quantity theory of money, while in policy terms it was centered around a preoccupation with control of the money supply as the surest means of containing inflation and promoting orderly growth. The more general significance of monetarism lay in its vehement opposition to state intervention, in favor of the need to subordinate political choice to the dictates of the market (Clarke, 1988: 393; Stedman-Jones, 2012: 212).

Monetarist ideas in the UK had hitherto largely been confined to a group of ostracized academic economists. The rise of monetarism within the UK from the late 1960s had much to do both with rising inflation and a growing transatlantic intellectual synthesis. The interrelated decomposition of Bretton Woods and the associated Keynesian state underpinning it opened spaces for an epistemic shift in economic thought, with monetarist thinkers waging war against Keynesian orthodoxy (Laidler, 1981; Friedman, 1986; Stedman-Jones, 2012). Milton Friedman and the Chicago school of economics led the attacks against Keynesianism.[14] Friedman's 1963 book *A Monetary History of the United States* was the definitive text of the monetarist counterrevolution. It criticized the role of the Fed during the Great Depression in the first salvo of a sustained campaign against its policies that gathered momentum during the 1970s (Smith, 1987: 17–21).

The UK proved a fertile ground for Friedman's theory. The devaluation of 1967 and general awareness of economic decline produced a climate of dissatisfaction with the postwar Keynesian consensus. Monetarism's advancement moved almost in step with the disintegration of Bretton Woods and the steady rise of stagflation. At the *Financial Times*, Samuel Brittan became an influential champion of monetarism, facilitating a major shift in thinking within the City's financial community from 1968. Peter Jay also began to promote monetarism around this time, with a leading article in *The Times* entitled "Understanding the Role of the Money Supply." The influential City mouthpiece the *Banker* then took up the monetarist cause in December 1968 with a contribution from Friedman himself. The Institute of Economic Affairs (IEA), a think tank established to counter state control of the economy, began to trumpet monetarism as well (Smith, 1987: 35–36; Burk and Cairncross, 1992: 139–44).

Despite the growing interest in monetarism from the City and the financial press, the roots of the increased attention paid to the monetary aggregates by Bank and Treasury officials were not primarily endogenous. The initial impetus came, as we saw in the previous chapter, through contact with the IMF in 1965 (Capie, 2010: 450; Schenk, 2010: 189). During the 1960s, UK monetary policy was principally concerned with maintaining the fixed exchange rate, and, up until 1965, voices within the Bank in support of control of the money supply were "few and, when heard, quietly ignored or put down" (Capie, 2010: 450).

Within the Treasury, a 1965 draft document on credit control explicitly rejected consideration of the quantity of money and the role of interest rates. In that same year however, the letter of intent to the IMF required that the UK commit to quantitative targets relating to credit policy, including estimates for increases in bank lending to the private sector (Schenk, 2010: 189). This was the first time external pressure was exerted upon the Bank and the Treasury to make commitments on monetary growth. Despite the exertions of the IMF, the attitudes of the Treasury and the Bank toward monetary control were ambivalent.

When the UK was forced to turn to the IMF again between 1967 and 1968, the scrutiny of monetary targets was much greater, and the Bank and the Treasury were pushed to accept that there must be a clear and successful attempt to contain monetary growth. In response to the IMF's conditions, the Bank and the Treasury began conducting joint exercises on the issue of the money supply. These discussions were reinforced by an IMF seminar on the domestic credit supply held in Washington, DC, in 1970, at which Bank and Treasury officials were in attendance. The discussions, begun in 1968, were to carry on over to the next decade before reaching their apogee under the Thatcher government (Capie, 2010: 451–63).

The impacts of Heath's policies (and of CCC in particular) were shambolic, leading to a recession that brought about the infamous policy "U-turn." Taking its cue from a similar change in tack from Nixon's administration, the Heath government shifted from an emphasis upon market discipline to Keynesian reflation through the "Barber Boom" from 1972 to 1973 (Glyn and Harrison, 1980: 72; Gamble, 1991: 125; Overbeek, 1990: 159). The Barber Boom relied upon tax cuts, a continued expansion of the money supply, and increased public spending to provide a temporary boost to productivity. But the investment was largely channeled into a speculative property and stock market boom, which fueled inflation and further aggravated the balance of payments deficit by stimulating imports (Anderson, 1992: 175).[15] These dynamics were further intensified by the inflationary impact of CCC, with the removal of quantitative lending restrictions rapidly leading toward an unprecedented expansion in the money supply, followed by a major financial collapse during the Secondary Banking Crisis of 1972, which required concerted action between the leading clearing banks and the Bank of England to launch the "Lifeboat" rescue operation (Capie, 2010: 525). The Bank's minimum lending rate rose from 7.5 percent in July 1973 to 13 percent by the end of the year, as the government attempted to wrestle with rising inflation and a deteriorating balance of payments (Capie, 2010: 531).

But just as in the US, the Bank was forced to pull back from tight money due to the banking crisis that the interest rate hikes helped provoke. Both in the US and the UK, the conditions were not yet in place for the high interest rate regimes that would be enacted during the 1980s. Echoing the Fed's abandonment of tight money during the commercial paper crisis, the Bank's lender-of-last-resort function trumped its capacity to tighten the monetary supply and forced it to inject liquidity into the system in order to avoid a widespread collapse.

Where Heath's policy platform did curry more favor was regarding European integration. The proposal was enthusiastically championed by the banks of the City, who supported the principled commitment of the EEC to the free movement of all factors of production (Glyn and Harrison, 1980: 83). A report into the future of London as an International Financial Centre, composed by the Inter-Bank Research Office (IBRO), captured both the widespread support for EEC membership and the broader climate of anxiety that would characterize the City throughout the critical decade of the 1970s. The report, based on interviews with a wide range of City banks, was unambiguous in its support for European integration, suggesting that the best strategy to promote the long-term interests of the City and the UK would involve "encouraging unified financial markets in Europe, the free movement of trading and investment funds between Europe and the rest of the world, and a growing level of business in other European and world financial centres."[16]

Although supportive of deeper European integration, the City was nonetheless sternly opposed to the prospects of a fragmentation of the global economy into regional trading blocs, which would harm the City's wider global interests. The report suggested that London's entrepôt role, as a conduit for both European and global business, would be crucial to maintaining its international standing during the 1970s. The City's support for harmonization of banking regulation was not, however, unconditional; the report cautioned that accelerated harmonization should only be supported to the extent that it meant the liberal provision of "freedom to conduct financial operations throughout Europe," in which case the City and UK government should push for an accelerated tempo of integration. Conversely, if harmonization led to "new restrictions" on the way that London-based financial institutions could conduct business, the report said, it may be better "to delay the process." The overriding strategic emphasis was on the development of London as a "multi-currency centre," with the entrepôt orientation of the City now the priority.[17]

Preserving and fortifying London's entrepôt role inevitably meant defending the position of the Euromarkets too. European integration was viewed as a potential boon to the Eurobond market, with growing demand for capital on the continent. But the Eurobond market was also a source of concern, with an awareness that moves by the US to eliminate the Interest Equalization Tax (a measure subsequently taken through the liberalization of capital flows in 1974) and restrictions on US MNCs' investment abroad might lead the US dollar-denominated bond market to return to New York. Similarly, it was felt that a correction to the US current account deficit might drain the Eurodollar pool.[18]

With these considerations in mind, and more general international monetary disorder casting doubt over the dollar's international status, it was felt that the greater use of either major European currencies or the European Currency Unit—or perhaps even a resuscitation of sterling as a trade and investment currency—would need to be developed as a potential alternative to the Eurodollar. Of these potential diversification strategies, the promotion of a European Currency Unit was considered more beneficial to the City, as the increasing usage of a wider range of European currencies was harming the concentration of the market within London to the benefit of rival European financial centers. The City's interests were seen to lie in the sponsorship of rapid banking harmonization within the EEC, providing that "the British authorities can bring their influence to bear and make such regulation as liberal as possible."[19]

Sensitivity to international monetary uncertainty within the City, and the dynamics of the transatlantic regulatory feedback loop, encouraged its bankers to hedge the City's offshore role between the potential for continued dollar hegemony, on the one hand, and the possibility of increased dependence upon a European currency alternative, on the other. The offshore orientation of the City, developed through the Eurodollar, was now shaping European integration and building support for a unified European currency.

The report also noted the major growth of the foreign securities business in London since the early 1960s, with foreign security houses, particularly US ones, attracted by London's international role and the UK's "large overseas portfolio investments." These dynamics renewed in intensity through the UK's integration with the EEC, with many foreign security houses viewing London as "a springboard for opportunities in the wider EEC." Future capital markets integration and the potential for increased merger activity between US and EEC firms were considered "growth factors of the future."[20] European integration could be leveraged to strengthen London's position at the heart of financial globalization. By the mid-1980s, with the liberalization of the Stock Exchange through the Big Bang reforms, many of these aspirations would be realized, with London bridging US and European corporate financing and attracting a second wave of big US banking arrivals.

But European banking harmonization also caused anxiety within the City, particularly for the US banks. With the US now having a major presence there, the seismic changes of the 1970s, from the breakdown of Bretton Woods to the UK's accession to the EEC, posed serious regulatory challenges. These anxieties manifested themselves in concerns over the extent to which the BBA (British Bankers' Association) was effectively representing the views of US banks regarding EEC integration. Daniel Davidson, the senior vice president of Morgan Guaranty Trust Company, wrote to the president of the BBA, Eric Faulkner, in November 1972 and questioned the granting of only associate membership of the US banks within the BBA. Davidson suggested that "because we would only be associate members of the BBA it would be possible that our views—and those of the foreign banking community—would not be adequately communicated to the governing body of the BBA." Stressing the importance of foreign banks, and the US banks specifically, to London's financial markets, Davidson argued that "it might be desirable to give foreign banks some representation on the board" and suggested that "a number of banks have the same reservation."[21]

The response to this request showed that, despite the significance of the US banks within London, there was still a hierarchical organization of the representation of their interests vis-à-vis UK banks. In his reply to Davidson, Faulkner defended the associate member status of the US banks and the existence of two different categories of membership since "the Association is primarily a 'British' one" and suggested that "we would not feel it appropriate" for associate members to be presented within the BBA's general council or executive committee. Despite the refusal to give the US banks core participation in the top levels of the BBA, Faulkner was at pains to stress that the BBA would, nonetheless, consider any banking-related concerns voiced by the US banks.[22]

A further unsuccessful attempt to gain separate representation was made on behalf of consortium banks within the BBA. John Pryor, the managing director and vice-chairman of Western American Bank (Europe) wrote to the BBA in March 1973 addressing the issue of EEC banking harmonization, expressing concern that City banks were concerned that "we may continue to enjoy the environment which has been ours for many centuries," and asking for clarity over "who is particularly representing our point of view" on the subject.[23] The BBA replied, welcoming the recent development of an Association of American Bankers in London in response to the new regulatory challenges posed by EEC integration and invited the consortium banks to consider the same course of action. Crucially, though, the BBA rejected the possibility of giving both the US and consortium banks full membership, offering only "Associate" membership and refusing the consortium banks' desire for representation on the BBA's executive committee.[24] The City's anxious mood would only worsen as the UK's economic crisis intensified and political consensus disintegrated.

A Crisis of Sterling

As the UK economy spiraled out of control on the back of both Heath's disastrous policies and generalized international disorder, the pound came under sustained attack. Domestic and international financial instability became increasingly interactive. The UK was forced to float the pound out of the parity agreed upon at the Smithsonian meeting, causing exit from the European currency "snake" of which it had briefly been a part (Eichengreen, 2008: 131; Schenk, 20120: 356).

The short-lived participation within the snake demonstrated the renewed impetus given to European monetary integration by the UK's accession to the EEC and the breakdown of Bretton Woods. But it also revealed the continuing limitations blighting European alternatives to the Bretton Woods system. The publication of the 1970 "Werner Plan" by the European Commission signaled a new attempt to further European monetary integration, focusing upon a three-stage advance toward economic union that sought to create an irreversible fixing of parities between member countries. The Werner Report, which looked more deeply into the issue, proposed the progressive elimination of fluctuations between members' exchange rates, the elimination of margins in fluctuation between member state parities, and eventually the "total liberalisation of movements of capital," The European council adopted a March 1971 "resolution of intent" signaling members' collective resolve to tighten economic and monetary policy coordination and narrow the margin of fluctuations between member currencies as a step toward more robustly fixed rates (Apel, 1998: 32–34). This was a bold vision for an intensified process of European integration and liberalization, one that threatened to establish a parallel zone of strengthening European monetary cooperation alongside the structures established at Bretton Woods.

The timing of the proposal was inauspicious. Bretton Woods' final demise proved an extremely difficult context for a revamped European monetary integration strategy. As first the deutschmark and Dutch guilder floated against the dollar in May 1971—after Eurodollar flows wrought havoc on the foreign exchange markets—and then Bretton Woods broke down in August, attempts at pushing for greater integration stalled, and the EEC became more preoccupied with defensive attempts to stabilize their currencies vis-à-vis one another in a context of dollar devaluation. In 1972, the six member states of the Community signed the Basel Agreement, or "snake in the tunnel." The agreement created a narrower range of intra-European currency fluctuation within the wider structure of permissible movement that had been agreed upon with the US at the Smithsonian. Central bank credit lines would be opened within the EEC to facilitate currency interventions using European currencies rather than dollars (Apel, 1998: 36–38; Giordano and Persaud, 2013: 7).

Sterling entered the snake from May 1972, but it was never a stable pillar, nor did the Heath government make the required sacrifice of domestic monetary autonomy necessary for the maintenance of strict exchange rate commitments. The Barber Boom put paid to any aspiration of meeting the mandated exchange rate targets, with the chancellor arguing that it was "neither necessary nor desirable to distort domestic economies to an unacceptable extent in order to retain unrealistic exchange rates" (James, 1996: 239). It was clear that the UK was unwilling to bind itself too tightly into European monetary structures, a pattern that would repeat itself over subsequent decades. It was forced to withdraw in June due to a run on the pound.

Turbulence within the international monetary system forced even more EEC countries to turn to foreign exchange controls, which opened an important cleavage with the UK. As West Germany began to extend capital controls from March 1972, with a particular focus on tightening up controls over foreign borrowing, the UK moved in a very different direction. The floating of the pound in June 1972 was accompanied by restrictions on the use of sterling. From 1974, all direct investment abroad was rendered conditional upon being financed by foreign borrowing, purchase of foreign currency in the investment currency market, or from retained overseas profits. Crucially, while West Germany sought to *curb* foreign borrowing by its residents, the UK sought to divert overseas investment out of sterling and into foreign currency, thus *encouraging* foreign borrowing rather than discouraging foreign investment sui generis (Tsoukalis, 1977: 132–36).

This markedly divergent approach to exchange controls neatly encapsulated the different attitudes of West Germany and the UK to the offshore currency markets: while West Germany attempted to clamp down, the UK promoted greater borrowing in foreign currency to prevent the further accumulation of overseas sterling balances and, importantly, signal its continued commitment to the Eurodollar market at a time of growing international pressure. The UK became a key ally in the defense of offshore currency markets. With European solidarity under strain, attempts to relaunch monetary integration from 1973 onward were unsuccessful, with the 1970s turning out to be a stalled period for the acceleration of European monetary integration.

With sterling again under attack and forced out of the Snake, the dollar followed shortly afterward with a renewed wave of speculative activity against the greenback in 1973, as contagious currency instability spread under conditions of mounting international monetary disorder. By 1974, a four-week miner's strike had brought the Heath government to an ignominious end (Overbeek, 1990: 161). The government's policies were indicative of the way in which the UK's fragile Keynesian compromise was creaking under the pressure of growing class conflict and a deteriorating international economic climate. In response, new policy strategies emerged from both the left and the right, which began to move beyond the confines of the postwar consensus. The early free market radicalism of the Heath government was paralleled by the emergence of the Alternative Economic Strategy within the Labour Party and the rise of the party's left wing.[25] The failed modernization programs of the 1960s opened spaces for more radical responses to the malaise of UK capitalism, with socialist industrial programs becoming increasingly popular within the Labour Party membership and the trade union movement. Influential figures on the Labour left believed that social democracy had failed to deliver, with a strategy to transform the economy in a socialist direction the only remaining option (Gamble, 1991: 172–77).

Labour won the 1974 election on the promise of a more conciliatory relationship with the unions than the Conservatives had been able to deliver (Harmon, 2008: 5). The central policy platform for this promise was the "Social

Contract": a policy framework in which the Trades Union Congress (TUC) agreed to wage restraint in exchange for welfare concessions, with pension increases central. Alongside the pact with the unions, Labour's election manifesto pledged to deliver the most radical upheaval in UK industrial policy since 1945. The Alternative Economic Strategy hinged upon the proposal, made by Tony Benn and Stuart Holland, to form a major state holding company and undertake a compulsory nationalization of twenty to twenty-five of the largest manufacturing companies. Compulsory planning agreements would facilitate an expansion of state control over private capital, and a major redistribution program was to be undertaken with income, wealth, and social service provision adjusted in favor of the workers. Trade union power would be augmented, through the repeal of the Industrial Relations Act and the extension of worker control over industrial activity (Glyn and Harrison, 1980: 91–96).

The actual policy delivered by the Labour government in power broke sharply with the promises of the manifesto. That it did so was down to the effective marginalization of the Labour left, and Benn particularly, by the right wing of the party, with Wilson, Callaghan, and Healey the chief architects. It was also a consequence of the overall weakness of a minority government in Westminster. Resistance to the radicalism of the Alternative Economic Strategy also came from officials within the Treasury and the Bank, and, as we shall see, from the increasing hostility of the City to plans for radical reorganization of UK capitalism. The Labour strategy was further limited by the broader international context and the hardening stance of a US administration increasingly comprised by right-wing Wall Street affiliates who were hostile to social democratic welfare states and staunchly anticommunist (Panitch and Leys, 1997: 107).

Labour entered office faced with rapidly rising inflation, the aftermath of the secondary banking crisis, a liquidity crisis in industry, and a slump in the stock market alongside a rapidly deteriorating balance of payments. These difficulties were partly a legacy of the Conservatives' catastrophic policy experimentations, but they were also the product of a growing crisis of global capitalism. On top of the international monetary disorder that resulted from the Americans' termination of Bretton Woods and the onset of a world recession sparked by stagflation, oil prices rose by 400 percent between 1973 and 1974 as major oil-producing countries formed the Organization of Petroleum-Exporting Countries (OPEC) cartel (Glyn and Harrison, 1980: 20; Burk and Cairncross, 1992: xiii). By 1974, the UK was paying £2.5 billion more for 5 percent less oil than had been imported during 1973 (Dell, 1991: 9).

For the UK, the consequences of the oil crisis were particularly acute. It transformed the status of sterling as a reserve currency by leading to the build-up of large sterling reserve positions by oil-producing countries while traditional holders of sterling unwound their reserve positions (Schenk, 2010: 357). After the devaluation of 1967, the BIS had led multilateral action to rebuild the UK's reserves and stabilize sterling by encouraging countries to hold sterling balances. The problem was that the addition of OPEC balances on top of the multilateral rebuilding effort now meant that the sterling balances were much larger than before, rather than gradually being wound down in an orderly fashion, as had been planned. The build-up of large, liquid sterling reserves renewed the pound's vulnerability to sudden movements in currency markets. By 1976, the official sterling balances were over twice as large as they had been in 1968 (Burk and Cairncross, 1992: 12).

It was this dynamic that would draw the UK into the disciplinary orbit of US power. Although the 1976 crisis was the result of a specific historic conjuncture, then, it was also a product of the longstanding weakness of sterling that had been such a pronounced trait of the UK's postwar development. The weakness of sterling had already led UK bankers to draw in the dollar and US financial power through the Euromarkets. Now it would draw together a much less welcome intersection between UK capitalism and US financial power. What followed was a reconfiguration of UK sovereignty that involved a much more direct relationship between the state agencies of the US and the UK than had been the case with the Euromarkets. The Fed and the US Treasury would intervene to reorder the priorities of the Bank of England and UK Treasury.

If the Euromarkets embodied the reintegration of the City and the Bank within an internationalist (and particularly transatlantic) orientation, it was the IMF negotiations of 1976 that would prove crucial to opening up the UK Treasury to intensified international pressure. The disciplinary power of the US was deployed to steer UK development in a direction amenable to the US vision for a liberal international economic order. This intervention came at a decisive moment when the interactive decomposition of the social basis of the Keynesian state and the Bretton Woods order opened spaces for alternative forms of political-economic organisation.

The 1976 crisis was a critical juncture in the prolonged postwar demise of sterling. The UK's eventual appeal to the IMF for financing was both preceded and succeeded by broader multilateral negotiations over the future of sterling (Schenk, 2010: 369). The crisis was differentiated from prior episodes by the views of the foreign interests involved, principally the Americans, that this should be the last sterling crisis and that all pressure necessary to guarantee finality should (and could) be exerted (Burk and Cairncross, 1992: 3). In 1974, Chancellor Barber had warned Heath that massive sums would be required to defend sterling at its existing value. With the oil crisis feeding into the existing inflationary dynamics within the UK and a worsening balance of payments position, sterling began to depreciate in a sustained fashion from April 1975 (Schenk, 2010: 369).

Wages were now rising at over 30 percent per year, and Denis Healey's April 1975 budget provided a record £9 billion public sector borrowing requirement that was met with a "chorus of dismay" from the financial press, prompting international markets to rapidly lose confidence in the government's wages and spending policy. Financial commentators denounced profligate and inflationary borrowing, while the *Economist* went so far as to suggest that the official estimates of public spending were now viewed as "works of fiction." These sentiments were shared by the *Wall Street Journal* in an article entitled "Goodbye, Great Britain," which argued that the UK government was so clearly headed toward a policy of "total confiscation" that anybody with assets in the UK was left "discounting furiously at any chance to get it out of the country" (Burk and Cairncross, 1992: xiii).

Hysterical reactions by the financial media fed into the behavior of investors who began to speculate heavily against the pound. In the City, the climate of opinion was increasingly hostile to the Labour government. The banks and other financial institutions had become increasingly concerned with the state of the public finances during the 1970s. As the crisis worsened from 1974, the continued budget deficits produced a situation whereby, for the first time, potential lenders were no longer confident of the capacity of the UK government to credibly service its debts. The government was now forced to pay higher interest rates than before and to orient its borrowing more toward the requirements of investors and creditors. This was a watershed in the postwar relationship between the City and the government, which, up to this point, had largely been characterized by mutually beneficial cooperation. For the financiers of the City, the 1974 Labour government was viewed in deeply unfavorable and oppositional terms (Michie, 2004: 47).

In this climate of distrust, long-simmering dissatisfactions with government policy reached a boiling point, particularly from those interests within the City that depended upon the well-being of the faltering domestic economy. For the offshore sector of the City, however, which had grown rapidly via the Euromarkets, the instability of the 1970s represented a boom, as financial innovations such as derivatives created profitable opportunities for benefiting from currency instability (Michie, 2004: 47–49). But despite their booming trade in hedging against currency movements and recycling petrodollars emerging from the OPEC surpluses, the offshore interests of the City also had reasons to be fearful of the Labour government. The Alternative Economic Strategy, with its emphasis upon exchange controls, import restrictions, and selective insulation from the world economy, constituted a direct threat to the climate of international financial openness upon which the Euromarkets were so dependent. These threats increased as Benn and other members of the Labour left began to formulate alternatives to the acceptance of IMF conditionality that would challenge the sanctity of private financial power in the City.

Most concerning of all of the proposed plans for the clearing banks, though, was the talk of banking nationalization within the Labour Party. The proposal of banking nationalization created a persistent climate of fear and the increased politicization of banks within the City. In response to the Labour party home policy committee's paper and a report of the working party on the nationalization of banks in September 1973, the BBA began a prolonged campaign to monitor and oppose nationalization ambitions through the manipulation of public opinion and direct lobbying with politicians. This involved the formation of a BBA Working Party on bank nationalization, whose members were tasked with considering the plans for nationalization and "to take such action as they consider appropriate, with reference to the need to publicise the Banks' counter-arguments," as well as "improving the public attitude to the banks."[26]

The working party was formally established in February 1976 in response to the endorsement of a 1975 Labour Party Conference resolution requesting that the party's national executive committee draw up proposals for the nationalization of banking.[27] Members of the BBA had begun closely monitoring Labour Party Conference proposals from 1975 and voicing concerns about banks being caught "at the fulcrum of the tussle between the right and the left wings of the Labour Party." The magnitude of the threat was considered such that the banks needed to take a more explicitly politicized and interventionist stance, breaking from what they termed their traditional "impartial and strictly non-political role." In explicitly party-political terms it was noted that "the right wing of the Labour Party needs to be given the ammunition with which it can prevail."[28] This would involve encouraging the national executive of the party to "water down" nationalization proposals while also making sure that the Cabinet would not include any "adverse proposals" in their legislative plan.

It was suggested that the campaign should draw upon a wide network of financial institutions "subject to similar threat." It was hoped that the clearing banks' national network of branch managers could be used to influence Labour MPs, and, if all attempts at "backstairs influence" failed, it was suggested that an "all-out public campaign" would need to be adopted.[29]

Concerns over nationalization plans were put directly to the prime minister in January 1976, when Charles Villiers of the BBA wrote to Harold Wilson, stating that reports of planned bank nationalization "have caused considerable concern in the City" and suggesting that "reports such as these are definitely damaging, both at home and abroad."[30] In response to Villiers's enquiry, Wilson suggested that there had been "no Government initiative in these fields, and no Government consideration of such proposals." But Wilson acknowledged that the government and the wider public would have to consider such proposals if they emerged from any "responsible body," while also suggesting that adoption of such proposals remained unlikely.[31] Despite Wilson's reassurances, the working party continued to draw up plans for combatting nationalization, as well as dividing up cabinet members between banks and tasking them to lobby members of the Parliamentary Labour Party.[32] The BBA also reached out to the Conservative opposition, with shadow chancellor Geoffrey Howe suggesting in a lunch meeting with a BBA member that "nationalisation of the banks was conceivable" despite the prime minister's recent reassurances to Charles Villiers. Howe explicitly aligned with the BBA's antinationalization agenda by arguing strongly that the banks should begin "getting their viewpoint over to the public at large."[33]

As the Bretton Woods order collapsed and the crisis of Keynesianism accelerated, the lines between public authority and private business power were rendered ambiguous. Concerns over the intentions of the government combined with the rising tide of monetarist critique of Keynesian policy and the vociferous attacks of the financial press to create an increasingly oppositional climate in which the government appeared more and more to be a threat to private finance. This environment of distrust was a major contributor to the immediate crisis of 1976, forcing the government to go to the IMF both for financing and to restore credibility in the eyes of the increasingly powerful financial markets.

With sterling's plight worsening, the UK turned to the IMF for funding under the "Special Oil Facility" that had been established in response to the OPEC price hikes. Throughout 1975, UK Treasury officials worked out strategic responses to the growing economic crisis faced by the UK and began to work on drafting applications to the Fund for drawings from the oil facility and the first credit tranche. From late October 1975, the Treasury began to formulate a position on the impact of drawing from the Fund. The principal consideration related to whether the UK should draw from the IMF oil facility, from the first credit tranche, or from both simultaneously. Countries that drew from the facility would have to commit to the maintenance of an open trade policy and would not be allowed to undertake import restrictions. At this point, the Treasury was seriously considering the imposition of import controls as a temporary corrective to the balance of payments problems. This was the strategy formulated by Tony Benn and the Labour left, which would have meant a sharp reduction in the UK's openness to the international economy. Treasury officials anticipated that the proposal would, however, be opposed by the Fund staff, even if it were made on a temporary basis. In a revealing acknowledgment of the predominance of US power within the IMF, Treasury officials suggested that, in practice, "the decision of the Fund Board must ultimately depend on the views of the major countries and, in particular, the USA."[34]

It was hugely improbable that the US would look kindly upon a UK turn to import controls. US officials were now in favor of a system of floating exchange rates that would rely upon the disciplinary effect of market forces on national currency values. These principles were endorsed in an agreement reached by the US Treasury and French finance ministry officials at the Rambouillet summit in November 1975. The Rambouillet meeting was a product of the linkages between finance ministries that the US Treasury had developed during the 1960s. This multilateral infrastructure connecting major capitalist states formed the basis for the development of the Group of Six, which convened for the first time at Rambouillet, as the focus was now on creating the institutional and legal basis for floating exchange rates.[35] The Rambouillet agreement suggested that stable currency values would be derived from the operation of market forces in response to evidence of domestic price stability (James, 1996: 269; Bordo et al., 2015: 221). This was in line with the US desire to see the resuscitation of private sector confidence and a return to noninflationary growth. As part of this transition of the governing principles of the international monetary system away from the politically negotiated values of Bretton Woods, the IMF's role would be extended to enhance its capacity for surveillance over the policies of individual states, who were expected to demonstrate commitment to facilitating market discipline (Panitch and Gindin, 2012: 145–55).

The new policy stance of the US toward the IMF reflected the growing domestic momentum of financial liberalism and the commitment to an international monetary order that would maximize US policy autonomy. In the aftermath of the 1973 oil crisis, the US opposed plans that would have seen the OPEC petrodollars recycled through IMF channels and made clear that private financial markets should be the beneficiaries of these flows. They then abolished their program of capital controls in December 1974, breaking the commitment made in the Smithsonian Agreement (Helleiner, 1994: 110–12).

In doing so, the US administration was moving in the direction of firmer advocacy of liberal international finance. As we saw in chapter 2, that position had been advocated by the Republican government of the early 1920s to restore a postwar gold standard. It was a stance that had also been favored by the bankers of Wall Street after World War II, keen for a market-based international monetary system in which private capital flows would exert discipline over government policy. In the wake of Bretton Woods' collapse, a market-oriented approach to reforming the international monetary system could preserve US policy autonomy and the primacy of the dollar. The capacity to attract foreign investment was enhanced by the deregulation of Wall Street brought about by the transformation of the Securities and Exchange Commission's (SEC) oversight of Wall Street in 1975. Under these changes, the SEC broke from its traditional support for the cartelized relationships between brokers, investment bankers, and corporate managers. The SEC dismantled obstacles to price competition and market entry but also gained new powers: it was now able to impose debt-capital ratios on investment banks, make sure that competitive market practices were upheld, and intervene in patterns of self-regulation. Deregulation occurred alongside market innovation, with the rapid growth of the derivatives business within US financial markets and an increasing internationalization of the US bond market that facilitated greater inward investment into the US (Panitch and Gindin, 2012: 149–51).

As had been the case with CCC in the UK, the US regulatory order was coming apart and being reconstituted in step with the broader transformation of the international monetary order after the collapse of Bretton Woods. In both states, the changes were also a reflection of the competitive dynamics between London and New York and the attempts of policy makers to gain advantage by creating the conditions required for market growth. The transatlantic regulatory feedback loop set in motion by the Euromarkets gathered momentum during the 1970s (Green, 2016: 23).

Alongside the transformation of the SEC, US politicians began to develop legislation to regulate the growth and entry of foreign banks in the US as their number expanded rapidly (Goldberg and Saunders, 1981: 365).[36] This caused considerable consternation within the BBA and was monitored closely, signifying the intensified regulatory interdependency between the City and the US. But, in a sign of the deepening European financial integration prompted by the UK's accession to the EC, the BBA was acting not only on behalf of UK banks, but also of European banks more broadly, through its engagement with the French banking representative body, the Fédération Bancaire.

A senior official of the BBA played a "leading role" regarding the foreign banks legislation by giving evidence in Washington, DC, in 1975 on behalf of both the BBA *and* the Fédération Bancaire, in support of draft legislation proposed by the Fed that the BBA considered to be "less discriminatory, and therefore more acceptable" than the proposals being made in the Senate.[37] The City's position as the spatial linchpin of financial globalization meant that the BBA acted as a conduit for the voices of European bankers with respect to the US. The BBA again partnered with representatives of the Fédération Bancaire in 1976, with the president of the BBA giving evidence in a Senate subcommittee on the issue of foreign banks legislation. In a sign of the City's role as a leading voice for European banks, the president of the BBA was thanked for representing both the European and UK banks' views on the topic.[38] As the City's operations internationalized, both via the UK's integration with the EC and the extension of US banking into London, the BBA took on multiple representative identities, increasingly speaking not only for UK banks but at times for the interests of European banks vis-à-vis the US, and at others for US banks in London vis-à-vis Europe. The City and its agencies were now at the heart of the regulatory politics of financial globalization.

The reconfigurations of the US domestic money market through SEC deregulation facilitated the international financial liberalism advocated by the US Treasury. For the UK, the US stance imposed serious limitations upon the space available for policy maneuvering. But it appears that some within the UK Treasury were unaware of the degree to which US thinking had shifted. Officials rather optimistically suggested that recent US legislation and congressional pressure in favor of domestic protection meant that the UK "might reasonably expect support from the USA for the right of member countries to take genuinely selective protective action."[39] UK Treasury officials did recognize that support from the IMF for import restrictions would only be forthcoming if it was made explicit that these restrictions would be temporary and that associated measures would be taken to deal with the public sector borrowing requirement (PSBR) and questions of monetary policy.

Crucially, action on cutting the PSBR and imposing monetary restraint to satisfy the IMF was not viewed as a "major new constraint on policy" by UK Treasury officials, as it was assumed that the chancellor had already rejected a reflationary strategy and was aiming at reducing the PSBR.[40] However, it was acknowledged that appeal to the oil facility would lead to a great intensification of international pressure on the UK if a policy of import restriction was subsequently introduced.[41]

Import controls were further considered in a draft UK Treasury document dealing with the international repercussions of their implementation. If the UK were to unilaterally impose import restrictions for one to two years, this would likely run the risk of "retaliation, emulation, denial of international financial assistance and invalidation." It was now considered that the reactions of the US Congress and US industry might generate pressures for emulation that the administration "would find it difficult to resist." The full gravity of the implications of import controls were then laid out in stark terms: "If our action were copied by any other important country, the whole world could rush into protectionism, with great damage to economic activity everywhere, including the UK."[42]

These comments demonstrate the Treasury's awareness of the massive consequences that the introduction of import controls might have, not just for the UK but also for the international economy. In terms of winning over international opinion, the views of the US, Germany, and France were understood to be crucial to successfully implementing this strategy. Significantly, however, the strategy of import controls was not considered in terms of a broader strategy of reflationary expansion. Import controls would, it was felt, need to be implemented alongside curbing of public expenditure and action to control the money supply. Officials noted that some of the countries whose agreement would be key were in a "critical mood," and that other countries would likely press for greater domestic control over the money supply and public expenditure. The climate of opinion among the major advanced economies was hardening against the UK's economic strategy by 1975, and these considerations, and not simply predetermined "national priorities" were factored into Treasury strategy. Treasury officials remarked that "whereas a combination of some temporary import control with a significant attack on the public sector deficit or money supply in the short-term would strike chords of sympathy and provide useful debating-points, the argument over the combination of exchange rate depreciation and import controls must be an uphill battle."[43]

The implications of borrowing from the IMF and implementing import controls were not considered simply in terms of "depoliticizing" existing priorities, then, but were actually being factored into the formulation of national economic strategy.[44] Treasury officials were clear that out of the two available strategies for responding to the balance of payments crisis, austerity and monetary restraint on the one hand, and import controls and exchange rate depreciation on the other, the former would be much easier to sell to the wider international community (and the French, Germans, and Americans in particular). As the crisis of the 1970s intensified and UK dependency upon external financial support deepened, national economic strategies were steadily becoming interactive with the broader climate of international opinion and preference in economic strategy. UK policy makers were actively internalizing the international context. Indeed, the argument for seeing the role of the IMF as a mere stooge for the depoliticization of UK policy is further undermined by chancellor Denis Healey's acknowledgment that it might well be "politically counter-productive" if too close a link was made between the IMF borrowing and cuts in public spending.[45]

Talk of a UK turn toward import controls was extremely concerning to Johannes Witteveen, the managing director of the IMF. In a letter to Chancellor Healey on October 26, Witteveen warned that import controls should be avoided and that the government should adopt other policies to achieve a viable balance of payments.[46] The Fund's tough attitude regarding UK import controls reached the Treasury, where officials concluded by the end of October that UK controls would face severe opposition because of the UK's size and importance to world trade and the serious concerns of the IMF.[47] Discussion of import controls also met a hostile reception from the Americans, who viewed their implementation as contravening the agreements devised at Rambouillet.[48]

By late November, Denis Healey informally approached Witteveen to borrow one billion special drawing rights ($1.2 billion) from the oil facility and a stand-by credit for 700 million special drawing rights (Burk and Cairncross, 1992: 16). Healey had suggested that a simultaneous drawing from both the oil facility and the first credit tranche would be a good way of demonstrating that the UK was "firmly embedded within the international monetary system."[49] Healey's thinking here attests to a growing international climate of doubt over whether the UK's actions would contravene the principles of the international monetary system through use of import controls or devaluation. In the end, import controls were not seen as a viable corrective for the balance of payments in 1975. The decision was made both based on the likely inflammatory consequences that such a measure would bring about internationally, and because it was felt that import controls were a form of protectionism that would insulate business from exposure to the modernizing catalyst of international competition (Wass, 2008: 92). Within the Labour Party, the outmaneuver of the left over the referendum on membership of the EEC greatly diminished the power of leading left figures to turn the UK away from the IMF and austerity (Burk and Cairncross, 1992: 15).

Disciplining the UK State

A formal approach to the IMF was made in December, and by the end of January 1976 the UK had borrowed all of the money available under the oil facility, the gold tranche, and the stand-by credit. In doing so it had now exhausted the borrowing potential under the more lenient first tranche credit conditions (Wass, 2008: 161). Firmer conditionality now lay just around the corner. In March 1976, the Bank of England was detected selling pounds, even though sterling's value against the dollar was already falling. This led to a sustained period of speculation against the pound. During the next three months the rate fell from $2.02 to the pound to around $1.70, despite the fact that the Bank had expended $1.5 billion in reserves to support the rate over the first night, and a full 30 percent of the reserves between February and April (Burk, 1994: 358). By June, the UK had been forced to turn to the US for support, beginning a process of negotiation that would seriously compromise UK financial sovereignty and rapidly accelerate the internationalization of the UK state under the auspices of US disciplinary power.

The Republican administration in Washington was increasingly frustrated with UK policy. This was not helped by the conservative disposition of influential figures involved in negotiations with the UK. William Simon, the secretary of the Treasury, was a New York bond dealer with a fervent conviction in market forces. Simon's undersecretary, Edwin Yeo, was a banker hailing from Pittsburgh who believed in balanced budget orthodoxy. The staffing of these key positions within the Treasury by private financiers testified to the intimate relationship between the US Treasury and Wall Street. The influential head of the Fed, Arthur Burns, referred to himself as a "Neanderthal conservative" who thought that the Labour Government was "profligate" (Dell, 1991: 220; Burk and Cairncross, 1992: 37; Panitch and Leys, 1997: 116).

Both Simon and Yeo, in a sign of the hardening of the US position on the management of the international monetary system, now advocated a policy whereby access to deficit financing was to be curtailed for chronic deficit countries, as a strategy to push them toward adjustment. The West Germans adopted a similar stance between 1975–76, but with less severity (Harmon, 2008: 7). The hardening positions of the US and West Germany represented a broader shift in international opinion between 1975 and 1976. Whereas in the immediate aftermath of the oil shock the emphasis had been placed on accommodating the financing needs of deficit countries, the tide had now turned in the opposite direction, with the market-centered approach of the US steering the international community toward accepting the need for adjustment by deficit countries. By 1976, then, the US was intent on depriving countries of financing by any other means than through the IMF. If the necessary steps in the direction of domestic retrenchment were not taken, countries would be drawn into the conditionality and austerity ordained by the IMF.

In general, the US moneymen adopted a very stern stance vis-à-vis the UK. Edwin Yeo believed that the role of the US was to convince the UK that the "game was over" and they had "run out of string." Other members of the US central banking system thought that they had given far too much time to propping up the ailing pound. After more than a decade, the US was finally running out of patience with the UK's chronic balance of payments deficits. But the firm position of key staff within the Fed and the US Treasury was not mirrored throughout all core components of the US state. The State Department and, to a certain degree, the president and his staff, were opposed to the hard line taken by the Fed and the Treasury. Throughout the crisis of 1976 the US Secretary of State, Henry Kissinger, attempted to mediate the pressure applied to the UK and Callaghan. Kissinger viewed President Ford as an ally in his endeavors. Brent Scowcroft, the national security advisor to Ford, was also more sympathetic to the UK (Burk and Cairncross, 1992: 38).

These divisions between different institutions of the US state reflected a broader pattern of institutional relations between finance ministries, central banks, and executive power during the crisis. In the cases of all the major players involved—the US, West Germany, and the UK—there were tensions between the treasuries and central banks with respect to their affiliated political authorities (Burk, 1994: 352). In each case, the treasuries and central banks showed a stronger commitment to the implementation of austerity and market discipline.

Leaders of major US corporations matched the attitude of the hard-line elements in the US administration, creating a formidable alignment of public and private power. In September 1975, leaders of large US transnational corporations were invited to the UK to make an assessment of the investment climate. Twenty-one chief executives, responsible for annual sales of $26 billion, arrived in the country—an enormously influential group of visitors, with many serving on government committees or holding other directorships. In general, the visitors reported upon arrival that the UK was perceived within the US business community to have slipped from its former "unquestioned" standing as an attractive location for investment to a situation in which "other locations now appeared more attractive." The more extreme views within the party suggested that the UK was now a "high-risk, low reward location."[50]

American foreign investment was a major force within UK capitalism that could ill afford to be lost. It was therefore of the utmost political significance to the government. The changing conditions of the UK's political economy now repelled potential US investment. The UK's social democratic compromise with the unions, and the agenda laid out in the Alternative Economic Strategy, were anathema to US investors, who were all "believers in a vigorous free enterprise system" and were described as "quick to re-act when they consider that the free enterprise system is under challenge." Although reassured by their visit to the UK, the investors still expressed discontent with UK capitalism in a wide range of market-liberal critiques. They saw the public sector as too large a percentage of gross domestic product (GDP) and criticized the idea of government-run businesses alongside planning agreements; they attacked the UK's level of personal taxation for being too high while suggesting that a higher income gap between managers and workers would help release the talents of the UK's managers.[51] These sentiments, from the captains of US industry, added weight to the pressures from the US administration.

An appeal by the governor of the Bank of England for financing from the Fed presented the key moment for the Americans to begin the enactment of their strategy to enforce adjustment. Arthur Burns's response to the request was initially cool. Burns believed that the right course was for the UK to focus upon cutting the fiscal deficit rather than arranging bilateral financing with the US. He eventually agreed to provide the requested financing, but only under the condition that the UK make an associated commitment to approach the IMF for a drawing if it were required to repay the swap arrangement. To make this much more likely, the swap arrangement was limited to an unusually short three-month period. Indeed, Burns acknowledged in his notes to the Fed's Open Market Committee that the US had set out with the intention of using the swap arrangement to force the UK to change its policies (Burk and Cairncross, 1992: 40). The US was aligning its sovereign power directly behind the IMF to pressure the UK into conditionality.

The agreement was signed on June 6 and was made between the US Treasury Exchange Stabilization Fund and the Bank of England for $1 billion, with the Federal Reserve Bank of New York acting as agent.[52] Crucially, the Treasury provided part of the funding rather than the Fed supplying all of it, as was customary in bilateral swap arrangements. It seems likely that the Treasury was ensuring that the question of renewal of the funding should be in its hands rather than under the remit of the Fed (Wass, 2008: 198). Although no explicit connection was made between this swap arrangement and a borrowing from the second credit tranche of the IMF, the connection was implicitly acknowledged as a central part of the agreement. The important factor here was the six-month (after a three-month extension) time limit on the repayment of the swap. When Yeo came to London to finalize the details of the swap arrangement, Callaghan fiercely opposed the suggestion of a six-month time limit. In the end, however, the UK's desperation led Callaghan to accept it. Over the weekend following the negotiation, Chancellor Healey wrote to Treasury Secretary Simon acknowledging the six-month limit and confirming that the UK would turn to the IMF if they were unable to pay back the funds within that period.

Alongside the formal swap agreement, other informal compacts were made with the US. The government promised to reduce public expenditure and rein in excess liquidity in the economy (Burk and Cairncross, 1992: 42). In exchange for financing from the Americans, which was part of a larger $5.3 billion central bank package from the G10, Callaghan was forced to publicly announce in parliament that the UK would accept IMF conditionality if the six-month repayment could not be met. Edwin Yeo later characterized the June 1976 swap arrangement as "bait" that was designed to "hook the UK economy into IMF control when the loan had to be repaid" (Harmon, 2007: 10).

In response to the cuts agenda pushed by the Americans and increasingly accepted by the government, Tony Benn and Francis Cripps began work on an alternative anticuts strategy. Benn recognized that the government would have to maintain a relationship both with the TUC and the IMF. It was very unlikely that the UK could repay the US by December without recourse to the IMF, as the markets were likely to take further speculative action against the pound in the interim. Benn believed that the UK was in a much stronger bargaining position vis-à-vis the IMF than Callaghan and the Cabinet suggested. The UK's importance within the global economy, as well as the possibility that the fall of the Labour government might weaken control over the union movement, thus imperiling the UK's role within the international monetary order, were sources of considerable leverage over the US and the IMF (Burk and Cairncross, 1992: 48).

Benn's hunches about US fears over the UK political situation were, in fact, well placed. Those fears existed at the highest levels of the US administration and were understood by senior UK officials. During a meeting with a US embassy official in May 1976, Derek Mitchell of the Treasury said that although he did not foresee the possibility of a political collapse in the UK that might lead to a Communist government, he suspected that Yeo certainly did entertain that worry as part of a potential "domino" chain involving the collapse of governments in Italy and France.[53] The document shows the degree of US anxiety over the future of the international economy at this time, and the concerns about the stability of liberal capitalist governance within the West. Yeo later recalled that "we feared that if a country like the UK blew up, defaulted on its loans, introduced foreign exchange controls and froze convertibility, we could have a real-world depression" (Burk and Cairncross, 1992: 4).

Other US officials, such as national security advisor Brent Scowcroft, also feared that a left-wing government that would push for withdrawal from the North Atlantic Treaty Organization (NATO) and Europe might run the UK. While the Germans considered these fears to be groundless, the Americans were not so easily assuaged (Burk, 1994: 353). The existence of the Euromarkets and US banking within the City, sterling's role as a major international currency, and the importance of the UK's role as a historical supporter of an open liberal international capitalist economy: all of these factors made what happened in the UK hugely significant for America's management of the global political economy. US structural power was prominent, but the capacity for highly disruptive political-economic developments within the UK to be transmitted back into the structures of US capitalism was very real.

Given the degree of integration between the UK and the UK, the US could legitimately fear the feedback effects of the collapse of capitalist governance in the UK and the ways in which it might translate into the political economy of the US. Had the UK chosen to impose import and exchange controls, then the trajectory toward globalization would have been halted by one of its hitherto foremost proponents. US fears intensified when the National Executive Committee of the Labour Party endorsed the statement on "Banking and Finance" in August 1976. The statement called for the nationalization of the big four clearing banks alongside the seven largest insurance companies, to create a platform for financial planning. The statement was then subsequently endorsed at the Labour Party Conference later in the summer (Panitch and Leys, 1997: 124), leading to renewed fears and an intensification of the campaign against nationalization from the City's clearing banks.[54] Widespread support for such radical measures to challenge major elements of private control over the UK financial system seriously threatened the City's international role and endangered US financial interests in London.

Potential UK adoption of policies that jeopardized further liberalization also ran the substantial risk of emulation by other countries. In fact, these fears were explicitly voiced during the investment mission in 1975, when the CEOs of major US TNCs saw the importance of the revitalization of liberal democratic capitalism in the UK for their interests, both abroad and at home: "We want Britain to succeed; more—we need you to succeed; if Britain, as one of the few remaining democracies fails, then the challenge to us in the USA will not be long delayed."[55] These sentiments, prevalent within both the private and public power bases of US capitalism, go a long way to explaining why the US took such a firm stance with the UK during the negotiations.

Monetarism Ascendant

For the US, the international and domestic contexts had become highly interactive during the crisis years of the 1970s. As the fixed exchange rate regime crumbled and inflation increased in pace, the domestic basis of the US political economy came under renewed political attack. From the right, business groups went on the offensive against the corporatist and embedded liberal structures set in place after World War II. Existing business interest organizations were revitalized, and new ones formed. Big business became directly involved in producing and spreading pro-business ideas, through organizations such as the new "Business Roundtable," which became the dominant business lobbying organization, abundantly bankrolled by wealthy corporations (Blyth, 2002: 152–53). Between September 1974 and September 1975, high-ranking corporate executives from blue-chip firms such as IBM and Exxon held eight three-day meetings to strategize the role of business in America. They concluded that growing government intervention in the market was a threat to the sanctity of private control over investment (Stein, 2010: 123). From the left, labor organizations such as the AFL-CIO (American Federation of Labor and Congress of Industrial Organizations) pushed for capital controls and tax policies to keep jobs onshore. Left-leaning economists pushed for an extension of Keynesian planning, by shifting from a Keynesian macro-economic emphasis to a microeconomic focus on specific sectors and sections of the economy (Stein, 2010: 118).

These increasingly partisan political tensions reverberated through to the Fed as monetary policy became more politicized. The need to be strict with the UK in negotiations was a product of this growing politicization of monetary policy as the monetarist counterrevolution in the US gathered momentum. The rise of monetarism within the US preceded its development in the UK; by the early 1970s, the monetarist offensive was slowly gathering momentum in the US, although it had yet to achieve sustained institutional influence (Johnson, 1998: 145; Stein, 2010: 125). Monetarism's advancement moved in step with the recognition that the US was witnessing a period of sustained inflationary pressure. By 1969, the annual rate of price increases was over 6 percent, but, by 1974, the consumer price index was rising at a staggering 12.2 percent per year. For Milton Friedman, the source of this inflation was easily identifiable: it was the result of the Fed's wayward monetary policy (Greider, 1987: 88).

Mounting inflationary pressures contributed to the transformation of institutional power within the US. Inside the Fed system, the St. Louis Fed had become a government-funded bastion of monetarist thinking and research, with its monthly publication at the center of the debate between monetarists and their detractors. Within the US business and banking community, too, monetarism had started to take hold. In this climate, the operations of the Fed were placed under a degree of public scrutiny and debate not seen before in the postwar era. Monetarist economists like Milton Friedman set the agenda for the debate (Woolley, 1984: 99; Greider, 1987: 97). In 1973, Friedman and other leading monetarist economists began meeting as a "Shadow Open Market Committee," which monitored the activities of the Fed's Open Market Committee (responsible for monetary policy) and poured scorn upon what they viewed as the Fed's archaic and misguided practices (Woolley, 1984: 99).

As inflation mounted, the credibility of the Fed's sound money credentials steadily eroded. In response to pressure from the monetarists, the Fed was forced to make piecemeal concessions on the techniques of monetary control, agreeing to focus more upon the monetary aggregates as a guideline for policy. This contrasted with the Fed's traditional approach, which arrived at target interest rates based upon the consideration of multiple factors. For the Fed's chairman, Arthur Burns, the challenging domestic context was reinforced by downward pressure on the dollar from the international markets, which further intensified the inflationary dynamics of the US (Axilrod, 2011: 55–71).

Given these conditions, it is hardly surprising that Burns and the Fed adopted a firm stance toward the UK throughout the crisis, insisting upon the need to control monetary expansion before any more support could be secured from the US (Schenk, 2010: 375). The Fed had to be seen to be taking a hard line with the UK and not handing over promises of US financial support without something in return. Burns made clear his commitment to fighting inflation on a visit to the UK shortly before the June swap agreement.[56]

Developments in the UK paralleled the rise of monetarism and the growing discontent with the unraveling of the Keynesian order in the US. This was not just a case of the US pressuring the UK. Powerful interests within the UK that had lost faith with the postwar Keynesian class compromise, from City bankers to Conservative politicians, were actively seeking to harness the power of the US and the IMF to achieve their own domestic objectives. Aligning themselves with US power and policy by attacking the Keynesian welfare state enabled these domestic forces to steer UK development away from radicalized social democracy and in the direction of liberal international integration. Social forces in the UK, embedded within Anglo-American development and Atlantic integration, were actively leveraging US disciplinary pressure to further their domestic agenda for the transformation of the UK's state and economy.

The high degree to which UK capitalism had already been Atlanticized meant that distinctions between the external and internal pressures driving the transition away from Keynesianism were difficult to maintain. From 1975, when Margaret Thatcher became leader, the Conservative Party began to give increasing attention and support to monetarist ideas. The Tories were very keen to reduce borrowing and slash public spending. In October 1976, as the crisis gathered momentum, Thatcher announced that the budget deficit could be halved without causing much harm (Burk and Cairncross, 1992: 158).

Within the Treasury and the Bank, similar pro-austerity interests were supportive of the UK's need to accept discipline. When the Governor of the Bank of England, Gordon Richardson, approached the Fed to arrange the June swap, Callaghan was very wary. Callaghan believed that the swap, negotiated between the two central banks and the US Treasury, "seemed simply designed to embroil the Government with the IMF for the specific purpose of enabling them to impose cuts in public expenditure" (Schenk, 2010: 372). His suspicions regarding the Bank's intentions were well founded. In a memo to Kit McMahon, the deputy governor of the Bank, a Bank official lamented the disappearance of the "disciplinary virtues" of the fixed parities system and suggested that stable rates could only be recovered once price stability was restored. Price stability was the objective that "has always been sacrificed" in the UK's postwar economic strategy; the official opined that "all but the French now seem to realise that stable exchange rates will not guarantee price stability, it must be the other way round."[57]

Clearly, then, the need to achieve domestic price stability had begun to raise more concern within the Bank in the context of increased international monetary disorder. Implementing austerity was the most obvious way to achieve this. Inside the Treasury, the view was split between those who favored Keynesian proposals for escaping the crisis and those who supported deflationary measures (Dell, 1991: 248). Chancellor Healey himself had been a keen advocate of austerity prior to the crisis, and many officials within both the Treasury and the Bank were supportive of the position taken by the IMF and the US Treasury (Helleiner, 1994: 129). During the height of the crisis, officials from the Bank and the Treasury met secretly with Simon and Yeo at a London tailor. It was likely that Simon was seeking an inside scoop on the proceedings here, and the meeting gave the Americans a clear picture of the different positions taken by the IMF and Chancellor Healey (Harmon, 1997: 194).

The Americans also had direct linkages to City banks and financial institutions. Indeed, US banks were now a major force within the City of London, and during 1976 the chancellor and the prime minister both held meetings with the heads of major US banks. The chancellor met with the president of Chase Manhattan Bank, while the prime minister met with the chairmen of Citibank and Morgan Guaranty Trust.[58] Although the minutes of these meetings went largely unrecorded, one can easily imagine the pro-austerity message that would have been put across to the government. Throughout 1976, the stockbrokers W. Greenwell & Co. provided the US embassy in London with daily reports on the gilt-edged market, which could be digested by Simon, given his expertise as a bond dealer. It is likely that other City institutions were also involved in supplying information about the markets to the Americans (Dell, 1991: 221). These connections were a testament to the linkages brought about through Anglo-American developmental interdependence.

The final decision to go to the IMF was prompted by the concerted action of bankers and investors in London and New York, who anticipated that the UK would have to turn to the IMF and pay higher interest rates on gilts. Bankers on both sides of the Atlantic refused to buy government gilts in the run-up to the IMF appeal, because they knew that they would receive higher returns afterward (Burk and Cairncross, 1992: 52). When asked by the chancellor whether he believed that the markets had already discounted a Fund drawing into their assessments, Yeo replied that he was "partly responsible for the idea that a drawing from the Fund would be a good housekeeping seal for the UK."[59] Indeed, when the UK looked to US banks to finance its deficits in early autumn, the leading players fell into line with the US administration and the Fund by stating that they would not participate in further financing for the UK until negotiations with the IMF had been completed (Wass, 2008: 219). Private and public actors interacted intensely during the crisis with the US Treasury central to orchestrating operations in order to shoehorn the UK into IMF conditionality.

When Callaghan made his famous speech signaling the UK's break with Keynesian policy on September 28, the Americans were cock-a-hoop. Much to the chagrin of the Labour left, Callaghan denounced Keynesian demand management and publicly indicated a shift in the government's policy orientation. The speech came shortly before the UK's formal approach to the IMF and was intended to signal the government's austerity credentials before an approach to the IMF. Despite Callaghan's speech, however, the government were still confident that they could apply on the basis of third tranche conditionality without having to substantially amend their existing policies. They hoped that the IMF would merely rubber-stamp the UK's economic credibility with the effect of restoring gilt sales, stabilizing the exchange rate, and allowing interest rates to fall (Burk and Cairncross, 1992: 59). But they were in for a much rougher ride than expected.

October proved to be a very significant month in the unfolding of the crisis. Callaghan grew increasingly concerned by what he saw as a conspiracy by the US and UK treasuries to use the Fund to foist more severe retrenchments upon the UK. To circumvent the finance ministries and the IMF, Callaghan began to make direct approaches to President Ford and Germany's Chancellor Schmidt. Although Ford was sympathetic to Callaghan's plight, he was not in a position to override the wishes of the US Treasury and the Fed. With Burns, Simon, and Yeo all convinced of the need to change the UK's ways through the pressure of the Fund, "they were unlikely to transmit requests from the President or his advisers to the IMF to lessen this pressure" (Burk and Cairncross, 1992: 62–64).

The inefficacy of Callaghan's efforts to go over the head of the Fund to the executive power centers in the US and Germany demonstrates the limits of executive authority during the crisis. It was the treasuries and central banks that were endowed with the institutional power and expertise to push through the internationalization of the UK state and undermine the foundations of Keynesian welfarism. In both the US and Germany, central banks enjoyed a high degree of constitutional independence from the executive branch, while Ford's power was further limited by his status as an unelected president. Although Schmidt took a more sympathetic stance toward Callaghan by offering to use Germany's dollar reserves to help solve UK problems with the sterling balances, his power to do so was extremely limited. As Schmidt's state secretary in the finance ministry, Karl-Otto Pohl, pointed out, Schmidt was not constitutionally empowered to dispose of the Bundesbank's reserves in this fashion (Burk and Cairncross, 1992: 66).

UK officials from the Bank and the Treasury were left with no doubts about the resolution of the IMF and the US to enforce conditionality when they attended the IMF conference in Manilla. Bank officials reported that Arthur Burns's stringency was widely shared within the international community and that the Labour government had frequently been arraigned for placating its left wing rather than taking the necessary measures to restore economic balance. In summary, Bank officials suggested that the "general climate of opinion towards the UK is not propitious." When they discussed the prospect of an agreement to stabilize the pound by alleviating the problem of the sterling balances, they concluded that "among the people who count"—the Americans and the Germans—there was no appetite for discussing the sterling balances until the UK had enacted austerity and drawn from the Fund.[60] Financial officials from the US and Germany were determined not to let the UK off the hook.

By late 1976 international attitudes toward the UK had clearly hardened. The US Treasury played the definitive role in restructuring its UK counterpart. The disciplinary approach of the US Treasury and the Fed proved to be unwavering. Crucially, it was the process of disciplinary supervision enacted by the US Treasury and the Fed that steered the UK into the clutches of the IMF and away from the postwar class compromise. This was an active process of discipline through which the US steered UK development during a definitive moment of crisis.

The very capacity of the US to do this was, in part, a consequence of the way in which the Euromarkets, through extending the hegemony of the dollar and integrating global financial markets, had enabled continued US international financial dominance after the collapse of Bretton Woods. Anglo-American development and the Atlantic integration of the City and New York had contributed to the generation of the US structural power resources that were brought to bear upon the UK. These processes, and the linked ascendance of monetarism on both sides of the Atlantic, also meant that segments of the City and the UK state were receptive to US discipline and IMF-induced austerity.

Just how far the disciplinary supervision over the UK extended is revealed in a Treasury document outlining a proposed bilateral swap between the UK and the US at the height of the crisis in December 1976. The swap was valued at $500 million, with $250 million each from the US Treasury and the Fed. Crucially, the swap was explicitly tied to approval of IMF standby credit:

> Drawings and renewals for additional three-month periods shall only be agreed if the US Treasury-Secretary, having consulted with the Managing Director of the Fund, is satisfied that the Government of the United Kingdom is following appropriate economic and financial policies, including policies that permit the sterling exchange rate to reflect underlying economic and financial conditions, and that all conditions and performance criteria specified in the IMF stand-by arrangement are being fulfilled by the United Kingdom.[61]

By explicitly linking their funding package with the IMF negotiations, the US aligned itself with the IMF and pooled its sovereign power with the Fund's authority. The reference in the text to the requirement that the sterling exchange rate reflect "underlying economic and financial conditions" embodied the US commitment to an international monetary system based upon the primacy of market forces and internal price stability. The negotiations over the December swap demonstrate how tightly US strategic priorities were imbricated with those of the IMF. Discussing the details of the swap, a Treasury official commented that "no process of examination of the British economy by the US Treasury is contemplated so long as the programme agreed with the Fund is proceeding satisfactorily."[62] Had the UK accepted this swap agreement along these terms, violation of the IMF conditions would have led to direct supervision of the UK Treasury by its US counterpart. This would have amounted to a humiliating curtailment of UK sovereignty, and it showed the degree to which the US was intent on using IMF conditionality, and, failing that direct US supervision, shaping UK economic policy. The draft agreement shows the centrality of the relationship between the two treasuries to the politics of the crisis and the opening of the Treasury to deepened international integration. In the end, Chancellor Healey decided that the second swap agreement with the US was not required, that the IMF funds were sufficient.[63]

After much debate within the Cabinet, Dennis Healey announced to the Commons on December 15 that large cuts would be made in public expenditure as a condition of the UK's drawing from the IMF.[64]

Entrenching Globalized Finance

The events of 1976 were critical in the politics of financial globalization. As this chapter has shown, US disciplinary power played a key part in steering the UK away from a radicalization of Keynesian social democracy that would have jeopardized the UK's commitment to liberal international finance and threatened the City's entrepôt status. Instead, the US, in conjunction with domestic social forces in the UK hostile to the Labour government, corralled the UK into a form of internationally open and market-liberal development. The central role of the US during the negotiations exemplified the importance of US power in coordinating the international response to the collapse of Bretton Woods. While the crisis did not represent the beginning of the drive for austerity and the abandonment of Keynesianism, which had already developed momentum both from within and outside the UK, it accelerated and accentuated these processes during a definitive moment in the restructuring of the UK state.

Engagement between the US Fed-Treasury-Wall Street and the UK City-Bank-Treasury nexus, mediated by and through the IMF, was essential to this process. The crisis of 1976 reflected the outcome of more than a decade of developmental interaction between the UK and the US that centered around the dynamics of sterling and the dollar under the Bretton Woods system. Anglo-American development produced a situation wherein social forces that benefited from Atlantic integration pulled in US disciplinary power to further their domestic ambitions.

The US was able to use the structural power of the dollar, along with its influence over the IMF, to set the terms and conditions of UK borrowing. But the very continued centrality of the dollar to the post–Bretton Woods monetary order had been built up through prior processes of Anglo-American financial integration. This created both a constituency of Atlanticized social forces within the UK and *simultaneously* rendered the US increasingly vulnerable to the possible effects of a radicalized Labour Party and a challenge to liberal trade and finance, by extending the dependency of US banks and the offshore dollar upon the City of London. Only through a focus on the longer-term lineages of Anglo-American development can we arrive at an accurate assessment of just how mutually entangled US and UK finance had become, and how central the events of 1976 proved to the wider movement of globalizing finance. Viewing the decade of the 1970s through a US-centric lens obscures these wider Anglo-American foundations and the linchpin role of the City, while arguing over whether the determinants of the UK's abandonment of Keynesianism were either pristinely "national" or "international" overlooks the deep developmental entanglements of Anglo-American capitalism that made separating the national and the international as discrete levels of analysis an increasingly futile preoccupation.

This was a moment of great contingency in the politics of financial globalization. Without the crisis of 1976 and the failure of the Labour government to follow through on its commitments, the Thatcherite transformation that followed might never have occurred. By steering the UK away from policy options that would have severely challenged the liberal international economic order and threatened to halt the forward march of financial liberalization, the US, the IMF, and the UK's domestic opponents of the Keynesian state established the preconditions for Thatcher's radical break from the postwar consensus. They also secured the trajectory toward liberalized finance within the City and in doing so maintained its spatial and infrastructural centrality to the integration of international finance. Accounts that stress the importance of the "Winter of Discontent" as the critical turning point in the UK's postwar economic development have understated how the resolution of the IMF crisis in favor of those forces opposed to a radicalization of social democracy prepared the ground for the Thatcherite shift.[65]

The UK's postwar consensus fractured in tandem with the decomposition of the Bretton Woods order. In the unraveling of the domestic and international orders, and the reconstitution that began to emerge in place of Bretton Woods and the Keynesian state, Anglo-American development played a crucial role: not only in shaping the future of UK capitalism, but also in entrenching financial globalization by stabilizing the political and institutional commitment to liberal international finance during the crisis decade of the 1970s. Were it not for the UK's defense of the Euromarkets from the attempted regulatory encroachments led by West Germany, the politics of global finance might have looked very different. Were it not for the defeat of the Labour left, both the City's role as a key sponsor and leader of international financial integration and the power of large private banks within the UK's domestic political economy might have been in danger.

The Labour government's implementation of incomes policy and the acceptance of IMF austerity weakened Labour's relationship with the unions

and culminated in the Winter of Discontent, which was sparked by public
sector unions in August 1978 (Glyn and Harrison, 1980: 118). Labour missed
the opportunity to implement the AES and break from the dictates of the financial markets. By pushing the costs of the stagflationary crisis onto workers,
the Labour government destroyed the political basis for a socialist strategy in
the UK and "prepared the political conditions for the right" (Clarke, 1987:
418). Margaret Thatcher and a hostile right-wing press were able to take advantage of these weaknesses by shrewdly constructing the Winter of Discontent as a more fundamental crisis of the state, produced by Labour's failed
attempts to manage the unions and deliver a stable economic performance
(Hay, 1996; Matthijs, 2012: 117–19).

Labour did not abandon its commitment to a radicalized response to the
crisis of the 1970s independently. The power of the US, exerted through IMF
conditionality, played a key part. That part was facilitated by the endorsement
of monetarism and the rejection of Keynesian economic strategy by the City,
the Conservative Party, and those within the government and the state who
wanted to temper the UK's social democracy. During the defining rule of Margaret Thatcher, which began in 1979, those forces saw their wishes for a radical
restructuring of the UK state realized to an unprecedented degree. Alongside
Ronald Reagan in the US, Thatcher's policies would reset the terms of the
domestic social settlement, implement a radical project of central bank monetarism to combat inflation, and give further momentum to the politics of
financial liberalization within Anglo-America.

6

Internalizing Discipline

THE POLITICAL projects of Prime Minister Margaret Thatcher and President Ronald Reagan were central to the "neoliberal" transformation of capitalism that began in earnest from the late 1970s.[1] In the United Kingdom, neoliberalism was underpinned by a set of closely interrelated policy commitments, designed to roll back the social democratic welfare state and extend the scope of market power through selective pro-market state intervention and the restoration of a virile sense of law and order.[2] In the United States, Ronald Reagan's policies followed a comparable pattern, targeting corporatist structures in order to restore the sanctity of the "free market." Neoliberal ideas would go on to become the dominant framework through which capitalist globalization was intensified during the 1990s, under the rubric of the "Washington Consensus" (Gamble, 2001: 130).

Transatlantic dynamics were essential to the reconstitution of Anglo-American capitalism. Thatcher's project, resting on the twin ideological pillars of the "free economy" and the "strong state" (Gamble, 1994: 6), occurred in highly interactive synchronicity with the transformation of the US political economy. In both states, monetarist ideas and techniques were embraced to provide an epistemic justification for the break from postwar Keynesianism. And, in both states, tensions arose between the central bank and the executive, as monetary policy was accorded new priority in the management of the economy. Interest rate hikes helped spark off deep recessions that accelerated regressive redistribution and damaged manufacturing and export-led sectors. The Keynesian compromise, with its commitment to full employment and rising living standards, was torn apart in favor of anti-inflationary politics and induced recession.

The reconfiguration of Anglo-American capitalism during the 1980s sent shock waves through the global political economy and laid the foundations for the definitive dominance of neoliberal restructuring in the decades after. The increased financialization of the Anglo-American economies, and the decrease in wages associated with staunch anti-inflationary politics, had long-term consequences. They created the dependence on consumer borrowing and house price inflation that would gradually sow the seeds for the global financial crisis of 2008 (Montgomerie, 2006: 122; Gamble, 2009: 453; Hay, 2011: 1).[3] An Anglo-American heartland of debt-driven consumption and financialization would underpin the neoliberal model that imploded spectacularly during the 2000s.

Despite the interactivity of neoliberal transformation in both states, the interconnections between monetary dynamics in the UK and the US during the early years of the Thatcher-Reagan era have scarcely been analyzed.[4] These relationships have tended to be interpreted as products of ideological synchronicity rather than institutional symbiosis. Consequently, although many accounts of the development of neoliberalism point to the significance of the ideological similarities between Thatcherism and Reaganism (Krieger, 1986: 17; Gamble, 2001: 129; Harvey, 2005: 22; Peck and Tickell, 2007: 28), less attention has been given to the fundamental interdependence and interconnectivity of the monetary policy regimes adopted in the early neoliberal period. What we are left with, then, is a notion of neoliberal synchronicity without an understanding of the underpinning processes of institutional symbiosis.

Neglecting these institutional linkages has also led to IPE accounts of US financialization that overstate the endogeneity of liberalization and associated financial sector expansion (Greider, 1987: 155; Schwartz, 2009a: 211; Konings, 2011: 131–37; Panitch and Gindin, 2012: 169; Krippner, 2011: 73). Within CPE, the rise of neoliberalism in the UK and the US has been interpreted either as emerging from the comparative structural specificities of their national models of capitalism vis-à-vis other advanced capitalist states (King and Wood, 1999; Prasad, 2006), or a common historical trajectory of hegemonic decline (Krieger, 1986). Existing accounts overlook the broader Anglo-American developmental context of transatlantic regulatory and monetary interdependence that drove the turn to financial liberalization and new regimes of monetary control in the 1980s.

This chapter addresses the symbiotic aspects of transformation in the UK and the US, by focusing upon the principal dynamics and consequences of financial liberalization, monetarism, and monetary policy between 1979 and 1982. This was the first phase of the Thatcher government's economic strategy and the decisive period in which the "Volcker shock" was implemented in the US. I argue that the synchronized radicalization of monetary policy, regulatory transformation, and central bank innovation in Anglo-American capitalism emerged out of institutional interdependencies generated by Anglo-American development. The development of offshore markets in the City led bankers on both sides of the Atlantic to push for further domestic liberalization, as competition between London and New York intensified. The pressure from US banks on regulators to replicate the City's offshore conditions progressively eroded the New Deal–era financial regulations. These dynamics, alongside the Fed's failure to regulate the Euromarkets, demonstrated the limits on US monetary policy autonomy, and the importance of the transatlantic impetus to liberalization arising from Anglo-American financial integration. Anglo-America, once more, was at the heart of the transformative politics of financial globalization. In the UK, attempts to retain a competitive advantage against the US and other international financial markets undermined postwar Keynesian banking regulation. Despite their competitive thrust, these efforts at regulatory liberalization were also increasingly coordinated around a shared goal of maximizing the liberalization of financial markets. The UK's deepening integration with the EEC increased its centrality as a regulatory pivot within wider international processes of capital market integration, but also raised political antagonisms with the US over preferential liberalization toward European markets.

With financial markets increasingly liberalized, administered monetary controls became much harder to realize, and monetarist approaches relying on the market mechanism of interest rate adjustments became de rigueur in a context of spiraling inflation. Having departed from a commitment to fixed exchange rates, the UK and the US sought to internalize discipline through radical new paradigms of central banking, inducing recession and terminating the Keynesian compromise by sacrificing full employment in pursuit of price stability. These transformations marked a watershed in postwar Anglo-American capitalism, with significant ramifications for the wider global political economy. They set the tone for the renewed importance of central banking in an era defined by the massive growth in the power of financial markets and heightened dependency of economic activity upon creditors. They also highlighted one of the major democratic shortcomings of neoliberal capitalism—the growing influence of unelected central bankers.

The chapter begins by assessing the impact of the post–Bretton Woods monetary order upon central banking. It then examines both the abolition of

exchange controls in the UK and developments within the politics of transatlantic regulatory competition. The next section identifies the "shock monetarist" regimes employed to break the post-war Keynesian consensus and con-
trasts central bankers' pragmatic approach to monetarism with that of more
radical doctrinal monetarists within government. The chapter then traces the
market and regulatory infrastructures that enabled monetary shocks, as well
as briefly maps associated distributional consequences, and finally concludes
by reflecting on the significance of the early 1980s to the crisis of 2007/8.

Floating Rates and the Inflationary Challenge

As we saw in the previous chapter, the collapse of Bretton Woods led to the
gradual adjustment of national monetary regimes to the new system of floating
rates. With the pound floating from 1972 onward, monetary policy was no
longer shaped by the requirement to maintain a fixed exchange rate.[5] Relative
to fiscal policy, monetary policy now became more important than before. In
the UK, the emergence of new international monetary relations also presented
an opportunity for monetarists to further advance their priorities.

After the fall of Ted Heath in 1974, monetarists within the Conservative
Party, particularly Geoffrey Howe and Nigel Lawson, rose to prominence
under Thatcher's leadership. The Conservative Party's new economic strategy
was outlined in their 1977 document "The Right Approach to the Economy."
The paper set out their plan to reduce government spending, cut direct taxation, and contain inflation. Combatting inflation was to be achieved by controlling the money supply and allowing the exchange rate to rise, to lessen the
impact of imported inflation (Keegan, 1984: 70). Thatcher's new government
was convinced that Heath's "U-turn" in 1972 had been a major mistake; it now
viewed inflation as the principal threat to social and political stability and recognized that tough measures were needed to arrest it. Achieving price stability
required a more resolute commitment.

By adopting a staunchly monetarist approach to inflation, Thatcher's government distinguished itself from broader European anti-inflationary politics.
In March 1979, the countries of the European Monetary System (including
France, West Germany, and Italy), established an exchange rate mechanism by
fixing their exchange rates to the deutschmark (Johnson, 1991: 36; Stephens,
1996: 5). The new system was designed to insulate European exchange rates
from the weakness of the dollar (Schwartz, 2009a: 207). It had been resisted
in 1978 by the Labour prime minister James Callaghan, who feared alienating

the Americans by appearing to reject the prospects of a dollar-centered world monetary system and push for European insularity. The UK remained outside of the new system (James, 2012: 149–176).

The path to deeper European currency integration through a tighter European fixed exchange rate system took a different approach than either the UK or the US. While the Europeans would attempt to achieve price stability and arrest inflation by tying themselves into a regional fixed exchange rate system led by West Germany, the UK and the US went about internalizing monetary discipline through monetarism and unorthodox policies. This was never simply a question of technical adjustments to the intricacies of international monetary politics; monetarism, and the austerity that it advocated as a cure to inflationary dynamics, was always also about the restoration of class power. Workers' expectations of rising wages and improving living standards—a key component of the postwar capitalist compromise—would be driven down: not only by the monetary tightening, but also by the imposition of antiunion laws, and the provocation of set piece engagements between unions and the state.

Even before taking up the reins as chairman of the Fed in August 1979, Paul Volcker understood the need for the US to internalize discipline. Volcker felt that years of mounting inflation had undermined the validity of interest rates as a guide for monetary policy (due to the difference between nominal and real rates), weakening the Fed's credibility and leading to uncertain expectations over price fluctuations. Under pressures of monetary instability and inflationary forces, the "fabric of discipline" was "fraying at the edges" (Volcker, 1978a: 9) Whereas expectations were formerly stabilized through the gold standard, the doctrine of the balanced budget, and fixed exchange rates, those disciplines had either dissolved altogether or had become "so attenuated as to be meaningless" (Volcker, 1978b: 332). Consequently, the US would now have to discipline itself (Panitch and Gindin, 2012: 163).

Within this context, targeting monetary aggregates offered a useful tool for communicating expectations to the public and restoring credibility. Aggregates could also serve as a check on the monetary authorities themselves. But Volcker was not a card-carrying monetarist; he recognized that inflation was not exclusively a consequence of movements in the money supply, but rather stemmed from a complex combination of social, economic, and political factors (Volcker, 1978b: 338). As Volcker's stewardship of the Fed would subsequently demonstrate, he took a more pragmatic and politically expedient approach (Johnson, 1998: 179; Mayer, 2001: 194–95; Konings, 2011: 134).

The strategy outlined by Volcker could only be undertaken within the context of the post–Bretton Woods monetary order, in which, untethered from the commitment to fixed exchange rates, the dollar's value could now fluctuate much more widely (Schwartz, 2009a: 207). Within the Bank of England, the transformed international monetary context justified the use of monetary targets, which were now viewed by some officials as fundamental to "filling the vacuum" left by the abolition of fixed rates.[6] Mirroring the view taken by Volcker at the Fed, Bank officials were increasingly willing to employ monetary targeting in a pragmatic manner. With demand management policies now delegitimized by their supposedly inflationary impacts, as well as the absence of fixed rates as a reference point for the judgment of economic policy, monetary targets became the new yardstick for assessing macroeconomic performance in an inflationary age.

Outside of the European efforts to build a regional fixed exchange rate system and formalized monetary integration—and no longer restrained by the requirement to maintain fixed parities—monetary authorities on both sides of the Atlantic allowed interest rates to be pushed much higher with more severe fluctuations in the exchange rate. Internationally, it was this context that enabled the interest rate shock regimes that characterized monetary transformation in the UK and the US. National and international monetary orders developed in a highly interactive fashion. Unorthodox central banking regimes must be understood within the context of the constraints, contingencies, and capacities of the international monetary system.

For both the UK and the US, the desire was not only to dampen domestic inflation, but also to restore the international value of their currencies. For the US—given the international currency role of the dollar—this was clearly a central strategic priority. The world was now effectively on a pure dollar standard. Although the dollar was no longer constrained by its fixed link to gold, the system nonetheless required relatively stable expectations about the dollar's future value to effectively anchor the international monetary order, maintain the attractiveness of dollar-denominated financial assets, and prevent the movement into alternative reserve currencies (Parboni, 1981: 58; McKinnon, 2001: 227–35; Panitch and Gindin, 2012: 163). For the UK, the appeal of a strong pound is at first less clear. But examining the Bank of England's archival record illuminates the motivation to achieve it.

Within the Bank, the exchange rate of the pound was identified as a decisive weapon in the anti-inflationary battle. A further OPEC oil price hike in spring of 1979 meant that prices had nearly doubled over the last year. Speaking at the

Bank of England's Court meeting, Gordon Richardson, the governor, acknowledged that a fall in the strength of the pound during the 1976 crisis had led to increased inflation, with companies passing on increased import prices to domestic consumers. Richardson made clear the need to "avoid the inflationary impact of a lower rate" and mentioned that some sectors of the economy "sought to benefit from a high rate."[7] The anti-inflationary priority was now firmly entrenched within the Bank's thinking. A strong pound would be central to this objective.

The Bank's anti-inflationary stance reflected not only the priorities of the new Conservative government, whose monetarist economic advisors strongly favored a floating pound, but also a broader shift in international opinion. This emerging consensus on the need for anti-inflationary policies to be prioritized over and above the expansion of economic growth was clearly expressed in a Bank report on the October 1979 IMF meeting in Belgrade. Government officials from around the world had lost confidence in their capacity to curb inflation, with many now concluding that "gradualism will simply not work in slowing down inflation." In this context, it was felt that a sharp recession, at least as sharp as that of 1974, was now required to adjust inflationary expectations.[8] Despite the focus on monetary aggregates and targets, then, the real strategy for combating inflation was an induced recession to slacken demand, provoke unemployment, produce spare capacity, and drag down prices. Creative destruction would pave the way for stable accumulation.

For monetary policy to be effective, interest rates would have to be pushed much higher than before. This was a consequence of the effect of inflation upon real interest rates (making them negative unless they were sufficiently high) as well as a result of the Euromarkets. Euromarket liquidity had eroded the efficacy of monetary policy as a means of curbing inflationary pressures, meaning that it would now have to be much tighter than before to effect a comparable slowing down of economic activity.[9] The problem of Euromarket leakage frustrated transatlantic attempts to regulate the money supply. Opting for a higher interest rate was not, therefore, simply an act of ideological voluntarism. It was also a pragmatic adaptation to the evolving monetary conditions associated with financial globalization and high inflation. As we have seen earlier in the book, the offshore Euromarkets hosted in London punctured holes in national money markets, destabilized Bretton Woods, and eroded national monetary regimes. These developments combined with inflation to produce a requirement for the radicalization of monetary policy if price stability was to be restored. Because of their centrality to the Euromarkets and their attempt to stabilize their currencies through the internal control of inflation (rather than an external currency peg or gold-backed money supply), the UK and the US were particularly sensitive to these considerations.

A strong exchange rate was identified as the surest means to quell inflation by reducing import prices. But the exchange rate question was also important in terms of another policy development that defined the early years of the Thatcher government—the abolition of exchange controls and the acceleration of financial liberalization. These processes would come to undermine the tight interest rate policy employed in the UK, creating a central contradiction within the early neoliberal policy program: between attempts at heightened monetary control, on the one hand, and simultaneous moves toward liberalization that weakened traditional forms of monetary regulation, on the other. This contradiction was also apparent in the US (Konings, 2011). Controlling inflation and liberalizing financial markets formed an awkward policy pairing that proved difficult to reconcile. Nevertheless, wholesale liberalization was undertaken.

Opening the Floodgates

Abolition of exchange controls was one of the earliest actions of the new Conservative government. Financial liberalization accorded with the philosophical commitment to extend the scope of market forces to the widest possible degree (Keegan, 1984: 149). The Bank had long called for an end to controls and set to work providing technical justifications for the process. In June and July 1979, the chancellor removed all restrictions on the financing of outward investment, enabled UK merchants to use sterling to finance third country trade, substantially reduced controls on individuals, and began to liberalize portfolio controls by allowing securities denominated in European Community currencies or issued by international organizations of which the UK was a member to be purchased with official exchange.[10]

Bank officials were tasked with strategic planning for the further removal of the remaining portfolio controls and began to evaluate the actual and anticipated effects. In general, officials felt that once most controls had been removed it became logically necessary to dismantle remaining restrictions. They also expressed concerns that failure to do so would provoke a "very critical reaction" from media commentators and the City—the same interests that had championed the monetarist cause throughout the 1970s.[11] It was expected that abolition of controls would lead to greater purchases of overseas assets by

UK residents, producing net capital outflows. But the extent to which this occurred was likely to depend upon the strength of confidence in the UK economy. More specifically, the Bank's thinking on the issue can broadly be split into three distinct components—the impact upon fiscal and monetary policy, the impact upon international regulatory dynamics, and, finally, the impact upon the future of sterling.

Regarding fiscal and monetary policy, officials saw that the abolition of controls was likely to have profound effects. One important impact would be upon the potential growth of offshore banking. If UK residents could borrow sterling deposits from overseas, then a growth in offshore banking could occur, which might lead to "possible adverse consequences for the control of the UK money supply."[12] UK authorities were now facing a very similar dilemma to that faced by the US after the rapid growth of US banks' involvement in the Euromarkets. As we have seen in chapter 4, the offshore dollar pool reduced the Fed's capacity to manage the credit supply by providing an escape valve through which US banks could borrow abroad to lend to domestic branches and circumvent tight money policy at home. With sterling liberalized, the same erosion of national monetary control would affect UK authorities. The Euromarkets weakened monetary control for both states and the problem intensified as financial liberalization continued to develop.

It was understood by the Bank that the abolition of exchange controls ensured that the UK's banking system "loses a degree of insulation from the world monetary system."[13] This inevitably exposed the UK to new problems arising from the interaction between domestic and external pressures. The Bank clearly understood how this might undermine the government's policy goals, commenting that "it could pose problems for both the techniques and efficacy of monetary controls in the situation where effective controls of the money supply and declining monetary targets were the centre piece of the Government's economic strategy."[14] In the past, UK authorities had relied upon direct controls over lending (apart from the disastrous and abortive attempt to do away with them during CCC) in order to control the money supply.[15] The problem now was that full liberalization of sterling would produce a situation whereby banks could easily circumvent such controls by persuading their customers to switch their deposits and borrowing to an overseas branch. It would also enable overseas banks, which weren't subject to the same controls, to extend their sterling operations in the domestic money market.[16]

At the very moment when the new Conservative government had come to power espousing the virtues of monetary stringency and price stability, the abolition of controls was undermining the existing framework of monetary control. This was the great contradiction at the heart of the monetarist attempt to quell inflation. The government's incompetence here was unsurprising, given that monetary policy had received very little attention from the Conservatives while in opposition, leaving them unprepared for the technical details of monetary reform and confused over monetary policy matters upon arrival in office (Keegan, 1984: 124). The aspiration to price stability through reining in the money supply was entirely at odds with financial liberalization.

The decision over the liberalization of exchange controls was not, though, taken solely in accordance with considerations about monetary policy. Transatlantic regulatory dynamics were also central. Abolition of exchange controls occurred against a backdrop of wider international—and, more specifically, Anglo-American—regulatory competition. In the run-up to the decision to liberalize, the Bank produced detailed reports on the abolition of exchange controls in both the US and Japan.[17] With the transatlantic regulatory feedback loop now exerting renewed pressures upon financial authorities, Anglo-American competition to attract Eurodollar business provided the context within which the decision to liberalize took place. We should therefore consider the decision to further liberalize exchange controls and open the City's financial markets within the broader lineage of Anglo-American development and the competition between New York and London, which lay at the heart of this process. Liberalization was not simply a consequence of philosophical preferences for free markets, but also a response to the competitive challenge posed by New York. That this liberalization continued was nonetheless highly contingent. It hinged upon an important event—the Fed's failure to win tighter regulation of the Euromarkets and bring offshore markets under control.

The Fed's Last Stand against the Euromarkets

Between 1978 and 1981, the Euromarkets and offshore banking were central to the interactions between UK and US monetary authorities. Volcker and other officials at the Fed were wary of the Euromarkets' impact on the conduct of US monetary policy and believed that the absorption of Eurodollar funds into the US money market during a period of tight monetary policy would undermine attempts to squeeze the credit supply. This had been the case in the late 1960s, as we saw in chapter 4. But by the late 1970s the Eurodollar market had grown even larger, and by 1981 the Eurodollar market was estimated to have grown to the size of approximately 10 percent of the US M3 money supply. As such, it constituted a major source of additional money that was not directly subject to the policy operations of the Fed (Helleiner, 1994: 135).

Faced with the challenge of Eurodollar leakage, the Fed and the US Treasury attempted to build international support for an attempt to encourage central banks to impose reserve requirements upon the international operations of their national banks and thus introduce reserve requirements for all Eurodollar activity. This was intended to arrest the market's growth and limit its negative impact upon national monetary policy autonomy.[18] The Fed received support from the West German government, which had, as we saw in the previous chapter, already attempted to curb Euromarket growth earlier in the decade and was similarly concerned with the 20-percent annual growth of the Euromarkets during the late 1970s (Hawley, 1984: 148). But when the Fed took the plan to the BIS, it met stiff resistance from two central banks that were heavily committed to protecting the Euromarkets: the Bank of England and the Swiss National Bank.

By April 1980, after the Bundesbank had also rejected the plan, the proposal was entirely scuppered (Helleiner, 1994: 137). The Bank of England, in conjunction with major European banks, had already effectively resisted the implementation of a 1977 European Commission proposal to standardize banking supervision (Hawley, 1984: 147). The successful resistance of both US and European regulatory initiatives demonstrates the pivotal role of the Bank of England as the guardian of the Euromarkets and financial liberalization. This role became more important as the transition to floating rates and problems of high inflation threatened to arrest financial globalization throughout the 1970s. The failure of the Fed's attempt to win regulation of the Euromarkets also demonstrated the limits of US structural power in finance and the degree to which increased monetary interdependence with the UK as part of a deeply integrated transatlantic financial space had undermined the capacity for US monetary policy autonomy.

Through its failed attempt to regulate the Euromarkets, the Fed demonstrated the difficulty of trying to lead cooperative action to regulate international financial markets. If the plan had gone ahead, it might well have substantially arrested the trend toward deregulation and financial liberalization. But the failure of the Fed's regulatory efforts meant that the growth of international financial markets continued apace. Consequently, the international inclination to deregulation and openness persisted as foreign governments made every effort to match liberalizing Anglo-American financial conditions and draw global financial firms into their domestic markets (Helleiner, 1994: 139).

The failure of the Fed's attempt to regulate the Euromarkets was not, though, simply a consequence of opposition from foreign central banks. US banks themselves were now actively lobbying for further deregulation and the recreation of offshore conditions within the US financial system. They used the Euromarkets as leverage to work away at eroding the New Deal regulatory order, weakening the US government's capacity for effective demand management in the process (Hawley, 1984: 132). As part of the transatlantic regulatory feedback loop, the dynamics of the liberalized offshore conditions within the City of London continued to erode the New Deal regulatory framework within the US. US banks had begun to lobby for the replication of Euromarket conditions within the US from the late 1970s, attempting to escape restrictive New Deal regulations and compete more effectively with nonbank financial institutions that were creating disintermediation by offering higher interest rates (as they were not encumbered by New Deal rate ceilings) at a time of high inflation.

A year before Thatcher came to power, the New York Clearing House Association made a crucial proposal, stipulating that New York should be granted a specialized status as a "monetary free trade zone." The plan attempted to draw offshore banking back into the US by encouraging both US and foreign banks to establish "international bank branches" (IBBs) in New York.[19] This proposal posed a major competitive challenge to London's status as a center for offshore banking and was undertaken by the New York authorities with exactly this intention in mind. By drawing the rapidly expanding offshore banking business back into New York, it was hoped that major benefits would accrue to the city, the US Treasury, and the banks themselves. US regulators were now on the front foot in their attempts to restore New York's preeminence as a hub for global banking, and it was the City of London, given its status as the principal location for Euromarket business and for overseas US banks, that could potentially stand to lose out. It was no surprise, then, that Bank officials paid careful attention to these developments.

Under the new scheme, IBBs would be able to make loans to, and take deposits from, overseas borrowers, without being encumbered by the reserve requirements and interest rate controls that were applied within the US. This constituted an attempt by US regulators and bankers to consciously and strategically reproduce the conditions that had sucked US banks into the City's Euromarkets en masse during the 1960s. US transnational banks viewed the creation of IBBs as a means of eliminating reserve requirements and interest rate ceilings for domestic banking (Hawley, 1984: 156). This was clearly a major assault on the key pillars of the New Deal regulatory order. As such, the plan would require the amendment of the Fed's Regulation D, which, as part of the New Deal regulatory framework, governed the reserve requirements for banks in the US. And, crucially, the plan would also require the amendment of Regulation Q, which prohibited payment of interest on deposits that fell short of thirty days.[20]

Competitive dynamics between New York and London were now driving the further erosion of the New Deal regulatory architecture in the US and the convergence of Anglo-American regulatory regimes. US authorities attempted to bring offshore business back under US territorial auspices by aping the regulatory climate of the City of London. The transatlantic regulatory feedback loop continued to disrupt regulatory frameworks on both sides of the Atlantic. Existing accounts of US financial deregulation during the Volcker era have understated the centrality of these competitive Anglo-American dynamics (Greider, 1987: 155; Schwartz, 2009a: 211; Krippner, 2011: 73; Konings, 2011: 131–37; Panitch and Gindin, 2012: 169).

The Americans thought that bringing the business back into New York would deliver substantial benefits. Repatriating offshore banking business would recover tax revenue on which the federal government had previously lost out, while the plan could boost the local New York economy (at a time when the city had been through a major fiscal crisis only a few years previously) by restoring the city's prestige as an international banking center and drawing in some portion of the Eurobond underwriting activities that were currently undertaken in London. It was anticipated that these developments might create between four to six thousand jobs.[21] Unlike the UK, the regulatory transformations in the US were also motivated in part by internal competition at the federal level, reflecting the differential geographical and constitutional composition of the US regulators in New York who were keen to take action before rival states and cities *within* the US—such as Florida, Delaware, Chicago, and Houston—acted on similar schemes. In the US, then, the decomposition of regulatory regimes was motivated not only by transatlantic competition, but also by interfederal competition.

Although attentive to the potential competitive challenge from New York, officials within the Bank remained sanguine over the effects of the proposed changes. They understood that the Fed might well filibuster the proposal from New York, to maintain monetary control in the face of potential leakage of funds between IBB and domestic markets, and noted that the Fed had rejected a similar proposal in 1975 on precisely these grounds. The new proposal was emerging at a time when the Fed was aware of its weakening control over the US monetary system, with declining membership of the Federal Reserve System by US banks already a major concern.[22]

Beyond their circumspect appraisal of the Fed's likely attitude to the New York proposal, Bank officials also extolled the virtues of the London markets. Officials noted that London would still have numerous attractions compared to New York, even if the plan went ahead. It was felt that London had two major advantages over New York. Firstly, its geographic location gave it a temporal overlap with continental Europe that increased its appeal as an entry point into European markets. Secondly, the expertise built up in London over decades at the core of the Euromarkets was also an enduring strength. In general, Bank officials accepted the view expressed by New York bankers: that the scheme wouldn't pose any more of a threat to London than other offshore centers already did.[23]

The proposals of the New York Clearing House Association were clearly intended as a competitive challenge. The Fed initially began to support the initiative rather cynically, to win greater bargaining power over the UK as part of is project to toughen regulation of the London Euromarkets. Once that initiative was defeated, the Fed felt that bringing Euromarket business back into New York was making the best of a bad situation (Hawley, 1984: 156). The proposals were subsequently approved by the Fed's board of governors in June 1981 in the form of "International Banking Facilities." The Fed's eventual acceptance of the proposals was due in no small part to the failure of earlier attempts to regulate the Euromarkets. As banks on either side of the Atlantic pushed their governments to create regulatory conditions favorable to international competition, the existing regulatory orders gradually broke down. These effects continued to erode domestic US financial regulation during the 1980s.

Within the City, US deregulatory maneuvers had been causing consternation regarding London's competitiveness as an international financial center. It was feared that Eurodollar business might return to a revitalized New York market as simple onshore dollar business.[24] The announcement of plans for the IBBs in New York led to the formation of a small working group in June 1978, consisting of clearing banks liasing with the Bank of England to assess the "danger posed by current developments." The Governor of the Bank of England had also mentioned the New York Free Banking Zone as a "topic of particular interest."[25] The Bank was particularly concerned with the competitive position of the UK -based banks, given their much-greater contribution to the balance of payments than foreign banks based in London. UK banks' share of total banks' external currency claims and liabilities had fallen from above one-fifth of the total in 1973 to around one-sixth of the total by 1978.[26]

Questions of where offshore banking would be hosted were only one aspect of the broader regulatory interaction between London and New York. The UK was keeping a close eye on US deregulation through officials at the Treasury and the Bank. In a letter to the Bank, the UK Treasury delegation at the embassy in Washington noted that the US financial system was marked by a "discernible trend towards deregulation and greater competition in the financial environment." Most important, Treasury officials noted that the momentum behind the dismantling of Regulation Q was continuing to build and noted that a majority of regulatory agencies would "accept the eventual elimination of Regulation Q."[27] As the existence of Regulation Q had been crucial to the original establishment of the Euromarkets, its abolition would have significant implications for the City. Euromarket operators would no longer be able to rely on their interest rate differential with US banks to draw funds away from the more tightly regulated US money markets.

Keen observations of international regulatory dynamics were not confined to the UK. The US was also scrutinizing developments within the UK. In mid-1979, Harold Williams, the chairman of the US Securities and Exchange Commission, paid a visit to London. Williams was on a fact-finding mission that would take him to a number of key international financial centers, with London of foremost importance. Williams intended to "examine the regulatory system operated in the UK, as compared with the comprehensive US system" and was supposedly himself inclined to "prefer self-regulation to imposed controls."[28] Williams's arrival in London marked a broader understanding within the SEC that, with liberalization and internationalization in the UK gathering momentum, London's markets presented a growing competitive challenge to New York securities business (Landau, 1987: 470; Longstreth, 1988: 183–85).[29]

Although deregulation occurred within a competitive context, it also did so in a manner marked by remarkably high levels of cooperation and openness, with officials on both sides seemingly well aware of, and often in direct communication about, developments on the other. This was a relationship characterized by "coordinated competition"—the methods employed were neither underhanded nor antagonistic but engaged in a manner that was recognized and reciprocated by authorities in the other country as part of an overall goal of liberalizing international financial markets. The degree of integration between financial markets in London and New York, as well as the major presence of US banks within the City, meant that deregulation, although competitive, occurred in a highly symbiotic fashion and tended toward a transatlantic convergence of regulatory conditions, as offshore banking practices and financial liberalization became increasingly embedded within both states. This dynamic of coordinated competition between the UK and the US was mirrored in the way that UK financial markets were gradually integrated into the competitiveness predicates of the European Common Market.

Williams's reception by UK officials is instructive in this regard. Heading to London with the explicit intention of understanding how the SEC's rules impacted overseas borrowers, Williams sought to gauge foreign perceptions of the usability of the New York markets. Such perceptions were a key component in their overall competitiveness. To this end, discussions between Williams and his UK counterparts were open and frank. Senior Treasury officials openly discussed their perceptions of the Yankee bond market with Williams, raising the complaint that the New York market required borrowers to divulge too much information. The relative attractions of the New York and Eurodollar markets were also openly discussed, and Williams was keen to discover whether the introduction of the Banking Act would impact US banks in the UK.[30]

These open discussions between senior officials on both sides of the Atlantic were a symbol of just how extraordinarily integrated Anglo-American financial markets had become. The situation contrasted markedly to the earlier unawareness and suspicion of the US Treasury and regulatory bodies, during the early years of the Eurodollar market, as to what exactly it was, how it functioned, and what impact it might have on the US. Increased financial interdependence required greater cooperation, openness, and mutual knowledge, but it did not eradicate competitive dynamics between rival financial centers. Instead, the acceptance of international financial competition and openness was inscribed in the new regulatory regimes that were gradually constructed in both states.

Although cooperation was remarkably close, there was still considerable room for friction as the maneuvers around Euromarkets regulation demonstrate. But the potential for tensions within the broader context of coordinated competition was not confined to the transatlantic horizon; the UK's gradual integration within the EEC was also a source of potential disagreement.

The City welcomed the prospect of deeper integration with European capital markets, with UK banks having "consistently been in favour of UK membership of the Community and broadly in favour of Monetary Union."[31] The passing of the EEC Banking Directive in 1977 had prompted greater innovation in devising ways to promote a unified European banking market with the anticipation that UK banks would come to view Europe as a "single home market," and their Continental branches as "part of the domestic branch network."[32]

But there was also an awareness that this vision of ever-deeper European integration might present risks to the City by threatening its status as an IFC equally attractive to a range of foreign banks. This arose in the form of fears that a "more formal and rigid EEC-wide supervisory system could inhibit the flexible UK system," creating a clash of regulatory cultures and undermining the City's regulatory attractiveness to foreign banks.[33] Additionally, deeper EEC integration might provoke tensions with other foreign banks by dividing the foreign banks in London into two distinct groups: "a privileged group of EEC banks and an unprivileged group of other banks."[34] Because the EEC Directive required member states not to privilege non-EEC banks over EEC bank branches, there was a risk that if a group of non-EEC banks had historically received more favorable treatment than those from the EEC, "the favourable treatment will be extended to the EEC banks under the directive but will not be extended to other foreign banks." Additionally, the directive required EEC branches to be given certain privileges "by right," with a danger that these privileges would not be extended to other foreign banks. Critically, for London's role as an IFC, the risk was that foreign banks outside of the EEC would view this as "the first step in a continuing process," and that as a consequence there would be a "reappraisal of the relative advantages and disadvantages of operating in London."[35]

As EEC integration combined with prior processes of Anglo-American financial integration, the City was increasingly acting as a transatlantic regulatory pivot: the crucial geographical site upon which processes of international capital market integration stretching from the US to Europe turned. The potential unevenness of the regulatory transformations this would entail, and the political fallout in terms of jealousies surrounding perceived preferential treatment, were interpreted as a potential threat to London's broader entrepôt status and international competitiveness.

Precisely these sorts of worries were borne out by the ignition of US concerns around exchange control liberalization, demonstrating the political consequence of differential geographical tempos and biases of coordinated competition. The Americans felt that the July measures had unduly privileged the EEC by liberalizing the securities market preferentially toward European markets, while maintaining regulations on the US. Chancellor Howe was prompted to explain to the Americans that this was just the first step in the direction of the eventual goal of worldwide portfolio liberalization.[36] Indeed, the Americans were so put out by the European bias of exchange controls liberalization that Howe felt compelled to write a letter to the US ambassador, explaining the measures on technical grounds and assuaging their fears.[37] In their efforts to liberalize financial markets, UK monetary authorities increasingly had to negotiate a course that respected the broader context of coordinated competition within both the EEC and the Anglo-American sphere of monetary interdependence. If the Americans felt that the UK was leaning more toward European markets at their expense, frictions were likely to ensue.

The final major factor bearing upon the liberalization of exchange controls was the future role of sterling. Officials at the Bank and the Treasury were aware that exchange controls could only be liberalized if sterling was in a strong position.[38] But officials within the Bank did express concerns over the potential for sterling to reemerge as a major international reserve currency after liberalization. It was felt that too great an expansion of sterling's international role would violate the Basel facility and agreements made in 1976, which involved the phasing out of sterling's status as a major international reserve currency.[39]

Concerns about the impact of a major resuscitation of sterling's international role did not prevent the Bank from speculating about the pound's future trajectory. The thoughts expressed here are extremely revealing, both in terms of the Bank's perception of the evolving international monetary system and the anticipated impact of exchange control abolition upon UK capitalism. Looking ahead, Bank officials speculated that a number of factors were likely to make sterling an attractive asset to private investors and managers of official reserves over the following decade. The key factor was the relative decline of the dollar, which was expected to continue unchecked.[40] The value of the dollar had fallen precipitously throughout 1979, in the wake of sustained US inflation and the OPEC price hikes (Greider, 1987: 18). Clearly, then, the Bank's calculations about the impact of liberalization upon the pound were highly dependent upon expectations about the future value of the dollar. The global significance of US monetary policy, and the interdependence of financial

markets, ensured that UK policy decisions would have to be carefully calibrated with regard to US policy dynamics. By liberalizing exchange controls
and expanding the scope for sterling business, as well as making it easier for
businesses to conduct dollar transactions and hold offshore accounts, UK authorities were heightening the interactivity between interest rates on sterling
and other currencies, particularly the dollar (Johnson, 1991: 37).

Domestically, the production of North Sea Oil was expected to exert sustained upward pressure on the value of the pound. The continued predominance of the City as "the most important international banking centre in the
world," and the wider accessibility of sterling compared to other major currencies, were also key factors in the Bank's assessment. But the broader international context was paramount to their considerations. Bank officials were
convinced that a multicurrency system was on the horizon as the dollar's hegemony faltered.[41] As the multicurrency system developed, sterling's international role would be revived as investors diversified away from the dollar. Regarding the future of the UK economy, the Bank's assessment revealed the
differential impact of a strong pound on UK capitalism. A potential to boost
invisible earnings was identified as the main advantage of an enhanced international role for sterling. Banks and brokerage firms dealing in sterling would
experience growth in their business.

The benefits of a stronger pound had long been recognized within the City
too. The Committee of London Clearing Banks called for the revival of sterling's international currency role in a 1977 paper prepared for the chancellor.[42]
Individual bankers had also noted that the fall in the value of the pound during
the IMF crisis had damaged the interests of the City and depreciated the resources of the UK banks with the effect that it "lessened their ability to compete internationally with the big European and US banks."[43] This had occurred
because a depreciation in sterling impacted banks whose capital was denominated in sterling by putting pressure on their capital adequacy ratios (by undermining the value of sterling assets vis-à-vis nonsterling liabilities), and
through balance sheet losses.[44] The weakness of sterling was affecting the capacity of UK banks to expand Eurocurrency lending by weakening their capital base. It was also thought to have damaged sterling's acceptability as an international currency, impairing the country's credit rating and leading to "signs
of reluctance to place funds in London," this problem even extending to the
Euromarkets, where "the volume grew more slowly than in previous years."
Within this context it was hoped that the IMF loan and Basel Concordat in

response to the 1976 crisis would be used to "stabilise sterling and restore international confidence in the City, particularly among foreign institutions."[45] There was clear support for a strong pound policy within the City.

This enthusiasm also applied to the closely related issue of exchange control liberalization, which was viewed as integral to restoring sterling's international standing. Sir Jeremy Morse, chairman of Lloyds Banks, had argued during a Bank meeting in June 1978 that the UK's improved economic position meant that exchange controls should now be dismantled and "kept tight only in a howling gale."[46] Influential parties in the City aligned closely with the Conservative vision for exchange control liberalization and were tipped off about the full magnitude of the plans during a meeting with the Bank in April 1979.[47]

From within the Bank of England, then, the view on restoring sterling's international role was somewhat conflicted, with principled support for exchange control liberalization balanced by a wider set of political considerations. Given that the UK government had publicly committed to running down sterling's international reserve role as part of the Basel Agreement, the Bank was worried about the effect that reinternationalizing sterling would have on the UK's vulnerability to capital flows, particularly in the context of large debt burdens. With these considerations in mind, the Bank felt that London must continue to conduct international financial business in foreign currency.

Despite these concerns, the governor suggested that the Bank had in fact "actively pressed for exchange control relaxations, concentrating first on the business sector, including insurance and banking." The overall hesitancy was driven by the Bank's wider entanglement with political considerations, as there were "strong political feelings," particularly from the trade unions, in preventing outward direct investment. Any further progress would depend upon "political ramifications" and the broader move toward exchange liberalization within the EEC.[48] The Bank's position demonstrated both its principled support for exchange control liberalization, and the extent to which UK liberalization was increasingly driven not only by transatlantic dynamics with the US, but also the wider EEC liberalization trajectory.

The Bank also perceived that the attendant sterling inflows and the high value of the pound could prove damaging to the traded goods sector: exposed to a greater volume of international capital movements, the economy "might run at a lower level of activity than otherwise."[49] The Bank appeared to be under no illusions about the varied impact of a strong pound upon UK businesses. It would most likely be good for the financial sector, and potentially highly detrimental for the manufacturing sector and export industries. This assessment turned out to be incredibly accurate. The Conservatives' commitment to a strong pound and exchange liberalization would wreak havoc on UK manufacturing while strengthening banking in the UK.

Where the Bank proved less prescient, however, was in its assessment of the dollar's future standing as the linchpin of the international monetary system. With the appointment of Paul Volcker in October 1979, the Bank was in for a big shock. The dollar's decline would be arrested in a drastic manner, with important implications for the UK's own monetary policy framework. In order to arrest the dollar's decline and push interest rates up to levels that were extremely harmful to sectors within the US economy, Volcker would initiate an epistemological shift in central banking.

Shock Monetarism

The Anglo-American economies were not the first major states to endorse monetarist techniques of central bank policy making. West Germany's Bundesbank pioneered monetarist techniques in the early 1970s. But this earlier turn to monetarism was fundamentally distinct in both purpose and practice from the shock monetarist policy regimes in the UK and the US. In practice, Germany's introduction of monetarist techniques was gradual and limited.[50] It was also initiated by policy makers within the Bundesbank, rather than conservative economists inside or outside the executive (as was the case in the UK and the US). In purpose, West Germany's approach to anti-inflationary policy was regime-conserving: designed to preserve the existing postwar corporatist balance between capital and labor and maintain German price stability (Johnson, 1998: 101–4; Germann, 2014: 712). It was therefore fundamentally consensual, receiving widespread support from German business and unions.

By stark contrast, the purpose of the abrupt and intense turns to monetarist central banking regimes in Anglo-America was regime-transforming, intended to shatter the postwar consensus between capital and labor by breaking the union movement and stamping out inflation. The significance of the synchronized and interdependent Anglo-American turns to monetarist shock regimes of central banking, then, was in its radical termination of the Keynesian compromise through induced recession and unemployment.

In the US, one man played the central role in leading the transformation. In one of the most important political appointments in the history of postwar

US capitalism, Paul Volcker took charge of the Federal Reserve in August 1979. Jimmy Carter's presidency had been wracked by high inflation and faltering economic performance. The problem of inflation, which had been simmering since the 1960s, reached a boiling point; it became the paramount issue within the US political economy, threatening to severely upset the existing distribution of wealth and power.[51] With inflation seemingly out of control, investors bet against the dollar, driving its value down in international markets. As inflation eroded the value of US government bonds, which were essentially offering a negative rate of return in real terms, bondholders and asset owners began to exert sustained pressure upon US monetary authorities to take anti-inflationary action (Greider, 1987: 40–45).

Power brokers on Wall Street identified Volcker as the right man to lead the war on inflation. After years of indecisive action from the Fed, which severely eroded the trust of investors and monetarist economists, Volcker was tasked with restoring its credibility and stamping out inflation in order to recover stable accumulation conditions. These pressures were echoed from within the international community, with West Germany in particular pressing the US to tighten its monetary policy and curb inflation during the IMF's Belgrade meeting in October 1979, shortly after Volcker's appointment as chairman of the Fed. The Germans, and other US trading partners, were concerned about the effects of dollar depreciation on their reserve values and resented the competitive export advantages that the weaker dollar offered to the US (Stein, 2010: 230).

Volcker immediately understood that an extremely tight monetary policy was required to exert pressure upon the credit supply and disincentivize borrowing. Under his stewardship, interest rates reached record levels.[52] Volcker pushed the discount rate up to 10.5 percent in his first month in charge, its highest level in the history of the Federal Reserve System. By October 1979, the Federal Funds rate had hit 16 percent, and by January 1980 it reached 20 percent (Greider, 1987: 76, 146).

As a veteran of the US political scene, Volcker understood that provoking a recession through extraordinarily high interest rates would be politically contentious, not least because it would lead to unemployment and business closures. The proposal for a sustained policy of tight money and austerity amounted to a conscious termination of the Keynesian commitment to full employment, in favor of a deflationary recession. Volcker's answer to this political problem was to bring about a paradigm shift in central banking techniques that would help insulate the Fed's decisions from political scrutiny by implying that interest rate decisions were taken on grounds of technical necessity rather than political choice (Greider, 1987: 106; Konings, 2011: 134; Krippner, 2012: 108).

This move to depoliticize interest rate policy was a key precondition of the central bank activism that ushered in the neoliberal era in the US. As we have seen, Volcker had championed the merits of practical monetarism prior to his appointment as chairman of the Fed (Volcker, 1978: 332). He put these views into practice by instituting a new monetary policy regime that involved a different approach to the traditional lever of open market operations. The new regime was designed to exercise tighter control over the money supply by enacting operating decisions on the basis of the aggregate level of reserves in the banking system, rather than targeting interest rate levels, as had traditionally been the case. The Fed's new operating system would be in place for the next three years, during the crucial phase of Volcker's attempt to quell inflation (Axilrod, 2011: 89–93). The Federal Open Market Committee (FOMC) would meet to decide a short-term path for money growth and would then task the market manager in New York with providing the system with a level of reserves that was thought to be consistent with the monetary targets. Under the new approach, interest rates would be allowed to fluctuate freely during the six-week period between FOMC meetings.

The stated aim of these measures was to restore the credibility of the Fed and provide a reliable basis (the monetary targets) according to which the markets could make judgments about interest rate directions. Yet it also came with the unstated benefit of passing off highly political decisions about interest rates as a consequence of pseudoscientific "laws" that were rooted in monetarist convictions about the privileged causal relationship between the money supply and inflation; it allowed the Fed to depoliticize controversial measures. The epistemological shift in favor of monetarism facilitated the political enactment of higher interest rates and regressive wealth redistribution. Monetarist theory was pragmatically employed in order to introduce radical interest rate policies that effectively ended the Keynesian commitment to maintaining full employment, regardless of any associated inflationary consequences. Now that the fight against inflation was sovereign, unemployment and recession were accepted as inevitable consequences, and monetarism reigned supreme. Internationally, the fact that the Volcker shock followed so closely on the heels of Carter's failed attempt to promote a Keynesian "locomotive strategy" through the Group of Seven (G7), in which Japan and Germany would stimulate global demand and drive growth, sounded the death knell of Keynesianism and paved the way for the ascent of neoliberal policy.

The UK experienced a comparable degree of monetary policy upheaval. Pressure from the IMF during the Callaghan government had, as we saw in the previous chapter, already initiated a more intensive focus upon monetary targets in the UK. But under the new Conservative government the intellectual commitment to monetarism became a central policy pillar. This was reflected in a raft of changes affecting the conduct of monetary policy, beyond the impacts of exchange liberalization previously discussed. These changes reflected a continuation of the failed attempt to reform monetary policy through the abortive CCC policy in the 1970s and were similarly geared toward expanding the scope for "market forces" within monetary policy. With the failure of CCC, monetary authorities had introduced the Supplementary Special Deposits Scheme to restrain credit creation and check competition for deposits within the banking sector. Under it, banks were required to hold non–interest-bearing deposits at the Bank of England if their portfolio of interest-bearing deposits grew beyond a certain level mandated by the Bank. This scheme, colloquially known as the "Corset," was abandoned in June 1980, as it was thought that the abolition of exchange controls rendered it ineffective (Artis and Lewis, 1981: 1; Buiter et al., 1981: 332–33). A new Banking Act had been introduced in 1979, to make clear which institutions could operate as banks within the evolving, institutionally diverse, and increasingly competitive monetary system. Reserve asset ratios were phased out from 1980, and new operational techniques for open market operations began in November 1980. From 1981, there were adjustments to the cash reserve requirement and experimentation with systems of monetary base control (Artis and Lewis, 1981: 1).

This amounted to a revolution in UK monetary policy—one that did not pass without producing serious tensions between the governor of the Bank and the prime minister, in a pattern of central bank versus executive tensions neatly mirrored across the Atlantic. In 1980 the Treasury and the Bank published a paper on "Monetary Control," which outlined that, in the absence of the Corset and other quantitative limits on bank lending, control of the monetary supply would now be achieved through adjustments in the level of interest rates and restraint of the Public Sector Borrowing Requirement (PSBR). Control over interest rates would be accomplished through open market operations and variations in the minimum lending rate.[53] The PSBR would be controlled through adjusting levels of taxation and spending (Buiter et al., 1981: 332–37). These related components of monetary and fiscal control were encapsulated in the government's Medium-Term Financial Strategy (MTFS), which mapped out medium term targets for growth of the money supply as part of a broad deflationary strategy that intended to lower the inflationary expectations of managers and trade union negotiators by tying the government into longer-term targets for monetary expansion (Stephens, 1996: 13).

Gordon Richardson, the Bank's governor, opposed the government's plans for the MTFS and argued that it would undermine the government's credibility by committing them to targets that were far too specific. But Thatcher's monetarist chief advisor, Terry Burns, stood fast and received the support of the influential Nigel Lawson.[54] The MTFS was rolled out in the March 1980 budget, with the only concession to the Bank and other critics being that the monetary targets were now given in ranges of percentiles rather than the firm figures originally proposed (Keegan, 1984:142). The adoption of the MTFS signaled to the Bank the severity of the government's commitment to deflationary policies. But the conflict did not end at this point. Chancellor Howe's announcement during the budget meeting that the Corset would be gone by June, proved to be "the harbinger of what turned out to be the worst period of diplomatic relations between a Prime Minister and a Governor of the Bank of England since the days of Harold Wilson and Lord Cromer during the mid-1960s" (Keegan, 1984: 150).

The government's high interest rate policy and the rising value of the pound were beginning to exert a heavy toll upon UK industry. By July 1980 officials at the Bank had decided that the situation, with increasing costs of borrowing and rapidly decreasing international competitiveness, was too grave to continue. Distress borrowing by struggling UK industrial firms was pushing up the money supply figures. The Bank determined to "de-rate M3": to push the government off its fixation with the measure for broad money in the economy. In practice, the Bank was already undermining the government's commitment to reducing the growth of M3 by using its contacts with the clearing banks to ensure a supply of credit to stuttering industrial firms. In the Bank's eyes, monetary policy was needlessly tight and in danger of creating very high unemployment, with GDP falling by 2.2 percent in 1980 (Smith, 1987: 90). The pragmatism of the Bank increasingly ran up against the ideological fervor of Thatcher's administration.

Events came to a head when Richardson visited Downing Street in early July. He implored Thatcher to lower interest rates, on pain of strangling the corporate sector of the economy. Thatcher grudgingly acceded to Richardson's request, but from that point on, with the M3 figures worsening and undermining the government's credibility, Thatcher's discontent with the Bank continued to grow. Tensions between the prime minister and the Bank were not, however, confined to disputes over the appropriate level of interest rates. The Bank increasingly came under pressure from Conservative politicians and their monetarist advisors to adopt a form of monetary base control derived from the quantity theory of money. This would have implied an attempt to achieve much tighter control of the monetary base by the Bank, but, as a consequence, interest rates would fluctuate unpredictably, as they were doing in the US (Johnson, 1991: 32).

At this key moment in the first phase of Thatcher's government, with monetary policy increasingly politicized within elite circles (ironically as a result of the attempt to depoliticize monetary policy) of the UK state and with high interest rates seriously undermining UK industry and intensifying the recession, the Fed was increasingly drawn in as an important voice in the debate. The Fed's intervention demonstrated the transatlantic interactivity of central bank regime transformation. Officials at the Bank looked to the Fed in order to fulfill their own domestic political objectives in thwarting some of the more radical Thatcherite proposals. By drawing upon the Fed's expertise, the Bank sought to navigate the institutional upheaval of the Thatcher government without sacrificing its institutional autonomy. With the Bank not formally independent like the Fed, the risk of being steamrollered by a fervently monetarist administration was graver than that faced by its US counterpart.

Thatcher and her advisors were clearly inspired by the adoption of the Fed's new monetary policy techniques under Volcker and wanted to apply these methods to the Bank. UK officials had been casting around for novel methods from a range of foreign central banks, but given its status and significance the Fed was a particularly important source of technical inspiration. This was the context within which Stephen Axilrod, a senior Fed bureaucrat, met with a series of UK Bank officials in order to discuss monetary policy. Axilrod went through the Fed's new operating procedures in detail with his UK colleagues and was also invited to attend a parliamentary committee setup to scrutinize UK monetary policy. While in London, Axilrod met with Gordon Richardson, with whom he discussed how and to what extent the Bank should bring monetary and reserve aggregates into the policy process. Crucially, the discussion was focused upon "how to go halfway toward meeting the Prime Minister's wishes without actually going quite that far" (Axilrod, 2011: 103–6). At a time of intense political struggle over monetary policy, institutional cooperation between the Bank and the Fed was employed to maintain central bank autonomy and navigate a pragmatic and conciliatory path through the prescriptions of monetarist politicians and their advisors. In the end, the Bank, with the support of officials from the Treasury, was able to resist the government's attempts to move wholeheartedly toward a system of monetary base control (Keegan, 1994: 156; Stephens, 1996: 20).

The defense of central bank autonomy under the duress of fervently monetarist political pressure was a defining feature of the monetary policy revolution on both sides of the Atlantic. These early struggles represented a key moment in the growth of central bank power that would come to characterize the neoliberal era in the UK and the US. Ronald Reagan's electoral victory in 1980 brought a monetarist president and a highly ideological government to power in America. During Volcker's tenure, the Fed came under pressure from Reagan's undersecretary of the Treasury for monetary affairs, Beryl Sprinkel. Sprinkel was a monetarist economist and former banker (Greider, 1987: 363). He was uncomfortable with the idea of the money supply being under the Fed's independent control and repeatedly made public announcements intended to undermine the Fed's credibility (Axilrod, 2011: 100). Jerry Jordan, a former economics professor who had participated in the Shadow Open Market Committee, served on Reagan's Council of Economic Advisors and was also highly critical of the Fed's anti-inflationary credentials.

Tensions between Reagan's administration and the Fed came to a head in the spring of 1981. Reagan's senior officials and advisors—men like Sprinkel and Jordan—vociferously criticized the Fed for allowing the monetary aggregates to rise at an unacceptable rate (Woolley, 1984: 125). They were convinced that Volcker's actions were undermining the president. Indeed, Treasury Secretary Regan later confided that he and the president had even considered "abolishing the Fed" (Greider, 1987: 378).[55] Volcker was called into the Oval Office to defend his actions in front of the president and his advisors. But Volcker drew on his wealth of political experience in order to defend the Fed's autonomy and evade answering questions transparently. He cloaked his analysis in the armor of complex technical details relating to monetary operations (Greider, 1987: 376–81). Ultimately, Volcker was able to maintain the Fed's independence despite pressure from the Reagan administration. Indeed, the constitutional basis of the Fed's independence gave the US central bank a more secure footing than that enjoyed by the Bank of England, but the scope for policy actions was nevertheless highly dependent upon the broader political context.

Despite different operating procedures and different degrees of institutional autonomy, both central banks consistently pursued a deflationary course of high interest rates between 1979 and 1982. That they were able to do so had much to do with the evolution of financial markets since the 1970s, but it was also very much a consequence of the lobbying efforts and political pressure applied by the banking sector. Regulatory and market developments enabled the banks to prosper from the high interest rate regimes while industry and workers suffered. At the heart of this new monetary policy regime, then, lay a partisan representation of certain interests within the financial sector that paved the way for the massive expansion of the sector's power in subsequent decades.

Infrastructures of Financial Transformation

In both the UK and the US, the high interest rate regimes and deflationary policies that ushered in the 1980s involved a dangerous game of brinkmanship with banks and the wider economy. In the past, the Fed had been forced to pull back from sustained attempts at tight money policy due to the possibility of major financial collapses resulting from the strain caused by increased borrowing costs. This had, as we saw in the previous chapter, been the case in 1969–70, when the US financial system had proved unable to deal with the high interest rate policy that had produced the commercial paper crisis and led to the collapse of Penn Central. In response to the crisis, the Fed had been required to rapidly inject liquidity into the banking system, undermining the original aim of tight money (Mayer, 2001: 186). US policy makers had been particularly sensitive to this possibility ever since (Konings, 2011: 134; Panitch and Gindin, 2012: 169). In the UK, the experience of the secondary banking crisis in 1974 had produced similar concerns, with interest rate hikes provoking a series of collapses within the secondary banking sector that forced the Bank to organize a support operation in concert with the major clearing banks (Capie, 2010: 525).[56]

That the Fed and the Bank were now able to implement policies of high interest rates and stick to them fairly consistently was partly due to a generally supportive political climate. But it was also an outcome of the development of Anglo-American financial market infrastructure. Sustained inflation during the 1970s affected nominal interest rates and changed the impact of interest rate ceilings and other financial regulations. Banks in both the US and the UK also became more dependent upon wholesale markets and were increasingly able to circumvent domestic tight money policies through the importation of offshore funds. Banks moved increasingly into loans and advances and away from traditionally safer assets such as government securities. As a result, they became more vulnerable to a sudden loss of earnings if market rates rose above loan rates. This led banks to switch toward variable rate lending contracts or "flexi-rate" loans (Lewis and Davis, 1987: 9). Flexi-rate loans increased banks' capacity to weather the interest rate shocks of the early neoliberal period by passing on the fluctuations in rates to their customers, thus insulating themselves from risk. Rapid innovation and technological development within financial markets continued apace during the 1980s (Llewellyn, 1985: 10).

The growth of wholesale banking and the Euromarkets meant that banking practices became progressively standardized on both sides of the Atlantic. Techniques of US banks were merged with practices in the UK and then exported back to America, driving homogenization. As new Eurocurrency markets emerged in other countries, the banking practices pioneered by UK and US banks in London began to be transmitted worldwide (Lewis and Davis, 1987: 9, 83). Another notable innovation was the introduction of rollover credits. These new loans "combined the interest-rate flexibility of British overdrafts with the legal formality of US medium-length term loans." Instead of a fixed interest rate for the entire span of the loan, the rate would be fixed for certain intervals of time (three to six months) and then adjusted in line with the changing market rates on bank deposits. The London Interbank Borrowing Rate (LIBOR) was used as the basis for these calculations, reflecting the international predominance of the London market. These innovations were part of a process whereby wholesale bankers pioneered techniques for passing on interest rate risks to borrowers at rollover dates that were directly linked to funding costs (Banking Information Service, 1985: 11; Lewis and Davis, 1987: 87, 111). Floating rate issues, adjustable to interest rate movements, also became much more widespread within the Eurobond market. High inflation and interest rate volatility led corporate borrowers to change their practices by shifting from fixed interest capital market sources of funds to floating rate bank sources (Llewellyn, 1985: 18).

Nevertheless, despite these adaptations, high interest rate policies still ran the risk of triggering major financial collapses. Both the Fed and the Bank realized that selective interventions in the market were required to provide support to systemically significant firms in both the financial and industrial sectors. The Fed was able to undertake selective bailouts for systemically significant banks. It did so with the bailout of the First Philadelphia Bank—the largest bailout in US history at the time (Panitch and Gindin, 2012: 170). In the UK, the Bank felt compelled to organize the clearing banks to provide support for significant firms that were struggling to manage within the context of higher interest rates and recession (Coakley and Harris, 1983: 194; Keegan, 1984: 146).

In both states, high interest rate regimes were also conditioned by, and contingent upon, a second dimension of the changing institutional infrastructure: regulatory transformations affecting the financial sector. Toward the end of the 1970s, City financial institutions had begun lobbying intensely for the abolition of exchange controls, which had limited the scope for postwar overseas investment—essentially a campaign for the City's freedom to export capital wherever in the world it chose, without politically instituted limitations (Coakley and Harris, 1983: 35–36). When controls were abolished, the impact was hugely significant. Pension funds substantially increased their overseas portfolio between 1979 and 1980, transforming the geographical spread of their investment by moving into the stock markets in Tokyo, Hong Kong, Singapore, and Australia (Coakley and Harris, 1983: 37). Holdings of foreign currency deposits also increased dramatically after liberalization, while the proportion of international business that UK banks conducted in sterling doubled between 1979 and 1983 (Banking Information Service, 1985: 15; Artis and Taylor, 1989: 14).

UK banks quintupled their overseas earnings between 1980 and 1984, with a large proportion of their increased earnings derived from areas that had been influenced by the abolition of exchange controls—for example, portfolio investment income and interest earned on lending abroad in sterling (Banking Information Service, 1985: 33). The abolition of the Corset enabled banks to expand and evolve their lending without the funding constraints that previously existed. As a consequence, they moved into the mortgage markets on a massive scale. The mortgage market had previously been a virtual monopoly of the building societies, but between 1980 and 1982 bank lending to the mortgage market rose from £50 million per month to over £3500 million per month. During this same period, banks' share of new mortgage lending increased from 6 percent to 40 percent, while the share of the building societies decreased from 80 percent to 54 percent (Llewellyn, 1985: 27). It is not hard to detect here the beginning of the intensified mortgage market competition that would eventually, as the next chapter shows, filter through to the subprime crisis several decades later.

After the abolition of exchange controls, the transformation of monetary policy became, to a certain extent, a fait accompli. By removing the protection for domestic banking activity, the abolition of controls "forced the reform of monetary regulation to take place on a very liberal basis" (Artis and Taylor, 1989: 1). This was particularly the case given the accelerated internationalization of financial markets during the 1970s, which meant that "monetarism's promotion of laissez-faire in financial markets became a necessity rather than a policy choice, given the City's growing international role" (Coakley and Harris, 1983: 207). So, although a move in this direction might have occurred regardless, exchange control abolition gave it a logical basis (Artis and Taylor, 1989: 1–2). By pressing for liberalization, then, the City set in motion a process that culminated in a wholesale reorganization of monetary policy, which had to be formulated within the constraints imposed by ever-deeper financial integration within the global economy. In this context, this enabled the move from quantitative and administered controls on lending toward a market-based system centered exclusively upon the role of interest rates in shaping the price and demand for money.

The tighter integration of national money markets also stimulated a convergence of interest rates, as financial operators could easily switch between markets in pursuit of interest rate arbitrage; thus, lower rates would lead to potentially destabilizing capital outflows as investors sought higher returns elsewhere (Llewellyn, 1980: 1). With the Bank of England intent on maintaining a strong pound in order to dampen imported inflation, the need to follow suit with the movements of the dollar became even more urgent.[57] Therefore, when Volcker pushed up US interest rates, the Bank felt obliged to follow suit. Pursuing an independent interest rate policy became increasingly difficult as the processes of interest rate interactivity that began with the birth of the Euromarkets continued to develop into the neoliberal era. Despite the apparent promise of the floating rates system in allowing a more independent and discretionary monetary policy than had previously been possible under Bretton Woods, the reality was that intensifying financial integration increasingly undermined this possibility.

In the US, the financial deregulation that had been "gestating for more than a decade" came to fruition with the Depositary Institutions Deregulation and Monetary Control Act in 1980 (Greider, 1987: 156; Mayer, 2001: 196). The act was a major political coup for the Fed, with all depository institutions now legally obliged to maintain reserves with the central bank (Woolley, 1984: 70). Membership of the Federal Reserve System had been declining, and the Fed passed off the legislation as a technical prerequisite for effective control of the money supply. In reality, the act was intended to strengthen the Fed's political support base by tying it to the power of the private banks (Greider, 1987: 155).

The act's unspoken quid pro quo was that the banks would accommodate the political requirements of their chief regulator in return for favorable responses to their request for mergers, branches, and the extension of their powers. The act also included direct benefits for the banks and other financial institutions, by eliminating their interest rate ceilings (Meltzer, 2009: 1013, 1066–67). This was a key moment in the financialization of the US economy. With the old Regulation Q checks on lending now gone, credit could flow freely around the economy even if market rates rose. Whereas the old ceilings had served as stop valves within the financial system, choking off credit when market rates rose above the administered ceilings, now credit simply became more expensive. Higher and more volatile rates associated with the abolition of ceilings fed into the development of a macroeconomic climate that increasingly favored financial activities over investment in industry and manufacturing (Krippner, 2012: 58).

A series of associated legislative measures were passed through Congress in order to deregulate finance and win the support of the sector for the Fed's tight money regime. These measures repealed the New Deal regulatory rules put in place during the 1930s and set the US financial system firmly on the path toward deregulation, with the implication that "borrowers, businesses and consumers would pay higher interest rates and creditors would enjoy higher returns on their wealth" (Greider, 1987: 156). The act embodied something symptomatic of broader trends within financial regulation: a combination of expanded supervisory authority and control for the Fed *alongside* increased liberalization for banks and other financial institutions. The Act widened the state's regulatory purchase over the entire banking sector. It was this combination of increased liberalization alongside and through increased supervision that allowed the Fed and the financial sector to effectively steer a course through the Volcker shock (Panitch and Gindin, 2012: 170).

It was also this exact same combination—of increased supervisory authority alongside financial liberalization—that occurred in the UK as Anglo-American developmental interactivity drove a synchronized homogenization of regulatory conditions.[58] The Banking Act, which was introduced in April 1979, shortly before the liberalization of exchange controls and other measures, required that all institutions accepting deposits had to receive authorization from the Bank as either recognized banks or licensed operators. The Bank would then supervise deposit-taking institutions, with their advertisements for deposits, use of banking names, and descriptions all regulated. All institutions were also required to pay in to a deposit protection scheme for their clients (Capie, 2010: 635). Liberalization of finance in the neoliberal era was conducted alongside and through the increased formalization of supervisory authority held by central banks and other regulatory bodies. In reality, deregulation meant reregulation.

Winners and Losers of Monetary Restructuring

What was the impact of all these changes on transatlantic regulatory regimes and the interest rate shocks? The benefits were enormously differential, both in terms of business sectors and of the relationship between capital and labor, but they followed broadly similar patterns. The start of the Volcker shock marked the beginning of the most profitable period for US commercial banking since World War II. Despite the wider recession in the US economy, banking experienced an increase of 10.3 percent in its net operating income in 1980, which was followed by another increase of 9 percent in 1981. Within this context of overall banking profitability, the largest gains went to the biggest banks. While returns on many other business activities fell, bank profits increased by more than 25 percent. The banks were able to take advantage of wide interest rates spreads when rates began to fall, borrowing cheaply but continuing to lend to customers at very high rates. Volcker's measures were good first and foremost for the largest banks, which happened to be the Fed's key constituency (Greider, 1987: 411–13). But the experience of the financial sector was not uniform: there were casualties. Savings and loans companies experienced severe difficulties both during and after the Volcker shock, with the number of insolvencies in the hundreds (Greider, 1987: 413; Mayer, 2001: 217–19; Panitch and Gindin, 2012: 173).

Other groups also suffered. The strengthening dollar reduced demand for US exports, with grain farmers and the steel industry hit particularly hard, while manufacturers experienced falling export volumes and a reduced share of the domestic markets as foreign imports became cheaper (Greider, 1987: 415–16; Konings, 2011: 138). But the real losers during the Volcker shock were US workers. Given the contradiction at the heart of the Fed's tight money regime—between increasing financial liberalization on the one hand, and the aspiration to fuller monetary control on the other—it was not surprising that the most effective anti-inflationary strategy would be to use an induced recession and the threat of unemployment to reduce workers' wage share. Indeed, it is arguable that inflation was not squeezed out of the US economy, but merely redirected away from wages and consumer prices and into the financial sector and asset prices (Konings, 2011: 137).

Volcker's achievements in reducing inflation owed much to the accompanying stance of Ronald Reagan toward US labor disputes (Axilrod, 2011: 99). Reagan's stern position vis-à-vis the air traffic controllers' strike, where he resisted their wage demands and effectively broke their union, set in place a demonstration affect that contributed to the rapid fall in wage-push inflation (Axilrod, 2011: 99). Volcker's struggle to contain inflation was always about more than technical issues of monetary policy; it was part of a broader neoliberal attempt to shift the balance of class power in the US back toward capital, a project in which breaking the political capacity of the US working class in order to dampen their expectations of increasing wages and rising living standards was a key component (Greider, 1987: 430; Panitch and Gindin, 2012: 171). This point was not lost on Volcker, who always accepted that, in reality, inflation defended upon a broader sociopolitical context, rather than the level of the money supply (Volcker, 1978: 330–31).

Between 1979 and 1983, personal incomes from interest earnings grew by over 70 percent, whereas wage incomes grew by only 33 percent (Greider, 1987: 578). The differential benefits of the Volcker shock were clear. Volcker's high interest rate regime accelerated the trend toward financialization that was already underway as funds were drawn into the US banking system from corporations, savers, and foreign investors. With wages falling, workers became more entwined in the relations of consumer-credit dependence that came to define the neoliberal era. Internationally, the strong dollar pulled in capital inflows that helped cover the ballooning public debt of the US during the Reagan era of massive defense expenditure. The Volcker shock replenished the dollar's role as the dominant international currency and strengthened the international appeal of US financial markets (Konings, 2011: 139–40). The reorganization of America's domestic class relations was intimately bound up with the maintenance of America's position at the heart of the global political economy.

In the UK, the story of the early neoliberal austerity regime runs remarkably parallel. The strong pound exerted a crushing toll on UK manufacturing and export-led industries as UK goods were priced out of international markets and borrowing costs soared under higher interest rates (Stephens, 1996: 17). The consequences were, in fact, much more severe than in the US and rapidly accelerated the decline of UK manufacturing. In a period when measures of French and West German real exchange rates were roughly stable, the UK's rose from 106.3 in 1978 to 137.9 in 1980 and was still at the level of 135.2 by the end of 1981. The UK's effective exchange rate increased by 21.6 percent between 1979 and 1980 (Buiter et al., 1981: 330). The UK's economy experienced a fall in output on a scale not witnessed since the 1920s with a decline of more than 5 percent of GDP between 1980 and 1981, as well as a doubling of unemployment. Manufacturing output fell by a staggering 20 percent between 1979 and 1980 (Keegan, 1984: 127, 171, 196–203; Stephens, 1996: 18).

Beset by the same contradiction between increased financial liberalization and the aspiration to tighter monetary control, Thatcher's government failed spectacularly in its attempt to hit the prescribed monetary targets. Monetarism was always defined more by its political implications than any semblance of intellectual coherence—a case of the "uncontrollable in pursuit of the indefinable," as a member of one of Thatcher's early Cabinets stated (Buiter et al., 1981: 367). But the policies were much more effective in weakening labor through the inducement of large-scale unemployment and the weakening of traditionally well-unionized sectors. The real showdown with the unions would come later on than in the US, with the landmark defeat of the bitter miners' strike in 1984. But Thatcher's planning for a conflict with the union movement was deeply rooted, having first been outlined in the "Stepping Stones" policy document prepared while still in opposition in 1977.

For the City, the benefits of austerity were widespread, and Thatcher's free market–oriented credit policy was warmly received (Johnson, 1994: 39). The high interest rate regime was beneficial to UK banks. The profitability crisis of the 1970s had led to a decreased reliance upon internal funds for corporate financing, which led to a shift away from fixed rate bond issues and toward bank financing. Between 1972 and 1980, bank borrowing financed over 50 percent of the corporate sector's gross borrowing requirement. Banks also became more competitive and aggressive during the period, partly in response to the increased entry of foreign banks into the market, while high inflation increased corporations' requirements for working capital, with banks an important source. As the recession continued to bite under Thatcher, businesses were forced into "distress borrowing" in order to stay afloat (Llewellyn, 1985: 22). These factors combined to ensure that the demand for credit was actually highly inelastic, with the implication that businesses would continue to borrow despite the increase in interest rates.

Under the monetarist regime, the UK economy at large suffered while the City prospered (Coakley and Harris, 1983: 192). City banks accepted attempts to control the money supply, as long as this did not entail direct restrictions on their freedom (Coakley and Harris, 1983: 200). Viewed from the perspective of the banks, then, the contradiction between monetary control and

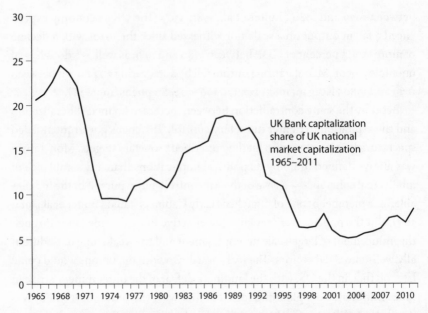

FIGURE 6.1. Capitalization as a share of national market capitalization:
British banks, 1965–2011

financial liberalization makes much more sense. But the policy was not without its dangers to the banks, which might begin to suffer if the recession wiped out too many large-scale industrial customers. All in all, though, the City supported monetarism as long as control of the money supply was mainly achieved through fiscal retrenchment, and the government supported a laissez-faire approach to the markets for foreign exchange and credit (Coakley and Harris, 1983: 204). The benefits to banks in the UK are neatly demonstrated in figure 6.1: as the graph demonstrates, UK banks (all banks operating in the UK, not just UK-owned banks) witnessed a very large increase in their share of total market capitalization between 1979 and 1989.[59] The first ten years of the Thatcher government were therefore enormously beneficial to banks based in the UK, who saw their share values rapidly appreciating.

Despite the differential impacts of neoliberal austerity within business sectors, this was not a case of banking versus industry. By the end of the 1970s, US industry had by and large come to support the anti-inflationary stance of the Fed and recognized the benefits of a strategy to defeat labor (Panitch and Gindin, 2012: 163). And, as we have already seen, savings and loan associations (S&Ls) were major casualties of the Volcker shock. In the UK, Thatcherism was based upon an unstable alliance of interests, with the CBI (Confederation of British Industry), the chief representative of UK industry, welcoming the promise of lower inflation and reduced taxes for businesses. The possibility that a recession might allow the "reimposition of managerial authority" was also widely welcomed in the business community, and the "sound money" common sense of monetarism had appealed broadly (Jessop et al., 1984: 43–45). The real victims of the monetarist austerity regime, then, were the millions of unemployed workers that felt the squeeze on both sides of the Atlantic.

The development of Anglo-American high interest rate regimes and accelerating financial liberalization also had significant international ramifications. During the 1980s, in the US, high interest rates drew in foreign capital on a massive scale. These inflows allowed the Reagan administration to finance its deficit while also further contributing to the expansion of credit within the US, further fuelling financialization and driving up financial sector profits. Inadvertently, the Reagan administration had stumbled upon a solution to the fiscal crisis of the late 1960s and 1970s, with foreign inflows into US Treasury bonds and dollar assets enabling the US to avoid the kind of fiscal deflation or increased taxation that would have been required without the vast inflows to cover the deficit (Krippner, 2012: 87–92).

Not only did interest rate shocks and financial liberalization transform the United States' capacity to finance its deficit—it also exerted a crushing impact on developing countries. By responding to the difficult economic conditions of the late 1970s by inducing further recessionary conditions, the Thatcher and Reagan administrations dampened global demand and devastated the primary commodity economies of developing countries in Africa and Latin America, as demand for their exports dried up (Greider, 1987: 415; Kiely, 2007: 202). The interest rate shocks and austerity also aggravated the debt crisis in the Global South. Countries had borrowed heavily from the banks in the City and New York during the 1970s, with the vast OPEC surpluses generated from the oil price shock recycled through the Anglo-American financial systems and lent in turn to developing countries. Interest payments on this foreign debt rose from $24.3 billion in 1979 to $41.8 billion in 1981, with massive increase in the percentage of GDP attributed to servicing the debt (Kiely, 2007: 2002).

Terminating the Keynesian Compromise

The tight money regimes imposed in the UK and the US brought a stunning end to the postwar Keynesian compromise and signaled the birth of the neoliberal era in the West. As this chapter has argued, the transatlantic synchronicity of these regimes was not, as the story has so often been told, coincidental or merely a consequence of shared ideology. It was a result of the symbiotic transatlantic development of Anglo-American financial markets and central banking practices. The shared desire to rein in inflation and achieve price stability emerged from the manner in which Anglo-American officials sought to anchor macroeconomic objectives in an era of floating exchange, high inflation, and intensified pressures from bankers in London and New York to liberalize financial regulations. They achieved this through the adoption of monetarist shock regimes, rather than through the construction of a multilateral fixed rate system.

Restoring price stability was also very much about arresting the destabilizing impact of inflation upon investors and financial markets and restoring class discipline over labor by means of austerity. It was no coincidence, then, that the strongest attempts at monetarist policies were made in the two states that hosted the world's foremost financial centers. Bankers on both sides of the Atlantic wanted to see a return to stable accumulation conditions. The convergence of monetary regimes in the UK and the US was underpinned by the increasing integration of global financial markets, which was based on the interactivity between London and New York and the transatlantic regulatory feedback loop. Dynamics of "coordinated competition" between regulators in London and New York were central to the way in which the offshore conditions of banking—brought about through the earlier Anglo-American developmental interactivity of the 1950s and 1960s—were embedded within national monetary regimes through processes of financial liberalization and supervisory centralization. We simply cannot understand the synchronized turn to increased financial liberalization and novel forms of central banking in the UK and the US as purely a consequence of shared ideological commitments or of internally discrete similarities between their national models of capitalism. Nor can we view US financial liberalization and financialization as a pristinely endogenous process or an exercise of US structural power. As this chapter has shown, transatlantic processes of financial integration and competition were absolutely fundamental to the early Anglo-American politics of neoliberal restructuring. They constrained the policy options available to regulators in both states.

The central contradiction at the heart of the Anglo-American experiments with monetarism was that between financial liberalization on the one hand, and control of the money supply on the other. Attempts to tightly control the money supply were made when the further liberalization of transatlantic financial markets and expansion of the Euromarkets made monetary control ever harder to achieve, particularly when undertaken without recourse to the kind of quantitative and administered restrictions that were now rejected. Attempts to ration credit by adjusting interest rates to affect demand proved to have a limited effect, given the apparent inelasticity of demand for credit (Krippner, 2012: 83).

By tying themselves into austerity policies, the UK and the US demonstrated their commitment to countering inflation and restoring credibility. In the process, they showed that the 1980s would not be characterized by the rising wages and growing militancy of trade unions, nor the sustained inflation that had marked the decade before. Under this new orientation of capitalism, central banks and monetary policy were accorded a more prominent role than during the postwar era. The political struggles between the Fed, the Bank, and their respective executives during the early neoliberal period were critical to the pattern of increased central bank independence that came to define the neoliberal era in the UK and the US.

Financial liberalization in Anglo-America ushered in a new era of increasingly financialized capitalism under which more and more aspects of social life and economic activity would be drawn into the orbit of credit-debtor relations centered around liberalized financial markets. These developments had severe consequences. As the power of finance increased and wages fell or stagnated, workers became more indebted and dependent upon financial markets. The "politics of productivity" that had offered so much promise to workers was now shattered.[60] It was not until several decades later that the model instated during the 1980s would fully implode in a spectacular manner during the global financial crisis of 2007/8.

7

A Crisis of Anglo-America

SCENES OF LEHMAN Brothers' employees hurriedly clearing out belongings from their London offices in September 2008 became part of the iconic imagery of the global financial crisis (GFC). The bank had just filed for the largest bankruptcy in US history. Lehman's collapse was the pivotal moment in the unfolding of the crisis, causing interbank lending markets to seize up, demonstrating the enormous peril faced by the global financial system.

Beyond the immediate context of the crisis, though, these images had a wider significance. They represented the catastrophic culmination of the decades-long processes of Anglo-American development that have been the subject of this book. In an age of globalized finance, the collapse of a US bank shook global markets and sent tremors through London. This was a crisis in the heartland: a financial disaster incubated in liberalized and globally oriented Anglo-American financial markets that transmitted contagion around the world (Gowan, 2009).

That the United Kingdom and the United States were at the center of this catastrophe was no accident. The institutional infrastructures and prevailing ideas that made Anglo-America vulnerable to a crisis on this scale had (as we have seen) been established through a concerted and long-term dismantling of the postwar Keynesian financial order in both states. The full effects of those processes were now felt globally, as the world entered into the worst financial crisis since the Great Depression. The financial crash would be shadowed by a prolonged recession that gripped all of the major Western economies from 2009.

The events of 2007/8 marked the beginning of the first truly global crisis of the neoliberal order. It would provide the biggest challenge yet for the globalized financial markets authored in Anglo-America. And it would test the limits of the technical and political capacities of the Anglo-American central banks that presided over those markets, prompting the embrace of highly unortho-dox policy measures, as they grappled with the new challenges of deflation and secular stagnation.

Diagnoses of the causes of the GFC have been broad and varied, ranging from emphasis on misaligned microeconomic incentives that encouraged risk taking (Roubini and Mihm, 2010) and misplaced intellectual faith in the effi-ciency of markets (Irwin, 2013) to the regulatory capture of influential public agencies and public policies (Baker, 2010) or global payment imbalances that fueled asset price inflation (Bernanke, 2011). Within this broad literature, the Anglo-American accent of the crisis has also been acknowledged (Gowan, 2009; Hay, 2013). But the systematic transatlantic developmental processes linking the reconstitution of Anglo-American financial markets have not been adequately explored. The crisis has either been interpreted as an extension of endogenous US dynamics of financial market transformation into a "satellite" London market, missing the reciprocity of Anglo-American development (Gowan, 2009), or as emergent from a comparatively specific "Anglo-liberal" model of capitalism that has been effectively typologized, but without effec-tively historicizing the generative transatlantic dynamics underpinning it (Hay, 2013). Many of these processes had their deeper origins not in the neo-liberal transformation of the 1980s, but in the postwar Anglo-American finan-cial integration explored in previous chapters. That these processes got under-way in earnest from the 1960s, within the supposed prime of the embedded liberal order of Keynesian welfare states, demonstrates the limited success of that order in properly embedding Anglo-American finance within a commit-ment to stable economic growth, full employment, and domestic welfare.

This chapter examines the incubation and transmission of the crisis within and through the liberalized financial markets of the UK and the US. It takes a wider-angle lens than previous chapters, shifting focus from a finer-grained archival analysis to a broader mapping of the transformation of Anglo-American finance from the later 1980s to 2007/8. The chapter argues that the Anglo-American origins of the crisis had a deep historical-institutional lineage, resting in the critical transatlantic transformations away from the Keynesian order during the early 1980s that were themselves enabled and conditioned by prior decades of postwar Anglo-American development. Only from the perspective of the longue durée of Anglo-American finance can we properly apprehend the role of the core institutional nexus between treasuries, cen-tral banks, and private bankers on both sides of the Atlantic in generating the GFC.

The turn to a neoliberal order ushered in by Thatcher and Reagan created new crisis tendencies that exploded during the GFC. The war on inflation and financial liberalization, discussed in the previous chapter, led to a longer-term decline in wages and produced greater dependence upon credit-fueled consumption. In regulatory terms, the intensification of the transatlantic feedback loop—most notably through the "Big Bang" in 1986 and a new wave of US entry into the City—deepened financial integration and spurred important innovations in mortgage markets. Politically and ideologically, the shared reorientation of Tony Blair's Labour Party and Bill Clinton's Democratic Party toward a more right-wing and deregulatory agenda cemented the commitment to a liberalized and integrated Anglo-American financial order anchored in New York and London. These patterns of Anglo-American development had two important international effects. Firstly, domestic Anglo-American regulatory convergence around laissez-faire was diffused globally through the dominance of Anglo-American regulators within the wider financial community. Secondly, deeper Anglo-American financial integration from the 1990s placed the UK and the US at the heart of the financial market infrastructure that transmitted the crisis globally.

The chapter begins by assessing the Anglo-American foundations of the crisis, exploring the links between transatlantic financial liberalization and innovation, house price inflation, and increased household borrowing. These were the central causes of the crisis. The chapter's focus then turns to the intellectual and policy convergence between political elites in the UK and the US; in the years before the crisis, this convergence created a dangerous conviction in the sustainability of a low inflationary growth regime premised on liberalized and expanding financial markets. Finally, the chapter examines the initial uncoordinated attempts to arrest the crisis and the gradual emergence of a shared Anglo-American strategy to stabilize financial sectors through bailouts and unorthodox monetary policy.

Anglo-American Foundations of the Subprime Crisis

From the late 1990s to 2007, house prices in Anglo-America increased at a tremendous rate. House prices in the US rose by two-thirds in real terms between 1999 and 2008 (Eichengreen, 2014: 76). By 2006, the average home in the US already cost 5.2 times as much as the median US income, up from three times as much between 1985 and 2000. In the UK, house prices rose by 154 percent between 1997 and 2005. The total value of all housing in the developed world was estimated to have risen to $70 trillion by 2005, up from $30 trillion in 2000 (Irwin, 2013: 99–101). What was at the root of this remarkable process of house price inflation?

Inflationary dynamics in the housing market were driven by a number of interrelated factors that became central to Anglo-American growth under the neoliberal order. Foremost among these were the sustained liberalization of financial markets, growing private indebtedness, and the persistence of relatively low inflation and low interest rates as part of the "Great Moderation." The repression of wages ushered in by the tough anti-inflationary policies of Thatcher and Reagan produced a longer-term shortfall in demand that had to be compensated for. Increasingly, workers and households turned to debt as the solution. In this way, the policies that provided the way out of the stagflationary crisis of the 1970s generated the problems that generated the crisis of 2007/8. Added to this were the continuing liberalization of financial markets and a broader financialization within Anglo-America. It is to the genesis of these factors that we now turn our attention.

Liberalized financial markets provided the opportunity for spectacular growth in borrowing. The transatlantic regulatory feedback loop continued to spur financial deregulation as the neoliberal order was entrenched during the 1980s. In the UK, the landmark event was the "Big Bang" of 1986. This referred to a series of moves to liberalize the City of London and open it up to greater competition, both internally and internationally, beginning in 1983.[1] Crucially, these changes marked the start of the transition from a regulatory framework marked by informal "club governance"—whereby long-standing City elites shaped practice through coordination with the Bank of England—to that of laissez-faire, formalized self-regulation. Shaken up by the Big Bang, the City lobbied successfully for minimal bureaucracy within the new framework. A "light touch" approach became a distinctive feature of London's regulatory climate in the years that followed (Morgan, 2012: 377–78).

These regulatory reforms were shaped by fears over a growing competitive challenge to London's global role. The increasing internationalization of banking and securities dealing, the US moves toward greater domestic financial liberalized discussed in the previous chapter, and rapid technological change all conspired to push the Bank of England in the direction of a wholesale shake-up of the City's regulatory order (Plender and Wallace, 1985: 1–3).[2]

Facing multiple competitive challenges, the Bank campaigned persistently from the early 1980s, on behalf of interests within the City, to open up the London Stock Exchange. By 1984, power had begun to shift decisively toward

New York, with Thatcher's abolition of exchange controls in 1979 having exposed stark limitations in the competitiveness of many City institutions. ICI, a blue-chip UK corporation at the heart of the City's equities market, saw more of its shares traded in New York than in London during 1984. Alongside these developments, the aping of London's offshore regulatory climate by foreign financial centers—most notably the introduction of International Banking Facilities (IBFs) in the US discussed in the previous chapter—revealed the insecurity of London's global position and eroded its share of the Eurodeposit market. Japan's growing economic strength was reflected in the increased internationalization of its banks, with many now taking an important stake in the London Euromarkets and proposals under discussion for creation of IBFs in Tokyo. Within Europe, deepening integration provoked concerns over the maintenance of London's regional dominance (Augar, 2008: 46). Added to this, the Mexican debt crisis of the early 1980s burst the bubble of internationally syndicated bank loans, in which Barclays and Natwest had been prominent players, and posed challenges to international banking (Plender and Wallace, 1985: 37–42).

Both the Bank and the Treasury were increasingly concerned by the City's hemorrhaging of securities business to foreign-owned banks and securities firms as well as foreign financial centers (Plender, 1986). Under Thatcher's premierships, the government's relationship to the City changed substantially. The Labour governments of the 1970s had been concerned with the City's capacity and willingness to support domestic industry. But under Thatcher's government, the concern shifted to making sure that the City was as internationally competitive as possible. This new priority demonstrated just how effectively the UK state had been Atlanticized and opened up to global capital under pressure from theUS during the IMF crisis.

The changes brought about through the Big Bang were hugely significant, both for transforming the structure of Anglo-American capitalism and in laying the foundations for the incubation and transmission of the GFC. The transformation of the City ushered in a second wave of Americanization, comparable to the first wave of the early 1960s, but establishing a much more rounded US banking business in the City than had ever been the case with the comparatively ghettoized presence of US banks within the Euromarkets. Having recently undergone a further merger wave domestically and having benefited from the experience of US deregulation as well as a booming New York stock market, dominant US banks were now ripe to launch a further round of internationalization. Deregulation in London provided the perfect opportunity.

Although deregulation was already underway in the US, the most important piece of Depression-era banking regulation—the Glass-Steagall Act that separated investment and commercial banking—was still intact. Some US commercial banks saw the Big Bang as a way to create an investment banking wing in London through the purchase of UK brokerage firms. For their part, US investment banks saw London as the natural staging post for an assault on rapidly integrating European markets (Augar, 2008: 70–76). The City continued to serve as a key site for the reproduction of financial globalization, drawing in US banking by enabling regulatory arbitrage. This weakened the efficacy of US regulation at home and hastened the demise of the New Deal regulatory architecture.

This second wave of Americanization in the City had profound implications. Firstly, it led to the swallowing up of a vast number of smaller UK financial institutions that were ill equipped to compete with their larger and more sophisticated US counterparts; consequently, US investment banks rather than UK merchant banks would lead the intensification of financial globalization during the 1990s (Augar, 2008: 219). Secondly, the influx of US banks transformed the practices and understanding of finance in the City, notably in the area of mortgage markets, a transformation that would prove crucial in the unfolding of the GFC. Anglo-American development had now been at the heart of critical transformations within global financial markets stretching from the late 1950s to the 1990s, demonstrating the deep historical roots of the market infrastructure that incubated the crisis.

To understand the transmission of the crisis through Anglo-America and into the wider global financial markets, we need to examine the impact of two influential pieces of legislation contained in the Big Bang bundle of regulatory reforms. These were the 1986 Financial Services Act and the Building Societies Act of the same year. The former act "opened the markets to a myriad of new financial institutions such as banks and centralized lenders," while the latter enabled building societies to demutualize and become banks. These changes had hugely important consequences and led to the establishment of securitization processes that were at the heart of the financial crisis. US investment banks were now able to set up mortgage lending subsidiaries in the UK, and UK retail banks, which subsequently became the biggest securitizers in the UK, began to originate mortgages (Wainwright, 2009: 376; Blyth and Oren, 2019: 610).

American banks had first begun securitization in earnest in the 1980s, with the technique subsequently diffusing throughout the global economy to differing degrees. The process essentially involves the sale of financial assets such as residential mortgages, credit cards, and consumer loans to third parties, in order to remove these assets from the balance sheet of their originating financial institutions. Assets are packaged into different categories of risk by investment banks and then sold to investors (Wainwright, 2009: 374; Eichengreen, 2014: 74). The securities produced via this process were referred to as "collateralized debt obligations" (CDOs).[3] This model of asset securitization became known as the "originate and distribute" model and was central to the genesis of the subprime crisis.[4] The ability of large banks to move their loan book off their balance sheet, through the creation of special purpose vehicles (SPVs), enabled them to circumvent the capital adequacy requirements put in place under the Basel banking accords.[5] Consequently, there was an enormous increase in mortgage debt and a huge flow of credit into US financial markets, generating a huge house price bubble that burst spectacularly in 2007 (Eichengreen, 2014: 76).

Second only to the US, the UK's financial system was the most deeply involved in the process of securitization. The entry of US investment bankers following the Big Bang led to the transmission of US banking practices, knowledge, and skills into the City. These US practices were then modified into a local form that corresponded to the particular legal and institutional structures of the UK economy (Wainwright, 2009: 378). This was a continuation of the Anglo-American financial development set in motion by the Euromarkets, marking the continuity of these processes across both the Keynesian and neoliberal eras. Synthetic financial innovations within the City helped further integrate transatlantic financial markets, processes, and products while retaining local features that reflected the particularities of the UK's national economic system. It was because of the City's importance as a global financial node that US financial practices were disseminated and adjusted in this manner.

Locally developed innovations in securitization enabled financial institutions in the UK to draw a wider range of global investors, particularly those from the US, into the purchase of residential mortgage-backed securities (RMBSs). Widening the pool of RMBS investors further encouraged the expansion of mortgage lending in the UK and boosted the profitability of securitization. This meant that the UK's mortgage market became much more reliant upon the continued liquidity of RMBS markets and "an abundance of low-priced capital obtained through global capital markets" (Wainwright, 2009: 381; Thompson, 2013: 479–80). Although these dynamics stimulated the rapid growth of the mortgage market in the UK, they also drastically increased the economy's vulnerability to systemic risk from the global economy. The techniques of securitization and the deep embedding of the UK's booming mortgage markets within the global capital markets—traceable to the longer-term cross-fertilization of US and UK financial institutions and practices— were at the root of Anglo-America's centrality to the GFC. This would be evidenced catastrophically when the subprime crisis that began in the US rapidly infected Britain's financial system in the late summer of 2007.

The financial liberalization and Anglo-American financial cross-fertilization that instantiated the prevalence of securitization and rapidly expanding mortgage markets in the US and the UK were only one side of the housing price coin, however. They provided the financial market infrastructure that underpinned booming property prices, but that they did so was only because so many workers in both states were willing to run up huge debt burdens. Between 1980 and 2005, US household debt rose from 52 percent of economic output to 97 percent (Irwin, 2013: 100). Outstanding financial obligations of UK households hit £1 trillion for the first time in 2004 (Langley, 2008). Credit card debt relative to GDP grew briskly in both states from the early 1990s (Montgomerie, 2007: 6). Rapid growth in household borrowing occurred throughout the G7 economies, but it was marked by a distinctly Anglo-American inflection (Langley, 2008). As these debt mountains grew in size, they became ever more important to the functioning of Anglo-American growth, all the while intensifying vulnerability to interest rate shocks and financial market panics. In this way, the neoliberal fix to the crisis of the 1970s that had depressed wages in order to quell inflation fed into an increased reliance upon debt-driven growth to compensate for deficiencies in aggregate demand (Crouch, 2009: 390; Gamble, 2009: 459; Hay, 2013: 1).

The combination of sustained financial liberalization and growing indebtedness in Anglo-America ensured that, from the early 1990s, housing and housing finance became integral to the functioning of the global economy, creating higher levels of employment and GDP growth in those economies that had liberalized their housing markets and financial systems.[6] The US stood at the center of this dynamic. Low inflation and low interest rates in the Western economies provided a steady supply of cheap credit that boosted property markets and helped maintain aggregate demand (Hay, 2013: 1). Due to the huge size of the US domestic market and its role as global consumer of last resort, strong US GDP growth was the locomotive for wider prosperity in the global economy (Schwartz, 2009b: 90–97). Globally, the buildup of massive balance of payment imbalances, with huge volumes of savings held by export powerhouses such as China and Germany, fed into what was termed the "Wall of Money." Held in dollars, these savings were at the heart of a global search for yield within which New York and London competed to recycle huge volumes of funds. This global savings glut was relieved through the massive securitization of subprime mortgages (Morgan, 2012: 378).

The Extreme Folly of the "Great Moderation"

Within central banks, this period of sustained low-inflationary growth was triumphantly heralded as the "Great Moderation." Gone were the days of eye-watering inflation and correspondingly severe interest rate hikes that had hamstrung Western economies from the later 1970s. The perennial specters of inflation, deflation, boom and bust were now supposedly consigned to the annals of history. In an age of sophisticated technical central banking and efficient markets, the old foes of monetary instability were slain—or, at least, that was how it appeared. The US economy had been growing for twenty-five years, interrupted by only two brief recessions (Irwin, 2013: 94). Similarly, the UK economy had experienced sixteen years of uninterrupted growth from 1992, its longest period of sustained growth in modern history (Gamble, 2009: 450).

The political foundations of the Great Moderation rested upon a reconfiguration of the ideological and policy terrain after Thatcher and Reagan. Their successes drastically reshaped the orientations of their traditional political opponents. Desperate to prove their credibility and capacity to operate effectively within the brave new world of liberalized global financial markets, shareholder societies, and vast global capital flows, Bill Clinton's Democratic Party and Tony Blair's "New Labour" underwent important transformations as they embraced the Third Way in order to win over a center ground that had been steered to the right.

In the US, Clinton's Democrats, responding to twelve years of Republican rule, took on a more pro-business orientation after 1992 (Hacker and Pierson, 2010: 224). They dropped their traditional opposition to financial deregulation and began to embrace balanced budgets, private-public partnerships, and the importance of the financial sector for driving growth. Clinton signed a whole raft of deregulatory acts into law, leading to "a massive increase in the size, complexity, and leverage of US financial institutions" (Eichengreen, 2014:

72–73). Those who opposed further liberalization faced political ostracism, with increasingly tight connections forming between Wall Street banks and state agencies, exemplified by Clinton's appointment of Goldman Sachs co-chair Robert Rubin to Treasury secretary in 1995 (Kirshner, 2014: 63).[7] Concretely, the deregulatory zeal of the Clinton Administration led to the final repeal of Glass-Steagall, the keystone regulation of the Depression era. The 1999 Gramm-Leach-Bliley Act phased out the old regulatory order of US finance by enabling the combination of commercial banking, investment banking, and insurance underwriting (Eichengreen, 2014: 70).[8] It was an important step toward the formation of the "too-big-to-fail" banks that would gravely afflict the world economy during the subprime crisis.

Internationally, Clinton's administration supported the IMF's drive for further capital market liberalization. The Treasury cemented its strategic centrality within the global economy by managing, alongside the Fed and the IMF, the many financial crises that erupted as a consequence of increased financial liberalization during the 1990s (Panitch and Gindin, 2012: 247). The outbreak of the Asian Financial Crisis in 1997/8 was used as an attempt to impose harsh structural adjustment plans upon Asian economies (Wade, 1998).[9] Within the Fed, Alan Greenspan—appointed as chairman in 1987—maintained Paul Volcker's focus upon price stability, combined with a commitment to increasing the transparency of the Fed's operations. Greenspan's Fed was forced to play an active role in managing the intensified financial crises associated with deregulation. In 1998, the Fed organized a creditors' consortium between top Wall Street financial firms to prevent the collapse of the US hedge fund Long-Term Capital Management (Mayer, 2001: 266–69; Panitch and Gindin, 2012: 264), having already played an important role in arranging emergency funding during the 1994 peso crisis (Hetzel, 2008: 196–207). The Fed's participation in crisis containment during the 1990s helped further develop its institutional capacity as global lender of last resort: a role that was played out dramatically during the GFC.

In the UK, a parallel transformation was underway during the 1990s as New Labour broke from its social democratic policy traditions (Glyn and Wood, 2001: 50; Coates, 2009: 424). The watchword for their new economic policy was now "credibility" (Burnham, 2001: 129; Hopkin and Shaw, 2016: 356). Given the respect shown for the capacity of financial markets to form accurate judgments about the economy and their supposed "efficiency" in this regard, it was concluded that economic policy could only be implemented if it were viewed as credible by the all-powerful, and all-knowing, markets (Arestis and

Sawyer, 1998: 32; Clift and Tomlinson, 2007: 47–48).[10] This concern was manifest in the policy centerpiece of the New Labour government elected in 1997: granting the Bank of England full operational independence with the Bank of England Act of June in the following year.[11] This was seen as a move that could instantly assuage skeptical markets of a Labour government's commitment to credible economic policy (Burnham, 2001: 133; Glyn and Wood, 2001: 51). Monetary policy was to be given higher priority by the new government, with the scope for traditional Keynesian fiscal operations now substantially reduced under the new intellectual orientation and prioritization of price stability over full employment.[12]

Plans for independence had long been floated within Westminster.[13] But by 1994 Ed Balls, an influential advisor to shadow chancellor Gordon Brown, had begun to advocate the policy consistently as a means to convince markets of Labour's anti-inflationary resolve, which would enable the chancellor to concentrate on other areas of policy. Balls's desire for Bank independence bore the imprint of the time he spent studying at Harvard under Lawrence Summers, who served as Clinton's deputy secretary to the Treasury. Shortly after their engagement with Balls, Blair and Brown headed off to Washington to learn from the US economic model and Clinton's political success in moving closer to the Republicans in order to win back voters (Keegan, 2003: 136). These meetings included discussions with Greenspan over how to implement central bank independence in the UK (Keegan, 2003: 156).[14] Anglo-American ideological parallels now moved beyond shared right-wing endorsements of neoliberal policies to envelop social democratic parties as well, establishing a new consensus around appropriate macroeconomic policy.

Granting the Bank independence was seen as a way to end the long-running debacle of trying to secure a credible policy anchor to stabilize inflation. Both monetarism and the accession to the European Exchange Rate Mechanism (ERM) had proved unsuccessful, with the UK forced to leave the ERM under humiliating circumstances in 1992 as the pound came under sustained attack during Black Wednesday. But the very fact that the Bank was now granted independence was a testament to its successful capacity to resist—with support and advice from the Fed—the executive pressures that it faced during the highly politicized adoption of a monetarist shock regime in the early years of the Thatcher government. The successful negotiation of those executive pressures upon central bank autonomy, in both the UK and the US, was essential to the role that central banks would play in guiding monetary policy during the Great Moderation.

A wider package of regulatory recalibration accompanied Bank independence. This signaled New Labour's embrace of the City and drew a line under the often fractious relationship between Labour and the City during the 1970s. Brown announced the creation of the Financial Services Authority (FSA), which would combine the regulatory responsibilities of nine existing bodies, including those of the Bank. This move to denude the Bank of its regulatory remit was not viewed favorably by its governor, Eddie George, who had to be talked back from the brink of resignation by Tony Blair.[15] The issuing of gilts was now to be separated out from the Bank through the creation of the UK Debt Management Office. This was intended to avoid any possible conflict of interest between the Bank's interest rate policy and the issuance of gilts.

What was left after all of these changes was a meaner, leaner Bank of England, one empowered by formal independence but stripped of some of its previous responsibilities. Still, the Treasury did not fully relinquish government influence over the Bank, with the chancellor retaining the authority both to set the all-important inflation target and appoint external members of the newly created Monetary Policy Committee for three-year terms (Conaghan, 2012: 28).

With a newly independent Bank, free from government interventions and having drawn upon expertise from within the Fed during design and implementation, New Labour was well placed to prosper under the Great Moderation. Institutional reorganization laid the groundwork for a broader move to harness the dynamism of the City (Michie, 2004: 53). With the global savings glut and the search for yield in full flow by the late 1990s, the Labour government and the City did not want to miss out. Labour saw a flourishing financial sector as a way to compensate for a dramatic decline in manufacturing, which fell from 20.3 percent of GDP to roughly 12.4 percent between 1995 to 2007. The same period witnessed a substantial rise of the contribution of financial services and related professional services.[16]

The City was now seen to be indispensable: the goose that laid the golden egg. Consequently, Gordon Brown, who viewed the City as exemplary of the UK's global standing and economic dynamism, undertook its promotion with gusto. Added to this, a series of corporate scandals that blighted the US in the early 2000s nourished a growing sense that the UK system was now superior to its US counterpart and therefore needed to be protected at all costs, particularly with regard to the looming threat of intensified European Union (EU) financial regulation, against which the government lobbied actively (Morgan, 2012: 380–81). These concerns reactivated the City-Bank-Treasury nexus around the goal of promoting the City's international standing.[17]

Propitious global conditions and the Labour government's unequivocal embrace of the financial services industry guaranteed that the City prospered tremendously during the boom years of the Great Moderation. Financial services wages and bonuses rocketed upward in the decade before the crisis, with two-thirds of income gains for the top 1 percent generated by bonus payments in the sector (Lansley, 2011: 16). Just before the crisis hit in 2007, financial and professional services made up 11 percent of UK GDP. The UK was also the largest source of international bank lending and the world's biggest share of cross-border lending, at 20 percent. No less than 250 foreign banks were based in London, with a total of branches and subsidiaries that was more than double the figure of New York (Talani, 2011: 22).

The adjustment of the party-political and ideological terrain on both sides of the Atlantic enabled the continued commitment to a liberal regulatory stance toward finance. This had consequences far beyond the domestic political economies of the UK and the US. Domestic regulatory agencies were, as we have seen, beholden to the demands of the largest banks. This situation was reinforced by a revolving door between the upper echelons of private banks and prominent regulatory agencies in both the US and the UK, alongside a narrow orthodoxy of neoclassical economics training among policy makers (Baker, 2010: 652–64).

With the stability of deregulatory commitment secured at home, a comparable position was sought within the wider international arena, in a manner that echoed Anglo-American leadership over international banking regulation in the early 1980s, during the genesis of the Basel Accords is fine here. International regulatory agencies became increasingly deferential to the interests of US and UK regulators, due to their status as home country regulators of London and New York financial institutions that were responsible for the most cutting-edge practices and technologies of the largest banks. In this way, the dominant banks in the US and the UK were able to exert indirect influence over international regulatory debates within Basel owing to the "disproportionate international influence exercised by US and UK officials" (Baker, 2010: 650–51).

Domestic commitment to deregulation within Anglo-America—a product of decades of transatlantic regulatory interdependence—was thus transferred onto the broader international plane. This set in place an international trend of accommodating financial regulation, expressed through the Basel Accords, that served the dominant banks. These lax international regimes enabled the buildup of enormous leverage ratios and inadequate capital among systemically significant banks. With regard to hedge funds and derivatives markets, Anglo-American preferences were encoded within international rules that favored market discipline and self-regulation as their governing principles (Helleiner and Pagliari, 2009).

The Anglo-American light-touch approach to financial regulation was particularly influential within European integration. Continental regulatory changes from the mid-1990s largely harmonized European rules with the US and UK approaches. Similarly, transforming the process for making and implementing EU financial legislation through the "Lamfalussy process" led to a switch to US and UK-style public consultation over legislation. This had the effect of opening up the process to the power of London-oriented financial coalitions. Elliot Posner and Nicolas Veron (2010: 401–5) conclude that political pressures "swept EU decision-makers towards international practice as established in US-dominated bodies and Anglo-American regulatory models that allowed financial services firms large degrees of discretion." A UK-led coalition was thus able to exert the prevailing influence upon precrisis financial services integration in Europe, shaping key regulatory rules (Quaglia, 2010: 1017–18). With regard to hedge funds and derivatives trading in the precrisis period, UK and US regulators successfully resisted European pressures for tighter regulation (Helleiner and Pagliari, 2009). Decades of financial liberalization shaped by the core competitive relationship between the City and New York now came to help mold the wider international context of regulatory transformation, with the UK's membership in the EU influential in disseminating the Anglo-American vision across the continent.

Beneath the surface appearance of unbridled prosperity founded upon financial deregulation, the Great Moderation rested upon extremely flimsy foundations. An unprecedented period of sustained growth only helped to conceal, rather than eradicate, the underlying weaknesses in this model. The steady rise of house prices was founded upon the existence of a "low inflation-low interest rate equilibrium" (Hay, 2013: 8). Once this equilibrium was disrupted, beginning with the Fed's 2005 rate hike to cool an overheating housing market, the model's fragility became increasingly apparent. From the second quarter of 2006, inflation, interest rates, and oil prices all began to rise in tandem throughout the West. This shattered the delicate balance that underpinned growth (Hay, 2013: 8).

A hike in the federal funds rate posed immediate problems for subprime borrowers, who struggled to repay their mortgage debts. It soon transpired that what had initially looked like a problem of the US would be global in scope. The run on the UK bank Northern Rock in September 2007 signaled that this would be a far wider and deeper crisis than anticipated.[18] As news emerged of the bank's perilous condition, depositors queued outside branches in order to withdraw their savings, and the UK government rushed to guarantee deposits and supply emergency credit (Conaghan, 2013: 145–50). It was a sign of the scale of government interventions that would soon be widespread on both sides of the Atlantic.

The crisis began in the US, but it was London, and UK–based financial institutions, that were its second port of call. This was precisely because of the deep integration of Anglo-American financial markets, which had established a robust transmission mechanism from New York into London and from Anglo-America into the wider world economy. The global financial market infrastructure of London and its centrality to global interbank lending—the culmination of what began with the Euromarkets decades earlier—put it at the heart of the transmission mechanism that spread financial contagion through the world.[19] Politically, the convergence of Anglo-American political parties around a neoliberal and pro-finance worldview cemented the basis of authority to preside over continued financial deregulation and the deepening of the defective Anglo-liberal growth model. These dynamics were consequent to the broader context of Anglo-American development that, stretching from the heyday of postwar Keynesianism to the emergence and consolidation of neoliberalism, produced a transatlantic financial space and an increasingly shared political-ideological orientation at the heart of financial globalization. All this meant that the actions of government, central banks, and regulatory agencies in the UK and the US would become crucial to the stabilization of the global economy in the aftermath of the crisis.

Putting Out the Fire

Standing before the Congressional Financial Crisis Inquiry Commission in 2009, Timothy Geithner's justification for the major scale of government intervention within financial markets was straightforward: "None of the biggest banks would have survived a situation in which we had let the fire try to burn itself out" (Panitch and Gindin, 2012: 301). Instead, the Treasury and the Fed took to firefighting, flooding the market with liquidity and guaranteeing the security of troubled institutions. Geithner was well placed to report on the severity of the events of the late summer of 2008 during the apogee of the crisis. Before undertaking his new role as Obama's Treasury secretary, he had worked closely with Bush's treasury secretary Henry Paulson, in his capacity as president of the Federal Reserve Bank of New York. If the run on Northern Rock was the first indication of the wider geographical scope of the crisis, it was the collapse of Lehman Brothers that really demonstrated its depth and severity.

American policy makers had already decided to organize a bailout in response to the troubles of major investment bank Bear Stearns in March 2008, providing $29 billion of guaranteed financing to Bear and facilitating an acquisition of the bank by JP Morgan Chase. But when Lehman Brothers got into trouble in September 2008, with much larger debts than Bear and a larger share of toxic mortgages, the Americans decided that Wall Street, and not the Fed, should bail out Lehman (Eichengreen, 2014: 198–201; Irwin, 2013: 142).[20] Officials feared that further government bailouts might encourage moral hazard, signaling that it was fine for major financial institutions to overexpose themselves to risk through highly leveraged business models (Axilrod, 2009: 152).

The inadequacy of this stance was soon revealed. Geithner's attempts to coordinate Wall Street CEOs around a private sector bailout of Lehman proved unsuccessful, with collective action inhibited by the fear of being left with each other's bad debts (Panitch and Gindin, 2012: 314). Lehman's failure acted like an earthquake within financial markets, causing widespread panic and shaking the foundations of interbank lending markets. But the Fed's inaction over Lehman was not only a political choice; it was also a reflection of the legal and political limits that policy makers faced. The size of the financial sector and the severity of the crisis forced the Fed to stretch its authority in uncomfortable ways. Increasingly, it provided ad hoc responses through regulatory innovation to keep the liquidity flowing to a financial system on the brink of collapse (Axilrod, 2009: 151).

Learning from the Lehman debacle, the Fed proved more decisive when confronted with the prospect of the collapse of AIG. It extended a multibillion-dollar loan to the troubled insurance giant (Irwin, 2013: 146). The AIG intervention demonstrated the massive lender-of-last-resort role that Anglo-American central banks would have to play, blurring lines between fiscal and monetary policy in the process and pushing up against legal, institutional, and political limitations.

Whereas the Bank of England hesitated in this regard (under the stewardship of the prickly and imperious Mervyn King) the Fed acted with much greater urgency. The experiences of the Fed and the Treasury in managing the financial crises of the 1980s and 1990s left them well placed to respond, having built up substantial institutional expertise. Due to the dollar's global key currency role, the Fed's lender-of-last resort functions transcended national boundaries. Already in late 2007, the Fed had announced large swap lines with a number of globally significant central banks, including the European Central Bank and the Bank of England. With the collapse of Lehman, the global demand for dollars surged, prompting the Fed to massively increase liquidity. By December 2008, it had lent a staggering $585 billion to foreign central banks (Axilrod, 2009: 161). Additionally, the Fed lent money directly to distressed foreign banks, including $85 billion to RBS and $65 billion for Barclays. These were politically hugely controversial moves—so much so that the enormous scale of these interventions was kept secret from the public, with only two people at each Fed branch in the know (Irwin, 2013: 154).

In the UK, concerns over moral hazard prompted Mervyn King to take an even more cautious approach to financial firefighting. The Northern Rock episode demonstrated the failure of the FSA and the wider New Labour regulatory apparatus to identify the growing risk to the UK financial system posed by the sort of business model that the troubled bank had adopted. King himself put too much faith in the possibility of establishing market solutions to the crisis, underestimating the need for full-blooded lender-of-last-resort intervention (Eichengreen, 2014: 181–82).[21] King's distaste for action frustrated the chancellor Alistair Darling and revealed the strains that the crisis could place upon the key relationship between the Treasury and the Bank. With an independent Bank of England, the scope for a more instructive role from the chancellor had been diminished—a fact that King was keenly aware of (Conaghan, 2012: 143).

Differences of opinion between King and Darling underlined the failure of the UK to formulate a coherent crisis strategy. The apparent indifference and disorganization (Darling learnt of the escalating crisis from a copy of the *Financial Times* while holidaying) with which the crisis was approached by the Bank and the Treasury was a source of considerable disquiet for US officials, with Treasury Secretary Paulson making clear his dissatisfaction in a meeting with the chancellor (Conaghan, 2012: 135–48).

Yet, as the crisis deepened after Lehman's collapse, a concerted and boldly interventionist response, led by the Fed and the Bank, did begin to gather momentum. Bernanke and King, former officemates at the Massachusetts Institute of Technology (MIT), realized that concerted central bank action would be needed to extinguish an emergency of this intensity. Both central banks engaged in vast programs of liquidity provision, oversaw massive bailouts of troubled financial institutions in coordination with their respective treasuries, and, crucially, began to move toward a concerted adjustment of interest rates. Prior to the Lehman bankruptcy, the Fed, the Bank, and the ECB had pursued divergent interest rate policies. Now the Fed and the Bank lowered interest rates together and turned, as we will see in the next chapter, to "quantitative easing."

From Crisis to Stagnation

The unorthodox policies implemented by Anglo-American central banks would have very significant implications. In tandem with a turn to fiscal austerity they would usher in a new phase of stagflationary capitalism within a neoliberal order experiencing a deep structural crisis. As this chapter has argued, the GFC represented the culmination of decades of deepening financial liberalization and transatlantic integration that lay at the heart of Anglo-American development. These longer-term dynamics account for the centrality of the US and the UK within the crisis. The centrality of the "Anglo-liberal" model to the crisis must be understood within the context of these formative transatlantic processes emerging from the deeper historical-institutional interdependencies of Anglo-American development explored in this book. In that sense, the historical roots of the crisis ran much deeper than merely the conjunctural specificities of the Great Moderation, or the turn to neoliberalism in the 1980s, for these were merely the second-order proximate causes underpinning the more immediate causes that sparked an acute crisis in the subprime mortgage market. The ultimate cause, in the form of originating processes of postwar Anglo-American financial integration that eventually gave rise to the GFC, were incubated during the heyday of Keynesian capitalism. Beginning our account of the crisis from the endogenous reconfiguration of the Wall Street system in the 1980s, and reading the crisis as a consequence of that system's externalization into "satellite" London markets, overlooks the deeper dynamics of transatlantic financial interdependency that progressively weakened the New Deal financial regulatory order in the US. It also grossly understates the agency of the City in driving the broader politics of financial globalization and regulatory competition between London and New York, which stimulated domestic transformations in the US.

This longue durée of Anglo-American financial development, and its centrality to the broader politics of financial globalization, reveals the limited success of the Bretton Woods embedded liberal order in effectively socializing private finance in light of the requirements of stable growth, full employment, and domestic welfare. Finance was never sufficiently embedded in the Anglo-American economies. From the 1980s, the successful transition to a more neoliberal order of capitalism under Thatcher and Reagan, characterized by monetary shocks and intensified financial liberalization, gave full force to liberalizing and integrative tendencies that had been building since the 1960s. Politically, the electoral success of Thatcher and Reagan, as well as the hegemonic ascendancy of neoliberal ideology, pulled New Labour and the Democrats toward support for deregulated finance. This laid the institutional foundations for the Great Moderation and the spectacular growth of mortgage markets. As we will see in the following chapter, the implosion of this reconfigured order of capitalism has had globally significant consequences, presenting a series of seemingly intractable political and economic challenges that have gravely destabilized the Western liberal order.

8

From Crisis to Stagnation

THE NEOLIBERAL era in Anglo-America began with radical central bank policies intended to combat inflation, discipline workers, and restore the power of the financial sector. Almost three decades later, as the financial crisis reached its zenith, the Fed and the Bank presided over the beginning of a new era of monetary policy experimentation. Now the threat was that of deflation, as confidence and liquidity drained out of the banking system. The response was an unprecedented phase of sustained monetary loosening, with interest rates hammered down to the zero bound and an unorthodox policy known as "quantitative easing" inaugurated.

That the interventionist response to the crisis came predominantly through monetary channels was significant: it reflected the victory over Keynesian fiscal activism won by the cheerleaders of neoliberal restructuring. More pragmatically, it was politically expedient to funnel credit through large-scale central bank actions rather than fiscal expansion requiring congressional or parliamentary approval. This was demonstrated by the fractious politics of the Troubled Asset Relief Program (TARP) in the US.[1]

But the details of TARP, which was closely coordinated with private financial firms, also exemplified the dense institutional linkages between the Fed, the Treasury, and Wall Street (Eichengreen, 2014: 293–94). These linkages, equally evident between the corresponding institutions in the UK (the Bank, the Treasury, and the City), enabled a crisis-response strategy that effectively bypassed much of the wider economy, by channeling new funds directly into the banking sector, with very little by way of a quid pro quo. Where banks were nationalized, the normal structures of private corporate governance were left in place (CRESC, 2011). It was public ownership without public control, despite the massive transfer of public funds to bail out private institutions.

After a brief resurgence of Keynesian ideas in the early years of the crisis, governments in the West soon began to settle on a widespread endorsement of austerity (Farrell and Quiggin, 2017: 273–77). Monetary loosening paired with fiscal tightening would become the prevailing formula for the postcrisis recovery. It would impose the costs of the recovery upon those least able to bear them, while further cementing the regressive distributional settlement of the neoliberal order.

This chapter traces the emergence of a new stagflationary regime of zero-bound interest rates, lower growth, stalled wages, and low inflation alongside increasing fiscal austerity. Taken together, these features characterized the Anglo-American recoveries from the GFC. Drawing upon political economy perspectives stressing the deep structural malaise of postcrisis capitalism (Gamble, 2014; Streeck, 2014), the chapter maps these tendencies within the Anglo-American context by arguing that although unorthodox monetary measures led by the Federal Reserve and the Bank of England helped alleviate the credit crunch and stimulated stock market rallies, they have not alleviated the deeper crisis of the neoliberal order.

The postcrisis period displayed the continued dependence of the global economy upon Anglo-American central bank leadership and the continued sidelining, despite a brief resurgence, of Keynesian economic ideas. But it also illustrated the increasing inability of the neoliberal economic model to deliver continuing economic growth and distributional gains on a level sufficient to secure popular democratic consent for contemporary capitalism. These failings have been demonstrated by increased political polarization and the rising power of xenophobic authoritarian populism in both states, represented most spectacularly by the fractious politics of Brexit in the UK and Donald Trump's presidency in the US.

The hallmarks of the neoliberal order—rising inequality, growing public debt, financial sector predominance, and sustained environmental degradation—have intensified since the crisis. Added to this, the postcrisis conjuncture has opened spaces for geoeconomic rebalancing within a changing global political economy. Brexit is a critical juncture that opens up possibilities for a substantial transformation of UK capitalism. In the US, Donald Trump's presidency and his "America First" policy in international trade and diplomacy have cast doubt on the country's commitment to liberal multilateralism. Growing rivalry between the US and China threatens the international trading system and imperils UK attempts to simultaneously maintain US ties while pivoting toward China. Anglo-American interdependence will continue, but historians of tomorrow will likely view the postcrisis decade as a turning point. Further dispersal of power within the global political economy looks set to ultimately weaken both the dynamics and the effects of Anglo-American development.

The chapter begins by examining the monetary loosening that pushed central banks to the fore of the postcrisis era of stabilization, continuing the trend of an enlarged role for central banks within the neoliberal order; it then examines the rise of austerity in the years after the crisis and goes on to evaluate such policies with regard to a longer-term structural crisis of the neoliberal order of capitalism. Finally, the chapter reviews the emergence of a new global conjuncture for Anglo-America in the wake of the GFC, one that is marked by the UK's contentious embrace of China's rising economic might in a context of increased Sino-US rivalry, the political and economic transformations opened up by Brexit, and the reconfiguration of America's global role brought about by the Trump presidency.

Monetary Loosening

Late in 2008, the Fed, fearing weak economic growth and the specter of deflation, lowered the federal funds rate to the zero-lower bound. Threatened by similar conditions, the Bank of England followed suit, slashing its rate to 0.5 percent in the spring of 2009 (Christensen and Rudebusch, 2012: 385). These moves followed the first globally coordinated monetary easing in history, as the Fed, the Bank, and the ECB moved to cut rates in October 2008 (Irwin, 2013: 161). As we have seen in previous chapters, coordination of Anglo-American monetary policy had a long-standing precedent. The presence of a unified European Central Bank (ECB) made cooperation and coordination throughout the Western economies more streamlined than before. But the ECB—facing its first major crisis—was slower to act than its Anglo-American counterparts. This intensified the effects of the crisis when it hit the Eurozone economies (Gamble, 2014: 59). It also demonstrated the continuing importance of Anglo-American central banks in leading the response to the credit crunch and the recession that followed.

Anglo-American central banks, unlike their European counterpart, did not stop with the introduction of low interest rates. They went much further, by engaging in massive purchases of long-term government securities from the private sector. The strategy, known as quantitative easing (QE), was intended to provide a large-scale monetary stimulus to the economy. The Bank of Japan pioneered the approach during its long struggle against deflation and low growth during the 1990s. Now it was the Fed and the Bank, fearing the contraction of their vast financial sectors, that turned to QE.

The principle behind the policy was simple—QE would expand the central bank's balance sheet in order to raise the level of central bank money in the economy (Joyce et al., 2011: 114). The policy would work through a number of discreet "channels" to stimulate the economic recovery. Most important, the increase in broad money holdings achieved through the purchase of financial assets would help inflate asset prices and stimulate greater spending as borrowing costs were reduced and the wealth effect for asset holders kicked in. In adopting this strategy, the Fed and the Bank signaled a major break from the prevailing policy paradigm in place since the 1980s (Werner, 2005: 49; Epstein, 2005: 2).[2] Rather than attempting to regulate the price of interbank borrowing, by using open market operations to hit the overnight interest rate target, they would now rely upon a quantitative adjustment of funds within the system through QE.[3] The interest rate was no longer the predominant means for achieving monetary policy. Just as the inflationary challenge of the early 1980s had been met by coordinated Anglo-American central bank experimentation, now similar processes of synchronized institutional innovation were at work in dealing with the new deflationary crisis of capitalism.

Although the policy tools of QE were novel, the objectives were not. They demonstrated continuity with the prevailing ethos of monetary policy. The key stated objective of the Bank's implementation of QE was the maintenance of price stability (BofE, 2013: 55; Joyce et al., 2011: 115). This target was very much in line with the long-standing elevation of price stability over full employment as the main goal of central banking. Additionally, the concern with creating a "wealth effect" for those that already held financial assets was inscribed with a distributional bias that would favor the wealthiest sections of society (Gamble, 2014: 21; Green and Lavery, 2015: 11). Again, this was a feature of QE that fit comfortably with the privileging of the interests of the top percentiles of the income and wealth distribution under contemporary Anglo-American capitalism.

In total, the volume of central bank purchases of assets was enormous. The Fed's three rounds of QE and the Bank's two rounds majorly enlarged the balance sheets for the two central banks, with the Fed's QE2 purchases alone totaling $600 billion. The fallout of the crisis was warehoused on Anglo-American central bank balance sheets. Stock prices, commodities, and foreign assets rose on the back of the monetary policy interventions, and the policy did restore confidence in the banking sector (Koo, 2015: 76–77). But, despite the massive increases in central bank reserves, or base money, QE proved to have an insufficient effect upon the growth in private credit or the money supply (Prasad, 2015: 140). Even with interest rates at rock bottom, the large volumes of debt afflicting the corporate and household sectors within Anglo-America led to deleveraging, which drained demand as part of a classic liquidity trap (Koo, 2015: 8–12). With the growth of bank lending so low, the inflation rate has remained low or fallen in both states, while oil and commodity prices have dropped precipitously in recent years, indicating that the new stagflation will have staying power.

As the prevailing proactive policy response to the crisis, QE had malign consequences beyond the distributional prejudices with which it was inscribed. This was the "substitution impact" of QE—its role in providing an activist policy to satisfy public demand for a response to the crisis (Green and Lavery, 2015). By providing the major impetus of crisis-response policy, QE led to the subordination and occlusion of more progressive monetary and fiscal policy combinations. QE drove the policy response in a pro-market direction that relied upon a financialized demand strategy targeted at boosting the wealth effect experienced by privileged asset holders. There was, potentially, an alternative route of crisis-expansionary fiscal policy, targeted at large-scale job creation and public investment, but this was the road not taken. Instead, QE and monetary activism were the ordained remedies. Rather than opening up to broader progressive alternatives, the policy reinforced the narrow parameters of reigning macroeconomic principles and emphasized financial market efficacy and monetary activism paired with fiscal restraint. The "monetary doping" central to the maintenance of Western growth since the 1990s continued (Streeck, 2014: 46).

There was a further, externally facing dimension to QE, however. The drastic cuts in interest rates led to precipitous declines in the value of the dollar and sterling.[4] For the US, this undermined its traditional leadership of the international monetary system by raising widespread fears within the Group of Twenty (G20) that the Americans were attempting a beggar-thy-neighbor strategy of competitive devaluation. Only the UK and the US remained in favour of QE at the G20 meeting in Korea during 2010, with all other members "circumspect or outright opposed to it." This marked a turning point in international monetary politics. It was no longer an undervalued Chinese RMB that was the bugbear of the international community, but, rather, the perception of currency depreciation by the UK and the US, despite their pleading to the contrary (Koo, 2015: 78). And it was China now leading the forceful opposition to what it termed "reckless" money printing by the US, while Germany was also strongly critical (Prasad, 2015: 128). As currency wars and competitive depreciations became the new normal after the crisis, the sustained decades-long trajectory toward global financial market liberalization and free currency movements, of which the UK and the US had been key drivers, was imperiled by Anglo-American policies. In 2012, the IMF went so far as to officially endorse the use of capital controls, breaking from its previous zeal for capital account liberalization (IMF, 2012).

Fiscal Tightening

In stark contrast to the new methods of monetary expansion and historically low interest rates employed to arrest the crisis and the recession that followed, the fiscal remedy centered around the resuscitation of a well-worn policy: austerity. There was no inevitability in the adoption of this policy. Things might have been very different. Indeed, early political responses to the crisis suggested that there might even be a Keynesian renaissance of sorts (Farrell and Quiggin, 2017). UK chancellor Alistair Darling openly endorsed Keynes in October 2008, around the peak of the crisis, suggesting that "much of what Keynes wrote still makes sense." The stabilizing role of deficits came to be widely acknowledged, with first the US and the UK, and then the G7, announcing that they would bail out major banks. These actions transferred the banking sector's toxic assets onto government balance sheets and substantially increased fiscal deficits. By November 2008, the G20 had issued a communiqué promising to "use fiscal measures to stimulate demand to rapid effect." Even Germany, which had resisted initial calls for greater fiscal expansion, turned to a fiscal stimulus to restore stability in 2009 (Konzelmann, 2014: 724–25).

Yet the "return of Keynes" and the rolling out of deficit-financed stimulus programs proved fleeting. By 2010, the fragile policy cohesion had broken down altogether, echoing the disintegration of consensus among economists. The crucial watershed moment was the transformation of the financial crisis into a Eurozone sovereign debt crisis. What had begun with revelations about Greece's mounting public debt in 2009 now threatened to engulf a number of major economies, with the prospect of default looming large.[5] These fears found symbolic expression with the G20 communiqué that ended the Toronto meeting in June 2010; it marked the end of the brief Keynesian renaissance and the transition to austerity. Rather than endorsing reflationary deficit spending, the G20 now called for "growth friendly fiscal consolidation" (Blyth, 2013: viii). The austerity agenda was now in command.

Germany's crucial role in driving the austerity agenda, with enthusiastic support from the ECB, cannot be ignored (Blyth, 2013: 59–60). The power of German policy voices testified to the huge economic power that the Eurozone's largest member state wielded after decades of effective catch-up following World War II. This was certainly not an instance of Anglo-American leadership. Yet the austerity agenda was taken up wholeheartedly by the UK's new Conservative-led Coalition government that came to power in May 2010, along with important figures from within the City and, controversially, by Mervyn King at the Bank. King strained the Bank's independence by calling for austerity from June 2009 (Conaghan, 2012: 224–25). In the US, the Republican right, wealthy households, corporations, and elements within the Democratic Party all trumpeted the austerity agenda (Crotty, 2012: 81). Although cautious about an overzealous embrace of austerity, Bernanke stressed the need for long-term reduction of fiscal deficits (Konzelmann, 2014: 727).

The political processes that underpinned austerity within Anglo-America were, though, very different. President Obama's administration committed to deficit reduction from the outset (Koo, 2015: 45). But a hostile Congress advocated for deeper cuts. Obama had come into office with an ambitious plan for progressive reform, involving a fiscal stimulus, health care provision, and climate change legislation. But, despite early majorities in both Houses of Congress, the entrenched organizational interests within US politics blunted Obama's reformist edge. These interests included a massive corporate lobbying effort against reform, and the increased use of the Senate filibuster by Republicans and Democrats acting on behalf of business (Hacker and Pierson, 2010: 257–75). The partisan politics and moneyed interests of Washington stifled Obama's efforts.

In the UK, the executive itself led the charge toward austerity under both its Coalition form (2010–15), with the liberal Democrats quickly ceding to the conservative austerity agenda, and the 2015 majority Conservative government. Although the transatlantic routes to austerity were different, the goals were the same. In both states, the panic over deficits was used as an opportunistic whip with which to lacerate ailing welfare states, further entrenching the crisis-stricken neoliberal order. As Paul Krugman (2012) concluded, "The drive for austerity was about using the crisis, not solving it." There was very little by way of rebalancing away from overreliance on overmighty financial sectors and growth driven by increasing private and public debt.

The scale of cuts was quite unprecedented. In the UK, David Cameron's Coalition government quickly laid out their plan to set the UK upon a new fiscal course, marked by permanently reduced spending, lower debt, and market-led growth (Kerr et al. 2011: 196; Taylor-Gooby, 2012: 61). They outlined an austere vision of neoliberal restructuring that emphasized the importance of shrinking state spending and reducing public debt to boost consumer and business confidence (Carstensen and Matthijs: 2018). In practical terms, this meant a huge reduction in public sector employment and a slashing of the government's welfare bill. While the most extreme austerity measures were softened under the Coalition in the run-up to the 2015 election, due to stuttering preelection growth and pressure from the IMF (Clift, 2015: 166), the first budget of the majority Conservative government in July 2015 demonstrated what was in store for the UK. The plan was to wipe £35 billion off the welfare bill over the Parliament and raise £47 billion through tax increases, while corporation tax would be further reduced and the public pay squeeze continued (BBC, 2015a).[6] These new goals were locked in by chancellor George Osborne's legislative commitment to permanent fiscal surpluses (BBC 2015b). Overall, the government stated its intention to bring public spending down to levels not seen since 1948 (Van Reenen, 2015: 1).

In the US, the Republicans used the contested politics of the fiscal "shutdown" as a lever to wring further austerity from President Obama, who had already agreed to extend the Bush tax cuts for a further two years, at a cost of approximately $850 billion in lost revenue. Then a budget bill passed by the House of Representatives in 2011 called for nondefense spending cuts of $4.5 trillion over ten years, with cuts to low-income programs comprising two-thirds of the total reductions. In a move that mirrored Osborne's efforts to lock in austerity, Obama suggested that Congress legislate automatic triggers that would reduce government spending if deficit reduction targets were not met (Crotty, 2012: 86–100). The sequester that came into effect from March 2013 cut discretionary civilian spending and the military budget, drawing criticism from the IMF (Eichengreen, 2014: 333).

On both sides of the Atlantic, the class politics of austerity were clear: keep taxes low for the wealthiest segments of society and make the poor pay for the crisis by slashing social services. One of the most regrettable aspects of austerity as a policy, beyond its deflationary and growth-inhibiting impacts, is the uneven way it hits the poorest within society (Blyth, 2013: 8). Those that benefited very little from the house price inflation of the boom years have now been made to cover the costs of the crisis. Austerity premised upon squeezing back welfare spending and stoking asset prices through monetary expansion was a toxic macroeconomic blend, marked by its regressive effects.

Viewed in the broader lineage of postwar Anglo-American political economy, the austerity measures represented attempts to roll back the social democratic gains that were made before and after World War II. There was an eerie echo of the damaging austerity regimes that strangulated global demand in the wake of World War I, feeding into the dysfunctional and desperate politics of the interwar years. The brief period of embedded liberal welfarist redistribution that marked the golden age of Western capitalism looks evermore to be anomalous within the longue durée of capitalist development. That era resulted from peculiarly propitious conditions that will likely never be replicated. Indeed, inequality has now returned to levels not seen since the 1930s (Piketty, 2014). With the neoliberal order that supplanted the postwar compromise now itself wrapped in crisis, we must inquire as to the prognosis for the future of Anglo-American development and the globalizing capitalism the UK and the US have stewarded.

The Structural Crisis of Neoliberal Capitalism

How effective have monetary loosening and fiscal tightening been in arresting the present crisis of neoliberal capitalism? Initially, despite fiscal austerity, both the UK and the US had enjoyed growth rates beyond many of their OECD counterparts (IMF, 2015). The existence of independent central banks and sovereign currencies proved a boon to the Anglo-American economies, enabling a liquidity fix to the crisis that evaded Eurozone members constrained by a shared currency and supranational central bank. The reduction in borrowing rates and flooding of the money markets with liquidity helped rally stock markets and resuscitate the debt-driven growth regimes that characterized Anglo-America in the precrisis years. Employment has recovered, albeit in labor markets that are now marked by the embedding of low wages and precarity on a major scale.

But by historical standards, the recovery from the financial crisis remained extremely sluggish (IMF, 2016). The slowdown in growth has prompted fears that we may be entering an era of "secular stagnation," which is characterized by a sustained decline in demand linked to a series of structural transformations within the advanced political economies (Summers, 2016; Green, 2017).

With the vote to leave the EU on June 23, 2016, though, the UK began to regress to only stuttering growth, shifting from a leader to a laggard in terms of postcrisis economic performance within the OECD. When it comes to the large current account deficits that have characterized the international payments position of both the UK and the US, it is the UK position that now looks much more vulnerable, with the emergence of shale gas having enabled the US to go much further toward closing its deficit (Green, 2016). Brexit has rendered the UK economic position, with its higher dependence upon international trade, looking increasingly susceptible to further crisis and deeper stagnation.

The worst fears of a 1930s-style Depression were avoided in the aftermath of the crisis, yet so much more could have been done to restore growth and build a progressive route out of the crisis. Given a more favorable alignment of social forces, alongside a firmer institutional basis for more novel economic thinking, the crisis might have been used as an opportunity to rebalance away from a low-wage, debt-driven model defined by bloated financial sectors in Anglo-America (Stockhammer, 2015).[7] The crisis could have rallied countries to a new global commitment to much more stringent regulation of financial markets, as well as to a new distributional settlement that arrested the excesses of the neoliberal order and restored a more equitable and sustainable pattern of global economy. As it stands, the reform of the financial sector has been pallid. There was no sustained revival of a "Bretton Woods moment" of widespread and substantive global reregulation (Helleiner and Pagliari, 2009). In the US, the lobbying efforts of Wall Street dulled the sharpest edges of the regulatory package launched by Obama (Taibbi, 2010; Eichengreen, 2014: 323–28). The Dodd Frank Consumer Protection Act passed by Congress in July 2010 did not impose sufficiently severe restrictions on the behavior of too-big-to-fail banks, nor adequately prevent future reliance on tax-payer funded bailouts (Wilmarth, 2010). Under Trump's presidency, the crisis-era Dodd Frank reforms have been targeted for reversal (Rushe, 2017). We have seen no regulatory response on a scale comparable to the 1930s (Gamble, 2014: 15).

In the UK, the initial regulatory response under the Labour government was weakened by the commissioning of insider enquiries into the crisis, which drew heavily upon City professionals and informed the Treasury's tepid response to the crisis. Not surprisingly, these accounts continued to promulgate the narrative of the indispensable City and trumpeted the many benefits that it brings to the UK, while largely ignoring the devastation it wrought during the crisis and the enormous vulnerability it attaches to the UK's economic development (CRESC, 2011: 5–11). Despite institutional adjustments and the introduction of a "macroprudential" regulatory paradigm, embodied in the creation of the Financial Policy Committee (FPC) and the Prudential Regulatory Authority (PRA) within the Bank of England, there are still major concerns over the existence of too-big-to-fail banks (Bell and Hindmoor, 2015: 466). Although the ring-fencing of investment and commercial banking activities is set to be introduced, a welcome step in reducing the exposure of everyday banking activities to high-risk investment banking activities, there are already signs of considerable pushback against the regulations from the City and the admission that the ring-fence will be open to a broad range of interpretive scope by the PRA (Binham and Arnold, 2015). The door has been left wide ajar for the reentry of light-touch regulation.

In terms of the broader picture of the UK macroeconomy as a whole, too, there continues to be staggering reliance upon a bloated financial sector. There have been no serious efforts to rebalance away from finance by shrinking the sector and rescinding the policy privileges that scaffold the UK's comparative advantage in financial services (CRESC, 2011: 9). The Conservative government continued to endorse a light-touch approach to the City. George Osborne sacked Martin Wheatley—the head of the newly created Financial Conduct Authority and someone whose tough stance on banks was widely unpopular within the industry—in the aftermath of the 2015 election. This came along with a promise from the then-chancellor for a "new settlement" with the financial industry (UK Government, 2015)—a promise widely interpreted as indicating a return to light-touch regulation.

What has been perhaps most crucial about the politics of regulatory reform, in terms of the broader political economy of the Special Relationship, is the continuing power of the Fed and the Bank of England. If anything, the enormous responsibility they have been given to drive the recovery through QE and loose monetary policy has only augmented their power, enabling the maintenance of central bank power within Anglo-America. This is significant because these institutions have not been immune from political challenges in the years since the crisis.

In spring 2009, the Fed came under tremendous political fire for its role in the crisis. Senators Dodd and Shelby sought to "unmake the modern Federal Reserve" by producing a bill to denude America's central bank of one of its key policy mandates: the ability to supervise banks throughout the country (Irwin, 2013: 173–74). But the proposal came under immediate attack by banks small and large, as well as by Bernanke and Geithner, who both defended the Fed's power. They feared Dodd's model, which would reduce the Fed to the author of monetary policy without many auxiliary powers. A wide array of forces, including small and large banks, as well as provincial branches of the Fed who felt their regulatory remit under challenge, challenged the legislation and watered down its proposals. Crucially, key players within the financial industry and the state worked to lobby Senate in order to win support for the reappointment of Bernanke as chairman of the Fed. Bernanke was duly reappointed on a 70–30 vote, while the legislation that came to be known as Dodd-Frank left the Fed as regulator of almost all banks within the US. As Neil Irwin (2013: 199) concludes, "The battle for the Fed was over, and it was the mighty Federal Reserve System that had won."

Mervyn King's Bank of England was also brought into some disrepute by the events of the crisis. George Osborne commissioned the Tripartite Review, to look into the system of regulation in place during the crisis. The damning report formed the basis for the Conservative's regulatory shake-up once in power from 2010. The Bank was criticized for failing to take its financial stability role seriously and then for neglecting to conduct any internal inquiry into its own conduct during the crisis. Despite the criticisms, the report ultimately led to the enlargement of the Bank's regulatory mandate, restoring the broader scope that it had held pre–New Labour. With the FSA subsequently dismantled, many of its former responsibilities were handed over to the Bank. Additionally, the Bank was given principal responsibility for assessing systemic threats to financial stability (Conaghan, 2012: 246–47). The Bank's role was greatly enlarged and its power deepened by the addition of these new regulatory responsibilities (Conaghan, 2012: 253).

The disappointing level of regulatory reform within the financial sector, and the continued concentration of power within central banks, have left the core institutional basis of liberalized financial markets and overextended monetary authorities intact. The persistence of this combination, which has been increasingly crucial to Anglo-American development during the neoliberal era, suggests that future financial crises will be very likely and that the reliance upon activist monetary policies looks set to endure. The Fed and the Bank have now survived the political fallout of the two signal periods of neoliberal monetary shocks—that which we discussed in chapter 6, and the zero-bound postcrisis regime from 2008—with their powers intact.

Whatever the efficacy of the policy remedies and regulatory reforms enacted since the crisis, the longer-term prognosis remains discouraging. There must at some point be a limit to the "monetary doping" that the Western economies, led by Anglo-America, have employed to propel themselves out of financial market crises (Streeck, 2014). Each increase in systemic liquidity, each new bubble created by a rush of cheap money into the bull asset category of the day, enhances rather than diminishes the risks of greater volatility (Minsky, 2008; Wolf, 2015).

In dealing with the existential crisis of the GFC, the Anglo-American economies have only deepened a longer-term, more deeply embedded, and gradually evolving structural crisis of the neoliberal order (Gamble, 2014: 18–19). Public debt levels have risen precipitously, with huge volumes of that debt now warehoused on the balance sheets of the Fed and the Bank of England as a result of QE. Unraveling from the age of the zero-bound is fraught with danger (Koo, 2015: 106). The Fed has so far managed to gradually raise interest rates since December 2015 without sparking a recession or broader financial instability, while the Bank of England has moved much more tentatively toward recent rate increases in the context of the UK's Brexit malaise (Schneider and Dunsmuir, 2017; Mackenzie, 2017).

But it remains to be seen whether further rate rises, or sudden hikes, will trigger widespread financial instability. Household debt levels in the US had reached $12.96 trillion by the third quarter of 2017, $280 billion above the pre-crisis peak (McGeever, 2017). In the UK, household debt increased at 7.3 percent per annum between 2012 and 2017, with unsecured consumer credit increasing at a staggering 19 percent. This has led household debt to approach levels not seen since the GFC. The continuing dependency upon debt-driven consumption, in the context of economic "recoveries" marked by deep wage stagnation, renders the Anglo-American economies extremely vulnerable to interest rate adjustments that might spark widespread defaults. The institutional bedrocks of the neoliberal order—independent central banks empowered to wield monetary tools with great scope—are endangered by each Minskian fix for the inherent instability of giant financial markets hosted within the City and New York. The veneer of central bank independence and the depoliticized cure-all of monetary policy become much harder to uphold as the crisis response reveals the distributional prejudices of these interventions.

Viewed within a broader panorama, the Anglo-American economies continue to rest upon one side of a precarious seesaw of global imbalances (Wade, 2009: 542). With wages low or stagnant in the postcrisis period, and productivity gains modest, the Anglo-American economies will continue to rely upon the goodwill and interest of foreign creditors to fuel their current account deficits. If those flows of credit slow or seize up entirely, the future of the Anglo-American debt-driven model looks insecure.

A further foundation of the neoliberal order, the international monetary system anchored by the dollar, has been opened up to renewed uncertainty. The crisis has shaken confidence in the dollar standard and stoked doubts over the longer-term viability of the Anglo-American vision of liberalized global financial markets (Chin and Helleiner, 2008: Kirshner, 2014: 2). The rising East Asian powers, with their confidence in US financial leadership already dampened by the Asian Financial Crisis, now question more deeply America's exorbitant privilege. China in particular has grown bolder in its challenges to the US financial order, however incremental its attempts to boost its own standing may be.

Despite all of these indicators of trouble for the dollar, and the liberal Anglo-American financial order more broadly, the world remains uncomfortably bound to the United States' financial future. Herein lies a fundamental paradox: despite its shaky longer-term prognosis, there is no credible alternative to the dollar's status as a safe haven asset. And in an era where the safety of assets has become more important, dollar-denominated securities prove indispensable. As much as they might be troubled by their exposure to the domestic policy whims of the US, emerging market economies—most crucially China—have no easy way out. Even the downgrading of America's credit rating in 2011 and the fractious politics of the shutdown did not dampen the appetite for US Treasury bills (Prasad, 2015: xii–18).

As this book has argued, the foundations of the international monetary order have always been deeply interactive with the national institutional orders of capitalism upon which they rest, particularly those of the UK and the US during the twentieth century. And there is no less uncertainty hanging over the domestic foundations of the global liberal order that the UK and the US have done so much to author. The politics of public debt and the austerity regimes that have come to characterize the "consolidation state" mark a new phase in the deterioration of postwar democratic capitalism (Streeck, 2013: 143). The distributional settlement between capital and labor that was crucial to the embedding of the Keynesian welfare state has continued to be further dismantled with this signal crisis of the neoliberal era. The postcrisis period has been used as an opportunity to take care of the unfinished business of the early 1980s by political and market forces hostile to social democracy. Increasingly, the state presides over a grossly unjust distributional architecture. Low wages, high inequality, and growing debt levels have been hallmarks of the recovery

(Green and Lavery, 2015). Many of the fundamental flaws of UK capitalism persist (Hay and Berry, 2015). In the US, Trump's proposed corporate tax cuts look set to further entrench spectacular levels of inequality (Pressman, 2017).

The persistence of structural economic weaknesses within Anglo-American political economies has, though, had hugely significant political effects. We cannot understand the twin shocks of the Brexit vote and the election of Donald Trump without appreciating the impact of the neoliberal macroeconomic regime in generating widespread political disaffection (Blyth and Matthijs, 2017). Nor were these political upheavals nationally independent in their origins, with important webs of transatlantic personal linkages contributing to the successes of the Trump and Leave campaigns (Wilson, 2017: 544).[8] Within parties of the left in the UK and the US, the fallout from the crisis has also been highly significant. In the UK, Jeremy Corbyn's election to the Labour Party leadership in September 2015 broke from almost two decades of New Labour centrism and promised to restore a more virile sense of social democratic renewal. Labour's major gains in the May 2017 general election confirmed the sense of a revitalized left, even if much of it might be attributed to Labour's carefully calculated position of ambivalence over Brexit, which enabled an electoral coalition based on both staunch Remainers and ardent Leavers. In the US, Corbyn's triumph paralleled the unexpected traction garnered by senator Bernie Sanders's 2016 presidential campaign. The successes of these politicians in actively critiquing the neoliberal settlement are a testament to the breakdown of the neoliberal political consensus, and the opening of ideological rifts in both states, may prove to fundamentally alter the political foundations of Anglo-American development.

An important transformation of another kind is also afoot. Spatial rebalancing, geared toward reconfiguring the UK's relationship to the world, has now begun to emerge. This rebalancing, which challenges the future path of Anglo-American development more than any period since the IMF crisis of 1976, has arisen within the changed postcrisis conjuncture of global capitalism. It is to these emergent dynamics in the political economy of the Special Relationship that we now turn.

The Offshore City and Global Rebalancing

In the years after the financial crisis the City-Bank-Treasury nexus has been reactivated. This has occurred within an altered global context. Two key facets of this altered conjuncture are of particular importance for the City and the

UK state. The first is the growing financial power of China and its enthusiasm for extending the global reach of that power. This development has been embodied most concretely in efforts to promote the international use of China's currency, the renminbi (RMB). The second relates to the UK's changed relationship to Europe, embodied in the shock 2016 referendum result in favor of leaving the EU through Brexit. The playing out of these two tendencies will be central to the UK's future relationship with the US.

As has been argued in earlier chapters of this book, UK elites maintained the international standing of the City of London and key institutions of the UK state by embracing US financial power during the decades after World War II. This was facilitated by the development of "offshore": a regulatory innovation that enabled the City to play a prominent role within global finance despite the demise of sterling and the waning power of UK banks. From the 1950s onward, the City became first and foremost a key center for dollar-denominated flows of trade and finance. With the creation of the euro, the City began to play a comparable role for Europe's fledgling currency (Thompson, 2017: 217).

Offshore continued, in an institutionally modified form, the City's centuries-long role in mediating of global flows of trade and finance. Now firmly in place and with so much of the City's—and with it the UK's—comparative advantage within the international division of labor resting upon the existence of a laissez-faire offshore orientation, UK development has been imbued with a specific trait: a unique sensitivity to transformations within the international monetary order. This may prove to be the most durable impact of decades of Anglo-American development upon the character of UK capitalism. The City-Bank-Treasury nexus now functions as a pivot that adjusts its orientation according to shifts in the distribution of global financial power, subjecting it, in the process, to complex and uneven forms of interdependent capitalist development spatially concentrated in the City. The two facets of transformation identified above highlight this condition: both China's rising financial power and the UK's disengagement from the EU will hold a special resonance for the City of London and with it the future of UK capitalism.

Let us first examine Chinese currency internationalization. Under David Cameron's governments, the central forces within UK capitalism began to court China as part of a wider strategy of rebalancing in favor of emerging markets (Green, 2018). With the UK's membership of the EU wracked with uncertainty and the ever-present threat of EU regulatory encroachment upon the City's treasured liberties undimmed, George Osborne's Treasury led the charge toward alternative sources of future financial market growth. China emerged as the favored candidate, due to its intention to internationalize its currency, the renminbi (RMB), as it seeks to increase its international reach and lessen its dependence on what Chinese elites view as an increasingly fragile dollar-centered international monetary order (Chin and Wang, 2010: 4; Kirshner, 2014: 13–14).

Plans are underway to integrate the London and Shanghai stock exchanges. The growth in offshore foreign exchange dealing in RMB has been rapid, and the Bank of England anticipates a massive increase in global RMB transactions (BofE, 2013: 304–7). The first-ever overseas sovereign bond for China has already been issued in the City, and now Beijing plans to issue short-term debt there too. All of this is part of a grander vision in which the UK will seek to be, as George Osborne puts it, "China's best partner in the West," with London as the foremost offshore center for RMB business (Parker and Moore, 2015). This involves a series of bilateral trade and investment deals as well, with China taking major stakes in crucial infrastructure projects, such as the development of a new power plant at Hinkley Point.

The UK's ardent courtship of Chinese financial power may put strain upon the political economy of the Special Relationship. US bankers have criticized London's "love fest" with China, arguing that Chinese banks in London are now receiving preferential regulatory treatment (Jenkins et al., 2015). More important, a growing divide over the future of the global economy came to light with a rare public spat over the UK's application for membership of the newly founded Asian Infrastructure Investment Bank (AIIB), led by China. A senior US administration official rebuked the UK for its "constant accommodation of China" and rebuked the UK government for having taken the decision after "virtually no consultation" with the US (Dyer and Parker, 2015). The Americans view the AIIB as a rival to the multilateral institutional structure, notably the IMF and World Bank, established under their auspices and prevailing influence after the end of World War II. That infrastructure was deployed to promote unbridled financial liberalization under the Clinton administration, advancing a model of political economy now delegitimized in many parts of the world. A number of states have become more willing to countenance Chinese-sponsored alternatives.

The UK's support for the AIIB, which prompted a cascade of European endorsements, is loaded with enormous symbolic significance. The UK was, as we saw in chapter 3, the key coarchitect of the postwar Bretton Woods order. It has long been one of the United States' closest allies. Continued reorientation toward China may gradually lead the UK to what *Financial Times* journalist

Gideon Rachman (2015) has termed a "clash of special relationships," a situation in which uncomfortable choices have to be made, particularly if geopolitical relations between China and the US, already strained by Chinese territorial claims and expansion in the South China Sea, deteriorate further.

Clearly, then, UK inclination to integrate more deeply with China has the potential to place severe strain on the political-economic foundations of the Special Relationship. But what of our second facet—Brexit and its immediate fallout? Here the challenge is perhaps even graver. The City's centrality within the global political economy, its status as part of a deeply integrated Anglo-American financial heartland, and the prestige and influence that it lends to HM Treasury and the Bank of England, all rest on one particular foundation: the continuation of its entrepôt status. It is that status that enabled the City to become a major base for dominant US and global banks.

Brexit now imperils the extensity of the City's entrepôt status. The loss of the referendum on European membership by Cameron's government poses the biggest postwar political challenge to the City (Thompson, 2017). The City's role as a gateway into European financial markets was central to the motivations of US and other globally oriented banks that established operations there during the 1980s. But here is the catch. This gateway role now depends upon membership of the European single market and the associated "passporting rights" that allow institutions based in the City to conduct off-shore euro business and sell financial services within Europe. That business with Europe was valued at £20 billion in 2015. Brexit will undermine these rights, and their loss threatens the City's lucrative euro trading and European business. The EU has offered UK financial services firms the weaker status of "equivalence"—a form of access granted to non-EU companies if the European Commission decides that the financial regulations of the country are as tough as those in Brussels. It can be withdrawn by the EU at short notice and offers reduced access compared to passporting rights (Parker and Brunsden, 2018). The negotiations over continued market access have demonstrated the challenge that Brexit poses to the City's regulatory autonomy. Potential loss of regulatory flexibility will likely diminish the City's global appeal.

In this respect, the vultures have already begun to circle. The French prime minister wasted no time in advertising, within days of the Brexit vote, that Paris would warmly welcome financial services inclined to relocate from the City (Wilkinson, 2016). Added to rival attempts to lure business away from the City, there has been a substantial weakening of the City's political centrality within European finance. The announcement that the EU intends to move its banking regulator, the European Banking Authority, out of London demonstrates the extent to which the City's traditional structural privilege within the creation and oversight of European financial regulation has been forgone. This was mirrored by the immediate resignation of Jonathan Hill, the UK's EU commissioner who had steered the financial services component of the commission, presiding over the regulation of banks and markets across the EU (Brunsden, 2016).

These changes are likely to embolden efforts by French and European regulators—underway prior to Brexit—to clamp down on euro business in the City and rein in "Anglo-Saxon" finance. Attempts by the Bank of France and the ECB to mandate that clearing houses handling over 5 percent of euro-denominated products must be located within the Eurozone already threatened London's dominance in this market and led to an ongoing legal dispute between the UK and the ECB in the European Court of Justice, which was ultimately resolved in favour of the UK (Fleming, 2014; Barker and Stafford, 2015).

Anglo-American Futures

This chapter has argued that the postcrisis period has thus far embodied a peculiar combination of continuity and change. Despite the important transformation represented by the embrace of sustained unorthodox monetary policies, the fundamentally regressive distributional basis of the neoliberal order has been left intact. The response to the crisis, through a combination of monetary loosening and fiscal austerity, has succeeded in preserving the financial sector and stabilizing capitalism. In acting quickly and concertedly to flood financial markets with liquidity through QE, Anglo-American central banks proved crucial once more to the steering of a definitive turn in the politics of financial globalization. Yet the responses that they inaugurated have done nothing to resolve the deeper structural crisis of the neoliberal order of capitalism within which Anglo-American development has played such a central role. Stagnant wages, overweening financial sectors, mountains of debt, and now slowing growth and productivity continue to mark contemporary capitalism.

Within this context of deeper structural continuity, however, important changes have taken place. Politically, the neoliberal consensus has fractured under the pressure of widespread disaffection and economic stagnation, leading to the Brexit vote in the UK and the election of Donald Trump in the US.

But the postcrisis period has also witnessed the reemergence of a more assertive left within Anglo-America, embodied by Jeremy Corbyn's successes as leader of the Labour Party and the unexpected popularity of Bernie Sanders's presidential campaign. Regarding the UK's institutional orientation toward US capitalism, the combination of an energetic pivot to embrace Chinese finance and the shock of Brexit present the biggest transformation affecting the City-Bank-Treasury nexus in the postwar period. How the politics of this pivot and the post-Brexit conjuncture develop in the years that follow will prove to be the main determinants of the future place of Anglo-American development within global capitalism. As we will see in the conclusion, the fracturing of democratic political consensus over contemporary capitalism presents several potential paths that Anglo-American development and global capitalism may follow in the decades ahead. Whatever these paths prove to be, it is likely that the GFC and the irresolution of the structural weaknesses within the neoliberal order will be recognized as a crucial turning point.

Conclusion

IN THE postwar era, Anglo-American development shaped the politics of financial globalization. The interdependence and integration of finance in the City and New York, the interactivity of sterling and the dollar, and the close linkages between the City-Bank-Treasury nexus and the Federal Reserve-Treasury-Wall Street nexus were crucial drivers of this process. As I have argued, Anglo-American governments and bankers destabilized the Keynesian compromise and unleashed forces of liberalized finance. They did so by supporting processes of deregulation and integration that unfolded at two tightly interlinked levels. Domestically, they fueled the growth of the financial sector and the dependency of workers upon a rising burden of debt. Internationally, they undermined the limitations on the freedom of capital movement through the embedded liberal framework put in place at Bretton Woods, rendering the maintenance of fixed exchange rates much more difficult.

Within the domestic political economies of Anglo-America, financial integration, interdependence, and competition weakened the foundations of the postwar regulatory order. Over time, these transatlantic processes drove the transition from a Keynesian system of administered and quantitative controls over lending to a more market-based neoliberal system governed by interest rates and dominated by large universal banks. Undoing interventionist political controls over the workings of domestic finance accelerated the breakdown of the postwar order; it made macroeconomic demand management more difficult by enabling a massive expansion in the size and scope of financial markets that constrained governments' capacity to directly shape the flow of credit.

The rise of a neoliberal order and the centrality of Anglo-America within it was not simply a case of an ascendant ideology. Long-term developmental processes ensured that a particular kind of intellectual disposition accorded more closely to the emerging structures of Anglo-American financial markets. Neoliberal ideas provided a fertile ideological context for the liberalization of finance and the restoration of market discipline. Nor was the turn to

neoliberalism and financial deregulation a dynamic that was exclusively en-
dogenous to the US. Many of the regulatory recalibrations that dismantled the
New Deal order during the 1980s emerged from the wider context of Anglo-
American development and transatlantic regulatory interdependence.[1]

In terms of the broader international monetary order, we have seen that
transformations within Anglo-American capitalism were central. Those transformations undermined the Bretton Woods order by spurring the turn to liberalized and vastly expanded global financial markets. The Euromarkets hosted
in the City provided the foundational market infrastructure underpinning the
globalization of finance. Sustained Anglo-American deficits during the 1960s
undermined the key currency roles of sterling and the dollar and gravely weakened the fixed exchange rates that the United Kingdom and the US had put in
place at Bretton Woods. During the crucial decade of the 1970s, US disciplinary power, and the politicized engagement of bankers within the City that
were hostile to social democracy were central to maintaining the UK's commitment to openness and continued liberalization.

Within the regulatory sphere, the transatlantic feedback loop shaped
broader international tendencies toward freeing financial markets and increasing integration. In terms of central bank leadership, the Bank and the Fed were
key to shaping the broader conditions of financial globalization—both in
shaping the politics of Basel and international banking regulation, and in making a synchronized effort to stamp out inflation and tear up the postwar consensus through shock monetarism.

The power and influence of bankers in the City and New York was at the
heart of Anglo-American development: they undermined the Bretton Woods
order and drove the dynamics of financial globalization. The interdependence
of bankers on both sides of the Atlantic was critical to the restoration of the
City's role as the world's premier financial center within an international financial order that now had the dollar at its core. As the competitive challenge from
London intensified and the integration of transatlantic money markets accelerated, increasingly incorporating a widening sphere of European financial
market integration from the 1970s, the New Deal regulatory framework in the
US came under increasing pressure.

That the City's restoration occurred within a context of transatlantic financial integration ensured that the dollar and US banks became the dominant
players in London. The spatial centrality of London for the internationalization of US finance created important transatlantic institutional linkages between
finance and the state in the UK and the US. The social forces that benefited

from the City's restoration then drew in US disciplinary power in order to reorient the UK state away from the potential radicalization of social democracy during the crisis of 1976. The success of the US in disciplining the UK, through the dictates of the IMF and supported by the actions of financial markets, was a turning point in the furtherance of international financial liberalization and the politics of globalization.

At the root of these developments lay the continued concentration of power within the institutional complex of the City-Bank-Treasury nexus in the UK, and the Fed-Wall Street-Treasury nexus in the US. The interactions between these institutions, through a transatlantic financial space, contributed significantly to the collapse of Bretton Woods and the unfolding of financial globalization. They also provided a basis for the emergence of monetarism and the launching of the broader neoliberal project during the 1970s and 1980s. As banking power increased with the development of global capital markets and decades of increasing financial liberalization, central banks within both states became increasingly important to the management of economic development.

This historical trajectory of deepening integration and sustained liberalization was not an inevitable process; it was shot through with moments of profound contingency. Had the merchant banking community in the City not been able to establish political support for the Euromarkets from the Bank and the Treasury, the history of postwar global capitalism might have been markedly different. Had the Labour government of 1976 gone against the wishes of the US, the IMF, and domestic forces hostile to postwar Keynesianism, by adopting a radicalized social democracy and endorsing protectionism, then the momentum of the entire globalization project may have been halted. And had the Fed successfully managed to win tighter regulation over the Euromarkets in the interests of domestic monetary stability, perhaps the intensified financial liberalization of the 1980s might not have occurred. The crisis decade of the 1970s was, then, a critical moment in the progression of Anglo-American development. Financial integration and the effects of the transatlantic regulatory feedback loop slowed under political uncertainty over the viability of globalization. Doubts were cast about the future of the Special Relationship.

Yet Anglo-American development weathered the turbulence of the 1970s and emerged resurgent. That this occurred owed much to the political power of finance. The deep ties between banks and the central agencies of the state, as well as the robust political support that they received under the Thatcher and Reagan governments, guaranteed that the Anglo-American core of financial globalization would be revitalized during the 1980s. The ultimate legacy of decades of Anglo-American development was the global financial crisis of 2007/8, effects of which continue to slowly unfold as the neoliberal order continues to contend with a deep and seemingly intractable crisis.

Rethinking Systemic Transformation

What of the methodological implications of this study? As this book has shown, existing accounts of postwar systemic transformation have overstated the singularity of America's role in authoring financial globalization and, correspondingly, played down that of the UK. Even more contemporary revisionist accounts have failed to come to terms with the specificity of the UK's role, dividing the politics of financial globalization between a European rules-based, managed approach and a US "ad hoc" approach (Abdelal, 2007). In these accounts, the specificity of the UK's role and the structural centrality of Anglo-America are overlooked. By the time Europe began to codify financial liberalization, Anglo-America had already structured global financial markets in ways that made further liberalization a fait accompli if other capitalist centers sought to prosper globally.

The serial neglect of the UK's unique position within the politics of financial globalization, and the structural centrality of a broader Anglo-American financial space, owes much, as we saw in chapter 1, to the prevalence of a stage-based and state-centric historiography of the global political economy that views its modern history in terms of the cyclical transition between hegemonic powers. The US clearly did play a privileged and unparalleled role in shaping the development of postwar capitalism; this book has not sought to dispute that claim. But a more geographically sensitive methodology, one that recognizes the uneven and interdependent patterns of international capitalist development, shows that it did so in conjunction with other major capitalist states. In the area of finance, the relationship of uneven interdependence with the UK, which formed the bedrock of the political economy of the Special Relationship, was crucial.

Contrary to the hegemony story, then, the UK did not simply slide into decline and irrelevance once the sun had set on the Empire. US ascendancy and global financial dominance were channeled through, and conditioned by, the subordinate integration of the UK. This integration was brought about by processes of Anglo-American development that exerted a hugely formative impact upon the postwar development of UK capitalism. But the UK also exercised considerable agency and, in turn, structured the development of US capitalism. It did so both in creating the institutional and regulatory conditions that helped to draw US finance into the City during the 1960s and the 1980s, and in generating important feedback effects upon the US, which spurred internal deregulatory pressures. The most important consequence of this process was the gradual decomposition of the New Deal regulatory framework, which had shaped the development of US finance since the 1930s. Financial integration and interdependence with the UK gradually weakened the foundations of the New Deal order.

Therefore, this was not a case of a simple transition from one hegemonic power to another. Neither was it a case of monolithic US structural power imposed upon a pliant UK. Anglo-American development also structured the options available to policy makers and bankers in the US. In the 1960s, attempts to enact tight monetary policy in the US were undermined by the existence of the offshore Euromarkets based in the City. And again, during the 1970s and 1980s, the Fed was constrained by the mechanisms of Anglo-American financial integration, adjusting its monetary policy regime in response to these conditions.

As we saw in chapter 6, the UK resisted attempts to regulate the Euromarkets while US banks formed a domestic constituency opposed to the prospect of extending the Fed's regulatory reach. Similarly, as argued in chapter 5, when it comes to the IMF crisis of 1976 US power only gives us part of the story. US power was undoubtedly important; it was embodied by the capacity of the US to align its position with that of the IMF and ration the supply of emergency dollar support for the UK based on the acceptance of IMF conditions. But the capacity of the US to exert influence over the UK also owed a great deal to the manner in which decades of Anglo-American development had embedded the international hegemony of the dollar into the Euromarkets in a way that cemented its continued role after Bretton Woods collapsed, and they created a constituency of social forces within the City, the Bank, and the Treasury that were hostile to plans for a restoration of social democracy.

Over the longer term, Anglo-American development helped to generate US structural power within finance by developing the institutional conditions within which the dollar could prosper as the dominant international currency. But the dependency upon institutional forms and social forces based geographically within the UK also created new vulnerabilities for the US. It limited the domestic policy autonomy of US officials attempting to control monetary policy, and it meant that political developments within the

UK—most notably during the crisis period of 1976—presented obstacles to the effective functioning of the Anglo-American market infrastructure based within the City upon which continued financial globalization had come to depend. These dynamics blurred the lines between domestic and international forms of power and agency, prompting us to rethink how systemic transformation within the global political economy occurs. The hub and spokes model of singular hegemons structuring and underwriting the wider international context neglects the complex spatial interdependencies and patterns of reciprocal causality that drive international capitalist development.

These insights regarding systemic transformation are particularly pertinent in the present historical moment. Contemporary debates over the rise of China, undoubtedly one of the central themes of global political economy in the twenty-first century, risk falling into the familiar conceptual traps. We should not repeat the theoretical failings that hampered our understanding of the postwar era and the wider history of modern capitalist development. With this in mind we should refrain from interpreting Chinese development through the lens of hegemonic aspirations and grand cyclical theorization. To do so would be to overlook the deep networked interconnections and mutual vulnerabilities of capitalist development in a globalized world market context.

Unless the open global order is entirely rolled back and states engage in a new era of autarkic development, it is unlikely that we will see a simple displacement of US power by an ascendant China. If anything, China's rise already appears more deeply dependent upon the future of US capitalism than the US was upon the UK. It is only by tapping into the United States' vast domestic market that China has been able to achieve such astonishingly rapid export-led growth. And it is only by welcoming the establishment of US MNCs within the Chinese mainland that China's evolving position within the international division of labor has been secured. Mutual dependencies of this sort also create mutual vulnerabilities. Even as relative Chinese power grows, the path of continued economic integration will set limits upon the scope for autonomous action—unless, that is, Chinese elites are willing to suffer the massive economic costs of ignoring the parameters of action that such deep integration creates. The uneasy interdependence of this condition is borne out by the contemporary "balance of financial terror" that characterizes the economic relationship between the two states.

Every period of historical transformation within global capitalism relies upon particular developmental configurations within and between states. These involve different institutions, intellectual rationales, and social forces.

We should not comfortably fall back upon the notion of hegemony to capture China's contemporary ascendancy and the weakening of the Anglo-American and Western international order. The case for UK hegemony has been widely discredited, and this book has shown the limits of framing the postwar processes of systemic transformation led by the US in those terms. China's symbiotic relationship with US capitalism points to a different form of global order emerging—a form of order that requires its own distinctive conceptual vocabulary if we are to apprehend it in its fullest specificity. Dynamics of global capitalist development, framed within an expanded methodological internationalism, should be at the heart of our inquiries into the nature of systemic transformation, not the application of static and transhistorical concepts of rule that begin from uncritical state-centrism and attempt to delineate pristine phases of global political-economic order. Only a properly historically institutionalist and internationalist approach can move us beyond this.

This study has also produced important insights for understanding UK and US capitalism comparatively. The deep developmental interdependence generated through Anglo-American finance challenges the common understanding of the UK and US as similar but nationally enclosed "liberal market" or "market-led" models of capitalism (Dore et al., 1999; Coates, 2000; Hall and Soskice, 2001). We cannot understand the convergence between financial systems and economic ideas in the two states as the product of endogenous "institutional clustering" by functionally similar firms. Instead, with regard to transformations of financial institutions and macroeconomic paradigms in particular, we need to understand national capitalism in the UK and US as shaped by long-term and deeply interdependent processes of transatlantic development formative to both states. And to apprehend these developmental interdependencies, we need to set capitalist transformation more firmly in a rich appreciation of historical time and geographical space—by examining how institutions are shaped by both deeper and more conjunctural forms of historical transformation, and how these temporal dynamics play out within and across particular spatial scales. Finally, we cannot begin and end our comparative treatment of these two cases at the level of abstract national models characterized by the orientation of firms or the relationship between state and the market. The importance of the relationship between the financial sectors and centers in the UK and the US suggests that we need to provide a more rigorous sectoral and spatial disaggregation within CPE. Only then can the differentially internationalized and spatially oriented nature of specific sectors and sites within national capitalisms be properly apprehended, generating a

CPE that is both more thoroughly comparative and more accurately international. This study has begun that work for the UK and the US, but there is undoubtedly much more to be done to reveal how specific sectors within other national political economies have demonstrated their own histories of uneven and interdependent international development.

Anglo-American Fault Lines

This leaves us with only one task remaining. We must draw together some political conclusions from this book by evaluating the lessons of Anglo-American history and prospects for the future. One of the major lessons is that the recurrent commitment to austerity within Anglo-American capitalism should come as no surprise. Viewed within a broader historical panorama, it is the Keynesian heyday of the postwar period, and not the rise of a neoliberal order, that is the real anomaly. A further conclusion to be drawn from the experience of the Bretton Woods monetary order—and the troubled history of the postwar compromise between capital and labor—is that it is incredibly difficult to overcome the forces of economic and political orthodoxy within Anglo-American capitalism. This should leave us with a sober understanding of the task at hand if we are to transform the basis of contemporary capitalism, tackle inequality, and restore democratic vitality.

It took the unfolding of two cataclysmic world wars within twenty years, the experience of the Great Depression, and decades of popular struggle before the old gold standard orthodoxy of balanced budgets and deflationary adjustments imposed on the working classes was properly challenged. Postwar planners attempted to create the space required, at Bretton Woods, for countries to run deficits and implement expansionary economic policies that would enable full employment and high growth rates. But the Anglo-American banking elite never lost its appetite for the old austerity politics and international disciplines of the gold standard era. The Keynesian transformation of the UK state did not go far enough in reorienting the City toward the UK's national development goals or the politics of full employment. In its desire to maintain the international role of the pound and restore the City's prestige, the City-Bank-Treasury nexus undermined the foundations of a lasting Keynesian transformation and successfully attempted to restore the old orthodoxy of fiscal discipline and price stability. In the UK and the US, both of the major political parties came to accept and advocate this policy program wholeheartedly.

Within thirty years of the implementation of Bretton Woods, the visions of Keynes and White had largely receded from view. The birth of the Euromarkets had punctured holes within national money markets. The domestic commitment to full employment was cracking under the pressure of increasing worker militancy and stagflation. The IMF had been transformed into an agent that would impose market discipline and austerity upon debtors rather than afford them space to grow their way out of trouble and pursue Keynesian objectives.

In the UK—the country that had produced the founder of the most successful intellectual challenge to the old orthodoxy, John Maynard Keynes—it was the IMF that helped drive the adoption of monetary targets and the enactment of austerity. The system of fixed exchange rates and capital controls, designed to provide the domestic breathing space for expansionary fiscal policy and full employment, and to insulate states from the disruptive influence of speculative capital flows, had collapsed under the pressure of liberalizing global financial markets that were hosted within the Anglo-American twin engine rooms of financial globalization: London and New York.

Despite the positive experiences with planning and enlarged Treasury control over national economic management during the wartime years, it did not take long before the Bank and the Fed were able to recover their former institutional privileges in the early postwar period. Once those privileges had been regained, even in the wake of the Bank's nationalization in the UK, they were able to promote financial expansion and eventual liberalization in a manner that imperiled their own models of national capitalism and the broader international monetary system. These processes did not simply unfold in accordance with a grand strategic plan; they were at many points products more of the haphazard interaction of private finance and state agencies, as Anglo-American bankers sought to negotiate the crises, constraints, and opportunities of the international monetary order.

What is clear from the arguments that I have made in this book is that the Keynesian transformations of Anglo-American capitalism did not go far enough. The freedom of private finance was not sufficiently constrained, nor the required institutional transformations enacted that might have put finance more durably in the service of more egalitarian goals. In this respect, the postwar Labour government in the UK was a failure. It left far too much of the existing structure of UK capitalism untouched. In the US, the more radical elements of New Deal politics ran out of steam too early to affect the kind of changes that were required to put US capitalism upon a progressive trajectory over the longer term.[2] The incomplete transformation of the postwar state, and the unwillingness to confront the power of finance more directly, left the path open for the gradual reassertion of the old economic orthodoxies.

By the 1980s, the predominance of central and private bankers in shaping the global political economy had been restored. By 1997, with the Bank of England granted formal independence by the New Labour government, independent Anglo-American central banks were once again fundamental to the politics of the international monetary order. With a distribution of national wealth and levels of income inequality reminiscent of the interwar years, one could be mistaken for thinking that the politics of the 1920s had returned under the neoliberal political economy of the 1990s and 2000s.

In the wake of the global financial crisis of 2007/8, the age-old bankers' remedy of austerity rose once again to the top of the policy agenda. The response to the crisis in the UK and the US relied upon the adoption of coordinated policies of quantitative easing and loose monetary policy. These policies boosted asset prices, continued the regressive redistribution of wealth associated with the neoliberal era, and shored up the balance sheets of banks. But they did little to solve the problems of stagnant living standards. Just as the neoliberal era was ushered in by the adoption of unorthodox Anglo-American central banking practices, its most severe crisis has been met with a parallel response. Now, unlike in the 1980s, the concern is with forestalling deflation and the collapse of asset prices. However, the focus upon activist monetary policy in combination with fiscal austerity remains the same. If the failure of the postwar monetary order and the Keynesian state tells us anything, it is that the way to escape the recurrent politics of austerity in the longer term is through firmly challenging the power of private finance and reconstituting the commanding heights of the state in line with different goals and priorities. That will inevitably involve circumscribing the freedom of finance and democratizing the dominant financial institutions of the state—central banks and treasuries. For that to happen, progressive social forces will have to agitate for change in a much more convincing and consistent manner.

There are signs of forces building that may carry the conviction to challenge the basis of Anglo-American capitalism. In the UK, Labour's turn to the left and its encouraging attempt to build a social movement base for transforming capitalism holds promise; it poses the biggest challenge since the 1970s to the foundations of UK capitalism and the deeply entrenched orthodoxies that have stifled, time and time again, the possibilities for the establishment of a more progressive political economy. In the US, Bernie Sanders's campaign for

Democratic leadership mobilized huge numbers of young Americans who now support democratic socialism and reject the ailing pillars of US capitalism, dominated by corporate lobbying power and staggering levels of inequality. If the excesses of Anglo-American capitalism are to be tamed, then these movements to renew and radicalize social democracy in the twenty-first century will be key. For the well-being of the wider world economy, they must go much further in challenging the entrenched interests of the City and Wall Street, turning them toward communitarian ends. The challenges facing these initiatives to strengthen the democratic and egalitarian basis of Anglo-American capitalism are enormous. The shackles of political centrism forged during the Great Moderation created entrenched opposition by incumbents within the social democratic parties. The road to renewal is likely to be long and hard.

If social democracy cannot be restored in this manner, then the alternatives are dangerous. The rise of populist xenophobia whipped up in the UK's Brexit campaign and the insurgency of first UKIP and then the Brexit Party mirror the drift to racism within Donald Trump's Republican US presidency. At the time of writing, in late August 2019, UK politics is riven by the divisive politics of Brexit led by a controversial Conservative prime minister, Boris Johnson. Johnson's well-documented character flaws represent a new low for the office in postwar history. His attempts to drive the UK to depart from the EU by whatever means necessary have led to the prorogation of parliament. Elected by the dwindling membership of the Conservative Party and presiding over the thinnest of parliamentary majorities in coalition with the Democratic Unionist Party, Johnson has thrown the UK into a deepening constitutional crisis. He has endangered the principle of parliamentary sovereignty at the heart of UK democracy by attempting to shield the Brexit process from scrutiny by a House of Commons that has repeatedly demonstrated its opposition to the possibility of crashing out of the EU without a withdrawal agreement. Johnson is borrowing from the populist playbook that has been enthusiastically employed by Donald Trump in the US—pitting "the people" and a mythical general will against the supposedly corrupt or obstructive institutions of the state.

Should Brexit lead to a deep and acrimonious fissure with continental Europe, a newly intensified alignment between the UK and the US may emerge. Trump has been a vocal supporter of Brexit, having shown consistent hostility to the EU. He prefers the reassertion of national sovereignty and the reduced geopolitical power of a divided Europe. He has also spoken warmly of

Johnson, noting approvingly that Johnson has been referred to as "Britain Trump" (Holland, 2019). Both Trump and senior officials within his administration have suggested that the UK would be "at the front of the queue" for a trade deal following Brexit (BBC, 2019). Achieving a major free trade deal with the US and using it as an opportunity to transform the regulatory structures of UK capitalism has long been a major Brexit goal of free-market leaning Conservatives and associated neoliberal think tanks like the Institute of Economic Affairs (Lawrence, Pegg, and Evans, 2018). The full implications of a trade deal are unclear, but President Trump refused to rule out that privatization of the full range of NHS services provision through opening up to US businesses would be up for grabs. The threat to the UK's bedrock welfare state institution is one part of a wider challenge posed by a potential free trade deal; it threatens to push the UK further away from European regulatory standards and institutions across a range of sectors, making UK capitalism look much more like its US partner. The regulatory interdependence that has characterized Anglo-American finance for decades may now be spread across many other sectors through a potential trade deal.

Beyond the encouraging noises emanating from the Trump administration, however, the obstacles to a trade deal with the US remain formidable. The vulnerability created by the disorderly politics of Brexit, and the loss of the negotiating power that comes from being a member of the large EU market, puts the UK in a weak negotiating position. From the US side, the rapid fall in the value of the pound linked to Brexit will probably be a sticking point in the negotiations, as sterling's depreciation will be viewed as providing an unfair advantage for UK exporters (Mason, 2019). The US domestic politics of a post-Brexit trade deal also look inauspicious. Senior congressional leaders have made it very clear that any Brexit outcome that destabilizes the peace process in Ireland will lead to a dismissal of the prospect of a UK-US trade deal (Fuchs, 2019). More generally, the increasingly partisan political mood within Congress has made securing congressional approval of any significant trade deal extremely difficult in recent years. Finally, despite friendly talk of the UK's special place in US foreign policy and economic relations, the reality is that the Trump administration has consistently demonstrated a ruthless approach to international negotiations.

After decades of global economic integration and the hollowing out of social democratic redistributive programs, Anglo-American development and the neoliberal order more broadly have reached a crossroads. The momentum of globalization has slowed. History's echo is audible. The lessons of the interwar years must be heeded. As postwar globalization reaches its hour of judgment, the debacle of the previous breakdown of global economic integration, which ended in disintegration and war, still figures in the political consciousness. The path must now be trodden carefully. Progressive forces must seek once more to democratize global capitalism, bringing revitalized national and subnational democratic forms into harmony with a reconstructed international order. This will involve embracing a sustainable ecological basis, strengthening the voice and the hand of the losers of neoliberal globalization. It must avert a fall into nationalist rivalry, authoritarianism, and xenophobia.

Within this new conjuncture, the power of Anglo-America will continue to be critical to the future of the global economy. A continuing alignment between the nationalist goals of Brexit and Trump's doctrine of "America First" threatens to usher in a new age of fractious international politics that stirs nationalist sentiment but does little to tackle the glaring inequalities of contemporary capitalism. Although Asian powers have grown in in strength and importance, London and New York will continue to be the world's dominant financial centers. Despite rising trade protectionism, the challenges to the freedom of international finance are muted by comparison. The UK's break from Europe and turn toward China may weaken the political foundations of the Special Relationship and reorient the City's international focus, but the institutional linkages underpinning Anglo-American development are deeply ingrained and will be difficult to displace. They look set to withstand the rising nationalism of the global economy. The biggest challenge to the Anglo-American axis of global finance is likely to come from within—from the possibility that progressive forces in the UK and the US continue to make political gains and challenge the power of private finance. Hopes for a more equitable and sustainable role for finance in the world economy will rest in no small part on the fortunes of their efforts.

NOTES

Introduction

1. In this book I deploy the term "Anglo-America" in a narrower sense than is often found, referring not to the entirety of the Anglophone world (countries such as Australia, New Zealand, and Canada), but, rather, the UK and the US exclusively.

2. Indeed, it is very hard to recognize the longue durée of Brexit without an acknowledgment of this fact.

3. LMEs are characterised by flexible labor markets, a limited role for trade unions, high autonomy for economic actors, and a more hands-off approach by the state. This LME-type is counterpoised to the greater role that more heavily strategic, nonmarket coordination plays in organizing firm activities in their second key typology: the coordinated market economy (CME).

4. Regarding UK and US capitalism, I refer to the broad totality of state and societal relations pertaining to matters of "political" and "economic" power.

Chapter One

1. HST's historical comparative framework of two template "hegemonies" involved in the formation of a modern world economy, UK in the nineteenth century and US in the twentieth, has as its methodological prerequisite the notion of two historically distinctive and separate objects of analysis amenable to comparison.

2. Several scholars explicitly frame the UK's condition of decline within the wider context of patterns of rising and declining hegemonic international economic leadership (Brett, 1985; Overbeek, 1990; Gamble, 2002). For others, the connection to US hegemony is not that of a shared historical fate but rather of a more direct and delineated nature. These authors view the humbling terms of the UK's early postwar relationship with the US as both indicative of the collapse of UK power and liable as a cause of the entrenchment of postwar decline (Strange, 1971; Ingham, 1984; Anderson, 1992).

3. What Cohen (2008) has contentiously termed the "British School" of IPE.

4. Strange saw structural power as rooted in four distinct yet related spheres: security, knowledge, production and finance (Strange, 1988a, 26).

5. For an important argument identifying Germany's role in shaping America's transition towards neoliberalism see Germann (2014).

6. Here I disagree with Streeck's (2010: 674) notion that development has fallen into irreversible disrepute within the social sciences and that "evolution" is an effective substitute concept. Evolution evokes Darwinian notions of "natural selection," with the consequence that those institutions that have evolved are assumed to be the best suited and adapted to their broader social context. This associates evolution with exactly the inherently progressive connotations that Streeck seeks to avoid.

7. This framework shares the focus upon institutions and path dependency associated with contemporary historical institutionalism but does not subscribe to the rationalist and methodologically individualist premises underpinning much contemporary literature (Fioretos, 2011: 375). Rationality is itself socially and historically constructed, and historical transformations within capitalism are driven by the collective agency of social classes. This collective class agency is highly unequal and is structured by the foundational centrality of differential relationships to private property rights (Streeck, 2011: 141).

8. Partly in that it does seek to break through containerized notions of socioeconomic transformation but does not seek to demote the significance or centrality of national state institutions within an understanding of political economy.

9. The attempt to ramp up the dismemberment of the remaining social democratic welfare state in the aftermath of the 2007/8 global financial crisis should be seen in this light.

10. IR and IPE have engaged extensively with rational choice and sociological institutionalism, but there has scarcely been explicit engagement with historical institutionalist approaches (Fioretos, 2011).

11. Pierson (2004: 18) identifies these features as: unpredictability (in that outcomes can vary substantially), inflexibility (changing course becomes harder over time), nonergodicity (the enduring consequences of chance events), and inefficiencies (the road not taken might have proved more efficient).

12. When depositors "cash" a check or look to withdraw cash from their account, the private banks' IOU is converted into a government IOU. Banks therefore need access to government money to meet cash demands of their depositors. They meet these demands through "reserves" held at the central bank (Wray, 2012: 78). Banks try to minimize these reserves as they are not interest-generating. Instead they operate with the smallest fraction of reserves (deposit liabilities) relative to their total loan assets. This is known as "fractional reserve" banking (Ingham, 2004: 139).

13. The treasury or finance ministry often tends to have ultimate sovereign authority over the central bank too, despite conditions of formal central bank independence.

14. For a more detailed discussion of this process, see Wray (2012: 102–8).

15. This was spectacularly evidenced by the massive bailouts of ailing banks and the sustained monetary loosening and quantitative easing introduced by central banks throughout the advanced capitalist world in response to the 2007/8 global financial crisis.

16. For other important reflections on the City-Bank-Treasury nexus, see Longstreth (1979: 159–84), and Anderson (1964).

17. This is not, for Ingham (1984: 36–37), a consequence of "City hegemony" or the capture of the state by banking capital. Rather, this coincidence of interests has emerged from the desire of each of the players involved to maintain their power and standing within UK capitalism.

18. Investment banks were responsible for orchestrating the sale of corporations' own stocks and bonds on their behalf.

19. Friedman's disagreement with Keynes hinged on the centrality and efficacy of interest rates to shaping dynamics within the economy. Friedman argued that Keynes had underestimated the importance of a stable money supply to stable economic growth. The turn to fiscal policy under Keynesianism had neglected the importance of monetary levers (Friedman, 1968). Operating with a revived "quantity theory of money," through which inflation and the excessive expansion of the money supply were essentially synonymous, Friedman called for greater focus on monetary dynamics (Laidler, 1981). But he also challenged the technical basis of monetary policy, arguing that interest rates were an unreliable indicator, due to the lagged nature of their effects on inflation; instead, attention should be paid to regulating the quantity of money itself through subordinating interest rate policy to the adjustment of the supply (Stedman-Jones, 2012: 201–3). The ascendancy of this intellectual rationale led policy-makers to focus intently and unsuccessfully on identifying and controlling various measurements of the money supply. Friedman's work also provided a gateway for the broader "new classical" macroeconomics, associated with the work of Robert Lucas and others, whose belief in the rational expectations of market agents and the natural rate of unemployment was used to challenge Keynesian ideas (Hoover, 1984).

20. Unlike monetarists, the neo-Austrians, represented most famously by Friedrich Hayek, argued that inflation was not solely a consequence of an expanding money supply. They offered an alternative diagnosis that identified the wider condition of government intervention within the economy, and a consequent misallocation of resources, as the central cause. This critique of the Keynesian regulatory order, which focused more generally on obstacles to the operation of market forces, led to a wider challenge to the Keynesian state (Clarke, 1988: 324). In the US particularly, the attack on the Keynesian order was shaped by the ideas of "public choice theory," espoused by James Buchanan and Gordon Tullock, who argued that all political policies were effectively representative of the economic interests that underpinned electoral coalitions. These coalitions were, in their view, cynically shaped by politicians whose interests were confined to maintaining their own power (Fischer, 2009: 324). The theory therefore delegitimized the very notion of a distinctive public interest and benevolent governance embodied by the state.

Chapter Two

1. Bills of exchange were used in trade financing from the eighteenth century in order to overcome liquidity shortages arising from metallic monetary systems. They acted as postdated checks: promises to pay a certain amount of money to the designated payee at a specified time in the future. Secondary markets developed in which bills could be traded prior to their maturity (Ingham, 1984: 43).

2. Although the gold standard was associated with liberal trade and financial openness, it was not a "liberal" institution in the classical sense of laissez-faire. As the Bank's central international role suggests, in practice it relied upon consistent state intervention to maintain stability through the active governance of the financial system (Knafo, 2013: 5).

3. From the late eighteenth century, the UK's pioneer industrialization formed a template for later emulation by developing countries (Kemp, 2014). Given the distinctive early trajectory of UK jndustrialization, though, it lacked some of the key modernizing structures required for the refinement of the techniques, financing, and organization of production.

4. Proprietary capitalism was characterized by the fusion of ownership and control, a reliance upon community diffusion of industrial skills, market coordination mechanisms, and low levels of investment (Lazonick, 1993). It became increasingly uncompetitive as the newer technologies and production processes of the second industrial revolution placed greater demand on high capital investment and managerial sophistication for the achievement of productivity gains (Schwartz, 2009a).

5. Managerial capitalism was characterized by the separation of ownership and control, a scientific (and disciplinary) approach to the management of labor and production, the scientific application of knowledge, and much higher investment in the organization and technological basis of industry. Mangerial sophistication, advertising, and large horizontally integrated economies of scale allowed US corporations to more effectively regulate the relationship between supply and demand (Lazonick, 1993).

6. The geographically uneven but extensive internationalization of these managerial and productive techniques would be central to the global dominance of US capitalism in the post–World War II era.

7. Joseph Chamberlain's Tariff Reform League is a prime example of such calls for protection.

8. We begin to see in this period the first wave of US corporate expansion into the UK. Singer opened a factory outside Glasgow in the 1860s, while Ford opened a large factory in Manchester in 1908 (Taggart, 1999: 30; Temperley, 2002: 90).

9. Strength in shipping and other invisibles also continued to serve as a substantial source of national income.

10. This amounted to an implicit termination of the gold standard, because it violated the statutory relationship between the money supply and the stock of gold reserves, brought about through the Bank Charter Act of 1844, thus undermining the credibility of fixed convertibility, given the discrepancy between the gold stock and the supply of banknotes.

11. The US had net maturing sterling commitments to the UK of £60 million that needed to be settled in gold due to the decreased availability of sterling (the war had disrupted the sales of US commodities needed to raise sterling). New York bankers proposed a plan to establish a gold pool fund to meet obligations in sterling, but US Treasury Secretary McAdoo was unwilling to sanction the further release of gold from the US Treasury's gold reserve, as he feared it would weaken confidence in the dollar and undermine the nascent Federal Reserve System (Roberts, 2013: 174)

12. The House of Morgan grew out of the massive import of European capital into the US during the nineteenth century. Financial relations between the US and European countries gave rise to investment banking houses that dealt in foreign exchange and orchestrated the sale of US securities to European investors (Corey, 1969: 42).

13. In continental terms, Europe had clearly been weakened through its internal warring. The US and Japan both experienced an increase in their relative power.

14. The destruction of merchant vessels during the war hastened the introduction of oil-powered vessels, accelerating the obsolescence of coal (Holmes, 1976: 159).

15. The UK's trade deficit with the dollar area increased by £156.4 million during the war (Moggridge, 1972: 34)

16. This same "Open Door" policy would be pursued vigorously after World War II.

17. Prior to the war some two-thirds of the world's trade credit had passed through London and half the world's long-term investments (Ahamed, 2009: 130).

18. In fact, the Treasury resisted attempts by the US banking community to promote a large influx of US government financial aid to the struggling European economies (Abrahams, 1969: 577–80).

Chapter Three

1. In Ruggie's (1982: 382) influential constructivist interpretation, Bretton Woods arose from an alignment between America's hegemonic power and a shared sense of legitimate social purpose among participant nations, producing an "embedded liberal" compromise between a fully open international economy, on the one hand, and domestic macroeconomic autonomy, on the other. Others have interpreted Bretton Woods as a "restrictive" financial order, with its rejection of classical liberalism and free capital flows (Helleiner, 1994). From a more systemic and structural perspective, the agreement has been interpreted as the extension of the domestic social democratic compromise onto the international scale (Frieden, 2008: 16–17). While more US-centric accounts have attributed the agreement to the internationalisation of US New Deal–era dynamics through a newly internationalist alignment of US social forces (Maier, 1977; Schwartz, 2009a; Konings, 2011; Panitch and Gindin, 2012).

2. The agreement has been connected to the historical transformation of US capitalism (Schwartz, 2009a; Konings, 2011; Panitch and Gindin, 2012), but the continued relevance of Anglo-American development has been overlooked.

3. Existing accounts of Anglo-American relations in the early postwar years have focused primarily on the extent to which the UK ceded to US demands as part of the Washington Loan Agreement of 1946. No consensus has been reached, however, with scholars developing starkly polarized accounts. Edward Brett (1985: 139) argues that the period was characterized by a total capitulation of the UK to US hegemonic power. In his counterargument, Peter Burnham (1990: 2) suggests that Brett overstates UK capitulation and overlooks the degree of persistent interimperial rivalry; uneven interdependence more accurately captures the relationship between the two countries. Brett's notion of capitulation neglects the continuation of acute rivalry between the two countries, but Burnham's evocation of "inter-imperial rivalry," conversely, misses the distinctively militarily pacified form of relations whereby outright conflict was, unlike prewar interimperial rivalry, unthinkable.

4. Identifying changes of this sort requires us to situate political economy in and through time (Pierson, 2004: 2).

5. Grosvenor Square in London became the home of a huge US presence while in Washington; during the height of the war, around nine thousand UK officials were based around the British Embassy.

6. Although the overall context of allegiance was never in doubt once the US had entered the war, there were still significant strategic differences (Saville, 1993: 64). Kolko (1968: 21) neatly describes Anglo-American wartime strategy as a "synthesis of grudging compromises." US officials were, at times, concerned that the UK might attempt to form a postwar Western European bloc, based on an allegiance with France and independent of both the US and the Soviet Union.

7. Sidelining of Treasury authority enabled the development of a more expansive welfare state in the postwar period (Cronin, 1991: 151).

8. John Maynard Keynes and Ralph Hawtrey, the director of financial inquiries at the Treasury, played significant roles in drafting the Genoa proposals and made sure that the UK's perspective on monetary relations was paramount (Eichengreen, 2008: 60).

9. The Imperial Preference System was an exclusive trade arrangement that privileged trade between the UK, her dominions, and other associated territories. It was established through the Ottawa Agreement of 1932. The system was based on a set of mutual trading preferences through which the UK granted preferential access to the home market for dominions exporting raw materials, in return for the preferential access of UK manufactured exports to dominion markets (Glickman, 1947).

10. This approach, also known as the classical "Treasury view" or "Gladstonian orthodoxy" regarding macroeconomic policy, viewed public expenditure as a drain on private sector growth and advocated a more austere approach to economic adjustment. The maintenance of a balanced budget was viewed as essential both to the avoidance of "crowding out" the private sector and the guarantee of a stable currency. This view dominated UK economic policy from the mid-nineteenth century until the 1930s (Konzelmann, 2014: 711).

11. New departments emerged dealing with wartime planning, and for a time the chancellor of the exchequer was excluded from the meetings of the war cabinet.

12. The UK's wartime budget was inspired by Keynes's work *How to Pay for the War*. Keynes had begun to exert a growing impact upon Treasury thinking from 1937 onward (Skidelsky, 2000: 20). But although the budget used Keynesian principles of public finance and national accounting, it did not make use of fiscal policy to regulate the market economy, as the market continued to be regulated by direct wartime controls (Clarke, 1988: 246). This was more a Keynesian budget in principle than practice.

13. Under inflationary conditions the Treasury would be expected to increase taxation to curb excessive demand, while a deliberate budget deficit could expect to be implemented during a recession.

14. Restoration of the traditional orientation occurred within a new acceptance of US preeminence, however, with the UK Treasury now subordinated to that of the US in its responsibilities for the management of the international economy.

15. The administered prices approach, advanced by management economists and popular commentators, stressed the need to push monopoly within the US further to ensure socially optimal price fixing by large cartels able to arrest deflation (Blyth, 2002: 50). Underconsumptionist ideas were popular among the "Democratic Party intelligentsia, New Deal social reformers, and maverick economists." They stressed the importance of a demand-side focus and attention to the level of consumption within the economy (rather than a supply-side focus) as the means to escape the Depression (Blyth, 2002: 50). The secular stagnation thesis was pioneered by the US economist Alvin Hansen. Hansen (1939) identified a long-term (secular) decline in the level of demand within the US economy. His proposed remedy was to provide a permanent program of government investment to supplement private investment shortfalls. This vision was closer to a permanent commitment to planning than Keynes's prescriptions for countercyclical fiscal and monetary policy (Weir, 1989: 76).

16. By 1938 the Sterling Bloc accounted for one-third of world trade and was increasingly independent of dollar imports (Kolko, 1968: 246).

17. Keynesian advocates also gained traction in newly created wartime agencies such as the influential Office of Price Administration, steering efforts to maximize production without stoking inflation (Weir, 1989: 69). Morgenthau shared Keynes's distrust for allowing private bankers to govern interntional monetary affairs, considering them selfish in their motivations (Borgwardt, 2007: 33).

18. These agendas were contradictory, as the exhaustion of UK financial assets would inevitably increase the desire to maintain an Imperial privileged trading zone after the war.

19. Labour's early postwar chancellors resented the power of the Bank and opposed the use of monetary policy as a macroeconomic lever. They maintained strict regulatory control over many of the City's activities. The Labour government had a troubled relationship with the wider City during its first postwar government, with disagreements over fundamental policy objectives. Whereas the Labour government wanted to extend the role of the state in the provision of investment, the achievement of full employment, and social justice objectives, the City prized the maintenance of its autonomy above all else. When the City did converge on policy commitments, they tended to center on low inflation, a stable exchange rate, and low government borrowing (Tomlinson, 2004: 174–176).

20. The sterling balances were sterling assets accumulated by overseas countries (predominantly within the British Empire and Commonwealth) during the war. These UK overseas liabilities were potentially highly liquid and, because of the UK's weak financial position, could not be covered by UK foreign exchange assets (e.g., gold or dollars) that might be exchanged for them. Nor could they be absorbed through an increase of UK exports to the holders of the sterling balances, as the UK's capacity had been gravely weakened by the war (Schenk, 2010: 38). The existence of the sterling balances in the decades after World War II proved a recurrent problem for the management of the pound, with periodic bouts of flight from sterling requiring exchange controls, interest rate hikes, and curbs on public expenditure known as the "stop-go cycle" (Cairncross, 1985: 8).

21. These were the blueprints for the IMF and World Bank, which were created at Bretton Woods.

22. As evidence of the partial victory of these sentiments, the final agreement over the IMF contained certain ambiguities that would later be seized upon to push the remit of the Fund far away from the original emphasis of either Keynes or White (Block, 1977: 50; Pauly, 1997: 85).

23. The Bank's skepticism of the IMF and the Bretton Woods Agreement is neatly encapsulated by Robert Brand who, while representing the Bank in the US, reported back that "I did what I could in the case of the Bank, generally aiming at getting the conference to be sufficiently conservative" (Kynaston, 2011: 413).

24. Instead, policy was directed by the president's committee, appointed by the Cabinet, and led by Herbert Morrison, a man who showed little interest in Keynesian thinking (Weir, 1989: 67).

25. After the publication of the Beveridge Report in 1942, the City had pushed hard to restrain the expansion of postwar welfare and full employment commitments. There were very

few high-level City figures that publicly supported the new Labour government (Kynaston, 2011: 407–422).

26. In the earliest postwar years, much decision-making power had continued to be vested in the wartime planning committees (Cronin, 1991: 157).

27. The European Payments Union (EPU) was formally proposed in 1949 by the Economic Cooperation Association. It was designed as a temporary multilateral measure to achieve payments within Europe, which had been obstructed by the challenges of the dollar gap and the widespread balance of payments vulnerability of war-ravaged European economies. It would facilitate automatic adjustment between deficit and surplus countries within the EPU area but would not entail the scale of balance of payments credit provision entailed by Bretton Woods. The implementation of the EPU was initially held up by UK concerns about its effects on sterling balances, which might be drawn down to make intra-European payments. The UK also wanted likely surplus countries in the EPU to accept further sterling balances in settlement. Eventually, the UK was enticed into the EPU by $600 million in support for the Union from the US (James, 1996: 76–77).

28. Butler, the new Tory chancellor, enacted all of the Bank's proposals in November 1951, when it called for a rise in the Bank Rate and deflationary cuts in public spending (Cairncross, 1995: 75).

29. This reflected an unease with the impact of the Mundell-Fleming model (or "Unholy Trinity") under Bretton Woods. The Mundell-Fleming model specifies the incompatibility of independent monetary policy, stable exchange rates, and free capital flows (Cohen, 2000). Under Bretton Woods the commitment to fixed exchange rates, allied with increasing currency convertibility and (in practice due to the difficulties of policing capital flows once current account convertibility was restored) capital mobility, reduced the capacity for an autonomous monetary policy. Monetary policy adjustments beyond a certain parameter would threaten to violate the fixed exchange rates inscribed at Bretton Woods. Allied to these international regime restrictions was the domestic Keynesian prioritization of fiscal policy, which further inhibited monetary independence.

30. The central issue during the war was the level of interest rates for US Treasury bonds. The Federal Reserve was forced to accept lower rates than it had wanted (Epstein and Schor, 1995: 15).

31. It was Russell Leffingwell, the chairman of J. P. Morgan and Co., known by the head of the Federal Reserve as the "dean of the financial community," who was the most important individual player in pushing for Federal Reserve independence (Epstein and Schor, 1995: 16).

32. From now on, an independent Central Bank would use adjustments in interest rates as the primary mechanism for control over the economy. Conservative Keynesian planning is defined by a lower degree of "intervention to control prices, wage rates and resource allocation in the private sector" (Burkhead, 1971: 335).

33. Epstein and Schor (1995: 8) suggest that the accord laid the foundations for major victories for capital against labor, through the tight monetary policy of the 1980s and 1990s.

34. Catto and John Maynard Keynes were given rooms on opposite sides of the chancellor's office (Chernow, 1990: 460).

35. These ambitions were realized with the passing of the Glass-Steagall Act, which undermined the unity of investment and commercial banking functions that had been key to Morgan's dominance within the US (Ferguson, 1995: 149).

36. Warburg opposed the influence of gold standard thinking on the agreement in the form of the US dollar's fixed convertibility to gold. He also rejected the restraints on capital mobility that were accepted at Bretton Woods as a necessary counterpart to fixed exchange rates and independent monetary policies. Warburg was critical of the early termination of Lend-Lease and, importantly, thought that Anglo-American bankers should do all that they could to create a closer link-up between finance and industry within the two countries (Ferguson, 2010: 167–69).

Chapter Four

1. The term "Euromarkets" applies to transactions in two distinct but related markets: the "Eurocurrency/Eurodollar" and "Eurobond" markets.[1] But the prefix "Euro" is rather misleading. The term is used as an umbrella to describe transactions of offshore currency traded outside of nationally prescribed banking authority (Burn, 1999: 226). Essentially, it describes an offshore market in foreign currency. The market is wholesale, predominantly comprising of large-scale operators such as commercial banks, governments, and large companies (Higonnet, 1985: 30).

2. Much of the debate over the Euromarkets has focused upon identifying their origins (Martenson, 1964; Bell, 1973; Schenk, 1998). These scholars have unearthed many of the processes that spawned the Euromarkets. Alternatively, the Euromarkets have been explored in the context of either the UK's national development (Strange, 1971; Ingham, 1984; Overbeek, 1991; Burn, 2006), or the international transformations associated with the collapse of the Bretton Woods system (Block, 1973; Helleiner, 1994; Langley, 2002; Eichengreen: 2008). Another grouping of scholars has argued that the emergence of the Euromarkets was functional to the deepening of US structural and financial power (Strange, 1987; Gowan, 1999; Panitch and Gindin, 2010, 2012; Konings, 2011).

3. See Gowan (1990); Konings (2011); Panitch and Gindin (2009); and Strange (1987).

4. By missing these dynamics, Konings, along with other scholars (e.g., Krippner, 2011), overstates the domestic origins of the US turn to monetarism and neoliberalism from the late 1970s and obscures the developmental impact of the transatlantic regulatory feedback loop in driving financial deregulation.

5. In a display of their increased postwar monetary power and UK vulnerability, the US pressured the UK into abandoning military intervention by orchestrating a run on the pound via sterling sales by the New York Federal Reserve Bank, while also blocking the UK's access to IMF funds (Kirshner, 1995: 70).

6. Among the key facets of this period were the continued decline of sterling as an international reserve and trading currency; the reversal of the postwar surplus of the US on trade and invisible earnings along with growing US expenditure abroad; and the increasing strength of the Japanese, German, and other major economies (Jessop, 1980: 25).

7. The Bank feared that devaluation would damage sterling's international credibility by reducing the value of foreign holdings of sterling and weakening its role as an international reserve currency (Brittan, 1964: 64). In effect, the stop-go cycle represented continuity with the deflationary adjustment mechanism that was necessitated for deficit countries under the classical gold standard, with fixed exchange rates ruling out the potential for adjustment through currency devaluation.

8. The exact origins of the Euromarkets are murky. It is certainly the case that the Eurodollar market preceded its Eurobond counterpart. A very discreet Eurocurrency market began during the early stages of the Cold War, in the late 1940s and early 1950s. Dollar deposits were placed with banks in London and Paris by the Soviet and Chinese governments, who feared that US authorities would seize their assets (Higonnet, 1985: 27). Controls on sterling's use for trade between third parties and as refinance credits, prompted by UK concerns over a deteriorating balance of payments, as well as the return to convertibility of Western European currencies from 1958, were also contributory factors to the rapid growth of the Eurodollar market form the late 1950s (Martenson, 1964: 14; Bell, 1973: 8; Schenk, 1998: 223; Burn, 1999: 229).

9. Catherine Schenk (1998: 233) describes this regulatory context as one that "encouraged innovation as a means of evading controls while tolerating such innovations ex post."

10. The Chase National Bank merged with the Bank of Manhattan Co. and Bronx County Trust Co. to form the Chase Manhattan Bank, while the National City Bank of New York took over the first National Bank of New York. In 1959, the Guaranty Trust Co. merged with JP Morgan Co., Inc., to form the Morgan Guaranty Trust Co. (de Cecco, 1976: 386).

11. Not only did it damage US banks international competitiveness; it also made it difficult to attract deposits and corporate customers (White, 1992: 8).

12. This shift occurred during the interwar years, with London institutions restricted from the provision of international bonds.

13. Dillon's May 1962 speech in Rome was particularly important (Burn, 2006: 111).

14. Under the swap arrangements, the US and a foreign government would agree to exchange currencies at spot value and simultaneously commit to reversing the transaction at a specific forward exchange rate on a specified future date (Bordo et al., 2015: 18).

15. The participant governments were Belgium, France, Italy, the Netherlands, Switzerland, West Germany, and the UK. All participating governments made an initial subscription of $270 million worth of gold and contracted to take fixed proportions of gold sales up to their subscriptions. Participating countries would sell their own gold reserves to relieve pressure from the US gold stock. They also agreed not to purchase gold on the London market or from any other sources, and to avoid immediate conversion of the dollars that they received from gold sales into US gold, thus avoiding a drain on the US gold reserve (Eichengreen, 2008: 121–22; Bordo et al., 2015: 178).

16. This was a departure from the pattern of US macroeconomic policy that had emerged after World War II. Generally, macroeconomic policy was conducted with indifference toward balance of payments considerations and the well-being of the international monetary system (Gowa, 1983: 50).

17. Bank of England Archives 6A123/1, Economic Intelligence Department Files: Euro Currencies—Including Euro Dollars and Euro Bonds 1/1/65–31/7/64, report on meeting of experts on the euro-currency markets at the BIS, November 9–11, 1963.

18. In 1968 the Treasury requested information from the Bank in order to prepare the prime minister's annual speech at the Lord Mayor's banquet, specifically asking for guidance over what the prime minister's stance should be with regard to the role of the City in the development of the Eurodollar market.

19. Bank of England Archives 6A123/5, Economic Intelligence Department Files: Euro Currencies—Including Euro Dollars and Euro Bonds 1/1/68–31/5/69, memo from the Treasury

to the Bank of England requesting prime ministerial brief on the Eurodollar market, October 22, 1968.

20. Bank of England Archives 6A123/1, Economic Intelligence Department Files: Euro Currencies—Including Euro Dollars and Euro Bonds 1/1/65–31/7/64, letter regarding document to be prepared by the Bank of England in response to a Treasury request for information of the standing of the Eurodollar market, March 6, 1964.

21. Bank of England Archives 6A123/3, Economic Intelligence Department Files: Euro Currencies—Including Euro Dollars and Euro Bonds 1/8/65–31/10/66, memo from the Bank of England Overseas Office charting US. banks drawing dollars through London branches, August 22, 1966.

22. Bank of England Archives 6A123/3, Economic Intelligence Department Files: Euro Currencies—Including Euro Dollars and Euro Bonds 1/8/65–31/10/66, internal memo, the Bank of England ("Eurodollar Lending to the US"), August 9, 1966.

23. Richard Sylla (2002: 62) describes this transformation aptly, suggesting that while US banks gave little consideration to operations in Europe before 1963, they "thought about little else in the decade thereafter."

24. Bank of England Archives 6A123/3, Economic Intelligence Department Files: Euro Currencies—Including Euro Dollars and Euro Bonds 1/8/65–31/10/66, internal memo, the Bank of England ("Eurodollar Lending to the US"), August 9, 1966.

25. The "Eurodollar slop," an expanding pool of expatriate dollars that tended to move predominantly back and forth across the Atlantic, was the underlying root of the dollar crisis of 1970/71 that preceded Nixon's delinking from gold and the de facto termination of Bretton Woods (Strange, 1972: 198).

26. Bank of England Archives 6A123/6, Economic Intelligence Department Files: Euro Currencies—Including Euro Dollars and Euro Bonds 1/6/69–31/3/70, report on the Meeting of Experts on the Euro-Currency Market, July 12, 1966.

27. Bank of England Archives 6A123/6, Economic Intelligence Department Files: Euro Currencies—Including Euro Dollars and Euro Bonds 1/6/69–31/3/70, transcript of presentation given by Andrew Brimmer ("The Eurodollar Market and the US Balance of Payments"), November 17, 1969.

28. Battilossi (2002: 16) suggests that the Federal Reserve adopted a "permissive" approach, with foreign expansion "accommodated, if not actively encouraged," while Schenk (2002: 89) concludes that there was a "passive acceptance" of the multinationalization of US banks. Kennedy's administration had certainly understood that borrowing through the Eurodollar market would be beneficial to the balance of payments (de Cecco, 1976: 390). But Helleiner (1994: 89) is an isolated voice when he asserts that Eurodollar market expansion was "actively encouraged" by the Federal Reserve and the Treasury.

29. Bank of England Archives EID4/113, Home Finance: Banking—General Papers 7/12/64–17/11/66, internal memo, Bank of England ("New American Banks in London—Dealing Limits"), March 5, 1969.

30. Bank of England Archives EID4/113, Home Finance: Banking—General Papers 7/12/64–17/11/66, internal memo, Bank of England ("New American Banks in London—Dealing Limits"), March 5, 1969.

31. Bank of England Archives EID4/113, Home Finance: Banking—General Papers 7/12/64–17/11/66, internal memo, Bank of England ("New American Banks in London—Dealing Limits"), March 5, 1969.

32. Bank of England Archives 6A123/1, Economic Intelligence Department Files: Euro Currencies—Including Euro Dollars and Euro Bonds 1/1/65–31/7/64, letter regarding document to be prepared by the Bank of England in response to a Treasury request for information of the standing of the Eurodollar market, March 6, 1964.

33. The most prominent crises in this respect were the major losses of Lloyds's Lugano branch, the collapse of the Israel British Bank in Tel Aviv, the Franklin National Bank in New York, and—most notably of all—the failure of the West German Bankhaus Herstatt (Capie, 2010: 625).

34. In his 1968 speech at the Lord Mayor's banquet, after the devaluation of 1967, Harold Wilson proudly spoke of the "Europeanization of the City." Wilson's speech was informed by the experts at the Bank of England, who had earlier been asked to provide a summary of London's role in the development of the Eurodollar market. In an implicit recognition of the City's growing entrepöt status, Wilson commented that despite the decreased role of sterling as an international reserve currency and continuing balance of payments problems, London was maintaining and in fact increasing its role as an international financial center. See Bank of England Archives 6A123/5, Economic Intelligence Department Files: Euro Currencies—Including Euro Dollars and Euro Bonds 1/1/68–31/5/69, memo from the Treasury to the Bank of England requesting prime ministerial brief on the Eurodollar market, October 22, 1968; Bank of England Archives 6A123/5, Economic Intelligence Department Files: Euro Currencies—Including Euro Dollars and Euro Bonds 1/1/68–31/5/69, Harold Wilson's speech at the Lord Mayor's banquet, November 11, 1968.

35. Certificates of deposit are negotiable certificates received by the depositor in return for a time deposit placed with a bank. A large secondary interbank market for CDs developed during the 1960s.

36. Gamble (1990: 120) identifies this failure to challenge the internationalist orientation of UK economic policy and breakout of the stop-go cycle as the key reason for the failure of modernization attempts during the 1960s.

37. Treasury File National Archives IR40/16006," Discussions with Financial Secretary, Treasury, and Revenue on Whether Companies Should Be Encouraged to Borrow on Eurodollar Market, 1966–1978," memo from Treasury to Inland Revenue, n.d.

38. Inland Revenue argued that dismantling the regulations around Eurodollar borrowing could have a knock-on effect upon tax avoidance. This was hugely ironic, given that London was already the offshore haven par excellence. Treasury File National Archives IR40/16006, "Discussions with Financial Secretary, Treasury, and Revenue on Whether Companies Should Be Encouraged to Borrow on Eurodollar Market, 1966–1978," memo from Inland Revenue to Treasury Officials, May 29, 1968.

39. Treasury File National Archives IR40/16006, "Discussions with Financial Secretary, Treasury, and Revenue on Whether Companies Should Be Encouraged to Borrow on Eurodollar Market, 1966–1978," meeting between Financial Secretary, Treasury, and Bank of England Officials, May 17, 1968.

40. Treasury File National Archives IR40/16006, "Discussions with Financial Secretary, Treasury, and Revenue on Whether Companies Should Be Encouraged to Borrow on

Eurodollar Market, 1966–1978," note by the Financial Secretary on Eurodollar Borrowing, May 1968.

41. Treasury File National Archives IR40/16006, "Discussions with Financial Secretary, Treasury, and Revenue on Whether Companies Should Be Encouraged to Borrow on Eurodollar Market, 1966–1978," note by the Financial Secretary on Eurodollar Borrowing, May 1968.

42. Treasury File National Archives IR40/16006, "Discussions with Financial Secretary, Treasury, and Revenue on Whether Companies Should Be Encouraged to Borrow on Eurodollar Market, 1966–1978," memo from Inland Revenue to Treasury officials, May 29, 1968.

43. This is hugely ironic, given that the ease of switching out of sterling and into dollars through the Eurodollar market played a major role in destabilizing capital flows in 1966 and 1967 (Brittan, 1971: 329).

44. Treasury File National Archives IR40/16006, "Discussions with Financial Secretary, Treasury, and Revenue on Whether Companies Should Be Encouraged to Borrow on Eurodollar Market, 1966–1978," Treasury letter to the Inland Revenue ("Draft Paper on Eurodollar Borrowing"), October 4, 1967.

45. Niall Ferguson (2010: 276) suggests that "in the early 1960s it was S. G. Warburg & Co. more than any other City firm that appeared capable of helping UK governments to address their recurrent financial problems."

46. Treasury File National Archives IR40/16006, "Discussions with Financial Secretary, Treasury, and Revenue on Whether Companies Should Be Encouraged to Borrow on Eurodollar Market, 1966–1978," memo from the chancellor of the exchequer to the Treasury ("Financing National Investment"), September 13, 1967.

47. Treasury File National Archives IR40/16006, "Discussions with Financial Secretary, Treasury, and Revenue on Whether Companies Should Be Encouraged to Borrow on Eurodollar Market, 1966–1978," memo from the chancellor of the exchequer to the Treasury ("Financing National Investment"), September 13, 1967.

48. Treasury File National Archives IR40/16006, "Discussions with Financial Secretary, Treasury, and Revenue on Whether Companies Should Be Encouraged to Borrow on Eurodollar Market, 1966–1978," Treasury paper on the possibility of borrowing abroad to finance the nationalized industries and local authorities, May 25, 1967.

49. Under Bretton Woods, the proposed system of adjustable pegs had in effect become a system of rigidly fixed exchange rates. Within this system, both devaluations and revaluations became "politically untouchable" (Gowa, 1983: 37–38).

Chapter Five

1. Helleiner's (1994) brief account of the crisis is a notable exception in this regard.

2. The notable exception here is Harmon (2008: 1–2), who provides a more nuanced account of the crisis, delineating different phases during which the scale of determination shifted from one determined primarily by national priorities (1974 to early 1975) to one being shaped by US and international pressures and priorities (late 1975 to 1976). Harmon's analysis focuses upon the role of US structural power, but neglects how social forces within the UK, which were hostile to the Labour government and the Keynesian state, drew in US discipline.

3. Writing to the Bank of England governor, Lord Cromer, in 1965, Martin stressed the need for dramatic measures to restore market confidence in sterling and suggested that "a wages and prices freeze would probably do this" (Capie, 2012: 214).

4. The Martin-Cromer plan is an important example of these creeping austerity demands. The plan was created by Bill Martin and involved the employment of a syndicate of countries who would support the sterling exchange rate through concerted market intervention. But, to access the support, the UK government would have to agree to the announcement of a wage, price and dividend freeze to boost market confidence (Schenk, 2010: 165).

5. Discussions over the conditionality of IMF lending had been an important aspect of the postwar Anglo-American discussions on international monetary politics. Whereas the UK had wanted IMF funding to be delivered without insistence upon deflationary measures, the Americans were keen on deflationary stipulations.

6. The London gold market was closed in March 1968, after huge gold sales and a request by the Americans. The seven leading central banks agreed to replace the Gold Pool with a two-tier market. This separated the official stock of gold reserves from the market. Although monetary authorities would continue to transact gold among themselves at the official thirty-five-dollars-per-ounce parity, they would no longer participate in the private market. This decision allowed the private market price of gold to fluctuate significantly from the official price, becoming a "highly visible barometer of confidence in the dollar and in the Bretton Woods system" (Bordo et al., 2015: 180)

7. Treasury File National Archives T312/3106, "U.S.A Balance of Payments Deficit and Eurodollar Outflow 5/4/71- 3/72," address by Leslie O'Brien, governor of the Bank of England, to the Bankers' Club of Chicago, Illinois, April 27, 1971.

8. Treasury File National Archives T312/3106, "U.S.A. Balance of Payments Deficit and Eurodollar Outflow 5/4/71- 3/72," address by Leslie O'Brien, governor of the Bank of England, to the Bankers' Club of Chicago, Illinois, April 27, 1971.

9. Treasury File National Archives T312/3106, "U.S.A Balance of Payments Deficit and Eurodollar Outflow 5/4/71- 3/72," passage to be inserted for Treasury brief for prime minister's meeting with President Pompidou of France, May 14, 1971.

10. The opposition was partly a response to those who complained that capital controls disproportionately affected small banks and corporations that could not operate in the Euromarkets with the ease of their larger competitors (Gowa, 1983: 84).

11. The Federal Reserve Board were not heavily involved in the planning of the Volcker Group. The New York branch of the Fed—known as a staunch defender of Bretton Woods that was more likely to gear domestic policy towards balance of payments concerns—was excluded from the negotiations and more generally maligned within the Nixon administration due to its support for Bretton Woods (Gowa, 1983: 112–13). Indeed, at the Camp David meeting where the decision to end Bretton Woods was made, the Fed chairman Arthur Burns spoke forcefully in favor of maintaining gold convertibility in the interests of the financial markets. Burns's position lost out: he was opposed by Treasury secretary John Connally and hamstrung by his poor relationship with Nixon, which had been weakened by their disagreements over the stringency of austerity required to cool inflation within the US. Burns had pressed for tighter monetary policy than Nixon wanted (Frieden, 2006: 341).

12. The Smithsonian Agreement, named after its location at the Smithsonian Institution in Washington, DC, established a new pattern of exchange rates to salvage the fixed but adjustable Bretton Woods approach. Germany agreed to a 13.57 percent revaluation of the deutschemark against the dollar, while the Japanese agreed to a 16.9 percent revaluation of the yen vis-à-vis the dollar. France and the UK both appreciated by 8.6 percent against the dollar (James, 1996: 237).

13. Accepting houses, international banks, and nonclearing institutions such as secondary banks benefited differentially from this policy framework.

14. See: Smith (1987: 3–16) for a detailed analysis of the major theoretical differences between monetarism and Keynesianism.

15. The money supply was growing at an annual rate of 31 percent by the second quarter of 1972 while bank lending to individuals rose by 175 percent between July 1971 and July 1973 (Glyn and Harrison, 1980: 77).

16. British Bankers' Association Archives MS32157X/1, "The Future of London as an International Financial Centre, 1972–1977," IBRO Report No. 117 ("The Future of London as an International Financial Centre"), October 1972.

17. British Bankers' Association Archives MS32157X/1, "The Future of London as an International Financial Centre, 1972–1977," IBRO Report No. 117 ("The Future of London as an International Financial Centre"), October 1972.

18. British Bankers' Association Archives MS32157X/1, "The Future of London as an International Financial Centre, 1972–1977," IBRO Report No. 117 ("The Future of London as an International Financial Centre"), October 1972.

19. British Bankers' Association Archives MS32157X/1, "The Future of London as an International Financial Centre, 1972–1977," IBRO Report No. 117 ("The Future of London as an International Financial Centre"), October 1972.

20. British Bankers' Association Archives MS32157X/1, "The Future of London as an International Financial Centre, 1972–1977," IBRO Report No. 117 ("The Future of London as an International Financial Centre"), October 1972.

21. London Metropolitan Archives (LMA), City of London, British Bankers' Association Archives MS32054/002, Minutes, May 1959–December 1973, letter from Daniel P. Davidson, senior vice president of Morgan Guaranty Trust Company, to Eric O. Faulkner, president of the British Bankers' Association, November 30, 1972.

22. LMA British Bankers' Association Archives MS32054/002, Minutes, May 1959–December 1973, letter from Eric O. Faulkner, president of the British Bankers' Association, to Daniel P. Davidson, senior vice president and general manager of Morgan Guaranty Trust Company of New York, December 12, 1972.

23. LMA British Bankers' Association Archives MS32054/002, Minutes, May 1959–December 1973, letter from John Pryor, managing director and vice-chairman of Western American Bank (Europe) Limited, to R. K. C. Giddings, secretary of the British Bankers' Association, March 16, 1973.

24. LMA British Bankers' Association Archives MS32054/002, Minutes, May 1959–December 1973, letter from E. O. Faulkner, president of the British Bankers' Association, to John Pryor, managing director and vice-chairman of Western American Bank (Europe) Limited, May 23, 1973.

25. The key positions held by the left within the 1974 Labour government were Tony Benn's role as secretary of state for industry and Michael Foot's appointment as employment secretary in the Department of Employment.

26. LMA British Bankers' Association Archives MS32142/1, Banks—Nationalisation (Public Ownership) Volume 1, 1924–31, January 1976, Committee of London Clearing Banks strictly confidential note to Lord Armstrong, "Bank Nationalisation Working Party," January 13, 1976.

27. LMA British Bankers' Association Archives MS32142/7, Banks—Nationalisation (Public Ownership) Volume 7, July 1, 1977–September 30, 1979, Committee of London Clearing Banks report to the Committee from the Bank Nationalisation Working Party, July 29, 1979.

28. LMA British Bankers' Association Archives MS32142/1, Banks—Nationalisation (Public Ownership) Volume 1, 1924–January 31, 1976, strictly private and confidential note, "Bank Nationalisation: An Assessment of the Situation," October 1975.

29. LMA British Bankers' Association Archives MS32142/1, Banks—Nationalisation (Public Ownership) Volume 1, 1924–January 31, 1976, strictly private and confidential note, "Bank Nationalisation: An Assessment of the Situation," October 1975.

30. LMA British Bankers' Association Archives MS32142/1, Banks—Nationalisation (Public Ownership) Volume 1, 1924–January 31, 1976, letter from Charles Villiers to prime minister Harold Wilson, January 19, 1976.

31. LMA British Bankers' Association Archives MS32142/1, Banks—Nationalisation (Public Ownership) Volume 1, 1924–January 31, 1976, letter from prime minister Harold Wilson to Sir Charles Villiers, January 21, 1976.

32. LMA British Bankers' Association Archives MS32142/2, Banks—Nationalisation (Public Ownership) Volume 2, February 1, 1976–April 30, 1976, agenda of meeting of Bank Nationalisation Working Party, April 9, 1976.

33. LMA British Bankers' Association Archives MS32142/2, Banks—Nationalisation (Public Ownership) Volume 2, February 1, 1976–April 30, 1976, letter from A. Ritchie to P. J. Nicholson of the Committee of London Clearing Banks, March 9, 1976.

34. Treasury File National Archives T385/30, International Monetary Fund: Applications for Drawings by the UK 1/1/75–31/12/75, undated Treasury document, "Implications of a Fund Drawing in Relation to Policy Options," October 20—November 4, 1975.

35. The Group of Six was comprised of France, West Germany, the UK, the US, Italy, and Japan. It later became the G7, with the addition of Canada in 1976.

36. This initiative would eventually lead to the passage of the International Banking Act in 1978, discussed in the following chapter.

37. LMA British Bankers' Association Archives MS32015/2, British Bankers' Association Minutes 1937 to October 1981, minutes of the Annual General Meeting of the BBA, May 27, 1975.

38. LMA British Bankers' Association Archives MS32015/2, British Bankers' Association Minutes 1937 to October 1981, minutes of the meeting of General Council, March 29, 1976.

39. Treasury File National Archives T385/30, International Monetary Fund: Applications for Drawings by the UK 1/1/75–31/12/75, undated Treasury document, "Implications of a Fund Drawing in Relation to Policy Options," October 20–November 4, 1975.

40. Treasury File National Archives T385/30, International Monetary Fund: Applications for Drawings by the UK 1/1/75–31/12/75, undated Treasury document, "Implications of a Fund Drawing in Relation to Policy Options," October 20–November 4, 1975.

41. Treasury File National Archives T385/30, International Monetary Fund: Applications for Drawings by the UK 1/1/75–31/12/75, letter from principal private secretary of the Treasury to other Treasury officials, "Outstanding Questions Concerning a Fund Drawing," October 21, 1975.

42. Treasury File National Archives T385/30, International Monetary Fund: Applications for Drawings by the UK 1/1/75–31/12/75, undated draft of a Treasury document, "International 'Negotiation' of Import Controls," October 20–November 4, 1975.

43. Treasury File National Archives T385/30, International Monetary Fund: Applications for Drawings by the UK 1/1/75–31/12/75, undated Treasury document, "Implications of a Fund Drawing in Relation to Policy Options," October 20–November 4, 1975.

44. This is the prevailing argument within the literature on the IMF crisis, that the pressures from the IMF were simply used as a disguise to depoliticize domestic political priorities (Rogers, 2009: 972).

45. Treasury File National Archives T385/30, International Monetary Fund: Applications for Drawings by the UK 1/1/75–31/12/75, undated Treasury memorandum circulated to the Bank of England, "IMF Drawing: Chancellor's Dinner with Dr. Witteveen."

46. Treasury File National Archives T385/30, International Monetary Fund: Applications for Drawings by the UK 1/1/75–31/12/75, memorandum from Johannes Witteveen, managing director of the IMF, to Dennis Healey of the Treasury (chancellor of exchequer), October 26, 1975.

47. Treasury File National Archives T385/30, International Monetary Fund: Applications for Drawings by the UK 1/1/75–31/12/75, internal Treasury memo, "IMF Oil Facility and Import Restrictions," October 27, 1975.

48. Treasury File National Archives T385/33, International Monetary Fund: Applications for Drawings by the UK 9/11/75–12/12/75, Treasury memorandum, "IMF Drawing: American Reaction to Import Controls," November 27, 1975.

49. Treasury File National Archives T385/30, International Monetary Fund: Applications for Drawings by the UK 1/1/75–31/12/75, note of a working dinner at No. 11 Downing Street with chancellor of the exchequer, Mr. C. W. France, Dr H. J. Witteveen (managing director of the IMF), and Mr. D. Green, November 3, 1975.

50. Treasury File National Archives T385/29, Visits of United States Ministers and Officials to the United Kingdom 21/10/75–5/11/76, letter from G. Booth, director of general trade development, to Sir Peter Ramsbotham, ambassador to the British embassy, Washington, DC, "The US Investment Mission to Britain 18–27 September 1975," September 1975.

51. Treasury File National Archives T385/29, Visits of United States Ministers and Officials to the United Kingdom 21/10/75–5/11/76, letter from G. Booth, director of general trade development, to Sir Peter Ramsbotham, ambassador to the British embassy, Washington, DC, "The US Investment Mission to Britain 18–27 September 1975," September 1975.

52. Treasury File National Archives T381/76, Swap Facility with the Federal Reserve and the United States Treasury December 1976, 6/6/76–5/1/78, "Swap Agreement between US Treasury and Bank of England," June 6, 1976.

53. Treasury File National Archives T385/29, Visits of United States Ministers and Officials to the United Kingdom 21/10/75–5/11/76, confidential note for record, May 3, 1976.

54. LMA British Bankers' Association Archives MS32142/7, Banks—Nationalisation (Public Ownership) Volume 7, July 1, 1977–September 30, 1979, Committee of London Clearing Banks report to the Committee from the Bank Nationalisation Working Party, July 29, 1979.

55. Treasury File National Archives T385/29, Visits of United States Ministers and Officials to the United Kingdom 21/10/75–5/11/76, letter from G. Booth, director of general trade development, to Sir Peter Ramsbotham, ambassador to the British embassy, Washington, DC, "The US Investment Mission to Britain 18–27 September 1975," September 1975.

56. Treasury File National Archives T385/29, Visits of United States Ministers and Officials to the United Kingdom 21/10/75–5/11/76, internal Treasury memo, "Visit of Dr. Burns," May 17, 1976.

57. Bank of England Archives OV38/117, International Monetary Fund 1/9/75–30/11/75, internal Bank memo, "The Exchange Rate Regime," October 20, 1975.

58. Treasury File National Archives T385/29, Visits of United States Ministers and Officials to the United Kingdom 21/10/75–5/11/76, internal Treasury memo, "Visit of Mr Butcher (President of Chase Manhattan Bank)," August 13, 1976; internal Treasury memo, "Prime Minister's Meeting with Mr. Walter Wriston (Chairman of Citibank)," May 26, 1976; internal Treasury memo, "Invitation to the Prime Minister from Morgan Guaranty," November 2, 1976.

59. Treasury File National Archives T385/29, Visits of United States Ministers and Officials to the United Kingdom 21/10/75–5/11/76, note of a meeting held at No. 11 Downing Street, with the chancellor of the exchequer, Sir Douglas Wass, and Edwin Yeo, undersecretary of the US Treasury, August 5, 1976.

60. Bank of England Archives G1/210, Governor's File: The IMF and International Bank of Reconstruction and Development—Christopher William McMahon's Impressions of the Annual General Meetings 10/76–10/79, internal Bank memo to the governors, "Manila Impressions," October 11, 1976.

61. Treasury File National Archives T381/76, Swap Facility with the Federal Reserve and the United States Treasury December 1976, 6/6/76–5/1/78, internal Treasury memo, "U.S. Swaps: Draft Agreement," December 21, 1976.

62. Treasury File National Archives T381/76, Swap Facility with the Federal Reserve and the United States Treasury December 1976, 6/6/76–5/1/78, Foreign Office and Commonwealth Office telegram No.4025 for Mrs. Hedley-Miller of the Treasury from Bridges, "Swap Agreement," December 17, 1976.

63. There would likely also have been concerns about entering into an agreement with the Americans that contained the potential for direct supervision.

64. The package involved a £1 billion reduction of public spending from 1977 to 1978 and the sale of £500 million of the government's shares in BP. There would be a further £1.5 billion reduction of spending from 1978 to 1979 and then £500 million for 1978 to 1979.

65. Matthias Matthijs (2012: 99–100) treats the crisis as a marginal event within the development of postwar UK capitalism when compared to the politics surrounding the Winter of Discontent.

Chapter Six

1. As a socioeconomic process, neoliberalism (or neoliberalization) can best be understood as a drive toward selective market-disciplinary regulatory restructuring that seeks to extend and entrench market rule, sheltering privileged groups and targeting obstacles of the market such as trade unions and welfare dependents. Because of the fundamental dependency of social institutions upon nonmarket logics of social organization, however, neoliberal restructuring is an inherently contradictory and inevitably incomplete process, generating crisis tendencies that require extended state intervention to address problems generated by market extension (Peck, 2010).

2. The key policy measures included the reimposition of employers' "right to manage" their employees, the strategic engagement and defeat of the labor movement, high interest rates to defeat inflation and restructure domestic manufacturing, the abolition of corporatist institutions, cuts to personal taxation rates, the privatization of nationalized industries, and the deregulation of other economic sectors (Peck and Tickell, 2007: 28).

3. By "financialization," I here refer to the processes by which ever-more aspects of socioeconomic activity are drawn into the orbit of credit-debtor relations centered around liberalized private financial markets that promote the deepening and extension of these relations.

4. The notable exception here is a brief but revealing discussion of the impact of the adoption of monetary targeting within the Fed and the IMF upon the Bank of England and the City's attitudes toward monetarism and the eventual adoption of "technical monetarism" during the Callaghan-Healey administration in Bob Jessop, Kevin Bonnett, Simon Bromley, and Tom Ling (1984), "Authoritarian Populism, Two Nations, and Thatcherism," *New Left Review* 1, no. 147: 32–60, 44.

5. This repositioned the UK's standing in relation to the "Unholy Trinity" (Cohen, 1995). With fixed rates terminated and capital market liberalization intensifying, monetary policy could be geared toward a domestic inflation target rather than international currency stability, with the pound allowed to oscillate in value.

6. Bank of England Archives, C40/1440, Monetary Policy: Miscellaneous 18/9/78–31/10/79, internal memo, "Monetary Targets and Economic Policy," September 28, 1978.

7. Bank of England Archives G37/3, Court of Directors: Informal Records 16/1/75–31/12/80, notes from the Bank of England Court Meeting, May 24, 1979.

8. Bank of England Archives, G1/210, Governor's File: The International Monetary Fund and International Bank of Reconstruction and Development—Christopher William Mcmahon's Impressions of the Annual General Meetings 10/76–10/79, "Thoughts after the IMF/ Belgrade Meeting," October 1979.

9. Bank of England Archives, G1/210, Governor's File: The International Monetary Fund and International Bank of Reconstruction and Development—Christopher William Mcmahon's Impressions of the Annual General Meetings 10/76–10/79, "Thoughts after the IMF/ Belgrade Meeting," October 1979.

10. Bank of England Archives, EC5/649, Exchange Control Act File: Relaxations—Papers Covering the Relaxation and Dismantling of Exchange Controls 6/9/79–17/9/79, "The Next Stage in Dismantling Exchange Controls," September 7, 1979.

11. Bank of England Archives, EC5/649, Exchange Control Act File: Relaxations—Papers Covering the Relaxation and Dismantling of Exchange Controls 6/9/79–17/9/79, "The Next Stage in Dismantling Exchange Controls," September 7, 1979.

12. Bank of England Archives, EC5/649, Exchange Control Act File: Relaxations—Papers Covering the Relaxation and Dismantling of Exchange Controls 6/9/79–17/9/79, "The Next Stage in Dismantling Exchange Controls," September 7, 1979.

13. Bank of England Archives, EC5/649, Exchange Control Act File: Relaxations—Papers Covering the Relaxation and Dismantling of Exchange Controls 6/9/79–17/9/79, "Monetary Policy and the Banking System," September 13, 1979.

14. Bank of England Archives, EC5/649, Exchange Control Act File: Relaxations—Papers Covering the Relaxation and Dismantling of Exchange Controls 6/9/79–17/9/79, "Monetary Policy and the Banking System," September 13, 1979.

15. These controls operated by restricting the growth banks' balance sheets or by taxing the banking system by forcing them to hold additional assets with the central bank.

16. Bank of England Archives, EC5/649, Exchange Control Act File: Relaxations—Papers Covering the Relaxation and Dismantling of Exchange Controls 6/9/79–17/9/79, "Monetary Policy and the Banking System," September 13, 1979.

17. Bank of England Archives, EC5/649, Exchange Control Act File: Relaxations—Papers Covering the Relaxation and Dismantling of Exchange Controls 6/9/79–17/9/79, "Exchange Controls in the USA, July 26, 1979; Japan Exchange Control," July 26, 1979.

18. These efforts were also intended to strengthen the dollar's faltering international position from 1978 by creating tighter control over offshore dollar liquidity and restricting the growth of speculative Euromarket currency flows.

19. Bank of England Archives, 4A115/3, Monetary Analysis: External Development and Policy Meetings 4/1/78–28/12/79, memo from the Bank of England overseas department, "New York as a Free Trade Banking Zone," May 31, 1978.

20. Bank of England Archives, 4A115/3, Monetary Analysis: External Development and Policy Meetings 4/1/78–28/12/79, memo from the Bank of England overseas department, "New York as a Free Trade Banking Zone," May 31, 1978.

21. Bank of England Archives, 4A115/3, Monetary Analysis: External Development and Policy Meetings 4/1/78–28/12/79, memo from the Bank of England overseas department, "New York as a Free Trade Banking Zone," May 31, 1978.

22. Bank of England Archives, 4A115/3, Monetary Analysis: External Development and Policy Meetings 4/1/78–28/12/79, memo from the Bank of England overseas department, "New York as a Free Trade Banking Zone," May 31, 1978.

23. Bank of England Archives, 4A115/3, Monetary Analysis: External Development and Policy Meetings 4/1/78–28/12/79, memo from the Bank of England overseas department, "New York as a Free Trade Banking Zone," May 31, 1978.

24. LMA British Bankers' Association Archives MS32157A/2, The Future of London as an International Financial Centre Volume 2, August 1973–December 1977, letter from D. W. Kendrick, general overseas manager, Lloyds Bank Limited, to D. Lewis, assistant secretary of the Committee of London Clearing Banks, March 11, 1977.

25. LMA British Bankers' Association Archives MS32157A/3, The Future of London as an International Financial Centre Volume 3, January 1978–August 1979, extract from the minutes of the meeting of the Committee of London Clearing Banks, March 1, 1979.

26. LMA British Bankers' Association Archives MS32157A/3, The Future of London as an International Financial Centre Volume 3, January 1978–August 1979, "Matters Arising from Meeting at the Bank of England," June 7, 1978.

27. Treasury File National Archives T388/98, International Monetary System and the U.S. Dollar 15/12/78–23/5/79, letter from UK Treasury and Supply Delegation, British Embassy, Washington, DC, to R. Gilchrist, Bank of England, "Developments in US Financial Environment," March 7, 1979.

28. Treasury File National Archives T388/98, International Monetary System and the U.S. Dollar 15/12/78–23/5/79, "Visit by Mr Harold Williams, Chairman of the SEC," April 30, 1979.

29. This challenge was highlighted by a decline in New York's share of foreign securities issues, with the percentage of foreign issues slipping from 13 percent of total issues in 1977 to just

3 percent by 1986 (Longstreth, 1988: 183). SEC regulators began to reevaluate the appropriateness of their securities regulation within this context, as operators in the New York securities markets pressed for a relaxation of regulations for foreign issuers, calling for a lower threshold of information disclosure by foreign issuers. The UK was the primary competitive reference point (Landau, 1987: 470).

30. Treasury File National Archives T388/98, International Monetary System and the U.S. Dollar 15/12/78–23/5/79, "Visit by Mr Harold Williams, Chairman of the SEC," April 30, 1979.

31. LMA British Bankers' Association Archives MS32157B, The Future of London as an International Financial Centre, 1976–August 1982, memo, "The Banking and Financial Activities of the City of London, the British Banks, and the EEC," June 20, 1979.

32. LMA British Bankers' Association Archives MS32157B, The Future of London as an International Financial Centre, 1976–August 1982, "British Banks and the EEC: Speech for M. C. S. to Deliver to the City University Business School Seminar," June 20, 1979.

33. LMA British Bankers' Association Archives MS32157B, The Future of London as an International Financial Centre, 1976–August 1982, memo, "The Banking and Financial Activities of the City of London, the British Banks, and the EEC," June 20, 1979.

34. LMA British Bankers' Association Archives MS32157B, The Future of London as an International Financial Centre, 1976–August 1982, "British Banks and the EEC: Speech for M. C. S. to Deliver to the City University Business School Seminar," June 20, 1979.

35. LMA British Bankers' Association Archives MS32157B, The Future of London as an International Financial Centre, 1976–August 1982, address to the Building Societies' Institute by P. E. Leslie, chairman of the Executive Committee of the British Bankers' Association, "Harmonisation of the European Banking Industry and London as an International Financial Centre," March 17, 1979.

36. Bank of England Archives, EC5/649, Exchange Control Act File: Relaxations—Papers Covering the Relaxation and Dismantling of Exchange Controls 6/9/79–17/9/79, "The Next Stage in Dismantling Exchange Control," September 7, 1979.

37. Bank of England Archives, EC5/649, Exchange Control Act File: Relaxations–Papers Covering the Relaxation and Dismantling of Exchange Controls 6/9/79–17/9/79, brief note to the governor concerning US sensitivity about UK exchange control discrimination, September 11, 1979.

38. Otherwise the pound might be subjected to intense speculative pressure and major outflows.

39. Bank of England Archives, EC5/649, Exchange Control Act File: Relaxations—Papers Covering the Relaxation and Dismantling of Exchange Controls 6/9/79–17/9/79, note to the chancellor of the exchequer and Bank and Treasury officials, dismantling exchange control and the international role of sterling, September 19, 1979.

40. Bank of England Archives, EC5/649, Exchange Control Act File: Relaxations—Papers Covering the Relaxation and Dismantling of Exchange Controls 6/9/79–17/9/79, "Sterling as an International Currency," September 19, 1979.

41. Bank of England Archives, EC5/649, Exchange Control Act File: Relaxations—Papers Covering the Relaxation and Dismantling of Exchange Controls 6/9/79–17/9/79, memo by the Bank of England External Finance Group, "Official Sterling Balances," September 14, 1979.

42. LMA British Bankers' Association Archives MS32157A/3, The Future of London as an International Financial Centre Volume 3, January 1978–August 1979, "Matters Arising from a Meeting at the Bank of England," June 7, 1978.

43. LMA British Bankers' Association Archives MS32157A/2, The Future of London as an International Financial Centre Volume 2, August 1973–December 1977, letter from D. W. Kendrick, general overseas manager, Lloyds Bank Limited, to D. Lewis, assistant secretary of the Committee of London Clearing Banks, March 11, 1977.

44. LMA British Bankers' Association Archives MS32157A/2, The Future of London as an International Financial Centre Volume 2, August 1973–December 1977, letter from A. Davies of Barclays International to D. S. Lewis, assistant secretary of the Committee of London Clearing Banks, March 14, 1977.

45. LMA British Bankers' Association Archives MS32157A/2, The Future of London as an International Financial Centre Volume 2, August 1973–December 1977, letter from D. W. Kendrick, general overseas manager, Lloyds Bank Limited, to D. Lewis, assistant secretary of the Committee of London Clearing Banks, March 11, 1977.

46. LMA British Bankers' Association Archives MS32157A/3, The Future of London as an International Financial Centre Volume 3, January 1978–August 1979, "Matters Arising from a Meeting at the Bank of England," June 7, 1978.

47. LMA British Bankers' Association Archives MS32157A/3, The Future of London as an International Financial Centre Volume 3, January 1978–August 1979, letter from P. J. Nicholson, secretary general of the Committee of London Clearing Banks, to Sir Jeremy More, chairman of Lloyds Bank, April 20, 1979.

48. LMA British Bankers' Association Archives MS32157A/3, The Future of London as an International Financial Centre Volume 3, January 1978–August 1979, "Matters Arising from a Meeting at the Bank of England," June 7, 1978.

49. Bank of England Archives, EC5/649, Exchange Control Act File: Relaxations—Papers Covering the Relaxation and Dismantling of Exchange Controls 6/9/79–17/9/79, memo by the Bank of England External Finance Group, "Official Sterling Balances," September 14, 1979.

50. The Bundesbank did not target the monetary base (preferring instead the broader "monetary aggregate" measure). It attempted only indirectly to control the monetary stock, through manipulating interest rates and reserves. And, finally, it never tied itself to hitting precise monetary targets (Beyer et al., 2009: 19).

51. It was upper-income households that suffered the biggest losses during high inflation as the real rate of return on financial assets was steadily eroded. For the home-owning middle classes, house price inflation and wage inflation were beneficial. In broad terms, debtors were rewarded by inflation (which eroded the real value of the borrowed money and interest rates), while savers were penalized as their asset values depreciated (Greider, 1987: 17). Banks, as net creditor institutions, tended to be highly averse to unexpected and excessive inflation (Woolley, 1984: 71).

52. The Fed's key mechanisms for affecting the money supply were open markets operations and discount window transactions. The Federal Funds Rate (the price of borrowing between banks on the overnight market to cover shortages in their reserves relative to their portfolio), set through the Fed's open market operations, was the key rate for the US monetary system and was the most closely monitored rate in the market (Greider, 1987: 62–64).

53. "Minimum lending rate" was the term used to described discount window operations carried out by the Bank.

54. Lawson was perhaps the foremost enthusiast for monetarism within Thatcher's government.

55. Of course, the political fallout from such a drastic move would have been immense, and it is no surprise that this option was never attempted in practice.

56. Bank of England Archives, G1/210, Governor's File: The International Monetary Fund and International Bank of Reconstruction and Development, Christopher William Mcmahon's Impressions of the Annual General Meetings 10/76–10/79, "Thoughts after the IMF/Belgrade Meeting," October 1979.

57. Bank of England Archives G37/3, Court of Directors: Informal Records 16/1/75–31/12/80, "Economic Developments Abroad: March 1980," March 4, 1980.

58. This is not to make the argument that the regulatory systems in the UK and the US became identical; they clearly retained a high degree of institutional difference. Yet the tendencies to simultaneous supervisory extension and centralization alongside financial liberalization were remarkably similar.

59. The subsequent sharp drop from the early 1990s reflects the beginning of a prolonged period of recession and a simultaneous crisis within the UK's small banks sector.

60. The "politics of productivity," the blueprint for US postwar reconstruction policy in Western Europe, had sought to resolve distributional tensions between social classes by expanding the rate of economic growth through a depoliticized commitment to the goal of enhanced industrial productivity (Maier, 1977).

Chapter Seven

1. The two major deregulations of this process consisted of the abolition of fixed commissions for securities deals, opening them to greater price competition, and the removal of obstacles to foreign entry into the London Stock Exchange, which had up to this point been constituted as a "private club" (Plender, 1986: 39).

2. In the US, the Garn-St. Germain Act of 1982 allowed savings and loans (S&Ls) to engage in commercial banking areas that went beyond their traditional mandate of taking deposits and providing mortgage loans, ultimately feeding into the S&L crisis of the late 1980s. This development challenged the profitability of banks and, allied to the major problems with failed syndicated loans to Latin America and Eastern Europe in the early 1980s, led to a loosening of regulation to enable the banks to restore profitability. Crucially, this entailed a "creative reinterpretation" of Glass-Steagall by 1986, which allowed commercial banks to earn up to 5 percent of their income from investment banking activities (Eichengreen, 2014: 69). These reforms represented a further weakening of the existing regulatory order.

3. Investment banks packaged the securitized assets into different tranches of credit risk, with the assumption being that the first tranche (which would receive the first claim to the cash flow generated by the underlying loans) was very low risk, particularly given that complicit credit ratings agencies had attributed the top credit rating of "AAA" to these assets (Eichengreen, 2014: 74–76).

4. This was a departure from the previous "originate and hold" model of mortgage issuance. With loans now packaged up and sold off, there was far less incentive to scrutinize borrowers, as the risk had been dispersed into the wider financial markets. This meant that the caliber of borrower decreased and the housing boom intensified, and that the systemic risk posed by subprime lending increased dramatically, with far more investors and institutions imbricated in ownership of the assets (Kirshner, 2014: 10).

5. It is important to note here that the Basel Accords that banks now sought to evade were the product of Anglo-American financial leadership. Regulators responded to high-profile bank failures during the 1970s, such as that of German bank I. D. Herstatt, that threatened the stability of interbank lending markets. The debt crisis of 1982 and further problems for major international banks turned the attention of regulators to levels of bank capital. In January 1987, the Federal Reserve and the Bank of England agreed a common standard for capital adequacy. The Fed and the Bank then used the existence of this agreement to act as a bargaining lever, threatening to create an Anglo-American regulatory "exclusion zone" in order to pressure other countries to sign up. This successful strategy led to the first Basel bank capital accords (Kapstein, 1989: 339–47).

6. The US and the UK were, of course, the liberalizers par excellence.

7. John Moscow, the deputy general counsel of the Federal Reserve Bank of New York, was removed from the Fed "within weeks" after he dared to use a New York Times op-ed to challenge the probity of allowing bigger banks to form (Kirshner, 2014: 52–53). Similarly, Brooksley Born, the chair of the Commodity Futures Trading Commission, was forced out of his position under pressure from the Fed and the Treasury Secretary. His crime: daring to counsel against further deregulation of derivatives (Eichengreen, 2014: 70).

8. Senator Gramm had been inundated with campaign contributions from Wall Street firms and commercial banks between 1989 and 2002, with the financial services industry spending almost $400 million on lobbying in the two years prior to the passing of the act (Kirshner, 2014: 56). The Gramm-Leach-Bliley Act was part of a wider set of deregulatory process. This included the elimination of oversight of derivatives markets by federal and state bodies, with the 2000 Commodity Futures Modernization Act, as well as the removal of restrictions on cross-state branching, via the Riegle-Neal Interstate Banking and Branch Efficiency Act of 1994, which facilitated the formation of huge banks (Eichengreen, 2014: 70).

9. South Korea was pushed into a series of deflationary measures and structural reforms under duress from the IMF and the Americans (testifying once again to the intricate linkages between the power of the Fund and the US).

10. Conviction in the rational expectations of individuals formed the basis of the "efficient markets" hypothesis propounded by Robert Lucas, which came to form a key intellectual support strut of the consensus surrounding the Great Moderation and helped legitimize the financialization of Anglo-American economies (Irwin, 2013: 97–98; Kirshner, 2014: 7).

11. Granting independence did not mean that the Treasury divested all control. The chancellor retained the authority to set the inflation target and was also imbued with the power to appoint external members of the Monetary Policy Committee for three-year terms.

12. There is a lack of consensus regarding just how far New Labour moved from a commitment to activist fiscal policy as a means of securing employment growth and regulating aggregate demand. New Labour endorsed two fiscal rules in an attempt to internalize policy discipline as a means to enhanced credibility. Firstly, through Gordon Brown's "golden rule" the

government pledged to borrow only to invest rather than to fund current spending over the economic cycle. Secondly, the government pledged that net debt would be held at a sensible and stable level over the economic cycle (Glyn and Wood, 2001: 51). Despite this, as Clift and Tomlinson (2007: 48–57) argue, New Labour pursued a "broadly Keynesian" set of domestic economic policies after 1997, managing demand through the "coarse tuning" of the economy. Certainly, public expenditure and borrowing did increase substantially during New Labour's time in office.

13. Nigel Lawson initially proposed the idea, unsuccessfully, during Thatcher's first government. That it was New Labour that finally enacted this policy demonstrated how far the ideological gap between the two parties had closed.

14. Brown went so far as to publicly declare his "personal gratitude" to Greenspan for his advice during the years before independence was granted, when the Fed chairman visited the UK Treasury in 2002 (Keegan, 2003: 156).

15. The creation of the FSA had a serious impact upon the institutional breadth of the Bank. The Supervision and Surveillance Department had been the largest within the Bank, employing five hundred people, the vast majority of whom would now, much to their chagrin, be shipped out to a new superagency in Canary Wharf (Conaghan, 2012: 34).

16. In 2007, financial services accounted for 15 percent of total UK income tax and 26.5 percent of corporation tax, as well as a £44.5 billion balance of trade surplus (compared to a huge deficit in goods) (Morgan, 2012: 379).

17. Of particular importance in this regard was the creation of a "High-Level City Group," tasked with promoting the City's global competitiveness (Morgan, 2012: 382).

18. Northern Rock had expanded its mortgage lending at a staggering rate. In order to do so it had relied upon borrowing short term within the interbank lending markets at low interest rates, rather than building its deposit base. This highly leveraged funding model meant that the bank suffered a liquidity crisis as interbank lending rates rose, and those markets eventually seized up entirely as the US subprime crisis deepened. It was symptomatic of the heightened systemic risk faced by the UK's financial system as a consequence of the widespread embrace of securitization in preceding decades.

19. This was signified by the importance of the widening spread that opened up between the London Interbank Offering Rate (LIBOR) and the Federal Funds Rate as the Lehman Brothers failure came to light, demonstrating the declining confidence within the interbank lending markets centered around London.

20. Reluctance to intervene more directly to save Lehman may have been, at least in part, motivated by concerns over moral hazard. But the Fed's refusal to make an emergency loan to Lehman remains somewhat puzzling, given that funds were forthcoming to Bear Stearns. Inaction was perhaps also motivated by fears over the adequacy of collateral provided by the bank in return for Fed funding, or doubts over whether the action would have been able to win the required votes within the Fed's Board of Governors (Axilrod, 2009: 152–58).

21. From the onset of the crisis King had, fearing moral hazard, been stern in his response to private bank demands for emergency lending. During the Northern Rock crisis, King insisted that any lending from the Bank be provided covertly, only as a last resort and at a punitive interest rate (Iriwn, 2013: 127). King's tough stance toward led Bush's Treasury secretary Hank Paulson to remark, in conversation with chancellor Alistair Darling during the North Rock fiasco, that "your guy Mervyn has a high pain threshold" (Conaghan, 2012: 149).

Chapter Eight

1. The bill, which authorized a fiscal package worth $700 billion, was passed in October 2008 in order to bail out the ailing financial sector. It proved highly controversial politically and was initially met with stern opposition from Republicans, leading to its defeat in the House of Representatives. The initial defeat led to a further plunge in market confidence as doubts over the government's capacity to handle the crisis deepened (Axilrod, 2009: 158).

2. In addition to QE, both the Fed and the Bank opted for "forward guidance" as another new weapon within the monetary policy arsenal. Under this policy, central bankers announce in advance that interest rates will not be raised for a certain length of time. The reassurance that this indication of a stable interest rate trajectory provides is intended to encourage households and businesses to engage in consumption or investment that they had previously forgone due to concerns over rising rates (Koo, 2015: 43).

3. This represented a return to the basic edict of monetarism: that fluctuations in the quantity of money would determine price levels.

4. Within three months of the collapse of Lehman, the dollar depreciated by 18 percent against the yen while the pound fell 23 percent against the euro (Koo, 2015: 80).

5. The default risk existed because Eurozone economies were no longer monetarily sovereign and thus dependent upon bond sales to cover fiscal deficits (i.e., the gap between public expenditure and tax revenues). The Anglo-American economies, by contrast, were unconstrained by these limitations, able to create fiat money to cover deficits and expand their central bank balance sheets.

6. Osborne did introduce a National Living Wage, to replace the minimum wage and raise the base wage level. This was a move to head off political opposition to the UK's appalling wage growth performance in the wake of the crisis and signify the Conservative's apparent "One Nation" commitment to working families. But, crucially, research by the Institute for Fiscal Studies (Elming et al., 2015: 3) suggested that cuts to tax credits would leave lower-income families worse off overall, despite the wage increase.

7. One of the impediments to the development of new economic thinking within institutionally privileged sites has undoubtedly been the durability of the economics profession and the ability of its neoclassical doyens to rebound swiftly from the delegitimization occasioned by the crisis (Mirowski, 2013).

8. The former UKIP leader and prominent Leave campaigner Nigel Farage was actively involved in campaigning for Donald Trump. Farage and the Leave donor Aaron Banks made an early visit to Trump Tower to congratulate the president-elect on his victory. From the US, the billionaire backer of the US far right Robert Mercer made donations to the Leave campaign and funded electoral strategy work by the UK-based Cambridge Analytica (Wilson, 2017: 544).

Conclusion

1. Krippner (2011) and Konings (2011) both provide excellent accounts of US deregulation during the 1980s. But their analyses overstate the endogenous origins of these changes and overlook the important role of Anglo-American development.

2. Anderson (1992: 164) and Brinkley (1996: 4) address the limits of these transformational projects in the UK and the US, respectively.

BIBLIOGRAPHY

Aaron R. (1973) *The Imperial Republic: The United States and the World, 1945–1973*, London: Weidenfeld & Nicolson.

Abdelal R. (2007) *Capital Rules: The Construction of Global Finance*, Cambridge, MA: Harvard University Press.

Abrahams P. (1969) "American Bankers and the Economic Tactics of Peace: 1919," *Journal of American History*, 56 (3): 572–83.

Agnew H. (2016) "City of London Gets First Blueprint for Life after Brexit," *Financial Times*. Available from: http://www.ft.com/cms/s/0/35bb3208–58c6–11e6–8d05–4eaa66292c32 .html#axzz4G46Png9P (accessed August 3, 2016).

Ahamed L. (2009) *Lords of Finance: 1929, the Great Depression, and the Bankers Who Broke the World*, London: William Heinemann.

Aliber R. (1985) "Eurodollars: An Economic Analysis," in P. Savona and G. Sutja, eds., *Eurodollars and International Banking*, Basingstoke: Palgrave Macmillan, 77–98.

Allen H. (1955) *Great Britain and the United States: A History of Anglo-American Relations (1783–1952)*, New York: St Martin's.

Altamura C. (2016) *European Banks and the Rise of International Finance: The Post-Bretton Woods Era*, London: Routledge.

Anderson P. (1964) "Origins of the Present Crisis," *New Left Review*, 1 (23): 26–53.

Anderson P. (1992) "The Figures of Descent," in *English Questions*, London: Verso: 121–93.

Apel E. (2013) *European Monetary Integration: 1958–2002*, London: Routledge.

Arestis P., and M. Sawyer. (1998) "New Labour, New Monetarism," *Soundings*, 9: 24–41.

Arrighi G. (1990) "The Three Hegemonies of Historical Capitalism," *Review (Fernand Braudel Centre)*, 13 (3): 365–408.

Arrighi G. (2007) *Adam Smith in Beijing: Lineages of the Twenty-first Century*, London: Verso.

Artis M., and M. Lewis (1981) *Monetary Control in the United Kingdom*, Oxford: Philip Allan.

Artis M., and M. Taylor (1989) "Abolishing Exchange Control: The UK Experience," *Centre for Economic Policy Research*, 294: 1–60.

Attard B. (2004) "Moral Suasion, Empire Borrowers, and the New Issue Market during the 1920s," in R. Michie and P. Williamson, eds., *The British Government and the City of London in the Twentieth Century*, Cambridge: Cambridge University Press, 195–215.

Augar P. (2008) *The Death of Gentlemanly Capitalism: The Rise and Fall of London's Investment Banks*, London: Penguin.

Axilrod S. (2011) *Inside the Fed: Monetary Policy and Its Management, Martin through Greenspan to Bernanke*, Cambridge, MA: MIT Press.

Baker A. (1999) "Nebuleuse and the 'Internationalization of the State' in the UK? The Case of HM Treasury and the Bank of England," *Review of International Political Economy*, 6 (1): 79–100.

Baker A. (2010) "Restraining Regulatory Capture? Anglo-America, Crisis Politics, and Trajectories of Change in Global Financial Governance," *International Affairs*, 86 (3): 647–63.

Banking Information Service (1985) *International Banking: The Role of the Major British Banks*, London: Banking Information Service.

Bank of England (2013) *The Red Book: The Bank's Current Operations in the Sterling Money Markets*. Available from: http://www.bankofengland.co.uk/markets/Documents/money/publications/ redbookqe.pdf (accessed January 16, 2014).

Bank of England Quarterly Bulletin (1964) "UK Banks' External Liabilities and Claims in Foreign Currencies," 4 (2):100–106.

Bank of England Quarterly Bulletin (1968) "Overseas and Foreign Banks in London: 1962–1968," 8 (2): 156–66.

Bank of England Quarterly Bulletin (1970) "The Euro-currency Business of Banks in London," 10 (2): 31–50.

Baran P., and P. Sweezy (1966) *Monopoly Capital: An Essay on the American Economic and Social Order*, London: Modern Reader.

Barker A., Stafford P. (2015) "Victory for UK over Eurozone Clearing Houses," *Financial Times*. Available from: http://www.ft.com/cms/s/0/425aeeeo-c24f-11e4-bd9f-00144feab7de .html#axzz4G46Png9P (accessed July 20, 2016).

Bartlett C. (1977) *A History of Post-war Britain: 1945–1974*, London: Longman.

Battilossi S. (2000) "Financial Innovation and the Golden Ages of International Banking: 1890–1931 and 1958–1981," *Financial History Review*, 7: 141–75.

Battilossi S. (2002a) "International Banking and the American Challenge in Historical Perspective," in S. Battilossi and Y. Cassis, eds., *European Banks and the American Challenge: Competition and Cooperation in International Banking Under Bretton Woods*, Oxford: Oxford University Press, 1–36.

Battilossi S. (2002b) "Banking with Multinationals: British Clearing Banks and the Euromarkets' Challenge, 1958–1976," in S. Battilossi and Y. Cassis, eds., *European Banks and the American Challenge: Competition and Cooperation in International Banking Under Bretton Woods*, Oxford: Oxford University Press, 103–35.

BBC (2015a) "Budget 2015: Osborne Unveils National Living Wage," BBC News. Available from: http://www.bbc.co.uk/news/uk-politics-33437115 (accessed September 5, 2015).

BBC (2015b) "Osborne Confirms Budget Surplus Law," BBC News. Available from: http:// www.bbc.co.uk/news/business-33074500 (accessed September 10, 2015).

Beeson M. (2013) "Can China Lead?," *Third World Quarterly*, 34 (2): 233–50.

Bell G. (1973) *The Euro-dollar Market and the International Financial System*, London: Macmillan.

Bell S., and A. Hindmoor (2015) "Taming the City? Ideas, Structural Power, and the Evolution of British Banking Policy amidst the Great Financial Meltdown," *New Political Economy*, 20 (3): 454–74.

Bernanke B. (2011) "Global imbalances: Links to Economic and Financial Stability," speech given at the Banque de France Financial Stability Review Launch Event, Paris, France.

Available from: https://www.federalreserve.gov/newsevents/speech/bernanke20110218a
.htm (accessed July 3, 2014).

Berry C., and C. Hay (2016) "The Great British 'Rebalancing' Act: The Construction and Implementation of an Economic Imperative for Exceptional Times," *British Journal of Politics and International Relations*, 18 (1): 3–25.

Best, J. (2005) *The Limits of Transparency: Ambiguity and the History of International Finance*, Ithaca, NY: Cornell University Press.

Beyer A., V. Gaspar, C. Gerberding, and O. Issing (2008) *Opting Out of the Great Inflation: German Monetary Policy after the Breakdown of Bretton Woods* (No. w14596). Cambridge, MA: National Bureau of Economic Research.

Binham C., and M. Arnold (2015) "UK Regulator Seeks to Quash Fears over Bank Ringfencing Rules," *Financial Times*. Available from: http://www.ft.com/cms/s/0/aa858c54–6eb2–11e5 -aca9-d87542bf8673.html#axzz4JemRLcxL (accessed October 12, 2015).

Blank S. (1978) "Britain: The Politics of Foreign Economic Policy, the Domestic Economy, and the Problem of Pluralistic Stagnation," in P. Katznelson, ed., *Between Power and Plenty: Foreign Economic Policies of Advanced Industrial States*, Madison: University of Wisconsin Press, 89–139.

Block F. (1977) *The Origins of International Economic Disorder: A Study of United States International Monetary Policy from World War II to the Present*, Berkeley: University of California Press.

Blyth, M. (1997) "'Any More Bright Ideas?' The Ideational Turn of Comparative Political Economy," *Comparative Politics*, 29 (2): 229–50.

Blyth, M. (2002) *Great Transformations: Economic Ideas and Institutional Change in the Twentieth Century*, Cambridge: Cambridge University Press.

Blyth, M. (2003) "Structures Do Not Come with an Instruction Sheet: Interests, Ideas, and Progress in Political Science," *Perspectives on Politics*, 1 (4): 695–706.

Blyth M. (2013) *Austerity: The History of a Dangerous Idea*, Oxford: Oxford University Press.

Blyth M., and M. Matthijs (2011) "Why Only Germany Can Fix the Euro," *Foreign Affairs*, 17: 117–35.

Blyth M., and M. Matthijs (2017) "Black Swans, Lame Ducks, and the Mystery of IPE's Missing Macroeconomy," *Review of International Political Economy*, 24 (2): 203–31.

Bordo M. D., O. F. Humpage, and A. J. Schwartz (2015) *Strained Relations: US Foreign-Exchange Operations and Monetary Policy in the Twentieth Century*, Chicago: University of Chicago Press.

Borgwardt, E. (2007) *A New Deal for the World*, Cambridge, MA: Harvard University Press.

Boyce R. (2004) "Government-City of London Relations under the Gold Standard, 1925–1931," in R. Michie and P. Williamson, eds., *The British Government and the City of London in the Twentieth Century*, Cambridge: Cambridge University Press, 215–35.

Brenner R. (2002) *The Boom and the Bubble: The US in the World Economy*, London: Verso.

Brett E. A. (1985) *The World Economy since the War: The Politics of Uneven Development*, New York: Praeger.

Brimmer A., and F. Dahl (1975) "Growth of American International Banking: Implications for Public Policy," *Journal of Finance*, 30 (2): 341–63.

Brinkley A. (1996) *The End of Reform: New Deal Liberalism in Recession and War*, New York: Vintage.

Brittan S. (1964) *The Treasury under the Tories, 1951–1964*, Middlesex: Penguin.

Brittan S. (1971) *Steering the Economy: The Role of the Treasury*, Middlesex: Penguin.

Broz J. L. (1999) "Origins of the Federal Reserve System: International Incentives and the Domestic Free-rider Problem," *International Organization*, 53 (1): 39–70.

Brunsden J. (2016) "UK's EU Commissioner Lord Hill Quits as British Departures Begin," *Financial Times*. Available from: http://www.ft.com/cms/s/0/c3a160fa-3ac7-11e6-8716 -a4a71e8140bo.html#axzz4G46Png9P (accessed June 25, 2016).

Buiter W., M. Miller, M. Baily, and W. Branson (1981) "The Thatcher Experiment: An Interim Report," *Brookings Papers on Economic Activity*, 2: 315–67.

Bulmer S., and W. Paterson (2013) "Germany as the EU's Reluctant Hegemon? Of Economic Strength and Political Constraints," *Journal of European Public Policy*, 20 (10): 1387–405.

Burk K. (1981) "The Mobilization of Anglo-American Finance During World War 1," in N. Dreisziger, ed., *Mobilization for Total War, The Canadian, American, and British Experience, 1914–1918, 1939–1945*, Waterloo: Wilfred Laurier University Press, 22–43.

Burk K. (1985) *Britain, America, and the Sinews of War, 1914–1918*, London: George Allen & Unwin.

Burk K. (1991) "The House of Morgan in Financial Diplomacy, 1920–30," in B. McKercher, ed., *Anglo-American Relations in the 1920s: The Struggle for Supremacy*, London: Macmillan, 125–58.

Burk K. (1994) "The Americans, the Germans, and the British: The 1976 IMF Crisis," *Twentieth Century British History*, 5 (3): 351–69.

Burk K., and A. Cairncross (1992) *Goodbye, Great Britain: The 1976 IMF Crisis*, London: Yale University Press.

Burkhead J. (1971) "Fiscal Planning-Conservative Keynesianism," *Public Administration Review*, 31 (3): 335–45.

Burn G. (1999) "The State, the City, and the Euromarkets," *Review of International Political Economy*, 6 (2): 225–61.

Burn G. (2006) *The Re-Emergence of Global Finance*, Basingstoke: Palgrave Macmillan.

Burnham P. (1990) *The Political Economy of Post-war Reconstruction*, Basingstoke: Macmillan.

Burnham P. (2001) "New Labour and the Politics of Depoliticisation," *British Journal of Politics and International Relations*, 3 (2): 127–49.

Burnham P. (2003) *Remaking the Postwar World Economy: Robot and British Policy in the 1950s*, Basingstoke: Palgrave.

Cain P., and A. Hopkins (2016) *British Imperialism: 1688–2015*, London: Routledge.

Cairncross A. (1985) *Years of Recovery: British Economic Policy, 1945–51*, Abingdon: Routledge.

Cairncross A. (1995) "The Bank of England and the British Economy," in R. Roberts and D. Kynaston, eds., *The Bank of England: Money, Power, and Influence, 1694–1994*, Oxford: Clarendon, 56–82.

Calleo D. (2005) "Hegemony and Decline: Reflections on Recent American Experience," *Sens Public Revue électronique internationale*. Available from: http://www.sens-public.org /article138.html?lang=fr (accessed June 6, 2017).

Calleo D., and B. Rowland (1973) *America and the World Political Economy: Atlantic Dreams and National Realities*, Bloomington: Indiana University Press.

Campbell H. (2008) "China in Africa: Challenging US Global Hegemony," *Third World Quarterly*, 29 (1): 89–105.

Capie F. (2010) *The Bank of England, 1950s to 1979*, Cambridge: Cambridge University Press.

Carstensen, M. B. (2011) "Ideas Are Not as Stable as Political Scientists Want Them to Be: A Theory of Incremental Ideational Change," *Political Studies*, 59 (3): 596–615.

Carstensen M. B., and M. Matthijs (2018) "Of Paradigms and Power: British Economic Policy Making since Thatcher," *Governance*, 31 (3): 431–47.

Cassis Y. (2010) *Capitals of Capital: A History of International Financial Centres, 1780–2005*, Cambridge: Cambridge University Press.

Chang H. J. (2002) *Kicking Away the Ladder: Development Strategy in Historical Perspective*, London: Anthem.

Chernow R. (1990) *The House of Morgan: An American Banking Dynasty and the Rise of Modern Finance*, London: Simon & Schuster.

Chin G., and E. Helleiner (2008) "China as a Creditor: A Rising Financial Power?," *Journal of International Affairs*, 62 (1): 87–102.

Chin G., and Y. Wang (2010) "Debating the International Currency System: What's in a Speech?," *China Security*, 6 (1): 3–20.

Christensen J., and G. Rudebusch (2012) "The Response of Interest Rates to US and UK Quantitative Easing," *Economic Journal*, 122 (564): 385–414.

Clarke S. (1967) *Central Bank Cooperation, 1924–31*, New York: Federal Reserve Bank of New York.

Clarke S. (1987) "Capitalist Crisis and the Rise of Monetarism," *Socialist Register*, 23: 393–427.

Clarke S. (1988) *Keyneisanism, Monetarism, and the Crisis of the State*, Cheltenham: Edward Elgar.

Clavin P. (1996) *The Failure of Economic Diplomacy: Britain, France, Germany, and the United States, 1931–1936*, Basingstoke: Palgrave.

Clift B. (2014) *Comparative Political Economy: States, Markets, and Global Capitalism*, Basingstoke: Palgrave.

Clift B. (2015) "The UK Macroeconomic Policy Debate and the British Growth Crisis: Debt and Deficit Discourse in the Great Recession," in J. Green, C. Hay, and P. Taylor-Gooby, eds., *The British Growth Crisis: The Search for a New Model*, Basingstoke: Palgrave Macmillan, 151–73.

Clift B., and J. Tomlinson (2007) "Credible Keynesianism? New Labour Macroeconomic Policy and the Political Economy of Coarse Tuning," *British Journal of Political Science*, 37 (1): 47–69.

Clift B., and J. Tomlinson (2012) "When Rules Started to Rule: The IMF, Neo-liberal Economic Ideas, and Economic Policy Change in Britain," *Review of International Political Economy*, 19 (3): 477–500.

Coakley J., and L. Harris (1983) *The City of Capital: London's Role as a Financial Centre*, Oxford: Basil Blackwell.

Coates D. (1994) *The Question of UK Decline: State, Society, Economy*, New York: Harvester Wheatsheaf.

Coates D. (2000) *Models of Capitalism: Growth and Stagnation in the Modern Era*, Cambridge: Polity.

Coates D. (2009) "Chickens Coming Home to Roost? New Labour at the Eleventh Hour," *British Politics*, 4 (4): 421–33.

Coates D. (2014) "The UK: Less a Liberal Market Economy, More a Post-imperial One," *Capital & Class*, 38 (1): 171–82.

Cohen B. (1986) *In Whose Interest? International Banking and American Foreign Policy*, London: Yale University Press.

Cohen B. (2000) "The Triad and the Unholy Trinity: Problems of International Monetary Co-operation," in J. Frieden and D. Lake, eds., *International Political Economy: Perspectives on Global Power and Wealth*, London: Routledge, 245–56.

Cohen B. (2008) *International Political Economy: An Intellectual History*, Princeton, NJ: Princeton University Press.

Conaghan D. (2012) *The Bank: Inside the Bank of England*, London: Biteback.

Corey L. (1969) *The House of Morgan: A Social Biography of the Masters of Money*, New York: AMS Press.

Costigliola F. (1977) "Anglo-American Financial Rivalry in the 1920s," *Journal of Economic History*, 37 (4): 911–34.

Cottrell P. (1995) "The Bank in Its International Setting," in R. Roberts and D. Kynaston, eds., *The Bank of England: Money, Power and Influence 1694–1994*, Oxford: Clarendon, 83–140.

Cox R. (1983) "Gramsci, Hegemony, and International Relations: An Essay in Method," *Millennium: Journal of International Studies*, 12 (2): 162–75.

Cox R. (1987) *Production, Power, and World Order: Social Forces in the Making of History*, New York: Columbia University Press.

Cox R. (1992) "Global Perestroika," *Socialist Register*, 28: 26–43.

Crawford B. (2014) "German Power and 'Embedded Hegemony' in Europe," in S. Colvin, ed. *The Routledge Handbook of German Politics and Culture*, London: Routledge, 329–48.

Cronin J. (1991) *The Politics of State Expansion: War, State, and Society in Twentieth-Century Britain*, London: Routledge.

Crotty J. (2012) "The Great Austerity War: What Caused the US Deficit Crisis and Who Should Pay to Fix It?" *Cambridge Journal of Economics*, 36 (1): 79–104.

Crouch C. (2009) "Privatized Keynesianism: An Unacknowledged Policy Regime," *British Journal of Politics and International Relations*, 11 (3): 382–99.

Culpepper P. (2015) "Structural Power and Political Science in the Post-crisis Era," *Business and Politics*, 17 (3): 391–409.

Curtis M. (1998) *The Great Deception: Anglo-American Power and World Order*, London: Pluto.

Cutler C. (1999) "Locating 'Authority' in the Global Political Economy," *International Studies Quarterly*, 43 (1): 59–81.

Dayer R. (1976) "Strange Bedfellows: J. P. Morgan & Co., Whitehall, and the Wilson Administration During World War 1," *Business History*, 18 (2): 127–51.

Dayer R. (1991) "Anglo-American Monetary Policy and Rivalry in Europe and the Far East, 1919–31," in B. McKercher, ed., *Anglo-American Relations in the 1920s: The Struggle for Supremacy*, London: Macmillan, 158–187.

De Cecco M. (1976) "International Financial Markets and U.S. Domestic Policy Since 1945," *International Affairs*, 52 (3): 381–99.

Dell E. (1991) *A Hard Pounding: Politics and Economic Crisis, 1974–1976*, Oxford: Oxford University Press.

Dimbleby D., and D. Reynolds (1988) *An Ocean Apart: The Relationship Between Britain and America in the Twentieth Century*, London: Hodder & Stoughton.

Dobson A. (1986) *US Wartime Aid to Britain, 1940–1946*, New York: St. Martin's.

Dobson A. (1995) *Anglo-American Relations in the Twentieth Century: Of Friendship and the Rise and Decline of Superpowers*, London: Routledge.

Dore R., W. Lazonick and M. O'Sullivan (1999) "Varieties of Capitalism in the Twentieth Century," *Oxford Review of Economic Policy*, 15 (4): 102–20.

Dyer G., and G. Parker (2015) "US Attacks UK's 'Constant Accommodation' with China," *Financial Times*. Available from: http://www.ft.com/cms/s/0/31c4880a-c8d2–11e4 -bc64–00144feab7de.html#axzz3eoxleik2 (accessed March 12, 2015).

Egerton G. (1991) "Ideology, Diplomacy, and International Organization: Wilsonism and the League of Nations in Anglo-American Relations, 1918–20," in B. McKercher, ed., *Anglo-American Relations in the 1920s: The Struggle for Supremacy*, London: Macmillan, 17–55.

Eichengreen B. (2008) *Globalizing Capital: A History of the International Monetary System*, Princeton, NJ: Princeton University Press.

Eichengreen B. (2011) *Exorbitant Privilege: The Rise and Fall of the Dollar*, Oxford: Oxford University Press.

Eichengreen B. (2014) *Hall of Mirrors: The Great Depression, the Great Recession, and the Uses and Misuses of History*, Oxford: Oxford University Press.

Eichengreen B., and M. Flandreau (2009) "The Rise and Fall of the Dollar (or When Did the Dollar Replace Sterling as the Leading Reserve Currency?)," *European Review of Economic History*, 13 (3): 377–411.

Eichengreen B., and P. Temin (2000) "The Gold Standard and the Great Depression," *Contemporary European History*, 2: 183–207.

Elming W., C. Emmerson, P. Johnson, and D. Phillips (2015) "New Analysis of the Potential Compensation Provided by the New 'National Living Wage' for Changes to the Tax and Benefit System," *Institute for Fiscal Studies*. Available from: https://www.ifs.org.uk /publications/7980 (accessed November 3, 2015).

English R., and M. Kenney (2000) "Decline or Declinism?" in R. English and M. Kenney, eds., *Rethinking British Decline*, New York: St Martin's: 279–300.

Epstein, G. (2005) "Central Banks as Agents of Economic Development," Political Economy Research Group (PERI) Working Papers: 104.

Epstein G., and J. Schor (1995) "The Federal Reserve-Treasury Accord and the Construction of the Post-War Monetary Regime in the United States," *Social Concept*: 7–48.

Farrell, H., and J. Quiggin (2017) "Consensus, Dissensus, and Economic Ideas: Economic Crisis and the Rise and Fall of Keynesianism," *International Studies Quarterly*, 61 (2): 269–83.

Federal Reserve Bank of St Louis (1968) "The Eurodollar Market: An Element in Monetary Policy," *Federal Reserve Bank of St Louis Review*, 50 (8): 102–9.

Ferguson N. (2010) *High Financier: The Lives and Times of Siegmund Warburg*, London: Penguin.

Ferguson T. (1995) *Golden Rule: The Investment Theory of Party Competition and the Logic of Money-Driven Political Systems*, Chicago: University of Chicago Press.

Ferris J. (1991) "The Symbol and the Substance of Seapower: Great Britain, the United States, and the One-Power Standard, 1919–21," in B. McKercher, ed., *Anglo-American Relations in the 1920s: The Struggle for Supremacy*, London: Macmillan, 55–81.

Fforde J. (1992) *The Bank of England and Public Policy, 1941–1958*, Cambridge: Cambridge University Press.

Fleming S. (2014) "UK and ECB Set to Clash in Court over Clearing Houses," *Financial Times*. Available from: http://www.ft.com/cms/s/0/17c32a34–06bc-11e4-ba32–00144feab7de .html#axzz3uxsq6e5D (accessed July 20, 2016).

Fraser S. (2005) *Every Man a Speculator: A History of Wall Street in American Life*, New York: Harper Collins.

Frieden J. (2007) *Global Capitalism: Its Fall and Rise in the Twentieth Century*, New York: W. W. Norton.

Frieden J. (2008). "Will Global Capitalism Fall Again?," Bruegel Essay and Lecture Series Available from: https://dash.harvard.edu/handle/1/25662473 (accessed March 1, 2015).

Friedman M. (1986) "Economists and Economic Policy," *Economic Inquiry*, 24 (1): 1–10.

Froud J., S. Johal, J. Law, A. Leaver, and K. Williams (2011) "Rebalancing the Economy (or Buyer's Remorse)," working paper, Centre for Research on Socio-Cultural Change, University of Manchester.

Fuchs, M. (2019) "Donald Trump's UK Trade Promises Are Hot Air—His Aim Is Brexit Chaos," *Guardian*. Available from: https://www.theguardian.com/commentisfree/2019/aug/20 /donald-trump-uk-trade-brexit-chaos-boris-johnson-us-eu (accessed August 26, 2019).

Gamble A. (1990) *Britain in Decline: Economic Policy, Political Strategy, and the British State*, Basingstoke: Macmillan.

Gamble A. (1994) *The Free Economy and the Strong State: The Politics of Thatcherism*, London: Palgrave.

Gamble A. (2000) "Theories and Explanations of British Decline," in R. English and M. Kenney, eds., *Rethinking British Decline*, New York: St Martin's, 1–23.

Gamble A. (2001) "Neo-Liberalism," *Capital & Class*, 25: 127–34.

Gamble A. (2009a) "British Politics and the Financial Crisis," *British Politics*, 4 (4): 450–62.

Gamble A. (2009b) *The Spectre at the Feast: Capitalist Crisis and the Politics of Recession*, Basingstoke: Palgrave.

Gamble, A. (2014) *Crisis without End? The Unravelling of Western Prosperity*, Basingstoke: Palgrave.

Gamble A., and S. A. Walkland (1984) *The British Party System and Economic Policy, 1945–1983: Studies in Adversary Politics*, Oxford: Oxford University Press.

Gavin F. (2004) *Gold, Dollars, and Power: The Politics of International Monetary Relations, 1958–1971*, Chapel Hill, NC: University of North Carolina Press.

Geisst C. (1997) *Wall Street: A History*, Oxford: Oxford University Press.

Germann J. (2014) "German 'Grand Strategy' and the Rise of Neoliberalism," *International Studies Quarterly*, 58 (4): 706–16.

Gerschenkron A. (1962) *Economic Backwardness in Historical Perspective: A Book of Essays*, Cambridge, MA: Harvard University Press.

Gill S. (1990) *American Hegemony and the Trilateral Commission*, Cambridge: Cambridge University Press.

Gill S. (1992) "The Emerging World Order and European Change: The Political Economy of European Union," *Socialist Register*, 28: 157–96.

Gill S. (1995) "Globalisation, Market Civilisation, and Disciplinary Neoliberalism," *Millennium Journal of International Studies*, 24: 399–423.

Gill S., and D. Law (1988) *The Global Political Economy: Perspectives, Problems, and Policies*, Baltimore: John Hopkins University Press.

Gilpin R. (1975) *U.S. Power and the Multinational Corporation: The Political Economy of Foreign Direct Investment*, New York: Basic Books.

Gilpin R. (1981) *War and Change in World Politics*, Cambridge: Cambridge University Press.

Giordano F., and S. Persaud (2013) *The Political Economy of Monetary Union: Towards the Euro*, London: Routledge.

Glickman D. (1947) "The British Imperial Preference System," *Quarterly Journal of Economics*, 61 (3): 439–70.

Glynn A., and A. Harrison (1980) *The British Economic Disaster*, London: Pluto.

Glynn A., and S. Wood (2001) "Economic Policy Under New Labour: How Social Democratic Is the Blair Government?" *Political Quarterly*, 72 (1): 50–66.

Goldberg L. G., and A. Saunders (1981) "The Growth of Organizational Forms of Foreign Banks in the US," *Journal of Money, Credit, and Banking*, 13 (3): 365–74.

Goodhart C. (2011) *The Basel Committee on Banking Supervision, A History of the Early Years, 1974–1997*, Cambridge: Cambridge University Press.

Gowa J. (1983) *Closing the Gold Window: Domestic Politics and the End of Bretton Woods*, Ithaca, NY: Cornell University Press.

Gowan P. (1999) *Global Gamble: Washington's Faustion Bid for World Dominance*, New York: Verso.

Gowan P. (2003) "The American Campaign for Global Sovereignty," *Socialist Register*, 39: 1–28.

Gowan, P. (2009) "Crisis in the Heartland," *New Left Review*, 55 (2): 5–29.

Green E. (1992) "The Influence of the City over British Economic Policy, c. 1880–1960," in Y. Cassis ed., *Finance and Financiers in European History, 1880–1960*, Cambridge: Cambridge University Press, 193–219.

Green J. (2014) "Beyond Coxian Historicism: Nineteenth-Century World Order and the Promise of Uneven and Combined Development," *Millennium-Journal of International Studies*, 42 (2): 286–308.

Green J. (2016) "Anglo-American Development, the Euromarkets, and the Deeper Origins of Neoliberal Deregulation," *Review of International Studies*, 42 (3): 425–49.

Green J. (2018) "The Offshore City, Chinese Finance, and British Capitalism: Geo-economic Rebalancing Under the Coalition Government," *British Journal of Politics and International Relations*, 20 (2): 285–302.

Green J., and S. Lavery (2015) "The Regressive Recovery: Distribution, Inequality, and State Power in Britain's Post-Crisis Political Economy," *New Political Economy*, 20 (6): 894–923.

Greider W. (1987) *Secrets of the Temple: How the Federal Reserve Runs the Country*, New York: Touchstone.

Grossman R. (2010) *Unsettled Account: The Evolution of Banking in the Industrialized World since 1800*, Princeton, NJ: Princeton University Press.

Hacker, J., and P. Pierson (2010) "Winner-Take-All Politics: Public Policy, Political Organization, and the Precipitous Rise of Top Incomes in the United States," *Politics & Society*, 38 (2): 152–204.

Hall P. (1986) *Governing the Economy: The Politics of State Intervention in Britain and France*, Oxford: Oxford University Press.

Hall P. (1989) "Introduction," in P. Hall, ed., *The Political Power of Economic Ideas: Keynesianism across Nations*, Princeton, NJ: Princeton University Press, 3–26.

Hall P., and D. Soskice (2001) *Varieties of Capitalism: The Institutional Foundations of Comparative Advantage*, Oxford: Oxford University Press.

Hall S. (1988) *The Hard Road to Renewal: Thatcherism and the Crisis of the Left*, London: Verso.

Hancké B., M. Rhodes, and M. Thatcher, eds. (2007) *Beyond Varieties of Capitalism: Conflict, Contradictions, and Complementarities in the European Economy*, Oxford: Oxford University Press.

Hansen A. (1939) "Economic Progress and Declining Population Growth," *American Economic Review*, 29 (1): 1–15.

Harmon M. (1997) *The British Labour Government and the 1976 IMF Crisis*, New York: St. Martin's.

Harmon M. (2008) "The 1976 UK-IMF Crisis: The Markets, the Americans, and the IMF," *Contemporary British History*, 11 (3): 1–17.

Harvey D. (2005) *A Brief History of Neoliberalism*, Oxford: Oxford University Press.

Hawley J. (1984) "Protecting Capital from Itself: US Attempts to Regulate the Eurocurrency System," *International Organization*, 38 (1): 131–65.

Hay C. (2011) "Pathology Without Crisis? The Strange Demise of the Anglo-Liberal Growth Model," *Government and Opposition*, 46 (1): 1–31.

Hay C. (2013) *The Failure of Anglo-Liberal Capitalism*, Basingstoke: Palgrave.

Hearden P. (2002) *Architects of Globalism: Building a New World Order During World War II*, Fayetteville: University of Arkansas Press.

Helleiner E. (1994) *States and the Reemergence of Global Finance: From Bretton Woods to the 1990s*, Ithaca, NY: Cornell University Press.

Helleiner E., and S. Pagliari (2009) "Towards a New Bretton Woods? The First G20 Leaders Summit and the Regulation of Global Finance," *New Political Economy*, 14 (2): 275–87.

Hetzel R. (2008) *The Monetary Policy of the Federal Reserve: A History*, Cambridge: Cambridge University Press.

Higonnet R. (1985) "Eurobanks, Eurodollars, and International Debt," in P. Savona and G. Sutja, eds., *Eurodollars and International Banking*, Basingstoke: Macmillan, 15–52.

Hogan M. (1984) "Revival and Reform: America's Twentieth-Century Search for a New Economic Order Abroad," *Diplomatic History*, 8 (4): 287–310.

Hogan M. (1987) *The Marshall Plan: America, Britain, and the Reconstruction of Western Europe, 1947–1952*, Cambridge: Cambridge University Press.

Holland S. (2019) "Different Kind of Guy—Trump Sees Kindred Spirit in Boris Johnson," Reuters. Available from: https://uk.reuters.com/article/uk-britain-usa-trump-johnson/different-kind-of-guy-trump-sees-kindred-spirit-in-boris-johnson-idUKKCN1UI2EE (accessed August 20, 2019).

Holmes G. (1976) *Britain and America: A Comparative Economic History, 1850–1939*, London: David & Charles.

Hopkin, J., and K. Alexander Shaw (2016) "Organized Combat or Structural Advantage? The Politics of Inequality and the Winner-Take-All Economy in the United Kingdom," *Politics & Society*, 44 (3): 345–71.

Hudson M. (1972) *Super Imperialism: The Economic Strategy of American Empire*, New York: Rinehart & Winston.

Hudson M. (2003) *Super Imperialism: The Origin and Fundamentals of U.S. World Dominance*, London: Pluto.

Ikenberry, J. G. (2001) *After Victory: Institutions, Strategic Restraint, and the Rebuilding of Order after Major Wars*, Princeton, NJ: Princeton University Press.

Ikenberry J. G. (2006) "Rethinking the Origins of American Hegemony," in J. Ikenberry, *Liberal Order and Imperial Ambition: Essays on American Power and World Politics*, Cambridge: Polity, 21–51.

Ikenberry J. G. (2011) *Liberal Leviathan: The Origins, Crisis, and Transformation of the American World Order*, Princeton, NJ: Princeton University Press.

IMF (2012) "The Liberalization and Management of Capital Flows: An Institutional View, International Monetary Fund." Available from: http://www.imf.org/external/np/pp/eng/2012/111412.pdf (accessed June 5, 2014).

IMF (2015) "World Economic Outlook October 2015: Adjusting to Lower Commodity Prices, International Monetary Fund." Available from: https://www.imf.org/external/pubs/ft/weo/2015/02/pdf/text.pdf (accessed November 5, 2015).

Ingham G. (1984) *Capitalism Divided? The City and Industry in British Social Development*, London: Macmillan.

Ingham G. (2008) *Capitalism*, Cambridge: Polity.

Irwin N. (2013) *The Alchemists: Three Central Bankers and a World on Fire*, London: Penguin.

James H. (1996) *International Monetary Cooperation Since Bretton Woods*, Oxford: Oxford University Press.

James H. (2012) *Making the European Monetary Union*, Cambridge, MA: Harvard University Press.

Jenkins P., P. Rabinovitch, and S. Fleming (2015) "US Bankers Attack London and China's 'Lovefest,'" *Financial Times*. Available from: http://www.ft.com/cms/s/0/1b00d4da-35c5-11e3-b539-00144feab7de.html#axzz3eYfCYnr2 (accessed October 15, 2015).

Jessop B. (1980) "The Transformation of the State in Post-war Britain," in R. Scase, ed., *The State in Western Europe*, London: Croom Helm, 23–94.

Jessop B., K. Bonnet, S. Bromley, and T. Ling (1984) "Authoritarian Populism, Two Nations, and Thatcherism," *New Left Review*, 147: 32–60.

Johnson C. (1991) *The Economy Under Mrs Thatcher*, London: Penguin.

Johnson P. (1998) *The Government of Money: Monetarism in Germany and the United States*, Ithaca, NY: Cornell University Press.

Jones G. (1991) "Competition and Competitiveness in British Banking, 1918–1971," in G. Jones and M. Kirby, eds., *Competitiveness and the States: Government and Business in Twentieth-Century Britain*, New York: Manchester University Press, 120–41.

Jones G. (1993) *British Multinational Banking, 1830–1990*, Oxford: Clarendon.

Kane D. (1983) *The Eurodollar Market and the Years of Crisis*, New York: St Martin's.

Kapstein E. (1989) "Resolving the Regulator's Dilemma: International Coordination of Banking Regulations," *International Organization*, 43 (2): 323–47.

Kapstein E. (1996) *Governing the Global Economy: International Finance and the State*, Cambridge, MA: Harvard University Press.

Keegan W. (1984) *Mrs Thatcher's Economic Experiment*, London: Penguin.

Keegan W. (2004) *The Prudence of Mr. Gordon Brown*, London: John Wiley & Sons.

Kennedy P. (1988) *The Rise and Fall of the Great Powers: Economic Change and Military Conflict from 1500 to 2000*, London: Unwin Hyman.

Keohane R. (1982) "Hegemonic Leadership and U.S. Foreign Economic Policy in the 'Long Decade' of the 1950s," in W. Avery and D. Rapkin, eds., *America in a Changing World Political Economy*, New York: Longman, 49–77.

Keohane R. (1984) *After Hegemony: Cooperation and Discord in the World Political Economy*, Princeton, NJ: Princeton University Press.

Kerr I. (1984) *A History of the Eurobond Market: The First 21 Years*, London: Euromoney.

Kerr P. (2001) *Post-war British Politics: From Conflict to Consensus*, London: Routledge.

Kerr P., C. Byrne, and E. Foster (2011) "Theorising Cameronism," *Political Studies Review*, 9 (2): 193–207.

Keynes J. M. (1941) "Post-war Currency Policy," in *The Collected Writings of John Maynard Keynes, Volume 2, 1940–1944, Shaping the Post-War World: The Clearing Union, 1940–1944*, Cambridge: Cambridge University Press, n.p.

Kiely R. (2007) *The New Political Economy of Development: Globalization, Imperialism, Hegemony*, New York: Palgrave Macmillan.

Kindleberger C. (1973) *The World in Depression, 1929–39*, Berkeley: University of California Press.

Kindleberger, C. (1981) "Dominance and Leadership in the International Economy," *International Studies Quarterly*, 25 (2): 242–54.

King D., and S. Wood (1999) "The Political Economy of Neoliberalism: Britain and the United States in the 1980s," In H. Kitschelt et al., eds., *Continuity and Change in Contemporary Capitalism*. Cambridge: Cambridge University Press, 371–97.

Kirshner J. (1997) *Currency and Coercion: The Political Economy of International Monetary Power*, Princeton, NJ: Princeton University Press.

Kirshner J. (2014) *American Power After the Financial Crisis*, Ithaca, NY: Cornell University Press.

Knafo S. (2013) *The Making of Modern Finance: Liberal Governance and the Gold Standard*, London: Routledge.

Kolko G. (1970) *The Politics of War: The World and United States Foreign Policy, 1943–1945*, New York: Vintage.

Konings M. (2011) *The Development of American Finance*, Cambridge: Cambridge University Press.

Konzelmann S. (2014) "The Political Economics of Austerity," *Cambridge Journal of Economics*, 38 (4): 701–41.

Koo R. (2014) *The Escape from Balance Sheet Recession and the QE Trap: A Hazardous Road for the World Economy*, London: John Wiley & Sons.

Krasner S. (1976) "State Power and the Structure of International Trade," *World Politics*, 28 (3): 317–47.

Krasner S. (1982) "American Policy and Global Economic Stability," in W. Avery and D. Rapkin, eds., *America in a Changing World Political Economy*, New York: Longman, 29–49.

Krieger J. (1986) *Reagan, Thatcher, and the Politics of Decline*, Oxford: Oxford University Press.

Krippner G. (2007) "The Making of U.S. Monetary Policy: Central Bank Transparency and the Neoliberal Dilemma," *Theory & Society*, 36: 477–513.

Krippner G. (2012) *Capitalizing on Crisis: The Political Origins of the Rise of Finance*, London: Harvard University Press.

Krugman P. (2012) "The Austerity Agenda," *New York Times*. Available from: http://www .nytimes.com/2012/06/01/opinion/krugman-the-austerity-agenda.html?_r=0 (accessed June 3, 2015).

Kynaston D. (2011) *City of London: The History*, London: Random House.

Lacher H. (2006) *Beyond Globalization: Capitalism, Territoriality, and the International Relations of Modernity*, London: Routledge.

Lacher H., and Germann J. (2012) "Before Hegemony: Britain, Free Trade, and Nineteenth-Century World Order Revisited," *International Studies Review*, 14 (1): 99–124.

Laidler D. (1981) "Monetarism: An Interpretation and an Assessment," *Economic Journal*, 91 (361): 1–28.

Lake D. (2000), "British and American Hegemony Compared: Lessons for the Current Era of Decline," in J. Frieden and D. Lake, eds., *International Political Economy: Perspectives on Global Power and Wealth*, London: Routledge, 127–41.

Landau D. (1987) "SEC Proposals to Facilitate Multinational Securities Offerings: Disclosure Requirements in the United States and the United Kingdom," *New York University Journal of International Law & Politics*, 19: 457–78.

Langley P. (2002) *World Financial Orders: An Historical International Political Economy*, London: Routledge.

Langley P. (2004) "In the Eye of the 'Perfect Storm': The Final Salary Pensions Crisis and Financialisation of Anglo-American Capitalism," *New Political Economy*, 9 (4): 539–58.

Langley P. (2008) *The Everyday Life of Global Finance: Saving and Borrowing in Anglo-America*, Oxford: Oxford University Press.

Lansley S. (2012) *The Cost of Inequality: Why Economic Equality Is Essential for Recovery*, London: Gibson Square.

Lawrence F., D. Pegg, and R. Evans (2018) "Right-wing Think Tanks Unveil Radical Plan for US-UK Brexit Trade Deal," *Guardian*. Available from: https://www.theguardian.com /politics/2018/sep/18/rightwing-thinktanks-unveil-radical-plan-for-us-uk-brexit-trade-deal -nhs (accessed August 27, 2019).

Lazonick W. (1993) *Business Organization and the Myth of the Market Economy*, Cambridge: Cambridge University Press.

Lewis M., and K. Davis (1987) *Domestic and International Banking*, Hemel Hempstead: Philip Allan.

Llewellyn D. (1980) *International Financial Integration: The Limits of Sovereignty*, London: Macmillan.

Llewellyn D. (1985) *The Evolution of the British Financial System*, London: Institute of Bankers.

Longstreth B. (1979) "The City, Industry and the State," in C. Crouch, ed., *State and Economy in Contemporary Capitalism*. London: Croom Helm.

Longstreth, B. (1988) "Global Securities Markets and the SEC," *University of Pennsylvania Journal of International Business and Law*, 10: 183–93.

Ludlam S. (1992) "The Gnomes of Washington: Four Myths of the 1976 IMF Crisis," *Political Studies*, 40: 713–27.

Mackenzie M. (2017) "Bank of England Rate Rise: What It Means for Markets," *Financial Times*. Available from: https://www.ft.com/content/fcc88c88-bfc2-11e7-9836-b25f8adaa111 (accessed December 17, 2017).

Mahoney J., and K. Thelen (2010) "A Theory of Gradual Institutional Change," in J. Mahoney and K. Thelen, eds., *Explaining Institutional Change: Ambiguity, Agency, and Power*, Cambridge: Cambridge University Press, 1–37.

Maier C. (1977) "The Politics of Productivity," *International Organization*, 31 (4): 607–33.

Martenson G. (1964) *The Euro-dollar Market*, Boston: Banker's.

Mason R. (2019) "UK Too Desperate to Secure US Trade Deal, Says Clinton's Treasury Secretary," *Guardian*. Available from: https://www.theguardian.com/politics/2019/aug/06/brexit-clinton-treasury-secretary-larry-summers-dismisses-desperate-uk-hopes-of-us-trade-deal (accessed August 28, 2019).

Matthijs, M. (2012) *Ideas and Economic Crises in Britain from Attlee to Blair (1945–2005)*, London: Routledge.

May C. (1996) "Strange Fruit: Susan Strange's Theory of Structural Power in the International Political Economy," *Global Society: Journal of Interdisciplinary International Relations*, 10 (2): 167–89.

Mayer M. (2001) *The Fed: The Inside Story of How the World's Most Powerful Financial Institution Drives the Markets*, New York: Free Press.

McGeever J. (2017) "Even Sticking to Cautious Rate Path, Fed Is on Thin Ice," *Reuters*. Available from: https://www.reuters.com/article/global-markets-higher-rates/column-even-sticking-to-cautious-rate-path-fed-is-on-thin-ice-mcgeever-idUSL8N1NN3IM (accessed December 17, 2017).

McGuire J. J. (1971) "The Edge Act: Its Place in the Evolution of International Banking in the United States," *Lawyer of the Americas*, 3: 427–45.

McKercher B. (1988) "Wealth, Power, and the New International Order: Britain and the American Challenge in the 1920s," *Diplomatic History*, 12 (4): 411–42.

McKercher B. (1991) "Introduction," in B. McKercher, ed., *Anglo-American Relations in the 1920s: The Struggle for Supremacy*, London: Macmillan, 1–17.

McKinnon R. (2001) "The International Dollar Standard and the Sustainability of the U.S. Current Account Deficit," *Brookings Papers on Economic Activity*, 1: 227–39.

McTague, T., and P. Nicholas (2019) "Inside Donald Trump and Boris Johnson's Special Relationship," *Atlantic*. Available from: https://www.theatlantic.com/international/archive/2019/07/boris-johnson-needs-trump-does-trump-need-him-back/595006/ (accessed August 7, 2019).

Mead W. (2007) *God and Gold: Britain, America, and the Making of the Modern World*, New York: Alfred A. Knopf.

Meltzer A. (2009) *A History of the Federal Reserve: Volume 2, Book 2, 1970–1986*, Chicago: University of Chicago Press.

Michie R. (2004) "The City of London and the British Government: The Changing Relationship," in R. Michie and P. Williamson, eds., *The British Government and the City of London in the Twentieth Century*, Cambridge: Cambridge University Press, 31–56.

Mikesell R. (1945) "The Key Currency Proposal," *Quarterly Journal of Economics*, 59 (4): 563–76.

Minsky H. (2008) *Stabilizing an Unstable Economy*, New York: McGraw-Hill.

Mirowski P. (2013) *Never Let a Good Crisis Go to Waste: How Neoliberalism Survived the Financial Crisis*, London: Verso.

Misraichi M., and Davis G. (2004) "The Globalization of American Banking, 1962 to 1981," in F. Dubbin, ed., *The Sociology of the Economy*, New York: Russell Sage Foundation, 95–127.

Moggridge D. (1972) *British Monetary Policy 1924–31: The Norman Conquest of $4.86*, Cambridge: Cambridge University Press.

Moggridge D., and S. Howson (1974) "Keynes on Monetary Policy, 1910–1946," *Oxford Economic Papers*, 26 (2): 226–47.

Montgomerie J. (2006) "Giving Credit Where It's Due: Public Policy and Household Debt in the United States, the United Kingdom, and Canada," *Policy and Society*, 25 (3): 109–41.

Montgomerie J. (2007) "Financialization and Consumption: An Alternative Account of Rising Consumer Debt Levels in Anglo-America," CRESC, Working Paper Series.

Moran M. (1986) *The Politics of Banking*, London: Macmillan.

Moran M. (1994) "The State and the Financial Services Revolution: A Comparative Analysis," *West European Politics*, 17 (3): 158–77.

Morgan G. (2012) "Supporting the City: Economic Patriotism in Financial Markets," *Journal of European Public Policy*, 19 (3): 373–87.

Morrison, J. (2016) "Shocking Intellectual Austerity: The Role of Ideas in the Demise of the Gold Standard in Britain," *International Organization*, 70 (1): 175–207.

Murray Brown J. (2016) "Hammond: UK Could 'Reset' Fiscal Policy After Brexit," *Financial Times*. Available from: http://www.ft.com/fastft/2016/07/22/hammond-uk-could-reset-fiscal-policy-after-brexit/ (accessed July 22, 2016).

Nairn T. (1979) "The Future of Britain's Crisis," *New Left Review*, 1 (113–114): 43–69.

Newton S. (2004) "Keynesianism, Sterling Convertibility, and British Reconstruction 1940–1952," in R. Michie and P. Williamson, eds., *The British Government and the City of London in the Twentieth Century*, Cambridge: Cambridge University Press, 257–75.

Nitzan J., and S. Bichler (2009) *Capital as Power: A Study of Order and Creorder*, New York: Routledge.

O'Brien R., and M. Williams (2016). *Global Political Economy: Evolution and Dynamics*, Basingstoke: Palgrave.

Olson M. (1982) *The Rise and Decline of Nations: Economic Growth, Stagflation, and Social Rigidities*, New Haven, CT: Yale University Press.

Oren T., and M. Blyth. (2019) "From Big Bang to Big Crash: The Early Origins of the UK's Finance-led Growth Model and the Persistence of Bad Policy Ideas," *New Political Economy*, 24 (5): 605–22.

Ovendale R. (1998) *Anglo-American Relations in the Twentieth Century*, London: Macmillan.

Overbeek H. (1990) *Global Capitalism and National Decline: The Thatcher Decade in Perspective*, London: Unwin Hyman.

Overbeek H. (2004) "Globalization and Britain's Decline," in R. English and M. Kenney, eds., *Rethinking British Decline*, New York: St Martin's, 231–57.

Oxford Dictionary of Finance and Banking (2008) 4th ed., Oxford: Oxford University Press.

Palan R. (2006) *The Offshore World: Sovereign Markets, Virtual Places, and Nomad Millionaires*, Ithaca, NY: Cornell University Press.

Panitch L. (1994) "Globalisation and the State," *Socialist Register*, 30: 60–93.

Panitch L., and Leys C. (1997) *The End of Parliamentary Socialism: From New Left to New Labour*, London: Verso.

Panitch L., and M. Konings (2009) "Demystifying Imperial Finance," in L. Panitch and M. Konings, eds., *American Empire and the Political Economy of Global Finance*, New York: Palgrave Macmillan, 1–15.

Panitch L., and S. Gindin (2004) "Global Capitalism and American Empire," *Socialist Register*, 40:1–43.

Panitch L., and S. Gindin (2009) "Finance and American Empire," in L. Panitch and M. Konings, eds., *American Empire and the Political Economy of Global Finance*, New York: Palgrave Macmillan, 17–48.

Panitch L., and S. Gindin (2012) *The Making of Global Capitalism: The Political Economy of American Empire*, London: Verso.

Parboni R. (1981) *The Dollar and its Rivals: Recession, Inflation, and International Finance*, London: New Left.

Parker G., and E. Moore (2015) "George Osborne Says UK and China 'Will Stick Together,'" *Financial Times*. Available from: http://www.ft.com/cms/s/0/be5c0e8c-607b-11e5-9846 -de406ccb37f2.html#axzz4Jevo2QM2 (accessed October 10, 2015).

Parker, G., and J. Brunsden, (2018) "UK Aims to Keep Financial Rules Close to EU After Brexit," *Financial Times*. Available from: https://www.ft.com/content/52515664-1278-11e8-940e -08320fc2a277 (accessed June 16, 2019).

Pauly L. (1997) *Who Elected the Bankers? Surveillance and Control in the World Economy*, Ithaca, NY: Cornell University Press.

Payne A., and N. Phillips (2010) *Development*, Cambridge: Polity.

Peck J. (2010) *Constructions of Neoliberal Reason*, Oxford: Oxford University Press.

Peck J., and A. Tickell (2007) "Conceptualizing Neoliberalism, Thinking Thatcherism," in H. Leitner, J. Peck, and E. Sheppard, eds., *Contesting Neoliberalism: Urban Frontiers*, London: Guildford: 26–51.

Pierson P. (2004) *Politics in Time: Institutions, History, and Social Analysis*, Princeton, NJ: Princeton.

Piketty T. (2014) *Capital in the Twenty-First Century*, Cambridge, MA: Harvard University Press.

Plender J. (1986) "London's Big Bang in International Context," *International Affairs* 63 (1): 39–48.

Plender J., and P. Wallace (1985) *The Square Mile: A Guide to the New City of London*. London: Vintage.

Pollard S. (2002) *The International Economy Since 1945*, London: Routledge.

Prasad M. (2006) *The Politics of Free Markets: The Rise of Neoliberal Economic Policies in Britain, France, Germany, and the United States*, Chicago: University of Chicago Press.

Prasad E. (2015) *The Dollar Trap: How the US Dollar Tightened Its Grip on Global Finance*, Princeton, NJ: Princeton University Press.

Pressman S. (2017) "Why Workers Won't Benefit from Trump's Corporate Tax Cut," *Salon*. Available from: https://www.salon.com/2017/11/25/why-workers-wont-benefit-from -trumps-corporate-tax-cut_partner/ (accessed December 17, 2017).

Pressnell L. (1986) *External Economic Policy Since the War, Volume 1: The Post-War Financial Settlement*, London: HM Stationery Office.

Prins N. (2014) *All the Presidents' Bankers: The Hidden Alliances that Drive American Power*, New York: Nation.

Rachman G. (2015) "Britain, China, and the Clash of 'Special Relationships,'" *Financial Times*. Available from: http://blogs.ft.com/the-world/2015/10/britain-china-and-the-clash-of -special-relationships/ (accessed October 18, 2015).

Rist G. (2002) *The History of Development: From Western Origins to Global Faith*, London: Zed.

Roberts R. (1992) *Schroders: Merchants and Bankers*, London: Macmillan.

Roberts R. (1995) "The Bank of England and the City," in R. Roberts and D. Kynaston, eds., *The Bank of England: Money, Power, and Influence, 1694–1994*, Oxford: Clarendon, 56–83.

Roberts R. (2013) *Saving the City: The Great Financial Crisis of 1914*, Oxford: Oxford University Press.

Roberts R. (2016) *When Britain Went Bust: The 1976 IMF Crisis*, London: OMFIF.

Rogers C. (2009) "The Politics of Economic Policy Making in Britain: A Re-assessment of the 1976 IMF Crisis," *Politics & Policy*, 37 (5): 971–94.

Roseveare H. (1969) *The Treasury: The Evolution of a British Institution*, London: Penguin.

Roubini N., and S. Mihm (2010) *Crisis Economics: A Crash Course in the Future of Finance*, London: Penguin.

Ruggie J. (1982) "International Regimes, Transactions, and Change: Embedded Liberalism in the Post-war Economic Order," *International Organization*, 36 (2): 379–415.

Rupert M. (1995) *Producing Hegemony: The Politics of Mass Production and American Global Power*, Cambridge: Cambridge University Press.

Rushe D. (2017) "Trump Orders Dodd-Frank Review in Effort to Roll Back Financial Regulation," *Guardian*. Available from: https://www.theguardian.com/us-news/2017/feb/03 /trump-dodd-frank-act-executive-order-financial-regulations (accessed December 17, 2017).

Russet B. (1963) *Community and Contention: Britain and America in the Twentieth Century*, Cambridge, MA: MIT Press.

Ryan C. (2016) "Britain Goes to China in Search of Life After Brexit," *Bloomberg*. Available from: http://www.bloomberg.com/news/articles/2016-07-21/hammond-seeks-u-k-business-in -china-following-brexit-vote (accessed July 22, 2016).

Salant W. (1989) "The Spread of Keynesian Doctrines and Practices in the United States," in P. Hall, ed., *The Political Power of Economic Ideas: Keynesianism Across Nations*, Princeton, NJ: Princeton University Press, 27–52.

Saville J. (1993) *The Politics of Continuity: British Foreign Policy and the Labour Government, 1945–1946*, London: Verso.

Sarai D. (2009) "US Structural Power and the Internationalization of the US Treasury," in L. Panitch and M. Konings, eds., *American Empire and the Political Economy of Global Finance*, London: Palgrave, 71–90.

Schenk C. (1998) "The Origins of the Eurodollar Market in London: 1955–63," *Explorations in Economic History*, 35:221–38.

Schenk C. (2002) "International Financial Centres, 1958–1971: Competitiveness and Complementarity," in S. Battilossi and Y. Cassis, eds., *European Banks and the American Challenge: Competition and Cooperation in International Banking Under Bretton Woods*, Oxford: Oxford University Press, 74–103.

Schenk C. (2010) *The Decline of Sterling: Managing the Retreat of an International Currency, 1945–1992*, Cambridge: Cambridge University Press.

Schmidt, V. A. (2008). "Discursive Institutionalism: The Explanatory Power of Ideas and Discourse," *Annual Review of Political Science*, 11: 303–26.

Schneider H., and L. Dunsmuir (2017) "Fed Raises Interest Rates, Keeps 2018 Policy Outlook Unchanged," Reuters. Available from: https://www.reuters.com/article/us-usa-fed/fed -raises-interest-rates-keeps-2018-policy-outlook-unchanged-idUSKBN1E7oIX (accessed December 17, 2017).

Schumpeter J. (1954) *History of Economic Analysis*, London: Routledge.

Schwartz H. (2009a) *States versus Markets: The Emergence of a Global Economy*, Basingstoke: Palgrave.

Schwartz H. (2009b) *Subprime Nation: American Power, Global Capital, and the Housing Bubble*, Ithaca, NY: Cornell University Press.

Sharp P. (2002) "Pushing Wheat: Why Supply Mattered for the American Grain Invasion of Britain in the Nineteenth Century," Department of Economics University of Copenhagen Discussion Papers, No. 08–08. Available from: http://www.economics.ku.dk/research /publications/wp/2008/0808.pdf (accessed June 5, 2017).

Skidelsky R. (1979) "The Decline of Keynesian politics," in C. Crouch, ed., *State and Economy in Contemporary Capitalism*, London: Croom Helm, 55–87.

Skidelsky R. (2000) *John Maynard Keynes: Fighting for Britain*, London: Macmillan.

Smith D. (1987) *The Rise and Fall of Monetarism*, London: Penguin.

Smith N. (2005) *The Endgame of Globalization*, London: Routledge.

Stacey K. (2019) "Trump to Threaten Curb on Intel Sharing with UK over Huawei," *Financial Times*. Available from: https://www.ft.com/content/2f850e66-8322-11e9-9935 -ad75bb96c849 (accessed August 30, 2019).

Stedman-Jones D. (2012) *Masters of the Universe: Hayek, Friedman, and the Birth of Neoliberal Politics*, Princeton, NJ: Princeton University Press.

Steil B. (2013) *The Battle of Bretton Woods: John Maynard Keynes, Harry Dexter White, and the Making of a New World Order*, Princeton, NJ: Princeton University Press.

Stein J. (2010) *Pivotal Decade: How the United States Traded Factories for Finance in the Seventies*, New Haven, CT: Yale University Press.

Stephens P. (1996) *Politics and the Pound: The Tories, the Economy and Europe*, London: Macmillan.

Stockhammer E. (2015) "Rising Inequality as a Cause of the Present Crisis," *Cambridge Journal of Economics*, 39 (3): 935–58.

Strange S. (1971) *Sterling and British Policy: A Political Study of an International Currency in Decline*, London: Oxford University Press.

Strange S. (1972) "The Dollar Crisis, 1971," *International Affairs*, 48 (2): 191–216.

Strange S. (1984) "The Global Political Economy, 1959–1984," *International Journal*, 39 (2): 267–83.

Strange S. (1987) "The Persistent Myth of Lost Hegemony," *International Organization*, 41 (4): 551–74.

Strange S. (1988a) *States and Markets: An Introduction to International Political Economy*, London: Pinter.

Strange S. (1988b) "The Future of the American Empire," *Journal of International Affairs*, 42 (1): 1–17.

Strange S. (1994) *States and Markets*, London: Continuum.

Streeck W. (2010a) "E pluribus unum? Varieties and Commonalities of Capitalism," Max Planck Institute for the Study of Societies, Discussion Paper 10/12.

Streeck W. (2010b) "Taking Capitalism Seriously: Towards an Institutionalist Approach to Contemporary Political Economy," *Socio-Economic Review*, 9 (1): 137–67.

Streeck W. (2010c) "Institutions in History: Bringing Capitalism Back In," in G. Morgan et al., eds., *The Oxford Handbook of Comparative Institutional Analysis*, Oxford: Oxford University Press: 659–86.

Streeck W. (2011) "The Crises of Democratic Capitalism," *New Left Review*, 71: 5–29.

Streeck, W. (2014) *Buying Time: The Delayed Crisis of Democratic Capitalism*, London: Verso.

Streeck W., and K. Thelen (2005) "Introduction: Institutional Change in Advanced Political Economies," in W. Streeck and K. Thelen, eds., *Beyond Continuity: Institutional Change in Advanced Political Economies*, Oxford: Oxford University Press, 1–39.

Summers L. (2016) "The Age of Secular Stagnation: What It Is and What to Do About It," *Foreign Affairs*, 95 (2): 2–9.

Sweezy A. (1972) "The Keynesians and Government Policy, 1933–1939," *American Economic Review*, 62 (1–2): 116–24.

Sylla R. (2002) "U.S. Banks and Europe: Strategy and Attitudes," in S, Battilossi S. and Y. Cassis, eds., *European Banks and the American Challenge: Competition and Cooperation in International Banking Under Bretton Woods*, Oxford: Oxford University Press, 53–74.

Taggart J. (1999) "US MNC Subsidiaries in the UK: Characteristics and Strategic Role," in F. Burton, M. Chapman, and A. Cross, eds., *International Business Organization*, Basingstoke: Palgrave, 29–46.

Taibbi M. (2010) "Wall Street's Bailout Hustle," *Rolling Stone*, 1099: 48–55.

Talani L. (2011) "The Impact of the Global Financial Crisis on the City of London: Towards the End of Hegemony?," *Competition & Change*, 15 (1): 11–30.

Taylor-Gooby P. (2012) "Root and Branch Restructuring to Achieve Major Cuts: The Social Policy Programme of the 2010 UK Coalition Government," *Social Policy & Administration*, 46 (1): 61–82.

Temperley H. (2002) *Britain and America since Independence*, New York: Palgrave.

Thompson H. (2017) "How the City of London Lost at Brexit: A Historical Perspective," *Economy and Society*, 46 (2): 211–28.

Tomlinson J. (2000) *The Politics of Decline: Understanding Post-war Britain*, New York: Longman.

Tomlinson, J. (2004) *The Labour Governments 1964–70: Economic policy*, vol. 3, Manchester: Manchester University Press.

Tooze R. (2000) "Susan Strange, Academic International Relations, and the Study of International Political Economy," *New Political Economy*, 5 (2): 280–89.

Triffin R. (1966) *The World Money Maze: National Currencies in International Payments*, New Haven, CT: Yale University Press.

Tsoukalis L. (1977) *The Politics and Economics of European Monetary Integration*, Reading: Allen & Unwin.

Van der Pijl K. (1984) *The Making of an Atlantic Ruling Class*, London: Verso.

Van der Pijl K. (1998) *Transnational Classes and International Relations*, London: Routledge.

Van der Pijl K. (2006) *Global Rivalries: From the Cold War to Iraq*, London: Pluto.

Van Horn R., and P. Mirowski (2015) "The Rise of the Chicago School of Economics and the Birth of Neoliberalism," in P. Mirowski and D. Plehwe, eds., *The Road from Mont Pelerin: The Making of the Neoliberal Thought Collective*, Cambridge, MA: Harvard University Press, 139–80.

Van Reenen J. (2015) "Austerity: Growth Costs and Post-Election Plans," working paper, Centre for Economic Performance, London School of Economics. Available from: http://cep.lse.ac.uk/pubs/download/ea020.pdf (accessed November 8, 2019).

Volcker P. (1978) "The Role of Monetary Targets in an age of Inflation," *Journal of Monetary Economics*, 4: 329–39.

Volcker P. (1978) "The Political Economy of the Dollar," *Federal Reserve Bank of New York Quarterly Review* (Winter): 5–12.

Wade R. (1998) "The Asian Debt-and-Development Crisis of 1997–? Causes and Consequences," *World Development*, 26 (8): 1535–53.

Wade R. (2009) "From Global Imbalances to Global Reorganisations," *Cambridge Journal of Economics*, 33 (4): 539–62.

Waddell B. (1999) "Corporate Influence and World War II: Resolving the New Deal Political Stalemate," *Journal of Policy History*, 11 (3): 223–56.

Wainwright, T. (2009) 'Laying the Foundations for a Crisis: Mapping the Historico-Geographical Construction of Residential Mortgage Backed Securitization in the UK," *International Journal of Urban and Regional Research*, 33 (2): 372–88.

Walton G., and H. Rockoff (2005) *History of the American Economy*, Mason, OH: South-Western.

Wass D. (2008) *Decline to Fall: The Making of British Macro-Economic Policy and the 1976 IMF Crisis*, Oxford: Oxford University Press.

Watt D. (1984) *Succeeding John Bull: America in Britain's Place, 1900–1975*, Cambridge: Cambridge University Press.

Weir M. (1989) "Ideas and Politics: The Acceptance of Keynesianism in Britain and the United States," in P. Hall, ed., *The Political Power of Economic Ideas: Keynesianism Across Nations*, Princeton, NJ: Princeton University Press, 53–86.

Werner R. (2005) *New Paradigm in Macroeconomics: Solving the Riddle of Japanese Macroeconomic Performance*, Basingstoke: Palgrave.

White E. (1992) *The Comptroller and the Transformation of American Banking, 1960–1990*, Darby: Diane.

Widmaier W. W. (2016) *Economic Ideas in Political Time*, Cambridge: Cambridge University Press.

Wilkinson M. (2016) "Paris Opens Doors to City of London Businesses Looking to Relocate After Brexit Vote," *Telegraph*. Available from: http://www.telegraph.co.uk/news/2016/07/02/paris-opens-doors-to-city-of-london-businesses-looking-to-reloca/ (accessed July 2, 2016).

Wilson G. (2017) "Brexit, Trump, and the Special Relationship," *British Journal of Politics and International Relations*, 19 (3): 543–57.

Wolf M. (2015) "The Risks of Central Banks' Radical Treatments," *Financial Times*. Available from: http://www.ft.com/cms/s/2/56c26346-fb50-11e5-8f41-df5bda8beb40.html#slideo (accessed May 25, 2015).

Woolley J. (1984) *Monetary Politics: The Federal Reserve and the Politics of Monetary Policy*, New York: Cambridge University Press.

Wray R. (1998) *Understanding Modern Money: The Key to Full Employment and Price Stability*, Cheltenham: Edward Elgar.

Wray R. (2012) *Modern Money Theory: A Primer on Macroeconomics for Sovereign Monetary Systems*, Basingstoke: Palgrave.

INDEX

Page numbers in *italics* refer to illustrations and tables.

de Gaulle, Charles, 120, 122–23
Democratic Party, 15, 234, 240–41, 250, 257
Democratic Unionist Party, 281
Department of Economic Affairs (DEA), 139
Depositary Institutions Deregulation and
  Monetary Control Act (1980), 223–24
deposit insurance, 40
deregulation: Democrats' embrace of, 15,
  234, 240–41, 250; Global Financial Crisis
  linked to, 10, 15; origins of, 138; stagflation
  linked to, 137, 249; in UK, 132, 208, 235,
  237, 244–46, 271–72; in US, 105, 132, 174,
  175, 203–8, 223–25, 234, 235, 236–37, 240–41,
  244–46, 271–72, 275
derivatives, 171, 245
Dillon, Douglas, 115
disintermediation, 41, 112, 204
Dodd, Christopher, 261–62
Dodd-Frank Consumer Protection Act
  (2010), 260, 262

Eccles, Mariner, 81
Economic Advisory Council (UK), 78
Eisenhower, Dwight, 113, 120
electrical industry, 51–52
"embedded liberalism," 101–3; as compromise, 41–42, 75, 90–91; limitations of, 96,
  249–50; undermining of, 4, 12, 259
Emminger, Ottmar, 153
Employment Act (1946), 98
euro, 266
Euromarkets, 63, 148, 169, 279; Anglo-
  American development shaped by, 9–10,
  12, 80, 103–5, 115–16, 117, 238; backdrop of,
  111–23, 145; Bank of England powers and,
  109–10; domestic vs. offshore, 110; in
  Eurobonds, 114–16, 140, 163, 221; in
  Eurodollars, 12, 39, 44, 111, 115–16, 125–36,
  140–42, 145, 146, 152, 163, 166, 202–3, 208;
  European integration linked to, 112; Federal
  Reserve and, 115, 132–33, 145, 188, 195,
  202–13, 275; growth of, 122; Japanese stake
  in, 236; lending restrictions in response
  to, 158; merchant banks' lobbying linked

to, 107, 142, 145; misconceptions sur-
  rounding, 5, 12, 106; monetary tools
  weakened by, 199, 201, 202; paradox of, 105,
  116, 136, 145; regulatory challenges of, 14, 42,
  43, 137, 144, 152–57; sovereignty redefined
  by, 107–8; UK domestic sphere reconfigured by, 138–43; US capture of, 124–34;
  West German designs on, 149, 191
European Banking Authority, 269
European Central Bank (ECB), 248, 257, 269
European Commission (EC), 165–66, 203
European Court of Justice, 269
European Currency Unit (ECU), 163
European Economic Community (EEC),
  117, 154; Banking Directive (1977) of, 209;
  exchange liberalization within, 212;
  formation of, 112; harmonization attempts
  within, 113–14, 165, 166; UK membership
  in, 108, 115, 120, 122, 138, 147, 158, 162–65,
  175, 178, 195
European Exchange Rate Mechanism
  (ERM), 242
European Payments Union (EPU), 82, 96
European Union (EU), 243
Exchange Equalization Account, 69, 78–79
Exchange Rate Mechanism (ERM), 242
exchange rates, 30, 242; under Bretton Woods,
  12, 19, 37, 41, 43, 90, 93–94, 96, 100, 102,
  104, 113, 144, 272; fixed, 12, 19, 41, 43, 85,
  90, 96, 100, 102, 104, 144, 146, 150, 154,
  160–61, 197–98, 271, 272, 279; floating, 39,
  90, 108, 146, 150, 156, 173, 195–200, 203; as
  inflation-fighting tool, 200; stabilization
  of, 63, 64, 70, 82, 91, 113, 117, 165, 187; of
  sterling vs. dollar, 53, 56–57; swaps and,
  118, 189; UK domestic autonomy and,
  166, 186; UK imports and, 176–77, 200;
  UK manufacturing and, 226–27. See also
  balance of payments; gold standard
Exchange Stabilization Fund, 119
exports: agricultural, 36, 49, 225; from
  developing world, 229; from UK, 49, 68;
  from US, 49, 52, 57, 214, 225
Exxon, 183

A NOTE ON THE TYPE

This book has been composed in Arno, an Old-style serif typeface in the classic Venetian tradition, designed by Robert Slimbach at Adobe.